DANCE OF THE MILLIONS

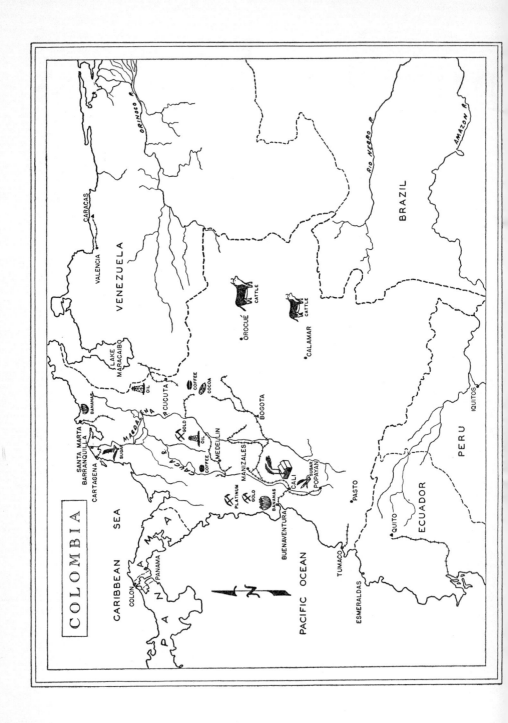

DANCE OF THE MILLIONS

MILITARY RULE AND THE

SOCIAL REVOLUTION IN COLOMBIA

1930–1956

Vernon Lee Fluharty

UNIVERSITY OF PITTSBURGH PRESS

Library of Congress Card Catalog Number: 57-7360
© 1957, University of Pittsburgh Press
PRINTED IN THE UNITED STATES OF AMERICA

Contents

Illustrations

Acknowledgments

Grateful acknowledgment is made to those Colombians who, through correspondence or in personal conversations with the writer, have contributed to an interpretation of the events covered by the scope of this study. The help of Dr. Julio Hernandez in assembling material relative to the causes of the Bogotá riots was of considerable importance, as was the assistance of Dr. Jorge Alonso Restrepo Robeldo, regarding the general course of political events in his country.

There is, unfortunately, no way to thank the scores of Colombians, both humble and mighty, who contributed to the writer's appreciation of them and their problems during the years he lived among them. May they be rewarded by a richer and fuller life for the whole of their people in the future.

To the writer's colleagues at the University of Pittsburgh go his sincere thanks and gratitude: Professor Albert B. Martin, whose invaluable counsel and advice were accorded the writer throughout the course of this study; Dr. Holbert N. Carroll, associate professor of political science; Dr. Michael A. DeVitis, professor of modern languages; Dr. William H. Dusenberry, associate professor of history; and Professor Louis W. H. Johnston, department of political science, all of whom offered helpful suggestions and criticisms.

Special thanks are due Dr. Miguel Jorrín of the School of Inter-American Affairs, University of New Mexico, who read the manuscript and gave the writer the benefit of his wide critical knowledge of Latin-American conditions.

To all these gentlemen the writer cheerfully acknowledges his debt and says: *un million de gracias!*

VERNON LEE FLUHARTY

Pittsburgh, 1956

I. Introduction

On June 13, 1953, a palace military *coup*, led by General Gustavo Rojas Pinilla, unseated the dictatorial Conservative president of Colombia, Dr. Laureano Gómez. This act terminated a bloody, five-year period of civil strife. With it, too, there ended the old political order in which two parties competed for power in a system which had caused many to look upon Colombia as the most stable democracy in Latin America.

Laureano Gómez was ousted from office by the military just five years after disastrous riots had razed Bogotá, disrupted the Ninth Inter-American Conference, and swept over other cities from border to border of the nation. These riots had exploded from deep, basic party differences, and from bitter social and economic cleavages that had set class against class. Attempts to suppress those differences had brought Gómez to power as the head of a determined counterrevolutionary force.

Until the blood bath of 1948 was loosed, Colombia had enjoyed almost forty years of relative peace and progress. Government was under civilians. The constitution was honored, if not always made explicit. The press was free, and public opinion was unshackled.

And then, as though at the wave of some malign wand, frightful violence swept the country. Civil liberties died, and opposition parties were silenced; partisan bands fought bloody pitched battles with the Army and the police; terror-stricken refugees swarmed by the thousands to the cities, depopulating the countryside; the jails bulged with political prisoners. Finally, when Colombians could stand no more, the Army stepped in to end the *danse macabre*.

Colombia's general course, until it was so radically altered, seemed to offer tangible proof that the whole of Latin America would eventually evolve toward stable political democracy. If Colombia could do this, ran the argument, so could the other Latin-American nations. Hence, the miserable failure of Colombia to meet modern demands with a representative system of popular government spread chagrin and disappointment among the friends of Latin America in general. They were left with the sickening feeling that comes when the star halfback at the crucial moment of the game seizes the ball and sprints toward the wrong goal posts, stiff-arming his teammates as he gallops toward defeat.

A solid, unpleasant, but unbudging fact emerges from the Colombian experience. The end result of "forty years of democratic progress" in Colombia is a military government which daily seems less willing to return the nation to the traditional political order. Rojas Pinilla seized power after some 100,000 lives had been sacrificed to partisan passion and madness. And still, the country lives in a state of siege. Censorship is swift and arbitrary. The military is in control of national and departmental administration. The constitution is in suspension, and government is by decree. Political parties are barred from the public arena.

At first glance, it would seem that Rojas Pinilla snuffed out the fabled Colombian democracy. But this conclusion assumes that a viable popular democracy existed in the first place. If it did not, Rojas may be something other than a typical Latin military Caesar. In either case, it is clear that the two-party system failed to meet the challenge of difficult and changing times.

The history of Colombia is liberally marked by social revolutionary urges. But characteristically, this proletarian striving, when serious enough to threaten the *status quo*, has always been met by a united front of oligarchs from both the Liberal and the Conservative parties. Temporarily discarding partisan differences, they have joined forces across party lines to halt land reform, labor unionism, agitation for higher wages, and other campaigns aimed at raising the general standard of living of the masses. This fusion of party oligarchies to maintain the old order in a changing social and economic milieu lies at the heart of the failure of the Colombian party system.

At this point, something should be said about "oligarchies" and "masses." The terms are overworked, distorted by emotional usage, and, therefore, they need qualification.

Quite frequently, oligarchies rule in backward countries because they have a logical right to do so. Often, theirs is the only social and economic competence in the society. Nor do they have far to look for justification of their role in organizing and directing the society: the masses, more often than not, are very poor, very ignorant, and very incompetent to make difficult public judgments.

But the awkward fact is that the masses "know where the shoe pinches." This places upon the oligarchy the responsibility of governing for the welfare of all the people. By their very nature, however, oligarchies are monopolistic, closed corporations. Often they are very loath to admit the mere existence of other groups. And yet, the masses are here to stay; they have demonstrated their ability to outlast the oligarchies, and they have become conscious of their potentialities. This embarrassing change of the last two or three decades poses a dilemma for the oligarchies: surrender at once, or make periodic strategic retreats tactically aimed at slowing down the advance of the masses toward their social and economic goals.

In these human struggles to reshape societies, it is difficult to maintain an unemotional view. Some bias seems to be necessary. But even intolerance must be moderated by the knowledge that the forces at work are not necessarily good or evil, but simply human. In social revolutions there are never villians or heroes, only conditions, and the men they affect. The kernel of the problem, then, seems to be that both the mass man and the oligarch are human. They are men. And because this is their great common denominator, an inflexible moral dictate, amounting to a social categorical imperative in our day, demands that the great masses of humanity be admitted to fuller living. Their very humanness requires that governments heretofore oligarchic in practice and objectives now take some official cognizance of that humanness.

In the main, governments in Colombia over the past four decades have failed in this regard. Consequently, the roots of most of the Colombian troubles are fairly easy to find. If the problem is complex, it is because of the mixed motives and the varied directions which the root-conditions engender in men. Most of those conditions are basic.

Spanish colonial-feudal society was transposed by the Wars of Independence into a Creole-feudal society in which the disjointments, cleavages, and unsolved problems of the former system were scarcely altered. To the dormant conflicts so perpetuated were added certain potent catalysts: the proletarian awakening following World War I; the advent of marxism as a practicing nostrum for all social ills; the influx of foreign capital into Colombia during the twenties; the rise of an urban wage-earning class; the development of air travel and the wider dissemination of ideas, as the press, now using air delivery, became a national force; the spread of national radio networks; a new era of high profits in industry and agriculture, accompanied by but little change in the wage level. All these things created new tensions and aroused new demands. Moreover, mass media of communication brought political issues down into the market place, where the people broke the former monopoly of the oligarchy on concern with the nation's destiny. When the masses realized that they had done this, there could be no turning back to the old ways which the oligarchy wanted to perpetuate. The pattern was permanently altered, the mold broken.

A number of important questions require answers before one can properly assess what has happened in Colombia. Among them, the following seem to be particularly pertinent:

Was the "forty years of democratic progress" authentically democratic, in that some substantial degree of popular democracy existed, or was created?

If democracy did, in fact, exist, why did it fail; and if it did not, what factors inhibited its growth?

As the product of social revolutionary forces run wild, what is demanded of Rojas Pinilla? What evidence has he given that he recognizes his true role, or that he may have chosen another?

What fundamental obstacles must he overcome in order to fulfill the mission given him by prevailing conditions, or by the processes which raised him to power?

What is his relationship to the social revolution that is coming to Colombia, as to most of the underdeveloped areas of the world?

The answers to these questions are rooted in the past. Finding them will entail the untangling of many elements: the cultural, ideological, economic, and legal-constitutional bases of policy and government in general; and particularly will it require close scrutiny of the manner in which the two parties have expressed these factors in their alternating hold on power over a century and more.

In order to get at them, we turn first to the raw materials of the Colombian political state: land, resources, economic structure, and people.

II. The General View: Land, Resources, and People

"All Colombia," says Kathleen Romoli, "is divided into two parts, the mountainous and the flat."[1]

One might well add, "And the greater of these is the flat."

More than half of Colombia is hot plains or drowned swampland and jungle. Double the size of Germany, her 440,000 square miles equal the combined areas of France, Spain, and Portugal.[2] This would be a truly impressive patrimony, if size alone were a criterion of potential prosperity.

For good or for evil, the main currents of Colombian life are channeled in the high Andes, along the mountain valleys and their slopes, and on the plains of the Atlantic littoral. This feature of Colombian geography has divided the people into two main location groups, the Caribs of the lowlands, and the *Andinos* of the upper altitudes. The psychological differences between capital and seacoast have been changed but little by the better transportation facilities of the modern age. "Colombia continues divided into Caribs and *Andinos*, who maintain between themselves differences not only physical, but in customs, temperament, and modes of expression."[3] But more important, the heavy concentration of population at the high altitudes has left two-thirds of the national territory still to be colonized: a great, empty domain where climate, terrain, and remoteness deprive the land of present positive value.[4]

The extremely irregular and varied relief of the country is due to the breaking up of the Andean range at the southern border of Colombia. There, three separate ranges fan out from the Pasto Knot and run parallel northward to the Atlantic littoral. This great Andean

[1] Kathleen Romoli, *Colombia: Gateway to South America*, reprinted by permission of Doubleday & Company, Inc. Copyright 1941 by Kathleen Romoli.

[2] *Investments in Colombia* (Washington; U.S. Department of Commerce, 1955), p. 3.

[3] "Eterno Retorno," *Semana* (Bogotá), August 8, 1955, p. 15.

[4] Pablo Vila, *Geografía de Colombia* (Bogotá: Librería Colombiana, 1945), p. 16.

5

region is breath-takingly contradictory, majestic, and clothed with a grandeur that defies description. Rich mountain valleys and savannas alternate with desolate, arid plateaus standing above the clouds, where the only visible life is the slow-wheeling condor. Snow peaks rise chill and grim above warm pastures and green-growing slopes. Half the year the region is gray, misty, and bathed in torrential rains, and the clouds drift low above the city streets at nightfall like swift gray ghosts. And then, during the remainder of the year, the sun warms cerulean skies, fleecy clouds hang high overhead like small balls of cotton suspended in a painted sky, and the air is pure and heady as a potent wine.

But this high heartland of the nation has its practical lures as well as its intangible magic. Many of the mountain slopes can be cultivated, and the mile-high valleys, though sometimes narrow, are bountifully fertile. In these great intermontane basins large cities have grown up, and commerce and industry, the arts and crafts, science and learning, have flourished. A harsh land, it has made of the Colombians a basically rugged people. Never could weaklings have peopled the high Andes.

In this often lonely land of crags and bulging mountain shoulders, there are a number of permanent snow peaks: Cumbal, in the Western Cordillera, rears skyward 16,000 feet; Tolima stands above the Central Cordillera at 17,000 feet, and Ruiz, gleaming white and icy, tops the Western Cordillera at 19,000. Near Santa Marta, on the Caribbean, is the Sierra Nevada de Santa Marta, a glacier peak of 19,000 feet which attracts climbers from many lands. With the blue sea at its feet, and ringed by banana plantations, the range is believed by geographers to be a dependent of the Central Cordillera.[5]

Reading from a geographic left-to-right, the Pacific littoral is jungle-covered, rainy, and extremely hot the year-round. Development has been impeded by disease, enervating climate, and the physical impossibility of chopping away a matted sea of jungle. But the port of Buenaventura, an excellent harbor, offers access to the interior. From the port a railroad and a highway wind in hairpin curves upward from the sea to a break in the wall of mountains. Beyond this pass lies the modern industrial city of Cali, a bustling hub of continental air communications.

[5] Ramón Carlos Goez, *Geografía de Colombia* (México D. F.: Fondo de Cultura Económica, 1947), p. 24.

Situated at 5,000 feet above sea level, Cali is the metropolis for the valley and the region which takes its name from the Cauca River. This river rises where the three cordilleras separate from the main Andean backbone, and it runs its course 635 miles northward to join the Magdalena, flanked along its course by the Western and Central Cordilleras.

The great Central Cordillera is literally the backbone of Colombia. With the Cauca Valley on the west, the long, rich valley of the Magdalena flanks it on the east. Colombian poets have traditionally been captivated by the romance of the Magdalena, dubbing it the "Life Stream of Colombia." For centuries it was the only line of communication with the interior, and it has transported, on their varied errands, the conquering Captains of Castile, filibustering rebels, viceroys and archbishops, warring Indians, courtesans and missionaries, presidents, generals, pleasure-seekers, and commercial travelers. Over it have flowed the imports and exports, the needs and the salable surpluses of a nation locked away from the world by towering mountain walls. In its basin, and in the Cauca Valley and the *Sabana* of Bogotá, 98.2 per cent of Colombia's people are born, live, and die.[6]

Of the three great Colombian ranges, the Eastern Cordillera is the longest and widest. Its contours are marked by several broad upland basins at an altitude of eight to nine thousand feet.[7] In such a lofty basin lies Bogotá, the nation's capital. The *Sabana*, as the great high plain is called, is a fertile intermountain valley approximately sixty miles long, with an average width of ten miles. Ringed by mountains whose crests reach 13,000 feet, the *Sabana* has literally been the mecca of the searchers for El Dorado. Jiménez de Quesada, Federmann, and Belalcázar converged there as though drawn by triple magnets, in search of the fabled Golden Man. And today, the politicians, the bureaucrats, the industrialists with an "angle," the aspiring provincial, and the hangers-on of the new society are drawn *hacia la capital* on the hunt of the modern version of the storied wealth.

This upland region of fertile valleys and large cities is today the effective portion of the nation. Within its 184,825 square miles are located not only the major cities, but the farms and factories, the great mansions, and the squalid huts of most of Colombia's people.

[6] William O. Galbraith, *Columbia, A General Survey* (London and New York: Royal Institute of International Affairs, 1953), p. 9.

[7] *Investments in Colombia*, p. 3.

Here, deep in the gashes of the hills and on the loamy plains between high mountains, human concentration is 57.3 per square mile. It is the scene of future important decisions. Here are the painful extremes of wealth, culture, and education. Here is the Great Questioning. Its center, Bogotá, is now a city of 700,000 people, whose level of culture has won it the sobriquet of the "Athens of South America." But just a few short miles from Bogotá, thousands of people exist on a level not far above that of later Stone Age Man.

From the high central area of Colombia, the Cauca and Magdalena valleys drop gradually from 5,000 feet to sea level, in a course veering slightly northeastward. Draining rugged slopes, they carry enormous volumes of water. During the rainy season they overflow, and as they reach the lower altitudes they leave along their courses vast areas of drowned, useless land, given over to jungle, to divers amphibious creatures, and to hordes of poisonous insects and reptiles. Farther on, where they join and become the Greater Magdalena, they leave the mountains behind and form an immense delta, where busy river and maritime ports stand in echelon.[8]

This northern littoral is not tropical in the extreme. Rich plains are favorable for stock raising, and for the cultivation of cotton. On this maritime margin are Colombia's two chief seaports, Barranquilla and Cartagena. On the west, the littoral boundary meets the frontier of Panama, and its northeastern extension becomes the flat, arid Guajira Peninsula.

The Guajira is essentially a region in itself. During most of the year, its scrub growth shimmers in infernal heat. And then the trade winds shift, the rains come, and grass shoots up as high as a man's head. It is the homeland of the Goajiras, a nomadic, stock-raising tribe of Indians who resisted Spanish conquest and enslavement. Recently this tribe has turned to civilized practices, and have begun to trade with Venezuela and the Dutch offshore islands.

To the east of the Eastern Cordillera lies another lost wasteland of Colombia, the Catatumbo, which borders the Lake Maracaibo region. A jungle of once-unexplored mysteries, it has recently been penetrated by geological parties of the large oil companies, who believe it to be a potentially great reservoir. Periodically, this region makes headlines in American newspapers, chiefly because of the pres-

[8] Georges Lafond, *Géographie Économique de l'Amérique* (Paris: Librairie Payot, 1947), p. 89.

The Andean range breaks up at Colombia's southern border; three separate mountain ranges fan out from the Pasto Knot and extend northward to the Atlantic littoral, providing the country with majestic scenery. Rivers and natural watersheds high in these mountains provide natural power for hydroelectric plants.

ence there of the Motilón Indians. These natives are an untamed tribe that has kept up an unremitting rear-guard action against the white man ever since the first Spaniard set foot on Colombian soil. They ambush exploring patrols, kill from the shelter of the dense forest with their long, slim-pointed arrows, and fade soundlessly into the green wall of jungle. Colombian Air Force planes have tried to quell them with machinegun strafing, but it is much like hunting quail from a Sherman tank.

More mysterious than the Motilones are the Catatumbo Lights. This name has been given to an extraordinarily luminescent greenish light that comes and goes over a large area of the Catatumbo, for reasons as yet unexplained. Ships have reported sighting the lights from over a hundred miles at sea. Of them, Kathleen Romoli says, "In the rainy season their mysterious glare waxes and wanes like a kind of constant sheet lightning, and science is baffled as to their cause."[9] Oil company scientists and engineers who have searched for their origin have been unable to offer any tenable hypothesis as to the source of the eerie glow. Like the Motilones, the last Treasure of the Zipa, and so many things in Colombia, the Catatumbo Lights remain a large, tantalizing question mark.

Perhaps, however, the nation's greatest contradiction is found when one faces eastward from the sharp drop of the Eastern Cordilleras. There, stretching away flat, harsh, and overpoweringly vast, from the mountain wall toward the far borders of Venezuela, Ecuador, Brazil, and Peru, lies the *Oriente:* called the *Llanos Orientales*, or Eastern Plains.

In all this great region of 270,500 square miles, a region forming part of the basins of the Orinoco and Amazon rivers, there live only 184,300 people. Although it comprises 60 per cent of the national domain, it contains but 1.7 per cent of the population. Human concentration in the *llanos*, in contrast to the high Andean region, is only .68 persons per square mile.[10]

Numerous rivers fall from the escarpment of the Eastern Cordillera, and their courses furrow the *llanos* until they lose themselves in the Orinoco or the Amazon. The plains of the northern part are fat and green, providing ample grass for large herds of cattle. But the temperature is torrid, and the uplands near the mountains are infested

---

[9] Romoli, *op. cit.*, p. 121.
[10] Galbraith, *op. cit.*, p. 9.

with disease-bearing mosquitoes, reducing the practical usefulness of the region. Even worse, perhaps, is the fact that the only road to market is five hundred miles in length over the roughest and most hair-raising part of the Eastern Cordillera. Starting at Villavicencio at the base of the ramparts, it has a bad reputation as a hazard to life and limb for those who undertake it, whether on foot or by motor vehicle. Improvements are now being made, but it still merits the description of one Colombian traveler who said of it, *"Por esta carretera no sube ni un gato con espuelas."*[11] (Not even a cat with spurs could climb *that* road!) Reduced to economic terms, this means that cattle driven from the *llanos* to market must be re-pastured for two months near Bogotá before they are salable at a profit.

The northern portion of the *llanos* is Colombia's Wild West. Proud, hard-bitten, hard-riding *llaneros* (of the race that provided Páez' redoubtable cavalry in the Wars of Liberation) follow great herds of cattle over the open range along the Casanare and Arauca rivers. It was these men and their fellows who fought the Army to a standstill in the civil war of 1948–53, and who laid down their arms only when Rojas Pinilla personally went into their territory to offer them a general amnesty.

To the south of the *llanos* begins the jungle—a tall green wall, matted and impassable save along the river courses—sweeping off toward the Amazon, seventy-five miles of whose course is navigable in Colombia. This is truly the lost world, the Green Hell, mysterious and virtually unexplored, totally unexploited, and possibly unexploitable. Despite proven oil fields of great capacity in the *llanos*, oil companies find it too remote to produce and market economically. Again, the difficulty of integrating this land into the total nation.

Rojas Pinilla seems to believe that the *llanos* can be incorporated into the national life. There is much talk and considerable action with regard to colonizing them, using both Colombian and immigrant agrarian populations. Aviation, too, has made a beginning at linking the *llanos* with the nation and the world, and Rojas' regime has constructed well-equipped airports in the region. But meanwhile, the mountains stand forbiddingly between the resources of the plains and those who could use them; they lie there, lonely, immense, inert, and virtually sterile: a contradiction per se to the words of a writer

[11] "En el Asfalto," *Semana* (Bogotá), May 30, 1955, p. 17.

who described them as "a region where the most formidable wealth sleeps."[12]

That sleep will probably continue until the Prince Charming of transportation can link the *llanos* up with the nation. Until then, the Eastern Plains spread their lonely, treeless immensity beneath the burning sun, "an immense territory, an endless plain, within a perfectly circular horizon, which reminds one of the horizon as seen from the deck of a ship."[13]

CLIMATE AND RESOURCES

The high mountains, the jagged rock barriers, and the river valleys between the ranges have marked more than the lay of the land. They have also shaped the lives and the character of the people who live upon it. "The nations carry the seal of the earth upon which they live, and man's manner of being depends on the skies which shade and warm him."[14] It would be hard to find a country where this observation is more literally true than it is of Colombia.

Although Colombia is situated almost on the equator and lies wholly within the torrid zone, still the varied relief produces a very gamut of climates. Colombians themselves say that their climate is "vertical" rather than "horizontal," and this is true because there are no seasonal climatic variations.[15] Twice a year the rains come, and it is "winter"; when the days are sunny, and cottony white clouds hang high in a blue sky, it is "summer."

The traveler crossing Colombia from west to east experiences something like the dizzying, slow-motion ride on a "roller coaster of the gods" as Romoli poetically describes it. From "sea level to 8,000 feet, down to 3,000 up to 10,000 or so, down to 800, up a mile and three quarters, down to a thousand feet—the whole in a little over two hundred air miles."[16] At sea level it is gaspingly hot; yet in Bogotá it is always topcoat weather. Medellín, at 5,000 feet, enjoys a suave 70 degrees mean annual temperature. Bogotanos occasionally take a day off to go down to "hot country," to drive the chill from their

---

[12] Jorge Bejarano, "Futuro y Destino de los Llanos Orientales," *Economía Colombiana* (Bogotá), August, 1954, p. 17.

[13] Vila, *op. cit.*, p. 50.

[14] J. M. Vergara y Velasco, cited by Goez, *op. cit.*, p. 55.

[15] Lafond, *op. cit.*, p. 90.

[16] Romoli, *op. cit.*, p. 7.

bones, and residents of *tierra caliente* who swelter in a perpetual Turkish-bath climate on the coastal littorals, go up to "temperate country" or "cold country" for a spell to activate sluggish livers and regain their vigor in the bracing air of the altiplano.

Entirely too much of the country lies in the sticky torrid zone to make for high effectiveness and zestful enterprise, but climate cannot be blamed for everything. Three hundred and twenty thousand square miles of the country lie at about 3,500 feet altitude, with a mild 75 degree mean annual temperature; the climate is somewhat brisker at 6,500 to 7,500 feet, and 74,000 square miles enjoy a 65 degree temperature at these altitudes; and for those who like a permanent autumn chill, there are some 44,000 square miles at an elevation of 10,000 feet upwards, with temperatures ranging from 55 degrees down to zero.[17]

When it rains in Colombia, it pours, to make explicit an old adage. Rainfall is heaviest on the western littoral, where landward air currents throw rain clouds up against the high escarpment of the Western Cordillera, causing them to break in torrential downpours.[18] Buenaventura claims a whopping fourteen inches in a twenty-four hour period, for something of an unenviable record. But Quibdó, on the summit of the range, once recorded 336 inches of rain in 229 days, after which, say the natives, the rains really set in.

In general, the high Andean plateaus and valleys receive more frequent rains, more equitably distributed over the season, than does the Pacific slope.[19] The *Oriente* is dry, but Goez counts it a region of torrential rains, which occasionally break the searing aridity of the plains.[20]

Actually, Colombia's spectacular variety of vertical climates is not unfavorable to national development. Its tropical location would be a blessing, did not the terrain inhibit transportation and communication. This latter fault has immobilized the people to a high degree, and also, the organic advantages which humans derive from physiological adaptation to changing seasons are lacking. On the debit side, too, are the low jungle areas, which are unhealthful and discouraging to colonization.

[17] Galbraith, *op. cit.*, p. 9.
[18] Goez, *op. cit.*, p. 61.
[19] Lafond, *op. cit.*, p. 90.
[20] Goez, *op. cit.*, p. 61.

However, the lay of the land has made possible a high degree of mineral and agricultural diversification. A wide range of minerals exists, and vertical climate favors a variety of crops, from bananas at sea level to wheat, hard grains, and orchard fruits at high altitudes.

To speak of natural resources is, of course, to use a term that is purely relative to markets, transportation, technology, and, above all, people. Farming methods in Colombia are backward, save in the commercial operations.[21] The land is vast, much of it very rich, but a total of 113,855,000 square kilometers finds only 3,000,000 devoted to agriculture, 14,000,000 non-arable, and 63,365,000 not exploited in any fashion.[22] Over half the land is forest-covered and about ten per cent is rivers, lakes, swamps, and drowned land. Many good mineral deposits occur where exploitation is difficult and economically unprofitable. But both land and subsoil are rich. The coffee lands of the Central Cordillera, the sugar-cane areas of the Cauca Valley, and the cotton-growing region of the Sinú are as richly productive as similar lands anywhere in the world.

Rare and common minerals are found in good supply in Colombia, although lack of transportation has impeded their exploitation. Large gold deposits in the Department of Nariño, for instance, cannot be touched because of the inability to move heavy machinery into remote areas. However, gold is steadily produced in good quantities in Antioquia, Nariño, the Chocó, Tolima, and Valle del Cauca. The world's richest platinum deposit (86 per cent pure as compared with Russia, 76; California, 63)[23] is located in the Chocó, and makes Colombia the world's leading producer. Internationally famous emeralds are mined in Boyacá, under a government monopoly. Heavy coal deposits occur in Antioquia, Boyacá, Santander del Norte, and Cundinamarca.

Limestone, too, is found in many parts of the country. Salt, for export above national needs, is mined in Cundinamarca, and in both Cundinamarca and Boyacá, there are important deposits of iron ore. Proven oil fields and producers yield enough for export in considerable quantities (1952 production, 38,683,000 barrels)[24] and it is esti-

[21] "El País," *Semana* (Bogotá), August 8, 1955, p. 15.
[22] "Eterno Retorno," *Semana*, p. 15.
[23] Lafond, *op. cit.*, p. 94.
[24] *Selected Economic Data on the Latin American Republics* (Washington: The Pan American Union, 1954), p. 24.

mated that these known fields will be able to meet the nation's needs for the next ten years.

In addition to these basic mineral requirements, Colombia has important deposits of quartz crystal (the main U. S. source in World War II), marble, gypsum, sulfur, mica, asphalt, tin, graphite, lead, and copper. Now worked only on a small scale, these minerals can become profitable as internal development progresses.

Colombia's fuel resources are great, for, although the native coal is not suitable for high-grade metallurgical purposes, it yields lower grades of coke. Also, the heavy rainfall, the rugged terrain, and the many rivers provide a hydroelectrical potential that puts Colombia high on the list of favored nations in this respect.

A balance sheet of Colombian geography and resources would show many fine assets and several substantial deficits. Rugged terrain, good soils, mountain barriers, a variety of climates and hydrography favor diverse agricultural pursuits. Mountain-born rivers provide high power potential. But the heavy rains leach out and erode the soils, and, while the existence of a large unsettled area would seem to be a still-untapped resource, climate, disease, remoteness, and other environmental hazards render the greater part of these regions in the main uninhabitable.[25]

There is currently much optimism regarding Colombia's potential for development. North American capitalists are singing the praises of the country as a capital investment market. Such zeal is not new. Lafond was in the vanguard of the new "boomers" in 1947, when he wrote, "Colombia enjoys an enviable economic position, and yet, if one envisages the brilliant future which is opening up before her, one can say that she is merely on the threshold of her prosperity."[26]

Such optimism must be flavored with caution. Colombia is harnessed to a one-crop economy. Coffee, almost alone, provides jobs, finances secondary industry, moves commerce, and regulates indirectly the employment index. The system of landholding strangles agriculture and makes necessary the importation of foodstuffs. Diversity is needed, as well as basic development. World price fluctuations in coffee sow panic in the Colombian economy, or create confidence. The little brown bean is the barometer of the whole economy,

[25] Galbraith, op. cit., p. 89.
[26] Lafond, op. cit., p. 89.

and the nation trembles when coffee drinkers in the United States are seduced by such price-protest slogans as "Take Tea and See."

The most important consideration, of course, is the fact that Colombia is experiencing a basic social revolution. The social, economic, and political institutions of the society are under attack. Mere political peace may have the appearance of basic stability, but the sicknesses of the nation have not been cured, even though the fever may have been temporarily reduced.

BASIS OF ECONOMIC GROWTH

Only after the industrial and commercial revolutions of the mid-nineteenth century did the Colombian economy begin to emerge from the vestigial colonialism of pre-independence. This emergence was linked mainly to the opening of international markets for coffee. Over the past half century, returns from coffee have supplied most of the funds for the nation's domestic consumers' market, and have been the main source of exchange upon which her capital formation has risen.[27] Lesser contributions have been made by petroleum, foreign investments, and private stimulation of fabricating industry. But coffee has carried, and still carries, the main load.

In 1952, for example, coffee accounted for 82 per cent of the value of all Colombian exports, as compared with 65 per cent in 1937.[28] Since World War II, in fact, high coffee prices and a strong market have kept the average percentage at about 78 per cent of the total. On the other hand, petroleum contributed 23 per cent of the total in 1937, but this share had fallen to 16 per cent in 1952, while other exports (tagua, gold, hides, divi-divi, balsa, etc.) fell from 12 per cent to only 2 per cent over the same period.

It is no exaggeration to say that coffee pays the bill for Colombian prosperity, and that prosperity is always subject to the habits of North Americans regarding coffee. Should all Americans cut their daily ration of coffee by one cup, misery would descend upon millions of Colombians.

Petroleum, running second to coffee in dollar importance, reached a peak of thirty-nine million barrels in 1952. Accompanying this rise was a wave of heavy foreign investment in the fields of transport, util-

---

[27] *Investments in Colombia*, p. 4.
[28] *Selected Economic Data on the Latin American Republics*, p. 7.

ities, mining, banking, and agriculture. Many Americans have joined with Colombian capitalists to organize new enterprises, and several companies from the United States have established branch plants in the country.

The growth of Colombian manufacturing activity since the early thirties is due, in large part, to substantial foreign investments. Under this stimulus, the national income rose from 1,049 million pesos in 1938 to 6,025 million in 1952, and the circulating medium increased from 81 million pesos to 514 million between 1938 and 1953. In this latter period, too, deposit capital (profits and income not reinvested) surged upward from 60.6 million pesos to 811 million.[29]

A similar trend is discernible in the nation's capital formation. High coffee prices and profits, often reinvested along with considerable foreign capital, ballooned capital assets from 153.5 million pesos in 1939 to 612.2 million in 1947, although inflation and the cheapening of the peso made some of this a "paper" increase. The industrial indices, however, bear out the story: 243 in 1948, using 1939 as the base year.[30] This internal growth is also reflected in the statistics of foreign trade. Between 1937 and 1952, the value of Colombian exports rose from 68 million dollars (U. S. currency) to 473 millions. Over the same span, imports climbed from 96 to 416 million, with a slight balance in favor of Colombia.

There is presently under way a drive to develop basic industries in the nation, but for many years to come Colombian industry will be essentially of the processing and fabricating type. The bulk of employment in industry now centers around textiles and food processing. Less important installations produce plywood, cement, asbestos-cement roofing, shoes, tires, and rubber goods, pharmaceuticals, boxes, soaps and fats, hats, pottery, and glass. In 1950 all manufacturing, including mining and construction, accounted for only 20 per cent of the national income.[31] It will be some time before Colombia can be classed as an industrial nation.

Nonetheless, the rise in productivity and the economic growth of the nation have been steady and impressive, despite the low productive rate of the Colombian worker.

[29] *Statistical Yearbook, 1953* (New York: The United Nations, 1953), p. 433.
[30] *Investments in Colombia*, p. 5.
[31] *Statistical Yearbook, 1953*, p. 433.

A decade and a half of this growth is shown in the figures below:[32]

Product Indicator and Amount

	1938	1948	1950	1952
Bags of coffee (thousands)...................	4,452	6,140	5,100	6,000
Bananas (thousands of stems)................	7,493	4,716	6,438	6,454
Corn (thousands of metric tons)..............	496	635	620	744
Gold (thousands of ounces)...................	521	335	379	422
Petroleum (thousands of barrels).............	21,306	23,801	34,060	38,683
Sugar (thousands of metric tons).............	45.7	108.6	146.4	142
Cement (thousands of metric tons)...........	142	364	580	704
National income (millions of pesos).........	1,049	3,741	5,547	6,600

These data demonstrate substantial progress in production apart from the main export crop, yet they do not reflect any great trend toward diversification. The Colombian dilemma is that nearly all her secondary industries depend on coffee exchange, and when coffee does not produce enough exchange to finance a lengthy import list, her secondary industries tend to run down.

In fact, agriculture has historically acted as the mainstay of the economy. From 1945 to 1950, agriculture contributed a steady 40–42 per cent of the rising national income. The most dramatic evidence of this is found in the case of coffee. And yet, "although coffee and bananas accounted for 80 per cent of the total exports [in 1948], these two crops ... represented only about 27 per cent of the aggregate value of agricultural production, not including animal husbandry."[33]

In simpler terms, crops grown for Colombians to consume at home were almost three times as valuable as coffee and bananas combined. But even so, high returns from coffee underwrote industrial production, employment, and consuming power. Dollar exchange is still the big problem for Colombia and coffee is the main provider of that exchange.

The recent expansion of the Colombian economy has been accompanied by a higher rate of capital formation; this capital accretion has, in turn, served to expand and create new industries. Productive capital assets in industry increased in value from 13.8 million pesos in 1938 to 103.6 million in 1947, including equipment, buildings, and labor costs of construction and installation. In the same period

[32] Selected Economic Data on the Latin American Republics, p. 24.
[33] Investments in Colombia, p. 5.

of time, agricultural capital increased from 11.5 to 56.5 millions, and over the whole economic sector in that time, the increase was from 72 to 612.2 million pesos.[34]

These impressive statistics have their deceptive side. Unfortunately, this piling-up of wealth for the capitalist, property-owning class has not been paralleled by a commensurate rise in the standard of living of the common people.

At best, figures on the distribution of wealth in Colombia are dreary. At worst, they are inaccurate and misleading. For example, the official figures show between 1948 and 1952 (when the greatest capital formation and deposit upsurge took place) a rise in the worker's cost of living of only 100 to 137; over the same period and by the same official count, real wages rose to *112*.[35] Perhaps there was a slight betterment of the condition of the workers during this period, but the United Nations Statistical Yearbook adds a qualifying footnote to these same data: "The figures should be interpreted with caution. Estimates of per capita real income are particularly subject to error, and in many cases are more appropriate to indicating general trends than precise year-to-year changes."[36]

The same trap lies behind official figures for per capita national income. These give 535 pesos for 1951, as compared with 118 pesos in 1939. The validity of such an index is undercut by the fact that a very few in the society enjoy fabulous incomes, while millions earn only a pittance, scarcely sufficient for subsistence. Dividing the total national income by a simple population figure gives a completely erroneous picture when set against reality.

Possibly a better indicator than real wages or per capita income is that found in the income tax returns. In 1947, 75,000 individuals "reported" incomes of more than 2,000 pesos. Of these, at least 350 persons had earnings in excess of 100,000 per year.[37] Mostly managers and owners, this group accounted for 30 per cent of the aggregate personal incomes reported, while those earning under 1,000 pesos

[34] *The Basis of a Development Program for Colombia* (Baltimore: Johns Hopkins Press, 1950), p. 40.

[35] *Estudio Económico de America Latina, 1953* (New York, Mexico: The United Nations, 1954), p. 85.

[36] *Statistical Yearbook, 1953*, p. 422.

[37] *Basis of a Development Program for Colombia*, p. 35.

comprised seven-eighths of the income earners making returns. This latter low-income group contributed 60 per cent of the total receipts.[38]

Were reliable income tax data available, the disparity of wealth and earning would appear much darker. Separate returns are made for corporations in Colombia, and their dividends, until 1954 were deductible from personal income declarations. Moreover, most Colombians, except for the very rich, simply have never paid taxes, regardless of the law.[39] All these factors tend to defeat any attempt to impale upon the sharp point of statistics the true distribution of Colombian wealth and earnings.

However, there is ample evidence of the great gap between the economic classes. Colombia's capacity for growth may have been great, but "the gains from this period of development have been unequally diffused. At the one extreme of the scale, the returns to owners of capital have increased more rapidly than returns to agriculturalists and general industrial workers. The bulk of the population has experienced some rise in the standard of living ... but the rise has been lower than what might have been expected to follow from the economic development already achieved."[40]

There is a minimum wage in Colombia. It calls for two pesos per day, with the peso worth about .25 in United States money at present. Many Colombian workers cannot make ends meet. They have "in general been faced with an increasing deficit, and ... this deficit has been met by them with privations and hunger."[41]

American capitalists, looking for investments in Colombia, might do well to look long behind the balance sheets of corporations, and behind the bank balances of the Colombian capitalists who invite them to participate in the country's development.

THE PEOPLE WHO LIVE THERE

The mountains and jungles, the sun and the rains, have their influence on where Colombians live, how they live, and what they do. The environment, as Vergara y Velasco says, forms not only the media

[38] The value of the peso at this time, approximately .57 U.S.
[39] *Basis of a Development Program for Colombia*, p. 35.
[40] *Ibid.*, p. 10.
[41] "Seamos Parcos," *Semana* (Bogotá), May 16, 1955, p. 8.

in which the tissues of animals and plants develop, but also that in which the moral fiber of men comes to fruition.[42]

This Colombian population, huddled in the confines of the high Andean valleys and plateaus, has been marked by its physical setting. Reduced to terms of heat and cold, lethargy and zest, 40 per cent of them live in the hot or tropical-humid region, 36 per cent in the temperate climates of higher altitudes, and about 24 per cent in the cold climates.[43] Consequently, climate has directly affected the rate of economic activity. Industry has concentrated above the hot, humid belts, and agriculture predominates near the coastlines and on the low plains. Says Miguel Samper: "Colombia is a country made backwards. If her population were rightly to exploit the territory which belongs to it, it would be concentrated along the coasts and in the river valleys."[44] And if the coastal littorals and the river valleys were not fever-ridden, humid, and debilitating, this might be true.

Contrary to prevalent opinion, Colombia is not an "Indian" nation, like other Andean countries. Originally Indian, Caribs peopled the lowlands and the coasts, and *Andino* tribes inhabited the higher levels. This simple classification was complicated, the racial character diffused and changed, by the Spanish conquest. It broke the Indians, as a people, as tribes, as a race. They, and later the Negro slaves, were the primary economic wealth upon which the conquering white men built their colonies. They were a cheap, abundant labor supply ready to be seized and exploited.

And, since the Spaniards who came to the New World were primarily soldiers without women, they mixed rapidly with the aborigines, weakening the white strain, and debilitating the red. "It was not an idle phrase when someone said that cross-breeding of the Americans [Indians] is due to the forgetfulness of the navigators and conquerors: they came without female companions."[45]

But the racial character of Colombia is far more complex than a mere mestizoism. The Spaniard, even before mixing his blood with another race, was a complex of explosive and contradictory factors. Behind a Jiménez de Quesada, a Cortes, an Orellana, move the shades of a variety of forebears: Phoenicians, Jews, Greeks, Carthaginians,

[42] Vergara y Velasco, cited by Goez, *op. cit.*, p. 55.
[43] Galbraith, *op. cit.*, p. 9.
[44] Miguel Samper, *Mejores Escritos* (Bogotá: Editorial Minerva, n.d.), p. 154.
[45] "Eterno Retorno," *Semana*, p. 15.

Romans, Goths, Visigoths, and Arabs. "The oriental ancestor of the original Americans went clear around the world, only to come face to face with his neighbor of Asia Minor and Africa."[46]

There is, then, no homogeneity in the Colombian population. The Indian as such is disappearing. There are a few pure white descendants of the Spaniards, and the Negro and the Indian are slowly being diluted in a three-way mixing of blood. Still and all, it is the white element which is effective, which runs the nation and makes the important decisions, although a tri-ethnic Colombian seems slowly to be evolving for some future day.

Pablo Vila, writing in 1945, divides the population as follows: whites, 26 per cent; Indians, 1.6 per cent; mestizos, 46 per cent; Negros, 4.4 per cent; and mulattos, 22 per cent.[47] Miscegenation seems to be reducing the Indian population, creating more mestizos, and, oddly enough, resulting in a rise of the white population as the crossing takes place chiefly on the "inferior" levels, while the whites with a higher survival rate, marry rather consistently into their own class.[48]

By far the largest percentage of Colombians work on the land. An estimate made in 1949 indicated that 70 per cent were so employed.[49] The balance has probably shifted slightly in recent years, as the lure of jobs in industry, the civil war in the provinces, and dissatisfaction with the land tenure system have combined to work a demographic revolution. Best present estimates hold that 60 per cent of the population is rural in character.[50]

Colombia's population is also growing rapidly. Between 1940 and 1953, the population rose from 8,701,816 to an estimated 12 million-plus.[51] This figure has probably now been surpassed, for it was based upon a 2.03 per thousand annual increase.[52] This growth takes place despite low levels of living and nutrition (2,280 calories per day as compared with 3,140 in the United States)[53] and in apparent disre-

[46] Ibid.

[47] Vila, op. cit., p. 89.

[48] Ibid.

[49] L. A. Scopes, Colombia, Economic and Commercial Conditions (London: British Board of Trade, 1950), p. 30.

[50] Elementos de Ingreso Nacional y Estructura de la Economía (Washington: The Pan American Union, 1953), p. 14.

[51] Demographic Yearbook, 1953 (New York: The United Nations, 1954), p. 74.

[52] Ibid.

[53] Statistical Yearbook, 1953, p. 273.

gard of an imposing list of epidemic and endemic social and nutritional diseases.

The rising birth rate and a declining mortality rate seem permanently to have thwarted such Malthusian controls as disease. Live birth rates between 1920–24 were 27.1 per thousand, but 1946 showed a rise to 33, while by 1952 the figure had gone up to 37.1. Meanwhile, the death rate declined from 15.6 to 13.1 per thousand. Better health facilities and public hygiene have also reduced infant mortality sharply—from 150.6 per thousand in 1946 to 110.7 in 1952, still another factor pushing the population upwards.[54]

The cold figures of statistics cannot, however, breathe life into the individual human being, cannot vitalize the story of the great contradictions of wealth and opportunity for the few, and poverty and misery for the many. At best they bear out the desolate generalities which the eye can discern, the mind comprehend. They are no more than the bare bones of a living class-economic fragmentation which sets the many against the few, the poor, ignorant, and permanently malnourished mestizos and mixed bloods against the rich, educated, well-nourished, and healthy whites and near-whites.

But there is another kind of fragmentation of the nation, a vitally important one politically, which has its roots in economic regionalism and in the basic Spanish "particularism" which works against integration at all levels. The Currie report recognizes this factor in the following terms: "It is a temptation to think of Colombia as four separate countries, united politically, but that would be an oversimplification. Actually, the zones are not clear-cut, and improvements in transportation will permit greater specialization and more inter-zonal trade. The zonal approach, however, does facilitate the understanding and treatment of Colombia's problems."[55]

These main economic zones are the Atlantic littoral, the Upper Magdalena or Eastern Cordillera, the Cauca Valley, and Antioquia. All four regions have long been self-contained, self-sufficient, and potentially autonomous in politics. Strong regional loyalties, tied to local economics, have led these regions to champion decentralization in government, revolution, general separatism. Each has its own transportation system, its metropolitan area, and its agriculture which meets the needs within its zone. The goods which move from zone to

[54] *Ibid.*
[55] *Basis of a Development Program for Colombia*, p. 4.

zone are chiefly those which can bear high transport costs: salt, sugar, oil, and imported and processed goods.[56] Characteristically, these four zones have resisted integration in thought, feeling, and doing on a national scale. This particularism may, of course, eventually disappear with better transportation and communication, but it will be long in doing so. Several centuries of tradition give it local meaning and vitality.

To begin with, each region was settled by different "nations" of Spaniards. They each found new environments in the New World, just as they had come from different ones in the Old. Particular interests, economic and racial, frequently brought them into conflict. The seacoast opposed the capital; the province, the city; the highlander, the plains dweller. Still, today, there is a great difference between the *Bogotano* and the *Costeño*; between the citizen of Cundinamarca and the man from Antioquia.

The *Costeño* is descended from a strong admixture of Catalan and Andalusian strains, with a tinge of African blood added. Catalan names predominate on the Atlantic littoral: Carbonell, Barcelo, Ferrán, Socarrás.[57] There are many mulattos, and the zambo is common. Diversion-loving, given to amatory gallantries, wordy and bombastic, the *Costeño* is an excellent companion. He is open, generous, witty, and a fine businessman with a practical man's contempt for the "long-haired poets" of Bogotá. Living and working by the sea, these people have, over the centuries, developed a more "outward" view, and have shown marked readiness to accept new ideas, possibly because of their continued contact with people of other lands.[58] Politically, they have opposed the politicians of the capital mainly because the latter, isolated in the interior, have in the past fostered policies restrictive of trade and commerce.

By contrast, the people of the highlands, particularly those of Boyacá and Cundinamarca, bear close resemblance to their ancestors in both manner and appearance. Even the Indians of the high regions have adopted much of the quiet courtesy which marks the people of birth and breeding, although they are understandably suspicious and withdrawn. The *gente*, however, are witty and subtle, natural dilettantes, "with more desire for information than capacity

[56] *Ibid.*, p. 5.
[57] Vila, *op. cit.*, p. 131.
[58] *Ibid.*

for organizing [their] knowledge."[59] Basically of Andalusian and Castilian stock, these people are given to passionate polemics, poetry (even the bootblacks of Bogotá know what happened yesterday in the Senate, and can recite the latest sonnet of the current literary lion), and to "causes" in general. Their personal demeanor is marked by a more than superficial cleverness, by love for, and a great talent with regard to, gracious living. But one learned *Bogotano* scholar is not too merciful with his own: "The Bogotanos," says Pablo Vila, "easily fall into abuse of the pun or witticism, and of irony. People from all over the country go to Bogotá in the hope of living more easily, amply and fully; they present a type which is most superficial, ingenious, and given over to an easy life; they are out after the support of the bureaucracy, or an opportunity in business, or an academic title; [they are] without interest in tenacious work or profound study."[60] This, essentially, is the people, almost unmixed with the Indian strain, who have directed the society since colonial days, and who hold it their just due to continue in that position. Their contempt for the pushing, energetic *Antioqueño* or *Costeño* is matched only by the derisive tolerance with which these two "races" treat them.

Basque and Andalusian blood created the energetic Antioqueño strain. Located as they were in the narrow mountain valleys of Antioquia, they were driven to colonization of fertile areas far afield, both by their natural energy, and by their truly extraordinary fecundity. Pushing down into Caldas, they developed trade, commerce, and industry, distinguishing themselves as colonizers and *hommes d'affaires*. The *Antioqueños* have retained their pure Spanish blood. They exterminated the Indian, and the Negro never reached these altitudes in large numbers. Consequently, the peninsular strain has been modified, if at all, chiefly by the environment. Many times in the past, Antioquia has raised the banner of revolt against the national government. She dominates commerce and industry, and her sons have always had weighty words in political councils. Regionalism is born into the blood and bone of the *Antioqueños*.[61]

The men who settled in the Cauca Valley (*Valle Caucanos*) found vast, rich lands, and there they mingled their blood—that of Castile, Andalusia, and Extramadura—with the descendants of slaves and with

[59] Juvenal Mejía Córdoba, cited by Vila, *op. cit.*, p. 131.
[60] *Ibid.*
[61] Vila, *op. cit.*, p. 131.

Indians. Today, the old aristocratic families of another, more genteel, day remain aloof, hugging their pride tight about them in a sea of slightly mixed bloods. But in general, the fusion of peoples has developed a regional "race" that is haughty, proud, slightly overbearing, intelligent, and somewhat soft and delicate as compared to the bustling, virile *Antioqueños:* in his person and his spirit, the *Valle Caucano* reflects the characteristics of his seductive *patria chica*.[62] These people, too, have often demonstrated their individuality. Bolívar was at his wits' end to "liberate" Pasto and Popayán, and tradition has it that in certain parts of the region, men still toss off their whiskey with a fervent toast to the King of Spain.

On the whole, the Creole population of Colombia has remained very pure.[63] In fact, it seems to be gaining over the other ethnic strains and crosses. The tradition of white rule and competence, and the parallel tradition of the inferiority of the dark and mixed bloods has come down strongly from colonial society which, itself, as Vila points out, was based primarily upon ethnical stratification. Inevitably, this heritage has been the cause of bitter clashes, particularly in an era marked by a proletarian ferment which is opposed by the dominant white society.

For these reasons, the social conflict in Colombia is really a two-phase struggle: that of the whites who oppose socially and economically inferior mestizos and darker bloods, and the rivalries, reaching far back into the history of Spain itself, between different races of Spaniards who tenaciously cling to their own regional, economic, and political particularisms.

From this fact of regional particularism has stemmed much of Colombia's political strife. The task of integrating semi-autonomous departments, the opposition of provincial interests and oligarchies to the national government, are merely a phase of the basic drive toward separatism, personal and collective, which is so characteristic of Colombians. Professor Eugenio J. Gómez puts it this way:

Every section, every valley, every hamlet of Colombia, is a unit which battles for its autonomy and demands its privileges. And this nation, so formed, is individualist, whether Conservative or Liberal; and it would say, if it were consulted honorably and truly, that it loves and defends its individual liberty and detests official co-action and government intervention in personal matters. We

[62] *Ibid.*
[63] Lafond, *op. cit.*, p. 90.

Colombians detest even the police ... our social organization, stemming from the Spanish roots and planted in the Indian [social] soil, was, for its greater glory, personalist from the dawn of the Republic. It would be bad to deform it with anachronistic regressions and exotic theories which do not square with the environment, nor with our hereditary training or our tradition.[64]

Commenting upon this same phenomenon, Eduardo Caballero Calderón, a great scholar and observer, held that "the constitution of the country [should be drawn] on the basis of its natural internal boundaries, so that political division might coincide with the divisions created by geography and political technique."[65] And Vila, whose study of the problem is probably the most comprehensive, himself says of the conflict of economics and of local interests and politics:

In the matter of continued territorial divisions which have taken place in Colombia, a great instability is observable, as though they were attempts to adapt new necessities, which mark the country's progress in general, and that of the various regions in particular, as the latter demand. But on repeated occasions local considerations and partisan calculations predominated more than the interests of the nation. For this reason, one constantly observes the small account that such division has taken of properly regional realities, physical, human and economic.[66]

But perhaps the final word should go to Professor Gómez: "The geography-environment has molded this individualism into the thousand sections which make up the national territory, many of them antagonistic, most of them disunited, and all ready for battle against the natural elements ... in short, [making] men of hard labor, of violent struggle, of incorrigible partisan ardor and, everywhere, men of strong-nerved valor."[67]

This, then, is the land, the wealth and the poverty of it, and what the people who live there have done with their natural and racial patrimony. This is but a swift glimpse of the raw material of Colombian politics. We now pick up the story of Colombian political directions in the modern era.

[64] Eugenio J. Gómez, *Problemas Colombianos, de 1863 a 1945* (Bogotá: Editorial Antena, 1945), IV, 175–80.

[65] Eduardo Caballero Calderón, cited by Vila, *op. cit.*, p. 21.

[66] Vila, *op. cit.*, p. 21.

[67] Gómez, *op. cit.*, p. 174.

III. The Old Order Changeth: World War I and the Great Depression (1910–1930)

Alberto Lleras Camargo, former secretary general of the Organization of American States and an ex-president of Colombia, has words pertinent to the recent troubled history of his own nation:

> Latin America has instability because it has not yet experienced the culmination of the process of social, economic and political integration; because the greater part of its political agitation represents the crumbling of situations that are essentially unstable; because it is still going through revolutions that did not take place at the proper time, and are now mixing explosively with those of our day ...[1]

It was not until the turn of the twentieth century that Colombia emerged from a long period of intermittent anarchy, and demonstrated capabilities for stable, mature nationalism, rather than the divisive, regional-based conflicts which had been her lot since the Independence.[2]

A similar lag occurred in the economic and social order. Necessary changes were not made. Business and industry, banking and government, were highly personalist. Commerce and industry were in the hands of small cliques of friends, and of those joined by family ties. These people, whom Antonio García calls the Great Families, lived, moved, and acted on an economic and social plane far above the common herd. It was the life of the Colony set down in the twentieth century, with its tradition of caste, of privilege, of power tenure. Its view was inward; it did not reflect the whole nation; it did not resist the demands of modern living—it simply denied their existence.

But events were to overtake this rich social narcissism. A rising new order was to clash violently with the old, and out of the clash was to rise the modern dilemma: whether to turn back, to conserve

---

[1] Alberto Lleras Camargo, cited in *Americas*, Washington, March, 1955, p. 37.

[2] In her first century of national existence, Colombia experienced ten revolutions of national scope, some seventy more limited uprisings. See Arrubla and Henao, *History of Colombia*, trans. J. Fred Rippy (Chapel Hill: University of North Carolina Press, 1938), p. 537.

the entrenched values of the past, or to move firmly toward a modern, balanced society in which the interests of all classes were equitably reconciled in a mood of mutual understanding. This is still the major dilemma of Colombia.

Three major influences cooperated to shake Colombia out of her somnolent colonialism. With the coming of World War I, she felt the impact of new markets and of participation in world trade, not to mention the later economic letdown which came with the drying-up of those markets. The old balances were further disturbed, and new norms created, by the spread of proletarian doctrines and ideas in the wake of the Russian Revolution of 1917, in particular, the growth of militant labor unionism. And, finally, a great influx of foreign capital in the twenties brought vast changes to the social and economic structure, and forced upon government the necessity of adapting to these revolutionary mutations. As a climax, world-wide depression struck the Colombian economy, sharpening the conflicts which had sprung from the changes already inaugurated. Colombians were faced with problems undreamed of in their experience.

Between 1910 and 1920, capital began to concentrate in new industrial and financial forms. Politically, the system of civil wars gave way to the operation of a parliamentary system where decisions were made, not by victor or vanquished, but by the majority or the minority.[3] As World War I closed many coffee markets, the administration of Dr. Jose Vicente Concha (1914–18) adopted a policy of retrenchment. Workers were discharged, public works in progress were suspended, and the government issued a flood of paper treasury notes, paving the way for the politics of finance.

Continued squabbling over finances quite naturally marked the Suárez-Holguín regime from 1918 to 1922, for a full-scale depression hit Colombia. Additional treasury scrip was issued, and in 1918, with a national income of sixteen million pesos, the national deficit stood at one-third of that figure.[4] Capital was still centered in small fabricating units, and had done nothing to better the lives of most workers or peasants. It was isolated from the main stream of the national life. Mining kept international trade alive, capital movements rarely went beyond family bounds, and the public credit con-

[3] Antonio García, *Gaitán y el Problema de la Revolución Colombiana* (Bogotá: Cooperativa de Artes Gráficas, 1955), p. 30.
[4] *Ibid.*, p. 38.

sisted of paper issues against the Treasury. Naturally, when such issues came into the hands of the well-to-do, they took effective control of the government. Thus they enjoyed a source of inflated fortunes as, from time to time, they redeemed the public indebtedness to themselves.

It was in this postwar period of social ferment that the masses began to shuffle tentatively toward the front of the stage. As capital expanded and the cities grew, the old patriarchial and "mutualist" labor societies were sharply challenged. Slowly, they were replaced by labor syndicates of a class nature. This epoch also saw the Indian insurrections in the signorial haciendas of the Cauca Valley; peasant uprisings in the Departments of Tolima and Cundinamarca, and increasing labor strife in the cities. A Socialist movement, and an intellectually-led Communist party came to life. The peasant-worker class grew clamorous and violence spread even to the coffee plantations of Viotá. In the Santa Marta banana zone, the Army was employed to massacre peasants who struck against conditions on the United Fruit Company's lands.

This potent brew of social ferment was ably stirred by a new generation of young intellectuals. Rejecting the old ideas regarding equality, these young men, many of whom were destined to become national political leaders, were irresistably drawn into the social fray. Gabriel Turbay, Luis Tejada, Hernández Rodríguez, and Moises Prieto organized the Communist party. Intrigued chiefly by the doctrine of the class struggle, they actually knew little about Marx, and cared less. Others, Díos Romero and Mario Cano among them, sponsored labor syndicalism, and men like Germán Arciniegas, Armando Solano, and Juan Lozano plunged happily into the strong current of socialism running through the nation.

It was a world burgeoning with change and tingling with challenge. The brash young men confronted the oligarchies and threw down the gauntlet. Inspired by the new ideas that came down every wind, they became the voice of Colombia's future, her nascent social conscience.

For the most part, they were laughed out of the arena. The oligarchy was certain that when they had established themselves, when they had made a mark and gained a stake in the society, these young firebrands would recant. The fever would die, the innovations pall, the challenging ideas lose their validity.

By and large, the oligarchy was right, but one of them remained unwavering and revolutionary to the end, despite honors, wealth, position: Jorge Eliécer Gaitán never abandoned his dream of a better society for the mass of Colombians. While others of his generation played intellectual footsie with Marx and Sorel, Gaitán, then at the University, organized the Center of University Cultural Extension, to bring to the humble and submerged the values inherent in learning and the understanding of new ideas. In 1924, he wrote his basic credo, *Socialist Ideas in Colombia,* not as a weapon for disunity, but to re-form his own Liberal party, to re-create the revolutionary fervor that had marked its beginnings and which was now needed in more trying times. Gaitán never went over to the "enemy," never compromised his program. There is historic irony in that fact. The Liberals were to desert him when Colombia stood at the crossroads and the people demanded of Gaitán that he show the way. He had warned liberalism: in a letter to Luis Tejada, an early organizer of communism he had said, "It must be from the files of Liberalism, a hundred times vocal and importuning, that the present generation accomplish its work against the bourgeoisie and for the economic liberation of labor."

But the Liberal party was to fulfill that role only briefly and timorously. It was to abandon its mission and the man who saw its role more clearly against the backdrop of changing times than any other Colombian. Its failure was to mean approach to the abyss, and Gaitán was to die.

But this is to anticipate. The impact of the delayed revolution and that of the present era—those twin social catalysts of which Lleras Camargo speaks—was to create an era of high social hopes, and their antithesis: the counterrevolution. The dance of the millions would leave in its wake not only reform-hungry proletarians, but a frightened and determined oligarchy, whose new wealth rendered it virtually impregnable to any assault upon it by the unorganized masses of the people.

Only logic and the basic social imperatives of history would keep the social revolution in Colombia in motion, after liberalism had abdicated.

"THE DAWN OF A NEW ERA":[5] THE DANCE OF THE MILLIONS

In 1922 General Pedro Nel Ospina became president of Colombia. Times were hard, and there was widespread popular agitation and

---

[5] See Arrubla and Henao, *op. cit.,* p. 531.

liberal complaint. The Conservatives were playing out a long string of victories, but increasing demand for a change was lending new strength to the long-powerless Liberal party. Liberals had cooperated in the cabinet of the previous administration, but had run a candidate against Ospina with impressive results. Although they lost the election, their showing was strong enough to cause Ospina to undertake an overhauling of the national administration. To this end, he brought to Colombia Professor E. W. Kemmerer of Princeton, together with a group of associated experts.

On the basis of Kemmerer's recommendations, Congress passed laws establishing a national bank, setting up an effective consolidated budget, and creating a Comptroller General's office. Along with the fiscal overhauling went other positive measures. An Agricultural Credit and Mortgage Bank was established, and the government pushed the construction of a pipeline from the Magdalena River oil fields to Barrancabermeja, for large-scale oil production was already underway.[6] As sops to quiet public clamor, government aid was extended to education, public sanitation, and public works. But the workers and peasants profited scarcely at all. Peasants received from ten to fifty centavos per day as field hands, and the average industrial wage was two pesos.[7]

The most notable innovation under Ospina was the beginning of a heavy borrowing program, mainly from United States bankers. After twenty years of internal peace, most Colombians were keenly interested in expansion. "The national spirit was ... manifesting itself in the demand for various activities such as the construction of railways, the increase of commerce, and the intensification of industries, and was tending to complicate the task of the magistrate."[8]

This influx of foreign capital, together with the revival of world markets, pulled Colombia out of the economic doldrums and swung her into a deadly spiral of inflation. The money madness was worsened by the payment, in 1921–22, of the United States indemnification of twenty-five million dollars for the Panama mutilation. Oil reserves of great extent had recently been discovered in Colombia, a fact which probably contributed to our sudden remorse (Senator Watson of Georgia remarked that "an oil proposition had been pipelined

[6] *Ibid.*, p. 532.
[7] García, *op. cit.*, p. 241.
[8] Arrubla and Henao, *op. cit.*, p. 532.

into the Treaty"),[9] but it is doubtful if the belated payment of damages was really a favor to the injured party.

All in all, eager Colombian hands received, between 1923 and 1928, 198 million pesos from the hands of investors equally eager to pass the money along. President Miguel Abadía Méndez, who succeeded Ospina in 1926, accelerated the boom-and-bust tempo. In his inaugural address, Méndez emphasized the need for the state to assist industrial development and transportation, because, "economic problems are those which tend at present to dominate national activity."[10] So it was that during the Ospina-Méndez epoch, the United States poured 280 million dollars into Colombia.[11]

It was, undeniably, a period of a certain material progress. The nation's foreign trade increased from 63 million pesos to 260 million between 1913 and 1928; by 1927 real estate was worth 2,000 million pesos; telephone line mileage went from 5,095 miles to 34,680 between 1913 and 1927; instruments in use, from 11,860 to 20,066, and messages from 2 to 6 million. The volume of mail quadrupled, railroad track mileage doubled, and the volume of freight rose 800 per cent. By 1929 there were 15,350 automobiles in use in the country, per capita exports had more than doubled, and revenues other than from loans had climbed 400 per cent from 1912. Improvements in livestock-growing and coffee-raising went forward, highways and railroads spread their networks into new areas, public construction and utilities boomed. Harbors were dredged and streets were paved, and public buildings seemed almost to spring from the ground as Colombia succumbed to the heady wine of "progress" poured from a cornucopia in the hands of U. S. bankers and their agents.[12]

But the benefits did not filter down to the masses. In many respects, the splurging in public expenditures was counter-productive.

Very little capital, for instance, went into the production of foodstuffs and raw materials, which have always been the true gauge of the nation's general prosperity. Mining concessions in gold, platinum, and oil did nothing much for Juan Fulano.[13] A great deal of ex-

---

[9] Thomas A. Bailey, *A Diplomatic History of the American People* (New York: Appleton-Century-Crofts, Inc., 1950), p. 543.

[10] Arrubla and Henao, *op. cit.,* p. 533.

[11] J. Fred Rippy, *The Capitalists and Colombia* (New York: Vanguard Press, 1931), p. 176.

[12] *Ibid.,* pp. 177–78.

[13] The Colombian "John Doe" or "Joe Citizen."

tracted wealth left the country, leaving behind it only royalties in the hands of the already-rich. Even the public works craze was carried out on miserably low salaries for the laborers. And, by drawing workers from agriculture, the program tended to lower food production and thus to raise living costs. Consequently, the worker who left the country to get his hands on "hard money" was the loser in the long run, for inflation robbed him of the imaginary gains in his economic status. Says Antonio García of this period:

> In proportion as the dollars flooded tumultously into the internal market, the migratory currents from the country to the city, to the roads and railroads and mines, grew. In 1926 and 1927 the fields of Boyacá were depopulated by the system of labor recruiting, to supply with cheap common labor the public works on divers fronts. Inflation began to operate like an endless screw: as the inflow of dollars increased, the programs of public works multiplied; and as these programs multiplied, more hands were drawn away from the fields and the demand for articles of consumption increased, without the State undertaking any policy whatever for the bettering of techniques of food production to the end, at least, of maintaining the old levels of productivity. And as these demands shot up, and the demographic potency of the cities swelled, the production of the countryside and the fields diminished.[14]

The flooding foreign investment increased the circulating medium considerably, but it stayed on the highest levels, as low wages together with rising living costs erased any benefits which might have come to the lower classes. Export values rose, but the rise was mainly in extractive materials. And so, the golden stream flowed past the peasant and the worker, past the producer of basic raw materials and foodstuffs. The people who had aligned with the foreign capitalists reaped the bulk of the golden harvest and called it prosperity. In the broadest sense, the boom did nothing organically constructive for the Colombian economy. Production and the use of the land, labor productivity, and the general consuming capacity probably were harmed rather than benefited. It was false, upper-level prosperity, which left the masses of people worse off than they had been. Writing toward the end of the boom, J. Fred Rippy says,

> It can hardly be contended that wages in Colombia are adequate. The cost of living has risen so rapidly during the last few years that the country has become one of the most expensive regions in the world.[15]

In fact, workers suffered a deficit in wages of a real nature between

[14] García, *op. cit.*, p. 242.
[15] Rippy, *op. cit.*, pp. 191–92.

1922 and 1929, a fact which, in itself, precluded the full exploitation of the internal consumers' market. Prosperity of the upper classes was "accompanied by the further improverishment of the poor classes."[16]

Voices were raised in protest. Intellectuals, writers, professional people, demanded planned production and conservation of natural resources, together with labor and agrarian reform. The capitalists waved them aside as "fuzzy thinkers." "It would have been worth more to the nation," wrote Alejandro López, "to build 100 kilometers of railway with money supplied by internal credit, than 1,000 kilometers with foreign loans."[17] And Laureano Gómez, in those times championing the people against the capitalists, said of the miners employed in the Chocó: "In order that the arrogant foreign companies may not lose one *castellano* of gold from the hands of the corn soup-eating negroes [in the mines], a whole sector of the Colombian population is condemned to misery."[18]

But this traditional system of extreme wealth and extreme poverty, typical of Colombia's past, was on the verge of crisis. It was a crisis created by the governing oligarchs, and their blind drive for personal profit had been the motive. In essence, they had widened two basic social gaps at a time when integration was demanded. The very rich had risen economically farther above the proletariat, and the country and the towns had grown farther apart in feeling and thinking. These years of peasant migration to the cities were as unproductive of organic economic growth as was the movement of the English yeomanry to the mills during the Industrial Revolution. The countryside was not prepared to lose strong hands; the city, not ready to feed, lodge, and care for the peasant who had suddenly turned up as an urban proletarian—rootless, penniless, without direction, and completely lacking in resources.

It was in this situation of falling real wages, of great prosperity for the oligarchy, of government for the benefit of the Great Families, that the Colombian proletariat shook itself awake and slowly stirred to life. The beginnings were tentative and badly organized, and in the main opposed by the government. "The acts of Colombia's rulers on an international plane," says Galbraith, "were in no way associated

[16] García, *op. cit.*, p. 242.
[17] Alejandro López, *Problemas Colombianos* (Bogotá, n.d.), p. 113.
[18] Laureano Gómez, *Interrogantes Sobre el Progreso de Colombia* (Bogotá, 1928), p. 162. Cited by García.

with the life or ideas of the mass of the people, who were not required to nor were in effect able to think beyond their immediate surroundings, needs and problems ... illiterate peasants voted as their employers indicated, while workers accepted low standards of renumeration without being able to refer to higher wages even in their own country."[19]

But the dance of the millions was ending, and the piper would present his bill. The masses were to become vocal and aware, and they were to find channels for their dissatisfaction.

Two events served mainly to break the power of the Conservative party and lift the Liberals up to power as the party of mass reform. A bloody strike in the banana zone of Santa Marta focused attention upon the ties between the oligarchy and foreign imperialism, and the world-wide depression discredited the policy of prosperity by loans.

From the repercussions of these events came the brief, abortive era of Liberal reform and progress.

PROLETARIAN RUMBLINGS AND LIBERAL VICTORY

When German ex-Luftwaffe pilots formed the *Sociedad Colombiana de Transportes Aéreos* (SCADTA) in 1919, and busily began to fly a network of air routes over the nation, time was compressed for all Colombians. Days and weeks became hours in terms of travel and communication. Provincial barriers crumbled, the Departments came closer to the national government, seacoast and capital rushed to meet one another, and national political integration appeared possible for the first time.

For the first time, too, the press found a national audience in place of its former local or provincial one. Newspapers went everywhere by air. Ideas were spread, opinions tested and reflected, on a wholly new scale. And when the national radio became a common medium, the politician, the idealist, and the demagogue took to it like the proverbial duck discovering water. In their competition for popular support, the parties often made extravagant promises, far in advance of the nation's true resources, and as Galbraith says, in excess of what either party intended to do or to grant. By creating expectations and awakening the masses without seriously intending to make good on their promises, the parties contributed to much unrest to come.

The masses fumbled blindly for vehicles of expression. Gaitán

[19] Galbraith, *op. cit.*, p. 127.

founded the *Unión Nacional Izquierdista Revolucionaria* (UNIR), and the Colombian Communist party rose out of the unrest of the middle class artisans and the university students. It was orthodox Marxist in strictest theory, but the peasants and workers knew it not, and its intellectual adherents later veered away into the Socialist party and the reformist wing of the Liberal party.

But despite the popular unrest and the bankruptcy of the Conservative regime, the people remained basically loyal to the traditional parties. Even UNIR, Gaitán's reformist party, was a bastard growth: half Liberal, half Socialist. The traditional Liberal party tie holding most people prevented it from gaining important strength.

Still, the lure of Russian communism drew and held certain Colombians. Colombian delegates attended the international labor conferences in Moscow in 1927 and 1928. They returned home anxious to adjust the tactics of international communism to Latin-American conditions.[20] Colombian Communists also took part in the creation of the Confederation of Syndicates of Latin America (CSLA), which was strong in the decade between 1924 and 1934.

For a short time, too, the proletariat found a voice through UNIR. Basically an offshoot of the *Aprista* movement which swept over Latin America following World War I, it clamored for agrarian reform, for the breaking up of the large estates, and for labor unionism. But paradoxically, it never reached deeply into the mass of the people. Probably it was premature, for the people for whom it was intended still believed strongly in the Liberal revolution, still were deeply traditionalist in politics. UNIR stood for orderly, parliamentary revolution, and rejected violence. It proposed, it is now believed, to wait for the people to become disillusioned with the two main parties. But Gaitán underestimated their patience. Many of the principles of UNIR are found in the *idearium* of Rojas Pinilla's regime today.

Through this period of change and ferment, certain rudimentary labor laws were in operation, although today they are termed "prehistoric" by Adan Arriaga, ex-minister of labor for Colombia.[21] Unions could be broken by employers, the strike was illegal, and often the Army or the police were used as strikebreakers. As the dance of

[20] Miguel Jorrín, *Governments of Latin America* (New York: D. Van Nostrand Co., Inc., 1953), p. 226.
[21] *Semana* (Bogotá), January 13, 1955, p. 14.

the millions swirled to its climax, the government openly used force to suppress the peasants in Santander, to discourage the action of UNIR in many places, and, most notably, to break the peasant revolt in the banana zone of Santa Marta.

The trouble in the banana zone grew out of the organized flouting of certain laws intended to protect labor. Statutes provided for a National Inspector of Labor, whose function was to insure safe and sanitary conditions for workers. There was a collective insurance system, and employers were liable for damages in certain instances. But, in general, officials connived frankly with employers to break these laws. Rippy gives a good account of how this was done in the banana zone controlled by the United Fruit Company:

> Native planters and the United Fruit Company escape direct responsibility for the provisions of Colombian law regarding medical attention, sanitary dwellings for labor, and collective and accident insurance. When regular wages are paid, the minimum until recently varied from $1.00 to $1.65 per day, depending upon climate and health conditions, which are generally very bad, but worse in some districts than in others. Until 1929 workers of all classes were paid twice a month, but had a portion of their wages advanced in the form of scrip, which would be exchanged for commodities at the commissaries of the companies or at the stores of the banana zone. A group of unscrupulous money-changers sprang up who often bought the scrip at a discount of 25 per cent just as they do in some southern cotton mill towns of the United States. Much of the clothing, food and other supplies consumed by the laborers is regularly brought into the region by the company, which is naturally interested in having cargoes for its vessels as they return from foreign fruit markets.[22]

Depressed and goaded by these conditions, workers in the banana zone, the mines, and the ports turned to class syndicalism. It was of a disorganized and anarchistic type, if not hazily objectiveless. But it was based upon a consciousness of class differences and injustices, and, vague as it was, it was to challenge the old order: "This imposing awakening of class syndicalism . . . in all the key points of the country . . . and this impulsive vigor of the new social mysticism, laid down the bases for the fall of the Conservative government in 1930," says Antonio García.[23]

Inevitably, there was sharp Conservative reaction to oppose the coalescing forces of the social revolution. Workers on the railway of the *Sabana* were fired for going on strike. The Tenant's League,

[22] Rippy, *op. cit.*, p. 181.
[23] García, *op. cit.*, p. 255.

formed to protest high city rents and speculation in real estate, was dissolved by government decree. The peasants in the Cauca Valley were stripped of their lands by the large *hacendados*, and Indian reservations were carved up and sold. At Guataquí, Cundiamarca, the homes of agricultural workers were burned when they claimed reimbursement for improvements made by their own labor. Strikes became subversive acts, and syndicalism was driven underground.

There were also prophets of the counterrevolution. In 1924 appeared a *Nationalistist Manifesto*, which denounced republicanism in general—a harbinger of the Hispanic nationalism of the forties—and deplored the rise of the working classes: "In opposition to the extreme anarchism of the urban proletariat, which is a systematic sedition of the individual against the species, we invoke the traditional feeling of the peasant classes, who are the very spirit of the land."[24] But the peasants had changed: more of them wanted their own land. The bitterness grew on both sides. Social struggle came to occupy first place in political matters.

In the summer of 1929, the condition of the workers under the hand of the oligarchy was dramatically portrayed for the nation. The peasants in the banana zone had struck against intolerable conditions, and the Army had been called in to suppress it. Brutality and bloodshed marked the repression, 1,400 peasants losing their lives, while 2,000 had been wounded and scores summarily tried and jailed.[25]

Jorge Eliécer Gaitán, even then the champion of the masses, and a member of Congress, went to the zone to make a personal investigation. In the summer of 1929, he laid his findings before Congress. The revelations shook the country. It was, as Gaitán painted it, a peasant revolt, one wholly justified by conditions. From the testimony emerged the fact that the Conservative Méndez government had used the Army to insure "social peace" for a foreign company, at a total and cold disregard for the welfare of native Colombians.

Colombians of both parties awoke with a start, as it became clear that Colombian bayonets had helped support the banana empire when challenged by poor peasants. During the congressional debates, the government was completely discredited. The Minister of War was forced to resign. And despite the evidence, there was a "cold op-

---

[24] Silvio Villegas, *No Hay Enemigos a la Derecha* (Manizales, 1937), p. 231. Cited by García, *op. cit.*, p. 256.

[25] See Rippy, *op. cit.*, pp. 181 ff.

position of Conservative and Liberal representatives" to the debate, as the finger of guilt pointed more directly to the oligarchy. Against these were Liberals and Conservatives who had been deeply shocked and alarmed. These men united in criticism of the government, and their charges "shook public opinion and prepared the civic upheavals" that followed.[26]

To the shock occasioned by the revelations regarding the banana zone strike, there soon was added the shaking impact of depression which brought the Conservative house of cards tumbling down. With foreign debts of two hundred million pesos burdening the country, stock values, coffee prices, and general equities plummeted. The bubble had burst. Colombia saw the Conservative regime in all its moral and political weakness, and sought a change.

The Conservatives had been in power since 1886. When Abadía Méndez succeeded Ospina in 1926, his election was partially due to the abstention of the dispirited Liberals, who neither presented a candidate nor voted. By the end of Méndez' term, however, Liberal fortunes were on the rise.

Méndez was leader of the "historical Conservatives" which, in free translation, means the reactionary wing of the party. Upon taking office he had asked the Liberals to join his cabinet, but following their refusal he organized his government along "historical" lines.[27]

Honest scruples probably had something to do with the Liberal abstention. The temper of the country was changing; trouble was ahead, and the Liberals sincerely wanted change. Tactically, of course, they could exploit Méndez' mistakes if they held aloof from his government. It seemed wise to let the Conservatives take the full blame for what appeared to be coming.

There was little difficulty in tagging the Méndez administration as "feudalistic." Socialists, Communists, leftist Liberals, regulars, thinkers, and intellectuals became apostles of the new ideas, the new philosophies. They made loud and odious comparisons of conditions in Colombia and other countries. They turned their big guns on borrowing as a national policy, upon the enrichment of the oligarchy, upon graft and corruption, upon the policy of foreign concessions which reduced Colombia to a colonial state in which foreign corporations oppressed Colombian workers and peasants. "It was alleged in

[26] García, op. cit., p. 257.
[27] Arrubla and Henao, op. cit., p. 533.

particular that there had been a lack of concentration upon the projects promising surest economic returns, as well as too much duplication ... occasionally accusations of inefficiency, waste or graft were
made."[28]

But the Liberal party was by no means homogeneous. Many Liberals had profited from loans, expansion, contracts, building. Many
were millionaires, or fondly hoped to be very soon. Still, the center
of gravity of poverty and reformism lay with the Liberals. "The
Liberal Party," says García,

> was two very separate things: a revolutionary movement of the people ... doc-
> trinally goaded by the new socialist generation and headed by a doughty general
> of the civil wars ... and a republican club. Of course, the dynamics of the party
> were revolutionary, because the people, and not the club, marked it character-
> istically: in the club, a republican, individualistic and bourgeois language was
> spoken ... after all, one of its best men had been found in the managership of a
> bank ... and among the people a class, socialist and revolutionary tongue was
> used. With one thesis or the other ... that of the conserving of the Liberal Party,
> or that of making new parties, the new generation understood that the people
> were obligated to battle, together, to gain their social rights, their political and
> their religious rights. All the revolutionary currents of the epoch ... Socialists,
> Communists, syndicalists and anarcho-syndicalists ... participated in the same
> doctrine.[29]

By 1928–29, this fusion of elements had blown up a tornado of suspicion and discontent with the "historical" Conservatives. At the
heart of the matter lay the mishandling of vast sums of money which
had come into the country from abroad. "The volume of these investments continued increasing year after year until many people
were fearful lest the foreign capitalists come to dominate the country
and its government. This naturally led to accusations of dishonesty,
fraud and graft, which, in turn, contributed to the political instability
of the Conservatives."[30] The banana zone scandals, the implication
of the Army, the depression and the collapse of the economy, the
growing enlightenment, and the increasingly obvious need for social
reform—all these had piled up into a vast potential of revolutionary
impetus. Liberals in general, of all denominations and colorations,

[28] *Ibid.*, p. 536.

[29] García, *op. cit.*, p. 257.

[30] William Marion Gibson, *The Constitutions of Colombia* (Durham: Duke
University Press, 1948), p. 357.

were convinced that the "oligarchic system" as Pereyra termed it, was desirable "only insofar as the transitory may consolidate itself."[31]

But division had occurred within the Conservative party also. The Moderates, having joined with the Liberals in attacking the government on the banana zone scandals, had moved apart from the "historicals." This schism was deepened when, as the time approached to find a candidate for the 1930 elections, the Archbishop of Bogotá began to meddle in the Conservative choice. First he approved the choice of one faction, then that of another, so antagonizing the Moderate wing and separating them from their brethren.[32] Many Conservatives, too, seemed convinced of the truth of the charges of graft and corruption against their party's government. "Some . . . appeared, in fact, to have been provoked to the point of being willing to give the Liberals a chance to guide the ship of state through the approaching economic reefs."[33]

So it was that the Liberals, scenting possible victory for the first time in forty years, approached for their candidate Dr. Enrique Olaya Herrera, Colombian minister in Washington.

Olaya refused. This act was significant simply because in the first instance only the Liberals asked Olaya to take the helm. Olaya was an aristocrat, a member from birth of the oligarchy. In the Méndez government were men who were of his class, who were his friends. Undoubtedly, too, he was aware of the reformist orientation of his own Liberal party. These new elements which were taking over were still strange, and to a degree untrustworthy, if not outright revolutionary. And so, Olaya refused the candidacy when it was tendered to him from the hands of Liberals alone. Sentimentally and spiritually, he was more comfortable with Conservatives.

But it did not end there. The challenge of the times was not a partisan one, but of a class nature. Therefore, Moderate Conservatives of the upper classes joined with the Liberals in asking Olaya to run for the presidency. This time, with the character of the backing made explicit, he accepted. A fusion ticket was drawn up. Olaya returned to Colombia, made a three-weeks campaign, and was elected

---

[31] Carlos Pereyra, *Historia de la América Española* (Madrid: Editorial Saturnino Calleja, 1927), IV, 318.

[32] Arrubla and Henao, *op. cit.*, p. 187.

[33] *Ibid.*

to head a government called *Concentración Nacional* (National Concentration). What the Liberals could not do, the Conservatives did for them. Parties had lost meaning. The issue was revolution, or holding the line against popular reform. Says García:

> The oligarchies of both parties felt the foundations of *their republic* shake beneath them, and in the face of the horror of revolutionary uprisings, took advantage of the union created by the Conservative split and the disconcerting schism within the Church, to present to the country a new road: that of National Concentration ... and Olaya Herrera, a representative figure of opportunist, ideal-poor republicanism. Just as in 1910, when the Republican Party was thrown together, National Concentration was a tactical maneuver to avoid revolutionary explosions, by transferring power to a Liberal chief of the privileged classes. While the ingenious Liberal public told itself that in Olaya's election it had found a tactical road toward the new revolutionary order ... falling victim to that amnesia so frequent in our history ... the upper classes, both Liberal and Conservative, had saved their dynastic kingdom by an able maneuver. They had saved their skin, but they could not save themselves from the harsh impact of the Great Crisis.[34]

The times called for revolution, and the people got a quasi-oligarch. With their *status quo* threatened, Liberals and Conservatives of the upper classes had joined hands across party lines to hold in check the pressure from below. It would not be conservatism, but neither would it be liberalism which would mark Olaya's government. He would be safe, and the very Liberal tag which he carried would appease the people to a degree. The oligarchy could look forward to this period of transition with some comfort, if not with complete faith that the line would hold.

[34] García, *op. cit.*, p. 258.

IV. The Rise of Liberalism and Reform: From the Depression to World War II (1930–1942)

OLAYA HERRERA AND "HOLDING THE LINE"

Olaya's basic purpose, the one for which he had been chosen and elected, was that of holding together a moderate front of Liberals and Conservatives in the face of an economic crisis that had revolutionary overtones. There is, therefore, nothing strange in the fact that his government sought mainly to conserve: of greatest interest to the men in both parties who supported him was a program which would protect them from the worst effects of the economic depression.

By his background, thinking, and philosophy, Olaya was destined for the middle ground. Nominally a Liberal, there was a wide streak of Conservative in him. In 1910 he had helped to organize the Republican party, an earlier version of National Concentration, which Luis Cano called "a layer of cotton between two crystals."[1] Its function had been the same as was Olaya's: maintaining the *status quo* under challenge. But now there were new factors to be dealt with. Olaya's government must cushion the growing friction between two major social classes. Accordingly, he chose the Golden Mean, and was generally acceptable to most people, for, "although the Liberals were proud to claim him as a great Liberal, the moderation which characterized him ... clearly distinguished him from the Colombian Liberals of the middle era of the nation's history. They were ... uncompromising Liberals of the impractical type; he was a sane and practical statesman ... a genuine progressive, but not a radical."[2]

Nor was Olaya heedless of the mass rumblings. Under his regime, a few needy citizens were given land carved from the huge estates; a start was made in providing cheap housing for the laboring classes; trade was spurred by abolishing customs barriers between the Departments; Colombians were given preference in employment in the oil industry, and the industry itself was placed under government

[1] Romoli, *op. cit.*, p. 289.
[2] Arrubla and Henao, *op. cit.*, p. 546.

regulation as a public utility. Public health and education came in for serious attention also. It was by no means a revolution of the society, but enough was done for the masses to keep them from erecting barricades in the streets.

In fact, radical reforms at this time might have brought serious disjointments, for the economy had gone into a tailspin. The state's income dropped from seventy-five million pesos to thirty-five million between 1929 and 1931. Foreign trade fell off to a trickle, and the internal market dried up. Credit was extremely tight. Many businesses failed, and were swallowed up by the banks: "Companies affiliated with the banks that were made up of stockholders of the former, auctioned away with borrowed money the property of debtors who could not pay up."[3] The dreary old saw came to life: "The rich got richer and the poor got poorer."

To save the situation, Olaya imposed a moratorium. Interest rates were reduced, suits for collection of debts were suspended, and land mortgage foreclosures were prohibited for the duration of the crisis. But in spite of these measures, much real estate, mortgaged during inflation, passed into the hands of bankers, "creating a new landed aristocracy ... with the money of the depositors themselves."[4]

For most Colombians, it was a time of *"sauve qui peut"* rather than for drastic revolutionary action. The big worry was whether the banks would take away one's land for less than the mortgage value. To meet the gap between credit and the need to refinance lands, the government established the *Caja de Crédito Agrario* and the *Banco Central Hipotecario* (Central Mortgage Bank) to ease conditions for the small coffee grower and for distressed mortgagees in general.

Nonetheless, these steps gave aid and comfort chiefly to those who already had some substantial patrimony, some established means of earning and saving. The land which was distributed to the peasant merely skimmed the surface of the problem. (Until the Land Reform Act of 1936, only 1,000 new proprietors had been made in the whole country; 14,513 *fanegadas* of land had been parceled out, a *fanegada* equaling 1.59 acres.)

This was not what the people had been promised, nor what they had expected. They had pinned their hopes in the Liberal party on

---

[3] *Debate Sobre la Situación Financiera y Económica del Pais* (Bogotá: Cámara de Representates, Imprenta Nacional, 1937), p. 120.

[4] García, *op. cit.*, p. 265.

the ideas expressed by Alejandro López, a Liberal spokesman, who had said, in 1931, "in a few years [redistribution will be made] of uncultivated lands lying between the cities of Facatativá, Bucaramanga, Manizales and Cáceres [as] the central zone of the country."[5] Consequently, this niggling program of Olaya's fell far short of popular goals. Reform laws were the rule, rather than true reform.

For all these reasons, social agitation grew. Jorge Eliécer Gaitán's UNIR again became active and vocal, calling for land distribution and relocation of the peasants on the land. In Cundinamarca there were peasant clashes with the police, and in Tolima and Valle del Cauca peasants and proprietors did sporadic battle.

But there was no revolution. The competent forces had found a leader who maintained a position just far enough off dead center to keep the troublesome elements in check. Even so, this policy might not have succeeded in the long run, had not the war with Peru intervened to divert the attention of all Colombians to other problems.

The trouble over the fever-infested strip of jungle known as the Leticia area in effect substituted an external crisis for the internal one. Colombians of all classes and conditions rallied to the banner. In one day the war budget of ten million pesos was subscribed, and social depression and agitation were forgotten as Peru, rather than depression, became the common enemy. Martial law was imposed throughout the land, and the psychology of the people was altered. The nation was in peril, and Colombia's fierce patriotism blotted out mere economic considerations.

It is just possible that the war with Peru may have saved Olaya's government. Internal conditions had come to a dangerous pass. But for the time being, solution of these problems was deferred for the attention of some more reform-minded government. That government was to come, under Alfonso López Pumarejo.

The fact that there was enough ready and available capital to buy up the war bonds in one day passed quickly over the national consciousness. Capital was there, in hiding, timid and fearful for investment in the bootstrap operation required to bring prosperity back to the nation.

That it came out of its dark recesses only to finance a foreign war, was put down to patriotism of the highest order.

[5] López, *op. cit.*, p. 211.

ALFONSO LÓPEZ AND "REVOLUTION ON THE MARCH"[6]

With the advent of Alfonso López to the presidency of Colombia, Liberal reformism reached high tide, and the concept of government as director and administrator of orderly revolutionary change made its indelible impress on the nation.

But the López reforms, his sponsorship of the rights and demands of the masses, brought forth opposition which, clashing with the Liberal thesis, created the tensions that eventually brought on the civil war of 1948–53.

López gave a new incentive to governing. Abandoning the old incentive of "occupation of the administration," he moved toward the incentive of gradual, planned revolution over the bitter opposition of the oligarchy. But when his first term ended, he had planted conflicts that tore the Colombian people and the classes violently apart. After López, the state as innovator, controller, and director was to be in constant struggle with the idea of the state as the maintainer and supporter of the privileged position of the oligarchy.

And yet it would be wrong to call López a revolutionary. He was, in fact, no more than the "most intelligent reformist of the Liberal bourgeoisie, an able administrator, pragmatic and dogmatic."[7] He gathered all the functions of command and administration into his office and person, and therefore he frightened the republicans and the moderate Liberals (not to mention the Conservatives), whose strength lay in a loose, chaotic republicanism which they themselves could control. In a sense, López made explicit the old heritage of *caudillismo*, operating through the thesis of "government of the Party as a convenient fact, but new and obligatory."[8]

An audacious agitator of social, economic, and political problems, he was also a cold, logical man whose enemies would not trust themselves to exposure to his personal charm and persuasiveness. Keenly aware of the needs of the masses, he mistrusted big business, yet was himself a big businessman, a charter member of the oligarchy, had he cared to exercise his membership. He was a reformer and an innovator, yet he was to offer nothing basically new, was eventually to fall

[6] López' first term, 1934–38, has often been likened to FDR's New Deal; he called it *La Revolución en Marcha*.

[7] García, *op. cit.*, p. 272.

[8] *Mensajes del Presidente López al Congreso Nacional* (Bogotá: Imprenta Nacional, 1938), p. 258.

victim to the timidity and the reactionary concepts of the oligarchy; and in his second term, when the cards were down, he was to abandon his supporters, and turn his back on the social revolution.

Because the man is so important to the recent history of Colombia, a quick sketch of his background is pertinent to an understanding of his policies.

López was a patrician, a wealthy man in his own right. He held a mild grudge against big business, although he had been an agent for the investment houses which poured money into Colombia while the dance of the millions was in full swing. From his youth he bitterly opposed the politics of civil war, espousing a kind of Creole radical-socialism.[9] This basic opposition to the old political methods and chiefs led him to fight against "the stratification of the nation, and of ideas." Believing that the republicanism of both the Liberals and the Conservatives had by-passed the country's needs, he refused to conform to the usual Liberal-Conservative mold, and gladly welcomed the challenge which they represented.

López began to stand out in politics between 1923 and 1929 (he had been a representative from Tolima since 1913), and soon gained a reputation as a critic of the financial policies of the Méndez government, which he called "prosperity by debt."[10] Having contributed materially to the discontent which brought Olaya to the presidency, it became clearer daily during Olaya's term that López was the man to succeed him. López spoke in phrases which coincided with the popular aspirations of the era. Many, of course, considered López a traitor to his class. Scion of a banking family, he firmly believed that big business had ruined the López bank.[11] Possibly this belief motivated some aspects of his program.

Following reverses in the family fortune, López worked in the coffee business, as a newspaper writer and editor, and as an agent for Baker-Kellogg, New York investment bankers. A learned, erudite man with much personal magnetism ("men listened to him and the eyes of women followed him")[12] he represented Colombia at the London Economic Conference, and was Colombian Minister to England in

[9] "Un Consejero de la Nación," *Semana* (Bogotá), February 21, 1955, p. 12.
[10] *Ibid.*, p. 14.
[11] Austin F. MacDonald, *Latin American Politics and Government* (New York: Thomas Y. Crowell Co., 1954), p. 394.
[12] "Un Consejero de la Nación," *Semana*, p. 15.

1931. By the time he was called to the presidency, his fortunes were remade, his reputation was secure, and by all ordinary standards he should have been a Conservative of the upper classes.

But still he harbored the lurking conviction that business and banking should be surrounded with safeguards for the public good, that the rich were not paying their fair share of the cost of progress. In the councils of the Liberal party he became known as the champion of the masses, a strong friend of labor. It was inevitable that he should be chosen to head the ticket when the 1934 elections approached.

As it came time to choose Olaya's successor, the Liberals began to engage in some earnest soul-searching. Those who had joined with the Conservatives to back Olaya wanted no one who would undertake the audacious reforms which the masses were demanding. The Conservatives were still discredited and weak, and the Liberals were divided among themselves regarding the extent to which they should sponsor reform. Austin F. MacDonald gives an analysis of this Liberal political schizophrenia which bears quoting:

> This [division] was not at all surprising, in view of the divergent groups comprising the party's membership. Many wealthy industrialists called themselves Liberals, either because they opposed the dominance of the Roman Catholic Church, or because they thought that the Conservatives were a shade too reactionary. Nearly all the employees of these industrialists, especially those who belonged to the trade unions, also claimed membership in the Liberal Party. So did many intellectuals, whose views were far from uniform. In fact, the Liberals could count on the votes of almost everyone except the representatives and followers of the feudal landholding classes, plus some very devout Catholics. This overwhelming Liberal support placed the party in a very enviable position, but it was also a source of weakness because it necessitated endless compromise in the selection of party candidates and the preparation of the party program.[13]

The very times tended to align men by class interest, to strain the ability to compromise. Actually, in most Colombian crises the differences between Conservatives and Liberals have been overstated and unreal. The oligarchs have never been embarrassed by party lines when united action is needed to oppose pressure from below. Much the same is true of the imagined differences over the Church question. Colombians themselves have a *dicho*, a saying, which expresses the shallow nature of the religious party difference: *"En Colombia, son Liberales los que toman el público y rezan en particular; son Conservadores los que rezan en público y toman en particular."*[14] The

---

[13] MacDonald, *op. cit.*, p. 393.

summation is apt enough. When basic issues threaten, neither Church matters nor party labels differentiate the Conservative and Liberal upper levels.

Consequently, the Moderate Liberals were uneasy about López. They, as well as the Conservatives, feared that he would initiate a "soak-the-rich" program. Yet a López was demanded by the times, and when the Liberals nominated him, the Moderates went along with the party. Many of them would have been happier with some Conservative party candidate.

There was, of course, violent opposition to López from the Conservative side of the aisle. It was headed by Dr. Laureano Gómez, leader of the most reactionary wing of conservatism. In fact, from the moment that López was nominated, the story of Colombian politics becomes, in a sense, that of López and Gómez in conflict: Siegfried and the Dragon, Caesar and Brutus, Maximilian and Juárez—the traditional story of sworn protagonist and antagonist, repeated and refined, but following its classical form and denouncement. It was destined to be a fateful political rivalry for Colombia. Hence, something should be said of Dr. Gómez.

Gómez: Sometimes-Loyal Opposition

John Gunther, in his *Inside Latin America,* says of Laureano Gómez, "he is a typical politician of the extreme Right, and we shall find one of him—with identical stigmata— in almost every South American country. He is strongly religious, strongly clerical, strongly Spanish. . . . His ideas, his instincts, his sympathies, are all bitterly anti-United States."[15]

Gómez was much more complex than this makes him appear. Trained as an engineer, he early foresook the drafting boards for politics. A thoroughgoing aristocrat in every respect, all his thinking stemmed from the frames of reference of the feudalistic, aristocratic landed gentry, and from the primacy of the Roman Catholic Church as the main force in the society after government. Physically a stocky, craggy-faced, hot-eyed zealot, Gómez was a polemician of the first rank, and he ran the Conservative party with iron discipline. Al-

[14] "In Colombia, the Liberals are those who drink in public and pray in private; the Conservatives are those who pray in public and drink in private."

[15] John Gunther, *Inside Latin America* (New York: Harper & Brothers, 1941), p. 166.

though magnetic and forceful, he often became as illogical as a spoiled, wilful child. In 1938, for instance, he suffered an apoplectic stroke after denouncing mild, scholarly President Santos as a "murderer . . . who 'sits in pools of Conservative blood.' "[16]

Oddly enough, this man, who was to bring Colombia, bloody and shackled, to her knees under a ruthless dictatorship modeled after Franco at the heighth of the repression, was anything but an *enfant térrible* in his formative political years. The Gómez who became the Grand Inquisitor of the era of 1948–53 arrived at that point by some strange, undetermined route.

In the twenties, he and López were one in questioning the Conservative policy of courting foreign capital. His attack upon the American companies for their treatment of Colombian labor was one of the most violent protests of the era.[17] Even more strange, he was at that time a close friend of Alfonso López. Always, their lives crossed: sometimes in amity, again, in bitter battle without quarter. "The life of the one has always been the point of reference of the other. If one of them were to disappear, the other would feel a secret, inner vacuum."[18]

Together, they attended the literary and political *cénacles* in which the ideas of the future were formed and discussed. The Gómez of that era was Conservative and strongly Catholic, but the intellectuals of the Right saw in him no *caudillo*, no positive force. As late as 1937, Silvio Villegas, a fire-eating totalitarian, was saying rather contemptuously of Gómez: "Doctor Gómez, who is impotent as regards violence, is even more so in the matter of civil action."[19] But this man who was "incapable of violence" was to author the most universal and thoughtless violence ever visited upon Colombia.[20]

Somewhere along the road of his intellectual development, Gómez belied his own ideas, foreswore his own philosophy. But before he could do so, he had to conquer his own basic, idealistic republicanism. On the eve of World War II he was writing his profession of faith, called *El Cuadrilátero*. "It was," says Antonio García, "a bitter protest against totalitarian imperialism, against the cynical Machiavel-

---

[16] *Ibid.*, p. 167.
[17] See Laureano Gómez, *op. cit.*
[18] "Un Consejero de la Nación," *Semana*, p. 13.
[19] Villegas, *op. cit.*, p. 216.
[20] García, *op. cit.*, p. 303.

lianism of Mussolini and Hitler, against the demonaic power of the
Georgian Stalin, against the paganization of political life expressed
in the systematic use of force."[21] It appealed to the youth of Colombia
to "renew in the prodigious life of Ghandi the eternal moral lesson
that ... the power of the spirit overcomes violence and destroys it;
that justice is stronger than the greatest fleets and the most powerful
cannon."[22]

What worked the metamorphosis in Gómez from enemy of violence
to that of ruthless suppressor by violence of all opposition will never
be known. This human drama of spiritual change may, in fact, be the
very drama of Colombian politics. Antonio García thinks that the
war destroyed the validity of the Gómez-Ghandian concept, and left
Gómez with nothing. From that time on, he opposed not the Liberal
party, not the working classes, but himself. He rose against his life,
his tradition, and became the Great Renegade. "This was," says
García, "not the most important victory of Laureano Gómez, but
the bloodiest, the most destructive."[23] It is an interesting theory.

Whatever the cause, the end result was notable: Gómez was to
mount a successful counterrevolution, and to bring fire and sword
to Colombia. He was to turn the course of the nation away from
popular republicanism toward the Hispanic state of Ferdinand and
Isabel. Once victorious in his battle with his friend-enemy Alfonso
López, he would try to replace the shade of Marx with the spirit of
Torquemada.

The López Program

Taken out of context, the López program seems commonplace,
even though it was, as Romoli says, "radical enough in relation to the
people to whom it was applied."[24] For the upper classes, it was daring
and unconventional,[25] although it made no basic reforms in the
structure of the society. López cleaned house, but did not construct
a new one.[26]

Soon after taking office on August 7, 1934, López asked the Congress

[21] *Ibid.*, pp. 302–3.
[22] *Ibid.*
[23] *Ibid.*
[24] Romoli, *op cit.*, p. 282–83.
[25] Gibson, *op. cit.*, p. 357.
[26] See García, *op. cit.*, p. 273.

for laws which would make the rich pay a higher share of the national expenses. At once a storm of protest swirled up from the Moderate Liberals and the Conservatives. The Congress, still controlled by the Conservatives, rejected López' land-partitioning plan, and, although he pushed through capital and income tax laws, these were declared unconstitutional by the Supreme Court.[27]

The humble people reacted angrily as they saw their revolution denied them. "The masses, poverty-stricken by the depression and as a result of influences already mentioned, began to demand that the big estates of absentee landowners be broken up and distributed among the landless and hungry, and López' policy included agrarian reforms with this in view."[28] In the forefront of the fight for reform was Gaitán, working to advance the interests of the commoners.

In the congressional elections of 1935, the Moderate Liberal-Conservative majority was toppled by a professedly reformist Liberal majority. López' program got the green light. However, still fearing the Supreme Court, López asked the new congress to amend the Constitution to permit the fulfillment of his program. Accordingly, certain amendments were approved by that body on August 1, 1936. Known as the Codification of 1936, these amendments and the laws passed pursuant thereto were to become the major targets of the Conservative counterrevolution. They remain issues down to the present. Therefore, they will bear scrutiny.

Article 17, Title III, provides that "labor is a social obligation, and it shall enjoy the special protection of the state."[29] With this legal sanction erasing the long, dreary history of union-busting and persecution, the scattered, timid locals of Colombia organized into a master union in the same year. Under the name of the *Confederación de Trabajadores de Colombia* (CTC), some 900 locals, totaling 100,000 workers, joined this group.[30]

Under this grant of power, interpreted as not only granting but *imposing* authority upon Congress to assist labor,[31] that body passed a series of laws to raise the status and condition of the workers. Article

---

[27] Galbraith, *op. cit.*, p. 128.

[28] *Ibid.*

[29] Rodrigo Noguera Laborde, *Constitución de la República de Colombia y sus Antecedentes Documentales desde 1885* (Bogotá: Fondo Rotaria, Pontificia Universidad Catolica Javeriana, 1950), p. 205.

[30] Jorrín, *op. cit.*, p. 293.

[31] Gibson, *op. cit.*, p. 361.

18, another innovation, provided that "the right to strike is guaranteed except in the public services. Its exercise shall be regulated by law."[32] To implement these constitutional guarantees, President López' Decree No. 2350 was made by Congress into Law No. 6, a Colombian Charter of Labor.

Law No. 6 spelled out the general form of the labor contract, relieved labor from judgments at common law, established a presumptive termination date of six months for parole and informal labor contracts, set up a minimum wage, provided for paid holidays and vacations, imposed employer responsibility for sickness and accident, established retirement benefits and severance pay, guaranteed further the right to strike without molestation, forbade the use of strike-breakers, set up the eight-hour day and the forty-eight week, and prohibited "parallelism" or duplication of unions in order to protect bona fide unions from those subsidized by employers.[33] In addition to those substantive gains, labor was given certain procedural benefits, such as the creation of a special tribunal, the Judicial Jurisdiction for Labor, to provide arbitration and conciliation services and to settle labor disputes.[34]

On the perennial land reform question, López met the agrarian agitation by shoving through Congress Law No. 200 of 1936. This act gave the peasants "squatters rights" on both public and private land, by making their eviction subject to difficult legal process if they had made even minimal improvements.[35] Both hailed and feared as a blow at the land-holding oligarchy, the law actually did little to add to the number of peasant holdings, and was, in fact, counter-productive since it was used to revaluate certain lands along ways of communication to a highly inflated figure.

But perhaps the most frightening aspect of the López reforms, for the oligarchy, was the philosophy of the state which López wrote into the constitution. Both the Moderate Liberals and the Conservatives saw the welfare state emerging from Article 19 which said, "Public assistance is a function of the state. It shall be given to persons who, being physically incapable of working, lack the means of self-support

[32] Noguera Laborde, *op. cit.*, p. 205.

[33] Adán Arriaga, cited in *Semana* (Bogotá), January 31, 1955, p. 14.

[34] *Ibid.*

[35] Luis Emiro Valencia, "El Problema Agrario en Colombia," *Economía Colombiana* (Bogotá), March, 1955, p. 295.

or the right to demand the same of other persons. The law will determine in what form assistance shall be given, and the cases in which the State should give it directly."[36] For a class which had always been accustomed to leaving the fortunes of the poor in the hands of nature, Divine Providence, or the private charities of Church and beneficent organizations, this was very dangerous doctrine.

And still the alarmed oligarchy had worse shocks in store. Article 20 shook the very foundations of property and business, in the view of the upper classes: "Property is a social function which implies obligations," said Paragraph 2 of this clause.[37] And, reasoning from this premise, "when enforcement of a law passed for reasons of public utility or social interest conflicts with the rights of individuals, private interests must give way to the public or social interest." And further, "For reasons of public utility or social interest, as defined by the legislature, property may be expropriated by judicial decree with prior indemnification ... nevertheless, the legislature, *for reasons of equity,* may deny indemnification by means of an absolute vote of the members of both houses."[38]

This provision naturally roused a storm of protest. A wave of wild surmise swept through the ranks of native and foreign investors and owners of property all over the nation. Uneasily, the upper classes of both parties studied the phrase, *"for reasons of equity."* What, indeed, was a "reason of equity"? The shape of the future loomed threatening and portentous for the oligarchy.

If they had any doubts about the shape of the new state, its role and function, Article 32 clarified them. "By means of legislation," this Article provided, "the State may intervene in the exploitation of public and private business and industry, for the purpose of rationalizing production to which it has a right."[39] In this phrase, the oligarchy almost detected the sound of the tumbrils rolling. But the reformist Liberals added insult to injury, religious heresy to economic unorthodoxy, by Title IV, which separated Church and state, stripped the Church of control over education, and permitted equal-

[36] Noguera Laborde, *op. cit.,* p. 205.

[37] *Ibid.,* p. 207.

[38] *Ibid.*

[39] This provision gave Congress, and not the government, the choice of methods of intervention. An extraordinary majority of Congress is necessary to use the power. See Gibson, *op. cit.,* p. 361.

ity of cults; barred priests from any public office, and rendered subject to ordinary law any acts "contrary to Christian morals or subversive to the public order done with or under the pretext of the exercise of any cult."[40]

Analysis of these main points of the López program indicate that they are progressive, that they meet changing times and needs; but they were nothing to topple a social order. Actually, when the smoke had cleared away, the real pinch on the upper classes came from López' tax reforms: always the theme for a song of disaster from the propertied classes. Romoli's analysis of the tax program indicates why this is so:

> Before 1936 Colombian taxation was extremely modest, and even such tributes as were due were ineffectually collected. *No one paid taxes*, except in the manner of a government making a symbolic payment on its external debt. Under the new law, the maximum tax on net income is 17 per cent; patrimony tax may reach 8 per cent in the highest brackets; that on excess profits ... can run as high as 30 per cent, but are susceptible to modification. Altogether, the revenue from these once dead-letter sources amounted in 1939 to more than nineteen million pesos. ... the number of tax-paying business concerns has increased by 256 per cent since the laws went into force.[41]

This tributary reform, then, disturbed the oligarchs simply because it was the first major direct, progressive tax laid upon income, patrimony, and utilities which they really *had to pay*.

In reality, the authentic innovation of the scheme was that it shifted from the customs receipts, to the income and direct tax base, the major responsibility for raising state income. The healthy effect of this was to remove the ancient stimulus to political parties to get their hands on the customs receipts as a reward for winning political power. Custom had long consecrated the practice of pilfering the customs receipts and of levying excises upon tobacco and liquor for the dual purpose of running the state and enriching public servants. López, in fact, referred to this necessary change in his last presidential message of the first term, when he laconically pointed out:

> The idea of reforming the tax system was born here not of the necessity of taking care of a vast program of armament, nor from a desire to punish a capitalist class of cruel and oppressive tendencies, but from that of creating a source

[40] Noguera Laborde, *op. cit.*, pp. 211–12.
[41] Romoli, *op. cit.*, p. 284.

of fiscal wealth different from, and more honest than, the tax upon popular vices which obliges the State to become an importunate inn-keeper for its clients.[42]

Basically, the fear that tax reform would ruin business was unfounded, for, like direct taxes everywhere, they were gradually absorbed by the payers into the balance sheets of costs of operation, transformed into prices, and passed along, in the last instance, to the same people who always pay such costs. Moreover, there was a false ring to the anguished cries from the upper classes, in view of the fact that even the new taxes exempted earnings from stocks and bonds, dividends, and capital associations generally.[43] In the end, the poor people paid the bill in increased costs for consumers' goods.

Nor were the benefits under López to the peasants and workers as great as the oligarchy claimed. The agrarian program was actually rather orthodox. It was limited in effect to parceling out a few haciendas, whose value was charged to the penniless grantees who had neither capital nor machinery to operate the land; to "agrarian colonies" which functioned as bureaucratic institutions for the benefit primarily of government employees; to carving up the Indian communities and shipping off small groups of peasants to fell the forest in remote and inaccessible regions of the country. Because the Law 200 of 1936 left ownership vested in mere registry of title, and at the same time provided rights for those who settled on and improved the land (without clarifying this title conflict), it resulted chiefly in a flood of lawsuits that swamped the courts. Naturally, most of these were won by the absentee landlords, whose titles could be proved with no difficulty under the Common Code. "Its application," says Carlos Mario Londoño, "has demonstrated to us that this law did not go beyond the fomenting of a veritable hatchery of lawsuits and disputes which brought no good to agriculturists, and as a result of which the nation has very few more proprietors."[44] And Antonio García says of it:

> In the Cauca, in Tolima, in Cundinamarca, the simple battle for the land left many peasants dead ... killed by the police of the "Revolution on the March". Law 200 of 1936 served as an instrument of the haciendas to resolve their problems

[42] *Mensajes del Presidente López al Congreso Nacional*, p. 330.

[43] García, *op. cit.*, p. 274.

[44] Carlos Mario Londoño, *Economía Social Colombiana* (Bogotá: Imprenta Nacional, 1953), pp. 158–59.

A view of the business district of Bogotá, Colombia's capital (population 700,000), which lies in a fertile intermountain valley called the *Sabana,* at an altitude of 9,000 feet.

with the sharecroppers or squatters, or touched only the mere periphery of the problem of property and landholding.[45]

As for the workers, their status had been legalized, their rights stated by statute. It was a beginning. But the additional burden placed on the rich was gradually shifted to the workers in increased costs, and the advances were not real. Worker education was scarcely touched. Nothing substantial was done to increase worker and peasant productivity. The façade of a labor movement was thrown up, but labor remained still an appendage of the Liberal party, and the unions lacked an organic political-economic consciousness of their power and their mutual objectives.

Consequently, since the laws did nothing to protect the labor movement from the psychological reaction of the oligarchy to syndicalism, the López reforms were vunerable before a determined counterrevolution. The mere destruction of the façade would leave labor weak, exposed, and disorganized before the purposeful onslaught of the managing class.

Beginning of the Counterrevolution

Tame and logical as it was, the López program caused the oligarchy to raise storm warnings against approaching communism. Both parties became jittery with fear of "Lopismo." In general, his measures "increased the resentment of many wealthy people toward the government, and also produced opposition from the more conservative elements among the Liberals, which defeated some of the administration's later reform bills."[46] In fact, by 1937 opposition within his own party had become so bitter that López no longer bothered to hide his feelings about it. At last he threatened to resign unless Congress became more cooperative. The people supported him, and the unions went out on strike to back him up. But Congress did not budge, and López remained in office, resigned to the opposition of a solid front of Moderate Liberals and Conservatives to every step of the Revolution on the March.

This Moderate Liberal wing of the party was headed by Eduardo Santos, owner and editor of the powerful *El Tiempo*. Santos parti-

[45] García, *op. cit.*, p. 275.

[46] Mary W. Williams, *The People and Politics of Latin America* (New York: Ginn & Company, 1945), p. 544.

sans fought the López program in Congress, in many cases joining with the Conservatives to defeat the reformist Liberals. Angered and disillusioned, López prepared to do battle with the reactionaries in his own party.

Other fronts were also forming their lines for political action. The employing classes united in the *Asociación Patronal Económica Nacional* (Employers National Economic Association); most of its membership were large landholders and entrepreneurs from both parties. And lesser groups soon sprang up as satellites to APEN. As early as 1936, when the reform bills were rolling out of Congress, the oligarchy had conceived the slogan, "Slow Down the Revolution on the March." Labor freedom, Communist agitation, the clamor of leftists of all stripes and colors, seemed to point to a proletarian dictatorship. All conservative and reactionary elements closed ranks to oppose it.

The election of a heavy bloc of Moderate Liberals of the Santos persuasion in the 1937 congressional elections presaged the character of the coming battle. These same Moderates were in the majority when the Liberal nominating convention met that year. Out of the clash of the two Liberal wings at the convention were to come strictures that would mean the failure of the social revolution. Hence, a word to distinguish between them.

The reformist Liberals, "apart from idealistic motives, perceived that a social revolution was under way, and held that the upward pressure from below should not be supressed by force, but could be controlled and directed towards useful development."[47] The Conservatives and the Moderate Liberals, on the other hand, favored meeting the upward pressure by screwing on the lid tighter. They favored minimum concessions, the suppression of leftist agitation and activities, and the restoration of the Church to a position of influence in education and government. Essentially, they believed in "the duty of everyone to conform to the station of life into which he [had been] born, and to leave the management of his affairs to the small, privileged and enlightened ruling caste, whose interests and capital were sacrosanct."[48]

Many of the Moderate Liberals hewed to the line of the Liberal party doctrine, but differed from the reformists regarding methods.

[47] Galbraith, *op. cit.*, p. 129.
[48] *Ibid.*, p. 129.

This was to become the most determined group in the nation. They felt that "their" party had betrayed them, that "[López] was going too far too fast. They were not, however, alienated to the point of leaving the party at the time of the election of 1938. This split was to come later."[49]

But as the time of decision approached, these men were nominal Liberals at best. They were determined that "the presidential candidate should be a man of less radical views than López." They had their way. Dr. Eduardo Santos was nominated by the Moderates of the convention, and they elected him president in May, 1938, to serve until 1942.

The Revolution on the March had been slowed down, and by the very party which had set it on its course.

SANTOS: THE REVOLUTION NO LONGER MARCHES

From the moment of nomination, Alfonso López opposed Eduardo Santos' candidacy. Himself a man who "threw out new ideas, who encouraged intranquility, who revised concepts," he publicly branded Santos a tool of reactionary interests who would turn the clock back on needed reforms. This blast stated at least one basic fact: Santos was to orient his regime slightly toward the *ante status quo*. López had rejected in advance the "pause in revolutionary rhythm" which Santos' government was to represent.[50]

By temperament and philosophy, Santos was heir to the political mantle of Olaya: measured and dignified, moderation was his outstanding characteristic. Like López a wealthy man, like him, too, a believer in democracy, the difference between the two was actually enormous. López rightly read Santos' nomination as meaning a doctrinal return to the near past. Fuming, he founded *El Liberal,* where, with a coterie of young intellectuals and reformist Liberals, he established an "inside opposition" to Santos which was to continue for four bitter years,[51] and to leave the Liberal party hopelessly divided and disoriented, an easy prey for the *coup de grâce* from the hands of Laureano Gómez. Gómez and the Conservatives were the direct beneficiaries of the founding of *El Liberal.*

But most observers agree that Santos provided the country with an excellent government. Even-handed and tranquil, it faced un-

[49] Gibson, *op. cit.,* p. 400.
[50] "Un Consejero de la Nación," *Semana,* p. 15.
[51] *Ibid.*

usual problems, and unusual opposition: not only from López, but from the Conservatives under Gómez, who grew daily more violent and irresponsible.

Santos lost little time in stating his position. Declaring himself in favor of bettering labor's condition, still, he let it be known that he would tolerate no violence, that unions might not intervene organically in politics.[52] Quite naturally, labor resented this, and henceforth identified the Moderate Liberals and the Conservatives as allies. Santos' action in using police to quell a student strike soon after he took office further tended to win his government a non-liberal reputation in the popular mind. Actually, he did not try to return to the past. He simply refused to push on into the future.

In justice to Santos, it must be said that he had his troubles. The country had undoubtedly been disoriented by "Lopismo." Such had been the nature of its organization and its prevailing psychology. But also, the disruptions of war brought to Colombia a loss of coffee markets, unemployment, importation troubles, a flood of European refugees, and a host of allied problems. As coffee fell on the New York market, so did the national income. Then, as coffee recovered and Allied war demands sucked up all raw materials, the nation was subjected to a triple inflationary tendency: deficit financing of the national budget, the shortage of imported fabricated materials and consumers' goods, and the piling-up of dollar balances.

To meet these problems, Santos adopted all-out cooperation with the United States' war aims. He suspended immigration, contracted loans through the Export-Import Bank, provided subsidies for coffee growers, and encouraged foreign exploitation of Colombia's mineral wealth. Administratively, he moved the government toward greater intervention and control. A whole host of agencies of one kind and another appeared, the most notable being the *Instituto de Fomento Municipal,* the *Instituto de Fomento Industrial,* and the *Instituto de Crédito Territorial.* Most of them, unfortunately, were not equipped, financed, or staffed to do their respective jobs, and obtained only rather superficial results.[53] But, where López had

---

[52] MacDonald, *op. cit.,* p. 396.

[53] Says Antonio García: "What could the *Crédito Territorial* do about a Plan for Peasant Housing, when in all its bureaucratic life up to 1948, it had made mortgage loans of only 8 millions? How could an Institute for Municipal Development, with a few million pesos annually, do anything about 600 municipalities without sewage systems, water, or electric light?" *Op. cit.,* p. 280.

gone through a period of economic recovery and relative prosperity, Santos caught the nation going into the low of the cycle. He did as well as he could. Early in his term he established the ministries of hygiene and of social welfare, to alleviate somewhat the condition of the poor. But mounting inflation and lagging wage levels could not be offset by the government's mild program of concern for the workers and peasants.

There was more positive action as regards cooperation with the United States. Acting in conjunction with the United States, Santos nationalized the German-controlled air lines, sent the Germans home, and placed the line under Colombian-American management. Shortly after Pearl Harbor, Colombia broke off relations with the Axis, and the Santos government quietly gave the American Embassy permission to operate a counter-espionage system through the Embassy and the Consulates.

This close collaboration with the *Pulpo del Norte* (Octupus of the North) was fuel for the heated Conservative opposition. Even the *Lopistas* exploited the issue as a matter of principle. López himself was thus credited with an anti-Americanism that he did not deserve. Says Hubert Herring on this score: "President Santos stands for complete Pan-American cooperation, offers Colombian aid to the United States for protection of the Panama Canal, and has proved his zeal by ending German control of Colombian air lines. Another faction of Liberals, headed by Alfonso López, condemns Santos' affection for Washington. However, those who know López have no fear that he will play with Washington's enemies."[54]

Thus, only for the sake of an issue upon which to oppose Santos, the López Liberals played into the hands of the Conservatives. Crafty old Laureano Gómez exploited every Liberal difference, preparing the Liberal party for the ultimate kill with the very weapons which Liberals were forging.

Gómez Exploits the Liberal Division over Reform

Breathing fire at every political snort, Gómez whipped the Conservatives into a militant, cohesive, and somewhat pro-Axis party. Something difficult to explain had happened to the man. Once merely conservative, he now appeared almost hysterically reactionary. His

---

[54] Hubert Herring, *Good Neighbors* (New Haven: Yale University Press, 1941), p. 286.

newspaper, *El Siglo,* the chief Conservative party line, kept up a campaign of opposition so wildly vitriolic that at times it seemed to border on insanity. Says Herring: *"El Siglo* . . . lays the lash on the Liberals, and especially on Alfonso López, who covets a second term in 1942. Gómez's editorials during the winter of 1940–1941 suggested everything short of murder for that ex-president."[55]

López and revolution had obsessed Gómez. By some involved mental process, he had swung entirely to the opposite pole. Taking Franco Spain as his model, he maintained that the damage could be repaired only by returning Colombia to the norms of the past. (In fact, under his guidance, the counterrevolution was to become Hispanic and feudalistic in concept. When it failed, he was to flee to that model of his political yearnings in exile, and from Barcelona he was to dream of Bogotá.)

Gómez swore that he would lead a revolution if López returned to office in 1942. No one questioned where he might find followers. In October, 1940, Jose de la Vega, editor of *El Siglo* and Gómez' chief lieutenant, talked openly in the Senate of a Conservative revolution because the Santos government was collaborating with the United States. When the Liberals jeered him down, de la Vega shouted angrily, "Laugh all you want! Don't think we have no arms. We can get them just where Franco Spain got them!"[56]

The Gómez newspaper, bellwether for the Conservative provincial press, led the way in invective for the Allies and praise for the Axis. In *El Siglo* appeared the Gómez thesis that if any foreign power must control the Panama Canal, Germany or Japan was preferable to the United States. In 1942 Gómez constructed a new plant for his paper, and the American Embassy reported that circumstances surrounding the project indicated that the Nazi Legation in Bogotá, through its Press Attaché, Herr Gottfried Schmidt, had put up the 100,000 pesos as part of its policy of subsidizing the friendly Latin press. At least six Conservative dailies in the provinces were as zealous for the Nazi cause as was *El Siglo.*

But praise of things totalitarian was not new for Gómez. In 1937 he had rendered public homage to Franco and the Falange, when emissaries of the latter visited Bogotá. On that occasion, the Con-

---

[55] *Ibid.,* pp. 206–7.

[56] This exaggerated broadside was considered by U. S. officials and many Liberals as tantamount to public admission of the Gómez-Nazi affiliation.

servatives organized an *acto de homenaje*. At the banquet honoring the Falangists, Gómez said,

> Spain, marching forward as the sole defender of Christian civilization, leads the western nations in the reconstruction of *Hispanidad*, and we inscribe our names in the roster of its phalanxes with unutterable satisfaction ... we bless God who has permitted us to live in an era of unutterable transformations, and who has given it to us to utter, with a cry that springs from the very depths of our hearts: "Up Catholic, Imperial Spain!"[57]

At some point in his spiritual transformation from staunch republican, Gómez had slipped back four centuries. It is a connection which one cannot pin down, but which persists. *Hispanidad* had claimed him. The spiritual nostalgia of Castile pervaded his thinking, whose core had become Church and state united, the Doctrine of the Two Swords, the rule of a landed elite, the unquestioned supremacy of the *Hijos de algo*.

According to Germán Arciniegas, the *Camisas Negras* (Black Shirts), Colombian version of the Falange, were organized in Gómez' office at *El Siglo*.[58] Certainly there was a Conservative-Falangist movement with strong Nazi overtones operative in Colombia around 1940–44. Among its chief apostles were Gómez, Guillermo León Valencia, Jose de la Vega, and one of Gómez' writers, Guillermo Camacho Montoya (who wrote under the nom de plume of *Américo Latino*). Here is a sample of Camacho Montoya's work, from the pages of *El Siglo*:

> We were born Spanish. ... We speak the tongue of Castile because we can speak no other. ... The twenty cowardly governments [of Latin America] have put themselves into the hands of foreign nations, dedicated to false liberalism and to masonic, atheistic democracy. ... The panorama is desolate. ... We are still conquered territory ...
>
> Hispanoamérica, the land of vassalage. ... Each day the yoke of Saxo-Americana [*sic*] is drawn tighter around our throats. Sometimes the yoke is of steel, sometimes of silk, soft and perfidious ...
>
> But — all is not lost. *There is still heard the voice of Laureano Gómez to tell the truth about the future, to direct us to the road of tomorrow, the Catholic Hispanic Empire.*
>
> *And we will go back to Spain.* The five arrows of Ferdinand and Isabella, the

---

[57] Germán Arciniegas, *The State of Latin America,* trans. Harriet de Onis (New York: Alfred A. Knopf, Inc., 1952), p. 163.

[58] *Ibid.,* pp. 163–64.

symbol of Catholic unity, will be our symbol also. It is written in the future of America by the inscrutable hand of Providence.[59]

This mental orientation of Gómez is important, for it was to color the course of the counterrevolution when, at last, Gómez came to power over the remains of the Liberal party. López' reforms had made of Gómez an authentic Hispanist. To him, López the reformer was the incarnation of the Antichrist. Morally committed, Gómez turned from opposition to hate. From this time onward, Gómez stands forth as Machiavellian, sinister, cruel; because of it, the madness which he brought to a nation makes him seem, in perspective, deranged.

New Era or Status Quo? The Liberals Split on Reform

The Santos regime, born of dissension over reform, had suffered the onslaughts of both the reformist Liberals and the Gómez Conservatives. Santos' timidity in social reform matters, his land policy and his treatment of labor, all served to line the masses up solidly behind the reformist Liberals. Facing them as in drawn battle lines were the Rightist Conservatives, threatening revolution should López be elected to a second term. It was in the nature of things, then, that the Liberal convention which met in 1941 should prove a stormy one.

By now, neither the Moderates nor the reformists were in a mood for compromise.[60] For a while the convention swayed in deadlock, while tempers rose and debate turned into acrimonious insult. The fact was that only one Liberal could capture and hold the interest of the people, and that was the man whose election, said Gómez, would precipitate a revolution. And already, López had carried on "an exhausting campaign for four years."[61]

Eduardo Santos was in firm command of the Moderates. While the reformists attacked him for not furthering López' reforms, Santos strengthened the delegations which might have wavered toward López. But even as López, four years earlier, had been unable to prevent Santos' nomination, so now was Santos unable to stop the

[59] Although this material appears on pp. 172–73, Gunther, *op. cit.*, it was made available to Mr. Gunther by the writer at the Ambassador's permissive request when Gunther visited the Embassy in Bogotá gathering material for his book.

[60] Gibson, *op. cit.*, p. 400.

[61] "Un Consejero de la Nación," *Semana*, p. 15.

swing toward López. Reformism won out. López became the candidate of the reform wing for a second term.

At that moment, Colombian liberalism entered upon its final agnony. The Moderates bolted, and chose for their own candidate Arango Vélez, a prominent, aristocratic Bogotá attorney. When this became known, the Conservatives, who had put forth no candidate of their own, threw their backing to Arango Vélez—a strategy of Gómez to exploit the Liberal division. For now the Liberals were placed before the nation as groping, fragmented, indecisive, lacking in the authority to speak for all their membership, much less for the whole nation.

But not all the Moderate Liberals were alienated by López' nomination. Enough of them voted for him to insure his victory, in a Pyrrhic choice that found them winning the election only to face the ultimate destruction of their party.

López beat Arango Vélez by two hundred thousand votes, and the Conservative press blasted the balloting with charges of corruption and intimidation of voters—charges which probably had considerable substance behind them.

Amid threats of revolution, charges of rigged elections, and general social unrest, Alfonso López took office for the second time.

V. Divide and Conquer: The Conservatives Regain Power (1942–1946)

LÓPEZ' SECOND TERM: THE REFORMER REFORMED

Many Colombians of progressive persuasion believe that López, in his second term, betrayed the hopes of those who elected him to bring to a climax the revolution that Santos had suspended.[1] Others see him as having lost his appetite for reform and wishing to rectify past mistakes. And there are those who "think that López, with his sudden swing toward the center, and toward what was then called the oligarchy, merely stopped short at the edge of the extreme Left because the country would not tolerate further agitation."[2]

For whatever reason, López did swing toward the Center. With that change, the program which he had begun was doomed to death by slow attrition.

In an analysis of this second term, *Semana* says:

> In any case, he changed friends. The young intellectuals who once had discoursed with him on the Constitutional Reform of 1936, on the Spanish Republic, on the English democracy, were replaced by solid financiers, particularly sensitive to the poetry of figures. The ministers, in this second government of López, did not become millionaires, but millionaires frequently became ministers. López lost the support of a great part of Liberal opinion, and suffered, once more, the pitiless assault of Laureano Gómez.[3]

Gómez did not make good his threat of outright revolution. But the moment that the returns were in, the attack began: a slow wearing down of the President by blasting him, his administration, and his family. Now, the opposition turned on a harsher, more brutal note—slander, scandal, lies, intended to break López' morale and to discredit him before the nation. Moreover, the country had changed: it was not the Colombia at whose head López had first found himself.

[1] "Un Consejero de la Nación," *Semana*, p. 14.
[2] *Ibid.*
[3] *Ibid.*

Writing of this period, Antonio García says:

> The country was not the same as before. The war, the sterile struggles, the growth of passionate partisan dynamics, had led it along a path that it scarcely noticed. Because of this, the political forces had polarized in two directions: that of capturing power and that of maintaining position in the State; that of holding power, and that of conspiring against the occupant of the presidency. The hour was one of revolution, but all the revolutionary forces had disappeared, through desertion. In the folds of Liberalism, there was not one single person—one voice is a symbol, even, and a principle—who spoke of the frustrated revolution ...[4]

Despite López' past criticism of Santos, he continued and even furthered the policy begun by Santos. In November, 1943, he declared war on the Axis. A defense council was created, and Axis interests were impounded or seized. Public holdings affecting the war were nationalized, and the government undertook the expulsion or internment of aliens engaged in espionage or propaganda on behalf of the Axis. Soon, the Colombian Navy was running an area of the Caribbean antisubmarine patrol.

Quite naturally, López' policy infuriated choleric old Laureano Gómez. Many Nazis were married into wealthy, highly-placed Colombian families. At every López move against them, Gómez' wrath rose to a higher pitch. He shouted of a "Yankee Gestapo." He accused López of "selling out to the rapists of Panama." But, more effectively, he emphasized the lack of shipping to move Colombian coffee to market, and blamed it on López' declaration of war. It was a telling argument. Many Conservatives and Moderate Liberals, who felt that it was not their war, agreed with Gómez. They openly expressed their dissatisfaction with the government. Cabinet members came and went with depressing regularity. "Within one period of eight months, there were five complete turnovers in the cabinet."[5]

In the Congress the legislators, reflecting the lack and loss of López' public prestige, blocked him at every turn. His labor laws were buried under a mountain of dissent, and labor blamed him. Hard times were upon the country, and inflation squeezed the masses. They cried out to their former savior, and he was powerless. Coffee could not move to market, fabricating materials could not be imported, and unemployment grew. The old López magic had lost its potency.

But at this time, too, a new evil mushroomed out of the multiplica-

[4] García, *op. cit.*, p. 292.
[5] MacDonald, *op. cit.*, p. 399.

tion of bureaus which had been created to control the economy, particularly imports and exports. Imports from the United States were
placed on a priority basis, and, since there was a mounting excess of
exchange together with a pent-up demand, a gigantic speculative
spiral rose that brought on runaway inflation. Cheap money, unfilled
demands, and myriad and unrelated control agencies quickly tended
to foster a thriving black market in import licenses and exchange
permits. The result was that the center of gravity of control stealthily
shifted from the state, to a social and economic apparatus of "inside
groups" which "constituted a privileged system of enrichment."[6]

> The acquisition of an import license, or an exchange license made more rich
> men in less time than any other activity, including land speculation. This is how
> the dominant families in the field of finance insinuated themselves into political
> channels, changing not only their skins, but their souls: in this tortuous twilight
> of the Liberal governments, there took place a metamorphosis of the "group of
> families" which co-allied incidentally for the purpose of negotiating with the
> state ... into stable, indissolubly-linked oligarchies to capture the organisms of
> political activity ... in the parties and the state ... and to establish not a tem-
> porary, fortuitous and clandestine regime, but a *system* of privilege.[7]

It is no exaggeration to say that dollar prosperity and the ability to
operate within a theoretically-controlled economy of foreign trade
made many fortunes at this time. The state grew, not organically, but
like some unhealthy, malign plant, and its fruit was the "fix," the
"angle," the knowing of someone on the "inside" of an agency or a
ministry. Between 1943 and 1945, 128.4 million dollars piled up in
unused exchange, providing an enormous pressure for inflation.
Speculative fever gripped the nation, and no coordinated plan was
put forward to halt this boom in speculation, or to curb the excessive
buying power. The great dollar balance could have been converted
into some well-conceived plan for economic development, for agrarian
reform, or for rural electrification, but nothing like this was attempted. Instead, the government demonstrated almost complete
financial confusion: even as it forced companies to purchase non-
negotiable bonds as forced savings to halt inflation, it added to inflation by issuing thirty million pesos worth of bonds, of which at
least ten million went into self-liquidating government schemes of
one kind and another.[8]

[6] García, *op. cit.*, p. 287.
[7] *Ibid.*
[8] *Ibid.*

It was natural under the circumstances that angry charges of Liberal mismanagement of the economy should be heard. An oligarchy of privilege feasted upon the control agencies and grew fat; the cabinet was permanently shaky and uncertain in support of the President; the masses, caught in a vise of misery, grew clamorous and sullen; and worst, there was no plan, no coherent view of the future. Discontent with the government grew daily. López had by now lost even the support of the reformists, who had witnessed his inability to control the situation and to press for necessary reforms. Moreover, the party strictures of the convention of 1941 worsened. The two wings of the Liberal party drew farther apart in a welter of public snarling and bitter acrimony.[9]

Such a situation was made to order for crafty, determined Laureano Gómez. Alive to the weaknesses of López' government, he moved forward, pushing aside Gaitán, López, and all the other public figures of the epoch as supernumeraries. He took to himself the lead in the national drama, turning the republican opposition of former days into terrorist opposition. The struggle for power in Colombia during this time was dominated on the Liberal side by the degeneration of public morals and a sloughing away of the values once associated with the old republican order. On the Conservative side, it was ruled by "the spirit of the Spanish war and totalitarian violence. The opposition to the Liberal government leaped the boundaries of the country, to acquire the character of a universal opposition to all that the government venerated or accepted. By reaction, by the counter-blows given, by the hate of the front which he was combatting in his own country, Gómez became transformed into the Great Renegade."[10]

Back-Alley Politics:
The Mamatoco Incident and Family Scandals

Gómez had marshalled a combination of forces to oppose the inertia of the government. The young men of the Right were drawn to him by a kind of revulsion against the existing order. The Moderate Liberals had always been more or less in opposition to López. The new corporations, the great concentrations of capital, the Church, and the plain misguided—all these joined to swell the ranks of the counterrevolution. But it must be remembered that the movement did not spring full-blown from the womb of events. Its roots lay in the past:

[9] Gibson, *op. cit.*, p. 400.
[10] García, *op. cit.*, p. 292.

the past when Gómez had helped to organize the Colombian Falange, and had feted the visiting Spanish members of the Falange Exterior. It was part of the basic Conservative thinking. In 1937 Silvio Villegas, an important Gómez lieutenant, had written, "The Conservative Party will not regain power as a political party, but *as the center of a counterrevolutionary* movement."[11]

Of all the elements of the counterrevolution, that which lent the most strength to Gómez was the emerging complex of national pressure groups composed of businessmen and industrialists. Two, in particular, are worth mentioning: the *Asociación Nacional de Industriales* (ANDI)[12] and the *Federación Nacional de Comerciantes* (FENALCO).[13] Vertical, class organizations which excluded workers and employees, they were organized for political action to protect their financial interests from reform. To this end they made their influence felt in the new atmosphere of privilege-control of government by the setting of tariffs, opposition to unfavorable trade and labor laws and regulations, and even in the choice of ministers of finance. "The economic oligarchy of ANDI and FENALCO participated, without involving themselves, in the conspiratorial atmosphere. Also, the party oligarchies, too, took part. The Liberal oligarchy itself saw the dangers of power based upon a resentful people who had been defrauded and now were without hope."[14]

But despite the diverse elements, the mixed motives, of the counterrevolution, the core of it, the *idearium* and the *élan vital* behind it, was provided by Laureano Gómez. Antonio García, whose study of the movement is the best available, makes this analysis of the purposes which moved Gómez:

> It was to be a return to the past, but not the past of yesterday ... to the golden, placid eras in which a revolution could be touched off by the killing of a student ... but to the past of *day before yesterday*. The Spanish War, the totalitarian conspiracy against the easy-going, inept Republic (made in the form and image of the Athaneum) was the best or the worst school for these forces: in it they learned the methods, the use of violence, the technique of terror, the well-remembered Golden Age of the Spanish Colony. The counterrevolution defined its political objectives during the war: wipe out the Republic and force a return to

[11] Villegas, *op. cit.*, p. 224. Writer's italics.
[12] National Association of Industrialists.
[13] National Federation of Businessmen.
[14] García, *op. cit.*, p. 300.

things as they were in the "imperial and Spanish era." All the theories of *Hispanidad* served only to mask this simple, terrible fact. From this moment onward is defined the feeling, the historic direction, of the counterrevolution and the counterreform. What Laureano Gómez did in 1952 and 1953 was to propose as constitutional norms what was in his heart and mind in 1940 and 1942. In 1952 the counterrevolution was triumphant ... and Laureano Gómez could say publicly that he wished a change in the course of the Republic, turning it back to *before* the Convention of Ocaña.[15]

Yet, Gómez was to destroy López not by violence, but by craft and insinuation. First, he was to break his spirit, then to pull him down from his place of power. Ironically, it was an exposé of the Conservative Right before the whole nation that sparked the Conservative counterattack which discredited López.

American Intelligence had uncovered a Creole Nazi-Falange group which ramified throughout the whole nation, and which was linked to both the Nazi party and the Spanish Falange. Documents subsequently seized by Colombian Secret Police directly implicated Silvio Villegas, Tomás Quiñones Uribe (a convicted seditionist), Graciela Escobar Moreno (organizer of the Falangist Youth Movement in the central Departments), and Guillermo León Valencia as organizers or sponsors. These persons were Gómez' aides and stood close to the National Conservative Directorate.[16] After the American Embassy had turned its files on *Acción Nacional*—the name of the party—over to President López, the latter gave the story to the press, naming names, calling it a Conservative-Nazi subversive plot, and issuing a decree which outlawed the party and membership in it.[17]

The fat was in the fire. The Conservatives were to retaliate with scandals and charges of scandals, in an effort to completely discredit López. Their opportunity came in the same summer of 1943.

Bogotá police found the body of a Bogotá prize fighter, known as "Mamatoco," in a public park, riddled with stab wounds. It seemed an ordinary crime of violence, of the kind not unknown to the Bogotá demimonde. The dead man had had a police record and a rather unsavory reputation, as well as a poor record as a pugilist. One thing distinguished him from the scores who passed over the marble slab of the morgue: he had published a small newspaper called *Voz del*

[15] *Ibid.*, p. 299.
[16] This material is drawn from the personal files of the writer.
[17] This incident is recounted from the writer's personal notes and experience with the affair.

Pueblo,[18] which had circulated widely in the workers' barrios, and which had been bitter of late about the condition of the masses. Mamatoco, it seemed, had been somewhat of a confused, resentful proletarian, rather disillusioned with the Liberal party.

Scenting political capital, a young Conservative judge began to push a full-scale investigation. With that, the press of both parties seized the issue, and charges and countercharges crossed in an atmosphere of mounting tension. Mamatoco, said the Conservatives, knew too much about the Liberals hierarchy, and they had gotten rid of him. Not so, cried the Liberals.

Unfortunately for the Liberals, the investigating judge turned up evidence implicating a number of highly-placed Liberals. An ex-Director of Police and the Chief of Police of Bogotá were arrested, along with a former secretary of President López. The *"Asunto Mamatoco"* pushed the war news off the front pages. And then, a high-ranking police officer confessed that he had planned the killing and had instructed a subordinate in all the details.[19]

Laureano Gómez and the Conservatives greeted this development with a howl of glee, masked, of course, as righteous outrage. Now, they said, there was evidence that Mamatoco had been assassinated by the Liberals to save important reputations. López was pictured by *El Siglo* as heading a gang of assassins. The Gómez paper boldly charged that the Minister of the Interior, fearing damaging revelations, had tried to block the investigation. The Minister countered with a libel suit against Gómez, and, when the latter did not respond, he was jailed for contempt of court.

Violence now erupted. Conservatives and their followers rioted in the streets of Bogotá, fighting Liberals, police, anyone who stood in their way. "Laureano Gómez in jail. The Assassins of Mamatoco in the Presidential Palace," screamed the headlines of *El Siglo*.[20] The mobs rushed the jail and tried to liberate Gómez by force. The police came in, swinging billies and cracking heads. After serious street

---

[18] "Voice of the People."

[19] A confidential investigator of the Minister of the Interior told the writer that this was purely a police-graft scandal involving irregularities in the "pay-off." It was ballooned into a political football, even as sometimes happens in the United States.

[20] "Las Bases," *Semana* (Bogotá), August 29, 1955, p. 16.

fighting in which many were hurt, the rioters subsided. But now the die had been cast. The issue could not again be by-passed.

López might have been unable to carry on; again, he might have weathered the storm. But his wife was very ill, and the Gómez campaign of vilification of the López family was endangering her health. In November, 1943, he asked the Senate for permission to leave the country and accompany his wife to the United States for medical treatment. Few believed that he would resume office when he returned. In fact, when he did so, he said that he would not resume his post. He appeared worn out, ill, harrassed. Still, he went back to his task.

But the merciless onslaught continued. Again, went the stories, it was a park, a corpse from the seamy side of life, a policeman—and this time, the President's son was allegedly involved. A painted lady from the *Zona de Tolerancia* was found dead in another Bogotá park. Another investigation. Witnesses placed the President's son at the scene, his car nearby, the arrival of the lady in a taxi to meet the young man. This was the last time she was seen alive. A policeman was found who claimed to have seen them meet.

This was too odoriferous to make the Conservative press, except by insinuation. However, the same effect was gained by a word-of-mouth smear campaign. The persistent whisper went around that the President had his son's confession, made at a family conference, and that Mrs. López' worsened condition was the result. Soon, rumor had it, the President would resign to spare his wife the mental torture. López and his family lived under a thick, black cloud of innuendo, slander, and gossip. "Gómez," says Galbraith, "also exposed and exaggerated the alleged scandals in the López family and twisted them for political purposes in furious and inflammatory fashion."[21]

Gómez, in jail on contempt charges, became a political liability to the Liberals, and soon they found a pretext to free him. However, it was too late to undo the harm. Disorders occasioned by the riots had spread to other parts of the country; clashes between Liberals and Conservatives in the provinces assumed the proportions of incipient anarchy. Meanwhile, Gómez called loudly for violence, for revolution, although he never quite got around to starting one himself.

This was a time of complete disorientation, "an instinctive search-

[21] Galbraith, *op. cit.*, p. 130.

ing among the ruins," García calls it. Gaitán began to emerge once more as a public conscience, as he tried to unite the scattered elements of reform. But the counterrevolution had seized the initiative. No better evidence of this could be found than the fact that the Socialist party, combining with other progressive elements into the *Liga de Acción Política* (Political Action League), could make no impression on either the people or the government. In a Manifesto it attacked the crisis in the traditional order and called for unity of the Left to reject the "old and the new oligarchies,"[22] but it failed to reach either the middle class, the universities, or the intellectuals, and the people heeded it not. Only the Right was organized.

One more blow was needed to unseat López, and it came in the guise of an abortive Army revolt.

In July, 1944, Colombian Army maneuvers took place near Pasto, close by the Ecuadorian border. On July 10, López and some of his cabinet ministers went to the scene. Colonel Diógenes Gil, commander of the Pasto garrison, took López and his retinue prisoners, issued a *pronunciamiento* calling on the Army to rise, and began negotiations with the Pasto branch of the Bank of the Republic for a loan. But the Army remained loyal, the Bank would issue no loan, and the people rose in support of López. Within a short time, the President and his ministers were freed, loyal forces arrested the conspirators, and the affair sputtered out.

But irreparable damage had been done to López' prestige.

Some observers think that the Pasto *coup* was brought on by Army jealousy of López' favoritism for the police.[23] This factor was certainly present. But military disaffection was not general, and the Army as a whole remained loyal. Given the situation which existed in the country, the Pasto *coup* was less an attempt to gain power than a conventional protest. Neutralism has always marked the role of the Colombian Army, and this aberration seems merely to have been a lapse in such neutralism as a protest against an intolerable internal situation.[24] In 1944 many of the younger officers were Liberals, keenly aware of the changing times, and privately bitter about the choatic

---

[22] *La Izquierda ante el Presente y el Porvenir de Colombia* (Bogotá, 1944), p. 5.
[23] Arthur P. Whitaker in *Inter-American Affairs*, New York, 1944, p. 34.
[24] Antonio García, "Exámen Político del Golpe de Pasto," Bogotá, July 10, 1945, in García, *Problemas de la Nación Colombiana* (Bogotá: Editorial Nuevo Mundo, n.d.), pp. 98–99.

state created by the government's weakness and by party conflict. In a very real sense, the Pasto *coup* foreshadowed Rojas Pinilla's move of June 13, 1953. But there was a deeper significance, too, for a certain prematurity of the Pasto action effectively blocked true Army intervention. Had the whole Army moved to take over at that time, the history of Colombia might have been spared the lamentable events of 1948–53. Says Antonio García in this regard:

> This was no *coup d'état* against López, but a blow against the possibility that the Army might direct a real blow against the state, with a program, and a certain number of great objectives of national transformation ... how much blood would have been saved, how many evils, how much misery, if the Army had then taken charge of the State. There being no revolutionary parties to bring in the revolution, the only force that remained on foot, to shield the nation from anarchy and blood-letting, was its Army.[25]

The years that followed were to make this explicit.

Upon his return to the capital, López issued a conciliatory statement, but the Gómez Conservatives leaped into the breach. The old scandals were re-ventilated, the old innuendos now pegged to the Pasto revolt. López appeared as a leader without popular sanction, minus the right to speak for the party or the nation. His prestige sank rapidly.

In this crisis, members of the *Liga de Acción Política* called upon the President and urged him to execute his own *coup d'état:* a revolution from above, which would lead to a democratic revolution and preserve the role of law. Antonio García, who was spokesman, as a member of the National Defense Council, says, "López was boiling, but not because of our proposal—as audacious as it was honorable— but because of the chaos which was entering like a schism into all circles of Colombian life. The courtesans of the regime did not see the bitter danger as clearly as López did, and our suggestion of a revolution from above ... was our mistake."[26]

Still another factor brought López' stock down. With the formation of the East-West alliance against nazism, Colombia, like other Latin-American nations, recognized the U.S.S.R. To Bogotá came a delegation of seventy-odd Russians, who were anything but self-effacing.[27] Colombian Communists flocked to the Soviet Legation as clerks, in-

[25] García, *Gaitán* ..., p. 309.
[26] *Ibid.*, p. 308.
[27] Gibson, *op. cit.*, p. 400.

terpreters, general functionaries. This was proof, to the oligarchy, that the Liberals—and López in particular—were offering aid and comfort to the Communists. He, and he alone, was blamed for bringing into the country a subversive force bent upon destroying the Colombian way of life.

By mid-July, the situation had become intolerable for López. His party was divided, much of his bitterest opposition came from his own ranks. The Congress held him at bay with snarling polemics, hate, and recrimination. Finding himself impaled "upon the horns of a dilemma whether to keep on fighting Congress or resign,"[28] he stepped down in August, 1945.

Gómez had won. The Dragon had slain Siegfried.

Named by the Congress to finish out López' term was Alberto Lleras Camargo, Colombian ambassador to Washington.

In his Message of Resignation, López said, "It alarms me that there should be created—as it appears there has been created—a political class far removed from the vital interests of the Colombian worker, from his present preoccupations and his legitimate ambitions."[29] Included, too, in his last message were passages from that of May, 1944, wherein he described what had been happening to the country, in particular the subversion of Congress by the oligarchies and the rotting away of the central power:

There has gradually taken place in the Capital of the Republic a concentration of the political chiefs of the Departments, which are gradually losing their former directive ties with the electorate and their familiarity with regional problems, acquired through assiduous contact with their constituents. This regional current [running] toward Bogotá, has cerainly not weakened those who were opposed to centralism, which on the contrary, exercised now from the captial by the most outstanding personalities of the Departments, is more oppressive and humiliating than ever. On the other hand, the regional political chiefs exercise upon the National Government, in order to maintain their electoral domain through remote control, a continual pressure, friendly or menacing according to the party to which they belong, and, without assuming any direct responsibility, co-administer the naming of administrators high and low, the preferential distribution of public expenditures, and the highest order of political matters as well as the most modest of activities. Debates on the course of the administration thus can take, unconsciously, the extravagant turn of frustrated or unsuccessful transactions between a subordinate executive and the members of Congress.

The executive power has been broken and diminished ... its functions, the

---

[28] "Un Consejero de la Nación," *Semana*, p. 15.
[29] *Mensajes del Presidente López al Congreso Nacional*, p. 20.

simple act of holding up or resolving conflicts created by private interests without feeling for national solidarity. The execution of the laws does not take place normally, because the laws, when Congress passes them with indifference, or because of complacency instead of *espirit de corps*, lack authority in themselves. . . .

Official action awakens threats of rebellion, or creates conflicts. Every interest thinks that it can exercise co-action, pausing, ceasing to act within its own orbit, invading that of others, creating a "shock" on the presumption that authority is created for the purpose of avoiding shocks or force, and thus the laws are relaxed . . . the members of Congress, and not only those of the opposition, stimulate and give rise to this criterion, constituting themselves voluntary spokesmen of the discontent against the government, and not infrequently against the judicial and administrative steps taken to resolve conflicts between private interests. . . . You may say to me, Gentlemen, that this is nothing new. But it is causing a crisis, because there are new factors of disorder which did not exist before. Such as the active industrial development which is causing and creating interests of such magnitude that they openly defy the force of the laws, the power of the Executive Branch and of Justice itself. Such as the awakening of a sleeping social consciousness which can turn toward violence more easily when it learns that violence produces concrete results. Such as, finally, the disorganization of the contemporary world, in which it was our lot to see abolished by force, and still not yet reestablished, the essential principles of our political and social civilization, and the victory, though fleeting, of other forms, all arbitrary and subversive of our classical tradition.[30]

The gentlemen of the Congress would have done well to heed these penetrating and prophetic words. They forecast the end of liberalism, and of the republican scheme of government in Colombia. López saw the meeting of the two revolutions of which Lleras Camargo speaks. But he was a prophet without honor, and the counterrevolution was now on the march.

LLERAS CAMARGO AND NATIONAL UNION: THE OLIGARCHY AGAIN CLOSES RANKS

Alberto Lleras Camargo came to the presidency of Colombia with the conviction that " 'National Union', coalition with the Conservative Party, [was] the only practical means of facing a situation verging on civil war."[31] It seemed a reasonable promise. But joining with the Conservatives at this time was much like a cornered, unarmed man forming an alliance with a hungry, man-eating tiger.

Lleras issued a measured statement upon taking office, in which he called for calm, and pleaded for national unity in the crisis. As evi-

---

[30] *Mensaje de Renuncia del Presidente López* (Crítica de la Reforma Constitucional de 1936), Noguera Laborde, *op. cit.*, pp. 143–44.

[31] Galbraith, *op. cit.*, p. 130.

dence of his sincerity, he offered cabinet posts to the Conservatives, and three moderate Conservatives accepted. At that, Laureano Gómez, who wanted anything but national unity, loosed a blast at them for "trafficking with the enemy."[32] But they stuck to their decision, and in support of them two members of the Conservative Directorate resigned their positions. Thus, a small rift opened in the Conservative ranks. With the backing of these few Conservatives and the Old Guard Liberals, Lleras was able to ride out the storm, while both parties feinted for openings in the coming elections of 1946.

This election promised to be decisive. Lleras' government, as López' had been, was under attack from the Gómez Conservatives and also from the reformist Liberals. This latter wing, now moving to the forefront under Jorge Eliécer Gaitán, had been gaining strength as the issue of counterrevolution versus reform was clearly joined and mass discontent grew. Basically, the battle was to be between Gómez and Gaitán. Hence, something must be said of Gaitán, the tragic figure of this entire political drama.

Gaitán: Spokesman for the Masses

Gaitán may or may not have been a "demagogue," but the word was frequently applied to him. Galbraith says, "[he] was an able jurist, but a demagogue with a vague policy which he defined in his party slogan 'Charge,' without making it clear against what, in what direction, or with what purpose."[33] And Don Julio Hernández, brother-in-law of President Mariano Ospina Pérez, says in a letter to the writer, "our *demagogues*, whose principal was Gaitán, taking advantage of the intellectual weakness and economic conditions of the poor people,"[34] were of great importance. But the term does not describe the man. It leaves too much unsaid, dismisses him with an airy wave of contempt which fails to take account of his role and his importance.

Gaitán's efforts on behalf of the masses reached far back into the history of the times, although he seldom made the headlines. It was he who investigated and broke the banana zone scandals of 1929; who sparked the congressional investigation that toppled Méndez' Minister of War and bought on the Conservative defeat; who organ-

---

[32] MacDonald, *op. cit.*, p. 402.
[33] Galbraith, *op. cit.*, p. 130.
[34] Private correspondence with the writer, Medellín, Colombia, June, 1948.

ized the UNIR party under Olaya's regime to push for land distribution and labor reform, thus making it easier, paving the way, for López. In 1924, Gaitán set forth his philosophy for all who would listen, in his *Las Ideas Socialistas en Colombia:*

> [We must] maintain that man has the right to enjoy the fruits of his labor. That man, by the sole reason of being Man, should not be treated as a beast. That it is not enough to assure him physical subsistence, but that he must be given the means of cultivating his spirit. [We must] ask that men who desire to work and ask for it, be not submitted to misery; that men who have given their health and their lives to labor, be not forced to die on the painful bedsteads of charity hospitals; that while there are women forced into prostitution by poverty, while there are children who, turned out of foundling asylums, then become candidates for prison, it is not human that others be forced into a life of dilapidation and of living off charity.[35]

His program, then, was on the record. It was not something hastily gathered up in the crisis of the forties. His credo was consistent and continuing, and he translated into actions the words which he spoke in explanation of his ideas.

There was nothing of the Johnny-come-lately professional political opportunist about Gaitán. He was of humble origin, of mixed blood, and had worked his way up to become a professor of law and an able lawyer. He was an excellent Minister of Education under Santos, in which post he did much to begin programs of rural and worker education. He was generally conceded to have been the best Mayor that Bogotá ever had. And as MacDonald points out, "He once served as Minister of Labor and had seized every opportunity to favor trade unions in their disputes with Big Business."[36]

Demagogue, perhaps, to those against whom his program was aimed. To the little people of Columbia, he was something else. "He was able to capture and hold the allegiance of certain of the intellectuals and idealists, some of the industrialists who believed that to give him his head would be the best protection against the inevitable pressure from below, and of the masses, who gave him almost fanatical allegiance as their savior from conditions of life becoming increasingly difficult."[37] And Germán Arciniegas says that Gaitán was the idol of the people, that his appeal to the submerged nine-

---

[35] Jorge Eliécer Gaitán, *Las Ideas Socialistas en Colombia* (Bogotá, 1924), p. 251.
[36] MacDonald, *op. cit.*, p. 401.
[37] Galbraith, *op cit.*, p. 130.

tenths was greater than that of any South American political figure whom he could recall.[38]

Some of this testimony may be prejudiced. The word of a Peruvian writer and statesman may, therefore, be more to the point:

> Gaitán was the most popular of the Liberal chiefs, the most loved by the people, and the most energetic standard-bearer of Liberalism. At least, one voice from an authoritative source said, only days before Gaitán's tragic death, "His prestige has grown formidably in popular areas. There are still some sectors on the coast ... which do not regard Gaitán with sympathy, but who are resigned to his leadership. Nonetheless, I think that these people are wrong, because Gaitán as a leader is growing steadily...." [39]

Possibly Alberto Niño H., chief of national security under Ospina Pérez, comes closer to the complex truth about the man. Alberto Niño H. was a Conservative, even though a friend of Gaitán, and his judgment would be a more balanced assessment between personal sympathy and political objections. He says:

> Gaitán was a living paradox. He was a revolutionary who hated disorder; he loved the people, but since his conception of the people was not the realistic Gorki view ... he attributed all virtues to them and exacerbated himself when, in his dealings with them, he discovered some of their defects. He liked politics, but lacked the tortuous and hypocritical discretion of the politician ... he believed in truth, his truth was the Good, and for it he was dogmatic ... incomparable leader of the masses, and an enemy of class conflict, still he roused in the country that very conflict by molding his actions and his words as an instrument for creating the consciousness of class among the popular masses.[40]

Such, then, was Gaitán. Essentially, he was the man who, at the critical hour, spoke for the commoners. Perhaps only they liked him. But that was enough. For, even with Gaitán dead, his shade still hovers uneasily over the social revolution in Colombia. The people have not forgotten.

Gómez Gives Gaitán the Kiss of Death: Liberal Against Liberal

Antonio García describes Lleras Camargo as "the most wonderful,

---

[38] Arciniegas, *op. cit.*, pp. 160–61.

[39] Rafaél Larco Herrera, *Por la Ruta de la Confederación Americana* (Lima, 1948), p. 153.

[40] Alberto Niño H., *Antecedentes y Secretos del 9 de Abril* (Bogotá: Editorial Pax, circa 1949), pp. 5–6.

but yielding and impressionable, intelligence of his generation."[41] Lleras' record was distinguished: brilliant writer, Ambassador to Washington, delegate to the Chapultepec and San Francisco Conferences, and President at thirty-nine. But he was not a Strong Man. Lacking a true mandate in his one-year term, Lleras was content merely to keep from rocking the boat until a new skipper could be chosen for the ship of state.

Perhaps this was a wise course. But in his transition term he did little to control the wild tides surging through the nation, save to offer a coalition government that did not include the really dangerous Conservatives. It was a time of agitation, of strikes, and disorders. And when Lleras put down the strike of transport workers on the Magdalena, the Conservatives learned that the unions had not the organic strength to combat repression, or to fight through for their demands. This was essential information to the counterreform:

> Syndicalism, in the past oriented by the Liberal-Communist bureaucracy, which had been accustomed to official complacency with its actions, simply could not get along with the government of Lleras. The government of Lleras was made the political *premise* upon which was to be founded ... by the Conservative Party the counterrevolutionary movement of which it [Conservatism] was the center and the spirit.[42]

At this twenty-fourth hour of the Liberal reign, the party was shattered. It had given up the fight with López' resignation, and its surrender came in the coalition government of Lleras Camargo. The basic differences between the wings of the party made it vulnerable: as the Moderate Liberals had feared López, so they mistrusted Gaitán. Consequently, they nominated Gabriel Turbay, a Santos Liberal, who had served as Ambassador to Washington. The reformist wing, of course, put forth Gaitán. Lleras' government declared a hands-off policy, and surrounded the candidates "with a barbed-wire barricade of guarantees" as Turbay bitingly put it. And so the Liberals embarked upon party suicide.

With two Liberal candidates in the field, the Conservatives seemed committed to nonparticipation. In fact, Gómez' *El Siglo* came out in favor of Gaitán. It was a clever stratagem of the old Conservative. Aware that the oligarchs would oppose Gaitán on reform, and that they would oppose Turbay because of his Levantine origin (he was

[41] García, *Gaitán* ... , p. 310.
[42] *Ibid.*, p. 311.

of Syrian parentage: "Turco" is the contemptuous term for such people in Colombia), Gómez effectively disoriented the Liberals and prevented them from making some unified effort.

For some time, the two Liberal leaders went up and down the land blasting one another, sowing confusion and division. And then, on March 26, the Conservatives announced the candidacy of Mariano Ospina Pérez. It was Liberal disaster.

As another mark of Gómez' craft, Ospinia was put forth as a candidate of "National Union," or a continuation of the coalition headed by Lleras. Thus, the Moderate Liberals and the Conservatives—the traditional oligarchs—were provided with a rallying point, with someone preferable to both Turbay and Gaitán.

But Gaitán was a hard man to beat, and he did wonders to awaken the Left to the basic issues. "With precise ideas and clear objectives ... he met head-on, reasoning, challenging and dominant, the directors of the party, the government, the press, the radio, the potentates, the politicians and *caciques,* large and small. He was against them all, alone, but the masses heard his talk, admired his truth, loved his justness, and ... they followed him, humble and fervid, as in the wake of an apostle."[43]

Gaitán had been taken in by Gómez' tactics. He had been proud of the Conservative support. When the Ospina candidacy broke, his first impulse was to leave the field to Turbay: "It is impossible for me to assume the responsibility for the fall of the Liberal Party," he told Niño H. "This Conservative candidacy means that I must defer my fight, but for you Conservatives, it means the loss of all hope. In Cali [where he was soon to go] I will announce my withdrawal from the race."[44]

However, the popular mainfestation of support in that city changed Gaitán's mind. Many progressive Conservatives came forward to support him. He came to believe that with their help he could win out over both Turbay and Ospina. But there was alarm and anger in his ranks. Some of his followers planned a general strike if he should lose, to show the nation's temper. They were determined to either "pull the country under" or demonstrate that Gaitán was the man for the people "who work and create wealth, whether they be called Liberals or Conservatives."[45]

[43] Niño H., *op. cit.,* p. 2.
[44] *Ibid.*
[45] *Ibid.*

In this dangerous frame of mind, the nation went to the polls. Gómez' strategy was justified. Ospina Pérez received 42 per cent of the vote, a plurality, totaling 565,894 votes. Turbay polled 437,089, and Gaitán ran last, with 363,049 votes. The Liberals had committed suicide. Conservatism was back in power, on the strength of a minority winner.

When the results were known, Liberal mobs surged through the streets of Bogotá calling for civil war. Unrest swept the whole nation. The people awaited Gaitán's word to touch off the violence. He witheld it. Instead, he called for order, and promised a return to the fight in 1950.[46]

Perhaps he sensed what had happened: the counterrevolution was now firmly in command of the march of events.

[46] *Ibid.*, p. 9.

VI. The Counterrevolution on the March: Leader without a Force (1946–1948)

THE LIBERALS REJECT GAITÁN: WHAT DOES A LEADER LEAD?

Soon after Ospina's election, Gaitán notified the President and the Conservatives in general that he would permit no regressive changes, nor the firing of employees for purely political reasons. If necessary, he warned, he would enforce this dictum with a general strike.[1] The threat seemed initially unnecessary, because Ospina had campaigned on a platform of National Union, stressing his desire to better labor conditions, to continue land parceling, and to extend social security to agricultural workers.

Before he took office, Ospina said, "A party government, and especially that of a group, invariably is actuated by ... the criterion of serving only partisan interests ... it is impossible to serve two masters at once: the nation and the party. Under my administration there will be no political reprisals on the part of the authorities against persons or property; no one will be barred from public office for party reasons; I faithfully guarantee to all the exercise of their natural and civil rights, and I shall make it my care to see that public liberties are respected. Neither the head of the state nor his associates or agents will take any step that even remotely smacks of political reprisals against anyone."[2]

True to his word, Ospina gave governmental posts to a number of Liberals, five of the party being asked into his cabinet. About half the departmental governorships also went to Liberals. But his most significant appointment was that of Laureano Gómez to the post of Foreign Minister. From this position the old war horse was to direct the reaction; the *Gomistas* became the power behind the throne.

Realistically viewed, national unity was doomed from the start,

[1] Niño H., *op. cit.*, p. 9.
[2] Arciniegas, *op. cit.*, p. 160.

for the nation's troubles could not be solved by mere superficial adjustments. No temporary agglomeration of bipartisan oligarchs was capable of dealing with deep social and economic cleavages, even had they been willing to tackle the basic issues.

Ospina made another major mistake when he failed to consult Gaitán on the Liberal appointments he did make. Gaitán at that time undoubedly spoke for the masses of Liberals. Hence, the snub by Ospina embittered the people and many Liberal politicians as well, thus undercutting the "unity" of which Ospina so glibly spoke.

And Gaitán had expected to be consulted. On the day after the election, he formally assumed the headship of the whole Liberal party. At that time he said, "The oligarchies and the half-Liberals caused Liberalism to lose its power. [The people] must regain it."[3] As spokesman for the people, Gaitán believed that he had the right of influencing the choice of Liberals in the coalition government. Even while Ospina was screening the names, Gaitán told Niño H., "I ask that Dr. Ospina and the Directorates of the parties work out with me a minimum program . . . and agree upon collaboration to attain it. . . . But union should be between party and party, and not between oligarchy and oligarchy."[4]

Consequently, as Niño H. points out, it was a mistake for Ospina to disregard Gaitán, if he sincerely wished national union. Any union without Gaitán amounted to no more than a union of Liberal oligarchs with Conservative oligarchs, allied for the purpose of defeating the plans and the program of that wing of liberalism headed by Gaitán, and which represented the social objectives of the vast mass of workers and peasants. Probably Gaitán would have worked reasonably with Ospina if asked, even though he considered the President "the top number of the plutocracy."[5]

But Gaitán, too, made grave mistakes. During the campaign, he had been a *popular* leader. The moment that he assumed headship of the Liberal party, he became a *Liberal* leader. In Colombian politics, this was enough to rob him of support: "How could one expect the peasants or the young Conservatives (who would have followed him as a popular leader) to accompany their great leader

[3] García, *Gaitán* . . . , p. 313.
[4] Niño H., *op. cit.*, pp. 11–12.
[5] *Ibid.*, p. 12.

into the very bosom of the Liberal Party? [They] would have followed him into the revolution itself, but never under the name of *Liberals,* since this is the fatum of our partisan psychology."[6]

Probably, too, Gaitán was in error in thinking that the disorganized masses, the people who wandered in *alpargatas* and *ruanas* processionally and aimlessly through the streets and market places, would provide him with a weapon to challenge the well-organized, firmly-entrenched oligarchy, now safe behind the barricades of the "double oligarchy" which controlled the government. It was not weakness that caused him to make these mistakes, however, but an excess of faith in the republican validity of "the people speaking." This almost naive faith in the masses was perhaps his greatest weakness." In another epoch," says Niño H., "Gaitán would have been The Leader; in that in which he lived, he was the leader."[7]

And so, despite Gaitán's injunctions toward moderation, the smoldering hates of the people awakened and flared. Partisan struggle within Ospina's coalition government served to increase the public tension. In scores of towns, Liberals and Conservatives clashed violently. The Conservative press claimed the martyrs as victims, even when they were Liberals, and the Liberal press did likewise. "And in this manner, with everyone collaborating, the atmosphere grew more heated, and mass demoralization increased, as the masses were prepared for subversion."

Ominously and significantly, a new term was now heard on the tongues of the people: *The Political Police.* Against Conservative denials, the Liberals charged the Conservatives with using the National Police as a force of repression. In fact, thousands of peasants fled their homes and sought safety in the cities. Many crossed into Venezuela. For this, Germán Arciniegas blames Ospina Pérez; Antonio García lays it at Gómez' doorstep. Says Arciniegas, "Little by little [Ospina] began modifying the organization of the police force, which in the provinces was transformed into shock troops at the service of the Conservatives ... thousands of country people stood by as their homes were burned down, many were killed, and a part of Colombia's inhabitants began to move to Venezuela in search of peace."[8]

[6] García, *Gaitán* ..., p. 314.
[7] Niño H., *op. cit.,* p. 13.
[8] Arciniegas, *op. cit.,* p. 161.

A major political break in the coalition came over the strike by the Petroleum Workers Union. While Ospina tried to negotiate a settlement, the Liberals withdrew from the government, but they returned when a solution was found, despite the fact that the Liberal congressional majority had disavowed in advance any settlement which the government might make. This difference of opinion deepened the conviction of the people that corruption had played a part, and that it was a maneuver of the oligarchy. "The belligerence and the class feeling of the people were inflamed by what they considered the 'remunerated desertion' of their chiefs."[9] There was talk of a popular *coup d'état*, of forcing Ospina to resign.

The violent trend was given impetus by Gaitán's failures in Congress. He had projected a program of reform covering banking and credit, state control of corporations and capital federations, and establishing a State Planning Commission to better conditions for the workers and peasants. All this was voted down by the Liberal Congress, and Gaitán stood discredited by what was nominally his own party. His fate was similar to that of López: he was a leader without a force to lead.

But the masses supported him and what he wanted to do. Sullenly, the people began to arm, to make caches of arms and explosives. Ammunition and cartridges flowed over the border from Venezuela into the country. In many places Liberals, harried by the Political Police, took to carrying long-range weapons. In Tolima, organized revolt broke out, and the Governor of the Department remained indifferent, even supported the revolutionaries. Detectives, ordered there to investigate, were sent packing back to Bogotá. In El Espinal, a Divisional Commander of Police was involved in planning a revolt, and "in one of the salons of the Chamber of Deputies, and in the Liberal National Directorate, precise instructions were given regarding the use of arms, and arms were promised. Numerous small arms deposits were seized [by police], demonstrating the insurrectionary atmosphere which existed in the country."[10]

As the Ninth Inter-American Conference drew near, with Bogotá preparing to act as the host city, the country stood on the verge of civil war. Conservative police, particularly in the provinces, had become an out-and-out force of repression. Refugees were flocking to

[9] Niño H., *op. cit.*, p. 19.
[10] *Ibid.*, p. 23.

the urban centers. "On the eve of the Pan American Conference that was to meet in Bogotá, terror reigned in the provinces," says Arciniegas.[11] Gaitán visited Santander, where the situation was the worst, and, upon his return, proclaimed the right of legitimate self-defense for the masses. To care for the peasants who were swarming into the capital, he ordered the creation of the *Casa del Refugiado* (House of Refugees). "After every move of Liberalism to recuperate its strength, there followed a wave ... cold, premeditated, exact ... of political violence. All the centers of resistance were hit. Political assassinations assumed massive proportions and drops of blood became wells of blood."[12]

In this worsening situation, Gaitán broke the slender thread of Liberal collaboration. He dissolved the Liberal portion of the cabinet in March, 1948. Immediately, a Conservative bloc moved in. On the heels of this move, the masses got another blow when Ospina Pérez passed over Gaitán in choosing the delegates for the Inter-American Conference. This snub was, in effect, a contemptuous gesture for the people of Colombia, for in degrading the importance of their leader, the masses were degraded by Ospina's action. Insult was added to popular injury when Laureano Gómez was named to preside at the conference.

By this time, Bogotá was swarming with hungry, homeless refugees from the provinces. The *Casa del Refugiado* had become a crying necessity, and Gaitán requested Antonio García to present the need for it to the city council of Bogotá. They refused, using these words, to quote García: "Should we create, in our very homeland, an institution which formalized the fact, at arms' length, of persecution and martyrdom? Political violence is now only an exception to the rule, a misfortune which will gradually disappear."[13]

Such blindness to reality was chronic among the ruling Conservatives in this latter hour of Colombian freedom. The ultra-Conservatives were now in effective control. Knowing this, Gaitán and the Advisory Board of the Liberal party had, as early as January, 1948, presented President Ospina with a memorandum charging that his followers and underlings were systematically sabotaging the principles of National Union. The memorandum accused the Conser-

[11] Arciniegas, *op cit.*, p. 161.
[12] García, *Gaitán* ..., p. 317.
[13] *Ibid.*

vatives of trying to "impose clerical education upon the nation, to persecute organized labor, to perpetuate electoral frauds, and to instigate general violence against the Liberals."[14]

Of course, the charges were rejected. So, in the same indignant terms, was organized aid to the swarming refugees from the provinces.

All down the line, the people were losing to the counterrevolution. Only days remained before they would lose their leader.

THE ECONOMIC STATE OF THE MASSES

The people were the helpless pawns in the struggle for power.

To understand the dynamics of the events of April 9, 1948, and the violent times which grew out of them, one must look at the hungry, the dispossessed, the misery-ridden, who had pinned their slim hopes on Gaitán. It was their revolution that had failed, and it was their price which was exacted for that failure.

World War II had a profound effect upon the Colombian economy. In the first years, many world markets were closed to Colombian coffee. The main problem then was the re-channeling of trade, but there were other ticklish aspects of the matter. Even when Colombia has ample foreign exchange from coffee sales (and the first effect of the war was to reduce and disorganize its sources), there is still the matter of being able to buy what is needed in the way of consumers' goods and raw materials for fabricating industries.

The war effort of the Allies sucked up into its greedy maw every available type of good to keep Allied armies marching and fighting. Supplies to noncombatant nations were strictly rationed, and the result for Colombia was a severe shortage of imports which ordinarily fed commerce, created jobs and employment, and generally affected nearly all wage-creating endeavors.

Colombian exports to Europe fell from 24 per cent of her total in 1936 to less than 1 per cent in 1942. Likewise, European imports declined from 46 per cent of the 1937 volume to a scant 9 per cent in 1942. This, while the United States, absorbing everything for its own war production, became increasingly unable to fill the gap left in the Latin-American–European trade.[15] Consequently, by the end

[14] Donald Marquand Dozer, "The Roots of Revolution in Latin America," *Foreign Affairs*, January, 1949, p. 283.

[15] *Colombia: Trade Problems* (Washington: U. S. Department of Commerce, 1943), p. 34.

of 1942, Colombia was exporting almost nothing to continental Europe. The value of United Kingdom purchases in Colombia (normally heavy), fell to the lowest point in thirteen years.[16] In time, of course, coffee again started to move as the United States bought great quantities for the armed forces, but imports (needed for fabricating) fell off in a steady curve as the United States concentrated on supplying the Allies.[17]

From this it resulted that, as dollar exchange piled up unused (because of gradual normalization of exports and a continued inability to make purchases), the Colombian economy was strained to the limit. A dizzying inflationary spiral set in. Lack of imports meant scarcity and increasing unemployment as many enterprises were forced to curtail production or shut down. Too, the scarcity on the internal market brought a rising price level, and, as living costs soared under the spur of scarcity and an excess of capital, wages remained static. Processing transactions declined, commerce clogged up, and, to replace normal commerical activity, the securities market began to climb under the pressure of idle, speculative capital looking for ventures.

Too tardily, the government initiated price controls. The economic momentum could not be halted. Manufactured, semi-manufactured, and consumers' goods became dearer, and food costs rose sharply. In order to evade controls, the governmental-control agencies often connived with the business community for graft and other reasons. The control system became not only useless, but vicious and chaotic. All imports were supposed to be subject to licenses on the basis of need-preference. Under the pressure of much idle capital, such licenses went at premium rates: there was frank evasion of the regulations by political, personal, and financial ties and pressures.[18] Moreover, such imports as did come in were not always channeled into the really crucial sectors of the economy. Those with political "pull" got what they wanted, often nonnecessities, while many badly-needed imports essential to employment-creating lines went begging.

When Ospina Pérez came to office in 1946, the channels of black marketeering and privilege-manipulation of government bureaus

---

[16] *Ibid.*

[17] *Ibid.*

[18] *Colombia's Economy in 1944* (Washington: International Reference Service, U. S. Department of Commerce, October, 1945), p. 6.

Coffee brings Colombia about half a billion dollars annually (mostly from the United States), and employs some six million people. Harvest season is in June and November when around nine hundred million pounds are picked and packed. Here, workers spread the coffee beans to dry under the sun.

had been formalized. Goods had begun to reappear, but the inflationary, speculative psychology had now taken possession of the country. Many deferred demands were gratified, as, in a wild spending spree, the surplus dollar exchange not only was depleted, but created a deficit. This buying urge maintained the inflationary pressure, in spite of attempts to ration the exportation of dollars and the expenditure of foreign coffee exchange.

To sum up, the period preceding the critical political era in Colombia had been one of constrictive inflation, induced by an export surplus which stemmed from heavy war demands for Colombian coffee and raw materials; by a simultaneous piling-up of exchange (as imports were reduced below the selling volume), and the use of the unexpended balances as speculative capital; and, finally, by a sharp, rapid increase in all prices, due to import controls and shortages of goods, which prevented buyers from spending and made money cheap, excessive in quantity, and ready for any reasonable venture as it had never before been.[19]

Socially, this economic situation brought direct ill effects upon the masses of people. Investment in real estate zoomed upward, raising rents for the poor, to add another burden to rising food costs. Meanwhile, the rich indulged their tastes for automobiles, travel, and durable consumers' goods which they had been unable to get before.[20]

It was an era of fat living for those who had money, but the concentrated nature of the economy let none of the benefits filter down to the masses of people. On the contrary, as inflation multiplied existing wealth, it pressed downward with greater weight. Workers, peasants, and the lower middle class wage earners were caught in a cycle of rising prices and wages that lagged far behind the cost-of-living curve.

It was dangerous and possibly unjustifiable, particularly since the government continued to favor the policy desired by the oligarchy, "Prosperity by Inflation." The masses could get no substantial relief. The plight of the common people is indicated by reports of the American Commercial Attaché in Bogotá during this time:

The cost of living index for Bogotá was 171.7 at the end of 1944, in comparison with 142.4 at the end of the previous year. In other cities the range was about the

[19] Secretariat Report on Economic Implications for Latin America of Defense Programs Abroad (Washington: The Pan American Union, 1951), p. 6.
[20] Ibid., p. 8.

same. Industrial wages rose at a slower rate than the cost of living, *and real wages had declined steadily since 1941.*[21]

And later, this report mirrored the worsening of the situation:

In November, 1946, the cost of living index of a [Colombian] workingman's family reached 229 (1937 as 100). It has continued to rise to record figures during each month since June, 1945. Food rose to 233.6, rent to 214.9, clothing to 223.5. The index for the Bogotá food market showed an increase, advancing from 384.6 in October, 1946, to 405.9 in November. As a result of public pressures against rising prices and the high cost of living, the Colombian government reinstituted price control in 1946. The measure was not very successful, and at year's end, inflation appeared unchecked.[22]

Finally, on February 25, 1947, the American Embassy, in its monthly airgram, analyzed the economic situation in this fashion:

Living costs have continued high. During January the cost of living index for a workingman's family rose seven points to 231. Scarcities continue in fats, oils, cocoa, sugar and panela. There has been considerable criticism of the fact that the new Bogotá price schedule, promulgated on February 17, allowed increased prices for panela and chocolate, *which are important staples in the diet of the masses.*[23]

These cold, bare figures display the other side of the picture: that of mass misery, of hunger, of wages lagging always behind living costs, of food becoming dearer daily, and of unemployment spreading. The violence in the provinces, the arming of the Liberals, the repressive measures of the Political Police and the counteractions, all these are understandable only in terms of want and economic hardship. The people were distressed and hungry. In 1948 the violence was accompanied by looting—a sure indicator of danger ahead. Terror was met by terror. And as police brutality spread through the countryside, as homes were burned and people killed, and the refugees limped into the cities for safety, the press added its voice to the clamor, castigating the government for permitting hoarding, speculation, and black marketeering.[24]

As of the moment immediately before the lid blew off, while the

[21] *Colombia's Economy in 1944*, p. 6.
[22] *Foreign Commerce Weekly* (Washington: U. S. Department of Commerce, March 1, 1947), p. 5.
[23] U. S. Embassy Airgram, Bogotá, February 22, 1947, p. 1.
[24] U. S. Embassy Airgram, Bogotá, April 10, 1947, p. 1.

city of Bogotá was decking the public buildings for the arrival of the delegates to the Inter-American Conference, Colombia was morally and politically bankrupt. It was ready for whatever violence might come, and the incentive needed not to be unusual. Donald Marquand Dozer gives a good summary of conditions in these words:

Meanwhile, the worsening economic plight of the masses of Colombian people, aggravated by the war and postwar dislocations, was exacerbating already serious social tensions and increasing popular dissatisfaction with the national administration. During 1947, living cost indices in Bogota rose to 253.2. These rises continued in 1948. During the single month of March, 1948, the cost of living index for an average workingman's family rose by 17.3 points, to a new high of 283.8. In the capital, where preparations for the forthcoming Ninth International Conference of American States had a further inflationary effect, the cost of living rose 20.6 points in the same period, reflected principally in sharp increases in the prices of bread, butter, milk, potatoes, fresh vegetables and meat. Control was powerless to curb speculation and prevent price inflation. However, *efforts of organized workers to secure wage increases commensurate with these increases in the cost of living appeared in several instances to be thwarted by government action.*[25]

The rejection by his own party of Gaitán's program; the victory and final entrenchment of the dual oligarchy; the terror of and in the provinces; the government's reluctance to materially help the workers, while it gave relief to those who sold food staples to the workers: these were all signs of the coming storm. Larco Herrera, in the city for the conference, recognized them, for he said,

The course of Colombian politics clearly showed unmistakable signs of illness, for months before the international assembly met. The Conservatives who were in power, and the Liberals who collaborated with them had been encountering differences of some importance, and soon the President, Ospina Pérez, had to meet a very delicate situation, such as the disturbances in January in Cundinamarca and other places, which continued to create an atmosphere propitious to the unleashing of the tragedy of April.[26]

Someone once said: "When a man is hungry, he will dream of bread." And when there is bread, and it is denied him, he will fight for it.

THE ROLE OF COMMUNISTS AND FOREIGN AGITATORS

Communists have been lavishly blamed for the violence of this period of Colombian history, but their role still remains essentially

[25] Dozer, *op. cit.*, p. 283.
[26] Larco Herrera, *op. cit.*, p. 151.

obscure. By the best accounts, the Colombian Communist party has never numbered more than 8,000 members. Arciniegas, examining the charges made by Laureano Gómez that the masses had "gone Communist" derides the idea,[27] pointing out that most were simply peasants who were fighting to protect their homes and families. Yet this is not the whole story.

Most of the nominal Communists of Colombia, even those who carry a party card, think of themselves as Social Democrats if they try to define an ideology at all. They back and support certain minimal social and economic goals sponsored by the Communist party, but they are strangers to Marx and dialectical materialism.

Communism in Colombia had, by 1930, gained some little strength in the labor movement, particularly in the petroleum industry. When the Conservatives returned to power in 1946, the Communists polled 25,000 votes and elected one senator and a member of the House.[28] However, this strength fell off in the congressional elections in 1947, for the party split into two wings, under Augusto Durán and Gilberto Vieira, respectively. In the 1946 elections, the Communists supported Turbay, the rightist Liberal; in 1947, pinning their hopes on Gaitán's congressional program, they shifted to Gaitán. But they polled only 16,000 votes over the nation, and Gaitán did nothing to win them over. A writer who supports the Conservative view of the epoch sums up Communist influence in these words:

> Between the unfortunate Colombian leader [Gaitán] and the Communist Party there existed discrepancies so fundamental, propositions and political ambitions so opposed, that if, occasionally, they feigned harmony and reconciliation to combat ... Ospina Pérez, they basically disliked and lay in ambush for one another, harrassed and persecuted one another, in a clever reciprocal game of deceit to see which would first lower his defense and let the adversary deal the decisive blow.[29]

The split which occurred in 1946 over backing Turbay or Gaitán was even deeper when the party met in Bucaramanga in July, 1947, to arrange strategy and find, if possible, a common line of action. There, an attempt was made to elect Gilberto Vieira as Secretary General of the party, but it was blocked by Durán, who vacillated

[27] Arciniegas, *op. cit.*, p. 387.

[28] Martin Ebon, *World Communism Today* (New York: McGraw-Hill Book Co., 1948), p. 326.

[29] Mario Fernández de Soto, *Una Revolución en Colombia* (Madrid: Ediciones Cultura Hispánica, 1951), p. 90.

between the two wings of the Liberal party as the proper vehicle for Colombian communism. Further disunity, therefore, came out of the Bucaramanga meeting. Vieira, the most doctrinaire of the two leaders, founded his own Colombian Communist party, and Durán sponsored the Communist Workers party. This move had been foreseen by the Colombian press, which reported in July: "Durán now is leading his party unconditionally toward adherence with Gaitán, who, on the other hand, has taken command of a large part of the masses formerly commanded by Durán ... without asking the latter's permission."[30]

But the adherence of Durán's wing to Gaitán was enough to cause the Conservative regime to crack down on the Communist movement. The Conservative dailies began to call for the outlawing of all unions even slightly tinged with Red, or whose Directorates included Communists. There were few of these, and the Liberal press deplored the possibility of destroying the budding organic nature of the labor movement for the mere sake of weeding out a few Communists.[31]

Nonetheless, there were forces in Colombia which might reasonably be feared. The Soviets had sent a diplomatic mission of scores of persons to Bogotá, but had accepted only a mission of three Colombians to Moscow. This great disparity, together with the lack of mutual interests between the two countries caused many Colombians to wonder. Then, too, within a short time after diplomatic relations had been established, the Soviet Legation began to disseminate its *chef d'oeuvre* of propaganda, the *Boletín de Información*, in whose pages Colombian writers, such as Jose Luis Salado, Ramon Mendezona, and others went straight down the party line with Russian Communists.[32]

There had also been a certain previous acceptance of the Soviet propaganda in Colombia. The Russians and their sympathizers had adroitly exploited their military victories, while playing down the feats of arms of the West; party workers paraded their democratic leanings; the Soviet Legation gave parties for its employees, where the minister and his secretaries toasted the chambermaids with vodka and danced with the charwomen. All in all, it was disgusting to the *gente*, and completely captivating to the lowly.

Moreover, even in Colombia many intellectuals were drawn into

---

[30] *El Diario* (Medellín). July 11, 1947, p. 8.

[31] "La Lucha Contra el Comunismo," *El Diario* (Medellín), May 28, 1947, p. 5.

[32] *Boletín de Información*, Legación de la Union de Repúblicas Socialistas Soviéticas, Bogotá, February 16, 1947; February 23, 1947; August, 1947.

"front" organizations, in particular, the *Instituto Cultural Colombo-Soviético* (Colombian-Soviet Cultural Institute). Among the sponsors of this organization were Baldomero Sanín Cano, Gerardo Molina, Germán Arciniegas, Alfonso López Michelsen, Carlos H. Pareja, Eduardo Zuleta, Antonio García, Juan Francisco Mujica[33]—a veritable Who's Who of Colombian culture, arts, and letters. Their sin was only that of permitting the use of their names, but, as was true in the United States in many cases, that was enough.

Unfortunately for the internal political situation, most of these respected gentlemen were Liberals. Naturally, the Conservatives saw them as offering aid and comfort to the enemy. They were proof that the Liberals wanted to turn Colombia into a Soviet satellite. *La Defensa*, a strong provincial Conservative daily in Medellín, the country's industrial heart, printed a photostatic copy of the masthead of the Cultural Institute, with the intellectuals' names on it, and wrote about it an editorial which said:

> Certain superior classes among the arts, letters and sciences, are surrendering without a whisper or a sigh, in the most unconditional adherence to the Russian experiment, to the Russian government and to the universal fatherland of the Red Proletarian Dictatorship. In this way, Russian Communism is founding in our country true spiritual hierarchies which, tomorrow, may hold over the masses greater directive power than the unmasked communists of the market place wield today. Perhaps we should run a picture of Lenin on the front page, but we purposely avoid this "about-face", since we have no desire to collaborate with Señor Sanín Cano in the exaltation of that shining Asiatic genius, the universal enemy Number A-1 of culture and of Christian civilization.[34]

On balance, Communist idealogical penetration was probably only mildly successful in Colombia, in spite of the Conservative apprehension. Basically, the core of the problem was Colombian, and Colombians identified their social and economic complaints with communism (when and if they did) only because they were complaints against a system that would have appeared defective even had Marx never been born. Still, the native Communists were active. And that activity increased as the date of the Inter-American Conference drew nearer.

The two wings of the party worked separately. Vieira frankly sponsored open and immediate revolution, while Durán, the crafty polit-

---

[33] "Comunismo in Edición de Lujo," *La Defensa* (Medellín), June 13, 1947, p. 5.
[34] *Ibid.*

ico, used infiltration, conspiracy, and subterfuge. One and the other agitated the people in the workers' areas of Bogotá around-the-clock; according to Niño H. "Both exercised notable and almost definitive influence in the workers' syndicates. The CTC has always been at the service of Communism. . . ."[35]

There is considerable doubt, nonetheless, as to the effectiveness of the Colombian Communists. Probably they were not too efficient because they were divided in the first place; again, many of the rank and file still thought of themselves as Liberals of the Far Left. Niño H., who, as Chief of National Security, thinks not too much of the threat, should know: "International or Russian Communism does not take seriously this bifrontal and ingenious Communism of ours, and although it uses and directs it without explanations, holds it in contempt which it does not try to hide."[36]

It should not be assumed from this, however, that communism was not a strong factor in the events which were to come. International agents of the party were on the scene, and events were playing into their hands. El Valle and Santander were the scenes of strikes, suspension of public services, minor rioting; strikes by the Chauffeurs' Union in Bogotá and Cali became violent and were broken by armed force; a general strike was called and fizzled out when some workers failed to obey the call. Employers then began reprisals, and further disturbances flared. In January the petroleum unions struck, and police seized explosives and handmade bombs in the homes of union officials. In Tolima, peasants were up in arms. "The Nation, the whole Nation, became aware that something very grave for the country was drawing near; on all sides people spoke of a *coup d'état*; the unrest was general and all horizons were touched by tragic lights and uncertain menaces; the economic crisis, the high cost of living, the propaganda which filled the press, the political pugnacity, the frequent arrival of foreign agitators, inflamed spirits and overcharged the national atmosphere of tempestuous clouds."[37]

It now seems fairly well established that the most important Communist aid came from Venezuela. President Romulo Betancourt's *Acción Democrática* government in that country was filled with old-time Venezuelan exiles who had made their headquarters in Bar-

[35] Niño H., *op. cit.*, p. 27.
[36] *Ibid.*, p. 28.
[37] *Ibid.*, p. 46.

ranquilla, Colombia, between 1929 and 1936. When they returned home, they kept up their ties with Colombian Liberals, and supplied arms and ammunition for the "Barranquilla Plan" of liberating Colombia, Ecuador, and Peru from "feudalism." Many of these men were one-time Communists, and they comprised the heart of the famed "Caribbean Legion."[38]

Among the foreign Communists who entered Colombia shortly before the explosion came were Gilberto Machado, a Venezuelan who traveled on a diplomatic passport and acted as liaison with the CTC; Salvador Ocampo, Communist senator from Chile, who, when arrested, had large sums of money in his possession which he could not explain away; Luis Fernández, Spanish Communist; Eugene Kerbaul, a French Communist; Milorad Pesic B., a Yugoslav party member, and Frances McKinnon, French in origin, but an American citizen. "Their mission was also revolutionary," says Niño H., "and from them were taken ... revealing documents which indicated that revolt was being prepared in Europe and Latin America. Regarding Colombia, there was found on them propaganda against the Pan-American Conference, orders to establish affiliates with the World Youth Movement in various places, and the names of contacts in Bogotá, Cartagena, Cali and other cities."[39]

While the foreign agents congregated, arms and ammunition came into Colombia in large quantities, and the material was traced by serial numbers back to Venezuelan armories. Suddenly finding itself discovered, the Venezuelan government claimed that the material had been taken without its knowledge. But when President Betancourt came to the Bogotá Conference, he took the long, hard way by road, stopping at every hamlet to be hailed by the humble people and to vary his official business by conferring with the leaders of the masses.

The condition of the masses was, in fact, desperate as events marched toward a climax. A gigantic mass demonstration began to gather force. Shock troops were organized in the capital. Liberals and Conservatives hurled charges hysterically back and forth as tension reached the snapping point. On February 7, Gaitán stood before a silent mass of poor people gathered in Bogotá's main square. Not a sound came from 100,000 people who looked to him as their savior—he had asked them to remain orderly, quiet, dignified. There was no

[38] Galbraith, op. cit., p. 132.
[39] Niño H., op. cit., pp. 50–54.

outcry, only the waving of hands and handkerchiefs at Gaitán as he said, in part,

> Mr. President, we are not here to present economic or political demands. All we ask is that our country desist from a line of action and conduct that puts us to shame in our own eyes and those of foreigners. We ask this in the name of mercy and civilization ... we ask that this persecution on the part of the authorities come to an end ... put a halt, Mr. President, to violence. All we ask of you is the guarantee of human life, which is the least a country can ask.[40]

But the die had been cast: it was too late.

The delegates met for the Inter-American Conference. Police arrested a worker trying to place a bomb in the capitol where the conference was meeting. Propaganda circulated on all sides, the Marshall Plan being the chief target. On the seventh of April a handbill flooded the city, attacking the oligarchs who "dined in state while the people went hungry," and calling for revolution. On Bogotá's main street a mob attacked the automobile of the Ecuadorian delegate to the conference. Rumors circulated that an attempt would be made on the life of the American Secretary of State, General Marshall, and the American Embassy notified the chief of National Security of a bomb plot against the Secretary. The same day, the Communists held two meetings, one public, the other behind locked doors.

On April 9, 1948, while the American States were assembled in conference at the capitol under the gavel of Laureano Gómez, Jorge Eliécer Gaitán was working in his office not two blocks away, across the great square which is the heart of the federal area. Snubbed by the Ospina government, still he had insisted that his followers, if named, should attend and serve their nation. Many were over there now.

At one o'clock in the afternoon, which is the start of the Bogotá lunch time, Gaitán left his office and went down to the street. At that hour there are always crowds of people of all classes and conditions on the square.

As Gaitán stepped to the sidewalk and started away, the dry, sultry report of a pistol rang out, four times repeated. Gaitán lurched, stumbled, and fell to the pavement.

With him there fell an era in Colombian history.

[40] Arciniegas, *op. cit.*, p. 161.

VII. Blood Bath and Dictatorship: The End of Republican Government (1948–1950)

As Gaitán slumped to the sidewalk, a vendor of lottery tickets made a rush for the assassin. Another man ran from a nearby cafe and smashed a chair over the killer's head.[1] In an instant a mob had gathered around the assassin, and quite literally they kicked him to death, disfiguring him so badly that his features were unrecognizable and identification had to be made from documents on his person.

While Gaitán was rushed to a clinic, an ugly mob formed in the great central plaza. Word quickly spread that Laureano Gómez, object of the people's hate, had ordered the killing of their leader. Howling for revenge, the crowd spilled across the plaza and into the capitol building, brushed aside guards and went on a rampage when it learned that Gómez had already fled. Records, furniture, paintings, were destroyed; the building was set afire, and rendered useless for the remainder of the conference. Then the mob surged back into the plaza, gathering in numbers. Looting and destruction began to spread to the center of Bogotá.

When word came that Gaitán had died shortly after reaching the clinic, the crowds simply went berserk. Howling mobs broke into liquor stores and hardwares, and, drunk as much with rage as with liquor, raced through the streets armed with dynamite, machetes, torches, gasoline. Rumors circulated that priests were firing upon them from the belfries of churches, and they put the churches to the torch and the sack, along with public buildings and commercial establishments. Dynamite destroyed Gómez' newspaper, *El Siglo*, and they watched it burn to a heap of rubble. Someone started howling for Gómez' head, and they took up the cry. A crowd of hundreds rushed for his suburban home, found him gone (he left the country for exile in Spain), and burned and looted his home. Streetcars were crisped to fiery hulls on the tracks where their crews abandoned them;

[1] MacDonald, *op. cit.*, p. 402.

buses, private cars, and police vehicles were overturned in the spasm of hate, and burned where they lay. The mobs, beyond all control, and thirsting for Conservative blood, moved toward the presidential palace. Only the presidential guard stood to defend it, for the Bogotá garrison, though called out, refused to leave the barracks[2] and the police everywhere were joining the rioters, even providing them with ammunition. The President's guard managed to hold off the attackers until tanks from an armored battalion arrived to offer support.

As night fell, flames lit up the ravaged city from scores of burning buildings. Damage to the city was immense. Foreign correspondents likened it to London or Plymouth after an air raid.[3] And the burning, looting and destruction was to go on for days until Army reinforcements arrived to impose order and martial law.

As has been shown, the security forces had been warned of many plots which pointed to the possibility of a general uprising.[4] The Soviet Embassy had moved its archives to Venezuela short weeks before the outbreak, and a few days before the riots, had taken from its offices quantities of material which it burned in a house rented in the suburbs for that purpose.[5] And some three weeks before the violence flared, Gilberto Vieira, leader of the authentic Colombian Communists, was quoted in the press by Alvaro Sanclemente, a columnist, as stating, "My party considers that the new political conditions created in the country require a full revolutionary battle of the working class and the people, in order to speed up the belligerent action of the masses and to defend democratic liberties, as well as to defeat the ... Conservative plans for reaction which conform to the slogan of Minister Jose Antonio Montalvo, 'Blood and Fire' "[6]

Communist work or not, the Conservatives had a good case. Moreover, the Liberals agreed with them. On May 16, 1948, Enrique Santos, Colombia's most influential and perceptive political writer (and brother of ex-President Santos), summed up the Liberal view:

Jorge Eliécer Gaitán was the first and most illustrious victim of the Communist Politburo's policy, as Colombia was another of the material victims. The un-

[2] Arciniegas, *op. cit.*, p. 161.
[3] The American Embassy estimated Bogotá's loss at $171,000,000, the country's as a whole, $570,000,000. See *Foreign Commerce Weekly*, May 8, 1948, p. 3.
[4] Niño H., *op. cit.*, p. 68.
[5] *Ibid.*, p. 75.
[6] Larco Herrera, *op. cit.*, p. 151.

chained multitudes, mad with grief and rage, might have limited themselves to protests, but they never would have thrown themselves into the destruction of the stores, to sacking and looting shops; to demolishing the work ... pride of the city ... which had been created for the Conference; to looting even the Colonial Museum, where many mementos of Bolívar are kept. Yet, they would have destroyed the very house in which the Liberator passed his last days in Bogotá, if the authorities had not succeeded in stopping them. Anyone who observed them, saw in Bogotá the functioning of the classical Communist action plan. They seized the radio stations, spread terror, directed teams of dynamiters, incendiarists and looters. To spread terror, to create panic, are fundamentals of the Communist offensive strategy. Looting, stealing things that might be useful, can be understood. But why destroy the Palace of San Carlos; why throw workers and modest employees out of work? Because all of this enters into the Communist plan: creation of panic, of desperation, of disorientation; the spreading of hunger among the workers.

On the radio we heard them urging on the incendiarists. And we saw them at the head of the mobs which set the torch to the governmental palace, which was just the beginning of the barbarism. Then, another Communist tactic, the jails were thrown open, bringing six thousand more malefactors into the wild melee and the wild hordes.

Is it possible to doubt the Communist direction of the uprising? Whoever listened on the radio would have been sufficiently convinced. They had everything ready and were prepared. They called over the radio to cities and towns, to specific individuals in those places to whom they gave specific orders and directions; and on the radio appeared the name of the mysterious "Doctor X," as head of the movement.[7]

Larco Herrera was also impressed by the apparent planning and organization behind the riots. He says, "On the radio stations, which were captured by the agitators, they were incited to murder and looting."[8] He concludes that the movement was Soviet-directed, for the purpose of sabotaging the Inter-American Conference.[9] And much the same view is taken by Fernández de Soto, "The Communist intervention and intention was manifest: prevent, if possible, the meeting of the Conference, or bring it to failure as a consequence of a series of subversive and tumultuous maneuvers intended to produce disturbance of the public order and create a climate of violence capable of compromising the security of the Assembly and of its delegates."[10]

On April 13, 1948, Secretary of State Marshall "declared emphatically that the *coup* which has just occurred in Colombia is manifestly

[7] *El Tiempo* (Bogotá), April 30, 1948, p. 8; also, May 16, 1948, p. 11.
[8] Larco Herrera, *op. cit.*, p. 150.
[9] *Ibid.*
[10] Fernández de Soto, *op. cit.*, p. 91.

Communist, and that the Ninth Conference should continue since the contrary would mean giving to Communism the battle for Latin America."[11] This served to convince most Colombians of what they wanted to believe. Foreign and Creole Communists were arrested, relations with the Soviet were broken off, and Scotland Yard was sent a hurried cable requesting investigators to sift the affair.

From this point on, the trail led off to nowhere. It was established that the man who killed Gaitán was a Rosicrucian, a mystic who heard "voices," a poor nobody of obscure background and few acquaintances, named Juan Roa. If, as some Colombians think, he was used as a tool of the Communist conspiracy to assassinate Gaitán and trigger a revolution, he served his purpose well. However, proof is lacking to link him to such a scheme.

The arrested Communists were eventually discharged for lack of evidence against them.[12] Scotland Yard investigated and went home. Its report has never been made public. Gaitán's death and its relationship to the Communist conspiracy remains an enigma–a tantalizing, persistent one.

One characteristic of the rioting bears the deep, red mark of Communist handiwork: the attacks upon the Church, which were characteristically un-Colombian, even for a time of extraordinary stress. In Barranquilla, priests were dragged from the altar, beaten, and hauled through the streets by their heels while rioters stoned them and beat them to death. "Churches, convents, ecclesiastical colleges, schools and institutions were burned, and the clergy were seized, killed, and in some cases, horribly mutilated."[13] In the first few hours, the leaders of the riots called over the National Radio to the people, telling them "that priests were assassinating the people, and firing upon them from the roofs and bell-towers of the churches."[14] And as a climax to this anti-Church fury, the directors of the violence "announced" that the Archbishop Primate of Bogotá was directing the priestly battle against the people—words which hurled the mob against the archepiscopal palace, putting the Primate on the run,

[11] *El Relator* (Cali), April 13, 1948, p. 1. Marshall later modified his view to blame the Communists only for taking over the riots after they had been touched off.

[12] MacDonald, *op. cit.*, p. 403.

[13] Galbraith, *op. cit.*, p. 133.

[14] Fernández de Soto, *op. cit.*, p. 105.

and destroying, in their blind anger, sacred and historical relics of great worth.[15]

Was there, if not a plot to assassinate Gaitán, a plot by the Communists to foster some general popular uprisings? From the hazy background of data something of the sort seems to emerge, even if one disregards the strong evidence of the security forces themselves. A letter to the writer from Don Julio Hernández, editor of *El Colombiano* and brother-in-law of President Ospina Pérez, says:

> Without doubt, the Communists were the instigators of what happened. We have, as you know, very few real Communists in Colombia, but the Russian Legation in Bogotá worked night and day, through its numerous employees (Colombian and Russian Communists) and, aided by other foreign Communists from Mexico, Cuba and Chile, created an atmosphere of violence and unrest in the country. That you may see in one of the copies of *El Colombiano* which I am sending you under separate cover.[16]

The evidence to which Don Julio refers is a photostatic copy of a letter which appeared in his newspaper. It is from Francisco Calderio (alias Blas Roca), to Don Luis Cardoza y Aragón, Guatemalan ambassador to Chile and serving at the time as his country's chief delegate to the Ninth Inter-American Conference.

Dated April 4, 1948 (five days before the outbreak), the letter indicates that Latin-American Communists, with the special assistance of the Venezuelan government, were planning revolt in a number of Latin countries, and were particularly bent upon wrecking the conference. The editors of *El Colombiano* "assumed full responsibility" for the authenticity of the letter, which, it was stated, came into their hands from a friendly, unnamed diplomatic source.[17]

The letter bears the heading of the *Federación Estudiantil Universitaria* (University Students Federation), of Havana, Cuba. Both the Federation and the University of Havana have been hotbeds of Latin-American communism, while Blas Roca, writer of the letter, was then head of the Cuban Communist party.[18]

There is an authoritative ring to the letter: "We have entered upon the month of trial, the period of our plans; if luck is with us,

[15] *Ibid.*, p. 106.

[16] Correspondence with the writer, Medellín, Colombia, June, 1948.

[17] The excerpts used here and the comments regarding the letter are based upon the article in *El Colombiano* (Medellín), June 29, 1948, p. 1.

[18] Ebon, *op. cit.*, p. 324.

we will see our banner flying in Mexico, Venezuela, Chile, the Dominican Republic, Panama, Ecuador, Peru, Brazil and the rest of Central America." The proximate triumph of the Costa Rican revolutionaries under Manuel Mora Valverde (Moscow-trained head of the Costa Rican Communist party) was to be the signal for the overthrow of all Central American governments, which then would be unified under a Guatamalan Communist leader. Panama was to be absorbed into the Central American Union: "No compassion must be shown to Panama; get rid of Arias without losing time."

As for Venezuela, "Everything is ready for Monday 12. All the oil-fields are controlled by Comrade Betancourt's men . . . the fields at Oriente and Maracaibo are crying for the match. I received a letter from Salvador Ocampo [Chilean Senator arrested by Colombian Secret Police], who says that Romulo [Betancourt] sent considerable assistance to Mora Valverde, and that our victory is assured in Costa Rica." Nor was Colombia far down on the agenda:

> The gringo Marshall and the negro Gaitán must be taken care of quickly, before the so-called Bogotá Conference warms up. And it must be remembered that our plans are ready for Monday. It is important that in Bogotá there not be left standing a roof where even a canary can hide. Comrade Betancourt will by now have sent the necessary trained men to accomplish that end. Ospina Pérez will not resist half an hour; but in any case, Bogotá must be destroyed as an example for other countries.

Later accounts of the affair in *Semana,* capital news weekly, quoted American Intelligence sources as stating that most of the arms and explosives had come from Venezuela (confirming both Niño H. and Blas Roca), while the funds had been provided by "Russian sources."[19]

The Blas Roca letter was never challenged, either by the governments or the individuals who were accused by its text.

On the whole, the evidence seems to indicate that the murder of Gaitán was a private affair, but that it accidentally triggered the events which anticipated a possibly well-laid plot by Latin-American Communists to create some major disturbance. It seems beyond question that the Communists took over and exploited the violence, once it was set off.

The Colombian government claimed that it had proof of Venezuelan intervention, in the form of a check for a large sum, paid

[19] *Semana* (Bogotá), April 30, 1948, p. 1.

by Romulo Betancourt to Gaitán.[20] And it is a matter of common knowledge that Venezuelan radio stations broadcast reports of certain events in Colombia before they occurred. But these things were quickly hushed up as too dangerous, for the angry people had idolized their fallen leader. In the final analysis, there is no facile explanation of the fact that the Venezuelan press and radio had reported that "Colombians had risen to throw off tyranny," or that rumors had spread among the Bogotá rioters that the Venezuelan Army had crossed the frontier to "help the people," under the leadership of Betancourt the "friend of the people."[21]

But on the whole, the impression gained from looking at this period is that the Communists themselves were "accidental." The villain of the piece, if one must have a villain, was the *system*, which reduced the great majority to misery and social debasement, while the very small minority became rich and waxed fat and prosperous. In its haste to find an explanation, the government reached for that convenient whipping-boy of distressed economies: communism. To admit that the parties, the system of feudalistic privilege, the institutions which the oligarchy had created, had buckled under the strain of modern demands, would have been to destroy the very thing that the oligarchs were trying to maintain. Therefore, the unreal theory, the tragically self-hypnotic delusion, that it had all "just happened"; that until the very day of April 9, 1948, Colombia had been orderly, peaceful, and democratic. No one repented, no one shouldered the blame. No one wanted to see the truth or admit the sickness of the society, for its sickness was a complex of the moral defects of whole classes.

But the society was sick, of a long, chronic illness. "For a long time the country . . . had been familiarizing itself with violence. Human lives, honor, wealth, were worth nothing, signified nothing, and national viability had ceased to exist. The dense cloud of smoke which emerged from the general conflagration prevented people from seeing the immediate, surrounding reality, the authentic reality, of Colombia. People held the illusion of living far away from tragedy, free from immediate danger. No one wanted to understand that it is not possible to live indefinitely under such torment, or that doing so in the end obliterates and destroys everything."[22]

[20] Galbraith, *op. cit.*, p. 132.
[21] *Ibid.*
[22] Fernández de Soto, *op. cit.*, p. 104.

Shocked, shamed, and helpless, Colombians believed what they wanted to believe, averting their eyes from the meaning of things that touched them. It is understandable, for these things "were the product of an unstable political and social situation which had been developing for years. What actually took place was a social revolution, and it is for that reason and not for their dramatic violence, that these days will deserve the careful attention of historians of Colombia. . . . Even the wildest demagogue must have been alarmed to see, after nearly fifty years of peace, the appalling savagery of a mob whose feelings had been constantly exacerbated over a period of time by the preaching of doctrines above its standard of political education against a background of unsatisfactory standards of living."[23]

And after it had passed with its fury, the men who ruled the nation only buried their heads deeper in the sands—sands which had started to run out for them and their system. But that way, they did not have to take the blame; they did not have to make the damaging admission that what had swept over the nation was, indeed, "an authentic social revolution . . . a revolution exactly the same as that which, from the steppes of Russia, has been convulsing and agitating the heart of the contemporary world."[24]

OSPINA PAVES THE WAY FOR GÓMEZ' DICTATORSHIP

In the evening of April 9, with the center of Bogotá in flames and drunken mobs still reeling through the debris-laden streets, members of the Liberal Directorate headed by Darío Echandía, successor to Gaitán, made their way to the presidential palace.

Theirs was a strange mission: they had come to ask Ospina Pérez to resign. Ospina, who had conducted himself with great courage and dignity when his own life was in danger, refused. Heated debate ensued, lasting until the small hours of the morning. When, finally, the meeting broke up, agreement had been reached on another coalition government, with Echandía as Minister of State, and General Ocampo, a Liberal, as Minister of War.

For the Liberals there was no other alternative to civil war.[25] Hence, the *marriage de convenance* was doomed to failure from that side. As for the Conservatives, they could coalign, or they could

---

[23] Galbraith, *op. cit.*, p. 133.
[24] Fernández de Soto, *op. cit.*, p. 84.
[25] García, *Gaitán . . .*, p. 319.

continue the violence. Neither side trusted the other. Ospina accepted the Liberals on his own terms.

But a crisis government did not mean the end of crisis. A general strike paralyzed Bogotá and brought the city to the verge of starvation. Echandía went to the radio and spoke in the name of Gaitán, pleading with the unions to restore normal services. Troops arrived in the city, the storm gradually abated, and an uneasy state of normalcy returned. But as the capital grew quiet, the tide rolled onward to the provinces, and violence became generalized. Revolutionaries held out against the Army in some towns for as long as a month. Systematic civil war gradually emerged from the spontaneous insurrection, and Liberals and Conservatives in the countryside took up arms against one another.

Under this goading, Liberal demands grew stronger, and soon the cabinet was split by dissension. In fact, Ospina Pérez had done more in the way of reform than the Liberals admitted, even though it was little enough. He had begun a program of workers' housing, had sponsored a law that required employers to provide workers with certain clothing and shoes, and had undertaken a minimal program of irrigation and rural electrification.[26] But what people needed was food, rather than a National Nutritional Institute; a good house and roof, rather than electric light; land, rather than irrigation; higher wages, rather than instruction from the government in how to "utilize the natural products of the country within reach of their subsistence."[27]

At first, Ospina heeded some of the Liberal demands. His Decree 1483 was aimed at land parceling, recognizing that *"in the present circumstances, it is necessary to bring about social stability by means of augmenting the number of proprietors."*[28] But this rather apologetic blow at the oligarchy was not implemented in practice. It was, rather, one of a number of "panic" concessions designed to quiet, rather than to satisfy, the people.

Confidence slowly returned to the Conservatives as the situation grew less frightening. Two months after the rioting, the financial-commerical-banking oligarchy was almost able to convince itself

[26] Fernández de Soto, *op. cit.*, p. 117.

[27] Daniel Valois Arce, "Colombia Necesita una Revolución," interview with Ospina Pérez, *El Colombiano* (Medellín), July 7, 1948, p. 1.

[28] Londoño, *op. cit.*, p. 167.

that the terror had been only a bad dream. A case in point is the mid-July analysis of the economic situation made by Dr. Gonzalo Restrepo, head of the Bogotá Stock Exchange. The report admits, in passing, that economic and social conditions were at fault, but considers them rather incidental: "It should not be overlooked, in considering the causes and consequences of the internal disturbances which took place in April, that economic causes contributed toward creating a situation favorable to popular insurgency, and to directing it toward abnormal objectives."[29] But the solution offered was, incredibly, that of additional guarantees for private property and the reduction of taxes, rather than an increase of levies or their diversion to finance social reforms. It was to be relief for the oligarchy, for already taxes were "the highest in Latin America,"[30] and by relieving business and industry, the masses would be benefited as prosperity seeped down to them. Less government interference would stimulate business and production; and the government must create a more favorable attitude toward "those who produce wealth, rather than holding them up as public enemies."[31]

The amazing assumption that workers do not produce wealth was typical of the "no-one-else-exists" view that the oligarchy seems steadily to have maintained during this troublesome time. The people had risen up and destroyed property. Therefore, protect the propertied classes. Remind the masses that the oligarchy is the source of all good—that is the basic assumption of this report. It represents the blind, inward view, the political Coueism which gripped the oligarchs at that time. They were, after all, frightened men, trying to convince themselves that it had not happened, that once the masses realized the true state of things, they would give up their foolishness. Moreover, the oligarchy was generous: it would pardon them their bad manners. They were, as Galbraith says, "Men who believed it the duty of everyone to conform to the station of life into which he had been born," and leave the management of all affairs for all classes in the hands of the privileged, enlightened, ruling caste.[32]

[29] Gonzalo Restrepo, "Analisis Espectral de Nuestra Economia," *El Espectador* (Bogotá), July 18, 1948, p. 20.
[30] *Ibid.*
[31] *Ibid.*
[32] Galbraith, *op. cit., p.* 129.

Not even Ospina Pérez was willing to admit that a social revolution had occurred. Shortly after the troubles began to die down, he indicated that a change from "coalition" might be in the offing: "Colombia [needs] an orderly revolution within the framework of peace. That is what we propose to bring about, from our position of power, in order to effectuate *an authentic national transformation* which will make Colombia a responsible and strong State."[33] The trouble, he indicated, had been caused by "small urban nuclei who have been led astray by demagogic propaganda, who do not see the worker's real interest, but only a chance to make political capital.... The Country is tired of anarchy ... it is not a question of repressing liberties, but of *making liberty responsible*. Every day I become convinced that we must make our national motto a reality: Liberty and Order. It is necessary to harmonize, not to oppose, these two factors of social energy."[34]

The government was, in fact, rotting away as a cohesive, directive force. There now seems little doubt but that Ospina was determined to break Liberal collaboration and use the firm hand. At least, that is what he did. And it may very well be that the violence in the provinces was agitated further by the Conservatives to provide justification for jettisoning the Liberal dead weight in the government.

The situation grew steadily worse. Armed forces of guerrillas in the hills frequently attacked police and Army units in bloody ambush; the Conservative forces retaliated by wiping out and burning to the ground entire Liberal pueblos. The Liberals would then sear to the ground some Conservative peasant center. And so it went: haciendas, villages, small towns, fell to the violence of fire, murder, rapine, vengeance. In the Army, a policy of discrimination was adopted against the Liberal officers, who complained that they were treated unfairly by the Conservatives, while the latter were given preference.[35] Many of these men deserted, fled to the hills with their entire units, and began partisan warfare against the government. Before long a large force calling itself the "Free Republic of Colombia" was ranging the countryside.

Striking back, the government declared the partisans and guerrillas outlaws, although they were strongly defended by the Liberals

[33] Valois Arce, *op. cit.*, p. 1.

[34] *Ibid.*

[35] MacDonald, *op. cit.*, p. 404.

in the cabinet and in the Congress. It was past time for a definite break with the Ospina government, but Echandía, convinced that such a move would bring on unrestrained civil war,[36] prevented the Liberals from walking out. There was open, unabashed talk of civil war in the halls of Congress, and even an empty, Quixotic attempt by the Liberals to force Ospina Pérez to resign or accept civil war. Actually, the Liberals could not have governed; and, since they would not fight, the gesture was at best dramatic and petulant, serving only to fire Conservative determination to be rid of them.

Finally, in April, 1949, the government removed the Liberal departmental governors, and instituted repressive measures against the "bandits" in the provinces. Protesting fruitlessly, the Liberal cabinet members resigned the following month. Soon they were followed by other Liberal functionaries in the provinces.[37]

Quickly, then, Ospina Pérez moved to replace Liberal governors, lesser officials, and cabinet members with stout Conservatives. The "authentic national transformation" was under way. Stories of atrocities in the provinces abounded. While it may not have been the "Reign of Terror" that the Liberals claimed, armed clashes and murder took place on a large scale.[38]

In the June congressional elections which followed the Liberal boycott of Ospina's regime, the Liberal party again piled up a strong majority. With a Liberal Congress and a Conservative executive and administration, with two parties literally at sword's point, the imbalance between the main branches of government became intolerable. The Liberal Congress, feeling that time would further reduce the party's influence, and that an early general election would return a Liberal to the presidency, pushed through a law which advanced the date of presidential elections from June, 1950, to November 27, 1949.[39] With Turbay dead in Europe, and Gaitán a martyr in the popular mind, a Liberal victory seemed assured.

The law was vetoed by Ospina Pérez, and then laid before the Supreme Court. But before the tribunal could render its opinion, hot-eyed old Laureano Gómez came storming out of exile in Spain, determined to take power for himself.

[36] Fernández de Soto, *op. cit.*, p. 103.
[37] Jorrín, *op. cit.*, p. 292.
[38] Galbraith, *op. cit.*, p. 133.
[39] Jorrín, *op. cit.*, p. 292.

GÓMEZ BECOMES DICTATOR OF COLOMBIA

When Laureano Gómez stepped from his plane in Medellín, on June 24, 1949, he greeted the assembled Conservatives with the Fascist salute and the Falange cry of greeting, "Presente!" Thereupon he delivered a harangue against the Liberals, branding them as unqualified Communists. In a speech of welcome to Gómez, Augusto Ramírez Moreno attacked the electoral college, the Council of State, and the Confederation of Colombian Workers as an "instrument of revolution ... which looks upon Colombia as a stepmother because Russia is the real mother of that organization." And he added, "Fortunately, the Conservatives number one-million stout-hearted, determined men who are moving even more swiftly to power."[40]

From the moment he set foot on Colombian soil, Gómez was a candidate for the presidency, and he soon set in motion the plan to gain his ends. His name was anathema to all Liberals, but the Liberals had abdicated. Consequently, under Gómez' guidance, the Ospina government moved rapidly toward the final liquidation of Liberal power.

Soon after his return, Gómez issued a blast declaring Congress incompetent, as *fuera de la ley* (acting outside the law), because of its action in advancing the election date. And, when the Supreme Court upheld the congressional act, Gómez turned, snarling, upon the Court itself: "The Court has lost its impartiality ... has lost its dignity as well. It is not, and cannot, continue to be a tribunal. It has become ... a contemptible political committee."[41]

The issue was now joined. During that July of 1949, violence was almost as marked in the Congress as in the provinces. Shortly after sessions began, Gómez' son, Álvaro Gómez Hurtado, a Conservative member, passed out police whistles for the Conservative minority. Thereafter, any Liberal who took the floor was drowned out in a horrible din the moment he began to speak. Roughhouse tactics replaced parlimentary decorum, presaging real violence to come.

It came on September 8, 1949.

In the heat of particularly acrimonious debate, Conservative members of the House opened fire on the Liberals with pistols. Gustavo Jiménez, who held the floor as the fusillade broke out, fell dead

[40] Arciniegas, *op. cit.*, p. 165.
[41] *Ibid.*, p. 166.

in his tracks. There was a wild scurrying and an exchange from armed Liberals. Others were wounded. Approximately a hundred shots were fired. The distinguished young Liberal, Jorge Soto del Corral, former foreign minister and ex-ambassador to France, received wounds which invalided him until the summer of 1955, when he died as a result of them.

The wounding of Soto del Corral was charged to General Amadeo Rodríguez. The General was indicted, fled to Ecuador, but soon returned. The indictment was pigeonholed, and Rodríguez remained at liberty. At about this time, Gómez was formally nominated as the Conservative candidate. "At a banquet held in his honor, General Amadeo Rodríguez was seated on his right. The young Falangists, who that day paraded in the manner of their confreres of Spain, mingled with their shouts of acclaim of 'caudillo Gómez' a joyous 'Long Live Amadeo's Pistol!' "[42]

As the presidential elections drew nearer, Ospina Pérez' tactics underwent an appreciable change. Once considered a Moderate Conservative, he now seemed to be bent on effecting the "national transformation" of which he had spoken to Valois Arce. He showed himself, says MacDonald, "much less moderate and much more conservative." Possibly he was influenced by the fact that Darío Echandía, the new Liberal leader, began to show strong possibilities of bringing about a Conservative defeat. Whatever the cause, the repression grew harsher. In the outlying regions, the death toll mounted, the armed clashes increased, the blood flowed more freely. Conservative goon squads roamed the countryside, backed up by soldiers, obliging the peasants to turn in their registration certificates and register "spontaneously" as Conservatives.[43] These safe-conducts bore the photograph of Laureano Gómez, and set forth the following:

The undersigned President of the Conservative Directory, CERTIFIES: that Mr. _____, bearer of card No. _____ issued in _____, has sworn that he does not belong to the Liberal Party. Therefore, his life, property, and family are to be respected.[44]

Since these oaths had to be sworn before parish priests, the Church was involved. Upon receiving proof that priests had taken part in

[42] *Ibid.*, p. 167.
[43] Jorrín, *op. cit.*, p. 292.
[44] Arciniegas, *op. cit.*, p. 167.

the fraud, the Archbishop of Bogotá issued a pastoral letter threatening all priests who participated with suspension from their duties. The Conservative censorship later suppressed this pastoral, since it implied criticism of Gómez' tactics.

By now, Ospina was using the police and Army openly to harrass Liberals.[45] Many of them fled the country. Since the departmental governors carried out the orders of the central government, which had appointed them to replace Liberals, the repression became generalized. So grave did the situation become that both houses of Congress began seriously to consider impeachment of President Ospina. Accordingly, they notified him that proceedings would begin, and asked him to present himself and make a defense.

Retaliation was swift and harsh. Liberal congressmen were beaten, threatened, their lives placed in danger. Under this attempt to terrorize them, they sent the Speaker of the House with a delegation to the Minister of War, to ask him to present to the President a note asking for police protection—a dreary commentary upon the state of constitutional government at that time.

The President acted, but not as they had hoped. When the Liberal delegation returned to the capitol, they found troops routing their colleagues out of their offices. Ospina had dissolved Congress for having "disturbed the public order."

With the Congress brushed aside, Ospina the same day issued a series of repressive decrees which provided for:

1. A state of siege, "owing to the disturbance of public order."

2. The dissolution of Congress for an indefinite term, or until the state of the nation warranted resumption.

3. The suspension of all state legislatures and municipal councils.

4. The outlawing of all public meetings and assemblies throughout the nation.

5. Extraordinary powers for the governors, which would make them "small dictators," carrying out the will of the authoritarian government in the capital: while the state of siege continued, the governors were to function as agents of the central executive; they could take such measures as appeared necessary for the maintenance of public order, and were empowered, without regard to existing ordinances, to create posts, make appointments, discharge office-

---

[45] MacDonald, op. cit., p. 133.

holders, draw on the public funds, and perform whatever acts might be necessary to the carrying out of these functions.

6. National censorship of the press and radio: local authorities and police were given the task of enforcement, and the Ministries of War and Interior were empowered to suspend any publication at their will.

7. The decrees themselves were to be judged by the Supreme Court on the basis of a three-fourths majority, and the application of the same standard was extended to all decrees of the government during the emergency.[46]

Only the mockery of an election was needed now to sanctify the dictatorship.

All controls over government were erased in one blow. The worst damage fell upon the Supreme Court: the extraordinary majority imposed upon it now made it possible for a few Conservative judges to defeat the Liberal majority. Quite naturally, the Justices protested. They admonished the President for unconstitutional action, in a letter which drew a withering blast in reply:

First, I wish to express the surprise of the government in the face of this unexplained occurrence in the history of the country, to wit, that a group of magistrates of the highest court of justice should express an opinion on a juridicial matter that has not yet been submitted to the consideration of the said tribunal. . . . I do not know whether you have realized, in writing me this letter, that you have already disqualified yourselves to pass judgment . . . if it should be brought before you.[47]

Since the Council of State also controlled the legality of government decrees, Ospina packed it with his own appointees. The Comptroller General, an appointee of the Congress, was replaced by a personal appointee of the President. Thus, as the election approached, Congress was dissolved, the Supreme Court and the Council of State were shackled, the Comptroller was a lackey of the regime, strict censorship was in effect, Army and police were actively enforcing the registration of Liberal peasants as Conservatives, the Liberal party was banned from public assembly and association, and the governors of the departments stood ready to carry out these and other repressive measures.

[46] *El Tiempo* (Bogotá), November 10, 1949, p. 1.
[47] Arciniegas, *op. cit.*, p. 172.

The Liberals bowed. They withdrew Echandía, and left the field to Laureano Gómez and the counterrevolution. But they did more than bow—they abased themselves; for, rather than leave the Congress, the elected Liberals stayed on, thus becoming a party to the farce. "The only thing that the Liberal representatives ... did then ... was to keep drawing their salaries. Not a single Liberal rebelled against the government which had robbed Congress of all dignity; they did not even cease to draw their *per diem* during the long period of closure and ominous silence."[48]

Two days before the elections, Echandía, his brother Vicente, and a group of supporters were ambushed by police as they walked through the residential section of Bogotá. In a fusillade of bullets that screamed for two minutes, Vicente Echandía was killed, along with four others. Several were wounded. A member of the party said, "Behind us several men were groaning with pain. We got up with our hands in the air and walked toward the police squad. Dr. Echandía called out, 'We are unarmed. Don't murder us; you can arrest us if you want to.' "[49]

In a farce that took place on November 27, 1949, Laureano Gómez was elected President. The Liberals did not vote. Gómez got all but 14 of the 1,140,634 votes cast.[50] Only *El Siglo*, straight-faced, published the returns. *Life* magazine reported the election in these terms:

Last week [Colombia's] liberty-loving people lost their precious heritage through a relentless power play by the minority Conservative Party. The main feature of [Gómez'] campaign was a reign of terror in the interior. Liberal towns were shot up. In the last two months, 2,000 Liberals were killed, hundreds were jailed, and other hundreds fled their towns. Seven thousand [came] ... to Bogotá alone. Troops took possession of the capital and patrolled the streets.[51]

So it was that the republican era ended and dictatorship came to Colombia. The great tragedy of the times was the complete bankruptcy, due to internal division and bickering, of the Liberal party as an organic force, a social movement with a mission, in the life of the nation. Its slow surrender to a weaker conservatism can be attributed only to the defection of its best men to the Liberal-Conserva-

---

[48] García, *Gaitán* ..., p. 321.
[49] Arciniegas, *op. cit.*, p. 175.
[50] Jorrín, *op. cit.*, p. 293.
[51] *Life*, December 12, 1949, cited in Arciniegas, *op. cit.*, pp. 176–77.

tive oligarchy, their abandonment of social action for the protection of economic class interests. "The victory of Gómez was even welcomed by certain Liberal capitalists and entrepreneurs who applauded his practical and businesslike outlook, and who were, as so frequently happens in such circumstances, so tired of the instability and uncertainty of the period 1946–49 that they felt that a 'strong man' as President might be a salutary change."[52]

The "salutary change" was to cost blood, tears, and misery of thousands, but it was, as the oligarchs hoped, to prove good for business.

[52] Galbraith, *op. cit.*, p. 134.

VIII. The Course of the Dictatorship: A Caesar Replaces a Strong Man (1950–1953)

REGIME OF BAYONETS

Laureano Gómez took the oath of office as President on August 7, 1950. Since Congress had been suspended, he was sworn in before the Supreme Court—an emasculated Court, demoralized and under the bans imposed by Ospina Pérez.

As the office changed hands, Gómez praised Ospina: "My gratitude is boundless. I hope to be able to imitate the proofs of courage and virtue so amply displayed by Your Excellency, which saved Colombia."[1] Then, stating that law and order would be maintained, he dwelt upon things dearer to the hearts of the oligarchy—the government would take rapid, firm steps to favor business, to develop industry, and to attract foreign capital.

One short month after taking office, Gómez issued a decree which disqualified Eduardo Santos (who was Second Designate, corresponding to Vice President in the United States) from succeeding to the office of President. Since Santos was a Liberal, Gómez thus insured *continuismo* of the Conservative regime. He was now free to put the counterreform into effect.

Gómez' choice as director of the repression was Roberto Urdaneta Arbeláez, who had organized the police shock troops at the beginning of Ospina's term. A former Ambassador to Spain, Jesuit-educated, and nationalist, Urdaneta became Minister of War, and announced that his mission would be essentially that of eliminating "banditry" in the provinces.

The most troublesome area was the *llanos*, where the wiry, tough little horsemen of the plains had risen in a fight to the death against the Conservative totalitarianism. To crush them, Urdaneta sent a full-scale military expedition over the eastern mountain wall and

[1] Arciniegas, *op. cit.*, p. 176.

down upon the burning flatlands. By his orders, commanders were to treat as bandits those over sixteen who fled from the military forces, all who violated the eleven to five curfew, and all civilians who carried firearms without authorization and were without a safe-conduct signed by the military.[2] Bandits could be summarily executed.

Unquestionably, many of the insurrectionists were truly bandits. But most of them were country people whose lands had been confiscated, whose homes had been burned or confiscated, whose women had been violated by the Political Police. For the forces of repression had enlisted many criminals, just as outlaws had attached themselves to the partisan forces. And so, the fratricide went on, in an expanding, bloody circle of violence without end. A letter to the writer, from a one-time supporter of Gómez, and who was also a member of the Conservative Directorate of Antioquia, mirrors both the impetus which the struggle had gained, and the growing disillusionment of the *Gomistas:*

Many things have happened in my country since we last spoke personally about it ... the armed resistance to the legitimate government increased and spread to many regions ... besides the *Llanos Orientales* ... formerly free of violence. This explains how some parts of Antioquia [the southwest, Urabá Puerto Berrío, etc.] became affected, and a great many people had to flee their homes and establish themselves in neighboring towns or in the over-crowded city of Medellín.

We have to admit that even if the largest number of abuses and violent acts were committed by the "guerrilleros", the Police and the Army in many cases took reprisals which, in turn, originated further attacks by the rebels. It got to a point where it seemed an unending circle. The government after some time, in an effort to placate hatreds, offered an unconditional amnesty to all those who had not committed crimes or thefts, but were only participating in the insurrection as political sympathizers or in reprisal for harm inflicted upon their relatives or friends. However, this measure was not adopted, and the fighting went on, at times calming down, but at others acquiring a marked ferocity. The "bandits"—as the government called them—always counted, if not on the open support, at least on the approval of the Liberal leaders, who never rejected their procedures.[3]

But the Army in the *llanos* stalled, unable to defeat, even to find, the main partisan forces. Thereupon, military planes flew over the sun-baked towns and hamlets, dropping leaflets which ordered the

[2] *Ibid.,* p. 180.

[3] Private correspondence with the writer dated Medellín, Colombia, May 27, 1953. The correspondent's name is withheld in order not to embarrass him in the present political circumstances in Colombia.

evacuation of the region. And so the women and the children and the men too old to fight shouldered their meager belongings and trudged wearily away, with the smoke of their burning homes making a greasy streak down the wide skies behind them. Where they could, they found homes. Their menfolk in the partisan bands fought on.

To make matters worse, the hate soon took on the coloration of a religious crusade. In the *llanos* were many Protestant missions. Soon after Urdaneta's "extermination" policy was inaugurated, a group of young men in ages between eighteen and twenty appeared in Soga-moso. They were of the Protestant faith. Their right hands had been cut off by the forces of the repression.

But the Church did not sanction this barbarity. Arciniegas lists some dozen pueblos in the Department of Valle del Cauca where, in 1951, Protestant chapels were burned, but he adds, "The violence has been carried out in the name of religion, against the will of the Catholic Church, to which the fanatical clergy paid no attention, as happened in Spain."[4] Nonetheless, Gómez' deep nostalgia for the wedding of the Hispanic Two Swords was the fiat upon which the repression was based, though translated into the will of the Conservative party and the Catholic Church. Occasionally, the latter was embarrassed. The account of a Catholic priest in Rionegro indicates that not all the clergy stood behind Gómez' methods:

> It was approximately eleven o'clock at night ... when a loud shout brought me to the window of the parish house.... I saw a group of some fifty people shouting "vivas" to the Conservative Party and the Catholic religion ... when I heard them shout "Long live the Catholic faith," I called out at the top of my voice from the window: "Listen to me, all you men and citizens of Rionegro: as a priest I forbid you to shout 'Long live the Catholic faith,' for the Catholic religion does not sanction violence."[5]

On the other hand, the Church offered an attitude only somewhere between the extremes, and deplored the "unchristian" attitude of the masses. In 1951, Father Felix Restrepo, S.J., wrote, "It is certain that our people are Catholic, but how far the great mass of them are from understanding and assimilating the doctrine of Christ!"[6] And he is corrected by Antonio García for this interpretation of the popular insurrection, in a public letter which bitterly criticizes the

---

[4] Arciniegas, *op. cit.*, p. 181.
[5] *Ibid.*, p. 182.
[6] Felix Restrepo, *Colombia en la Encrucijada* (Bogotá: Editorial Pax, 1951), p. 37.

Church's attitude: "In this case the argument is incomplete, because not only the great masses but also the rich minorities are outside true Christian militancy. Hence, the impenetrable feeling of caste which is theirs, their racial aristocratism, their insolence and their Hedonistic ethics. How can the heavy crust of their egoism be broken while their power as a class is maintained with their system of privilege?"[7]

In essence, it was the Crusades, the Inquisition, and the Castilian Reconquest from the pagan Moors, all over again in miniature. The worst of the Hispanic character systematically loosed: the cruelty, African and Semitic in origin, which can almost casually send a man howling to his death in flames; which shows its genius in obscene and inhuman tortures until human flesh can stand no more, and dies. The essence of it is in these words:

> The villages burned, the children mutilated in their schools, the jails filled to overflowing with prisoners denied a trial or a judge, the men castrated in cold blood, those tortured in police dungeons, the women killed after being subjected to ignominy, the gagged press, the dwellings leveled by some functionary under arms, these ... brought moral ruin and the most abject complicity. We all just let it go on, because we did not hear the weeping of wounded children, and because the river of blood did not physically reach up about our feet! These hundreds of thousands of dead, of exiled, of fugitives, killed or shriveled the souls of everyone. But especially they left their stain on the only spiritual and political power that might have been able to disarm the government and the parties. In place of religious and human reasons, the Church preferred "Political Reason."[8]

It is difficult to distill the essence of this violent epoch in Colombian history, but something of the unbridled hate and savagery should be set forth in this study, for the wounds went too deep, were too basic, to be forgotten; they are still there, demanding the healing of some government or another. They may break and reopen under social friction at some unforeseen day in the future, and for this reason, they are important. Philip Payne, a *Time* correspondent, caught the essence of it in a dispatch written in 1951, and it is quoted here in its entirety:

> Liberal guerrillas were in the neighborhood, and the stoutly Conservative residents of San Pedro de Jagua knew well that their homes might be struck next.

[7] García, "El Socialismo y la Iglesia," *Problemas de la Nación Colombiana*, p. 134.

[8] García, *Gaitán* ..., pp. 334–35.

... Early this year San Pedro's citizens organized a raid-warning system among the outlying plantations and ranches. Any farmer who spotted bandits coming was to sound the alarm by setting off a dynamite bomb.

At 4:30 one day recently, there was a dull boom in the east. The warning did not save San Pedro. Minutes later, a uniformed column approached the village. "Don't shoot!" cried one marcher. "We're the Army." By the time San Pedro's garrison [police] of 18 realized that the column was some 50 bandits in stolen army uniforms, it was too late. "Surrender or die!" the bandits roared, and with one brief volley they dispersed the defenders. Two hundred more bandits, not uniformed, poured into the city, shouting, "Long live the Liberal Party!"

The rising sun showed the villagers who their attackers were: mostly country boys, some as young as 14, every one with a good Mauser rifle (a few had automatic rifles), a revolver, a machete, a knife. Commanding the bandits from San Pedro's central plaza was a lightly-built man of about 25, clad in a new *ruana*. This was the storied bandit chief, Tulio Bautista.

Guns cracked all over town. A boy stepped from a doorway holding a five-peso note; a bullet dropped him, and a grinning bandit pocketed the money. Lighting hand-made grenades with cigarettes, the bandits routed out the hidden villagers. Once the town was subdued, Comandante Tulio, whose well-formed features and steady voice carried his authority, proceeded with the execution of the leading Conservatives. Three young boys were included among the victims. "They are *Godos* (Goths, the Liberal term for Conservatives) and will grow up," a bandit growled in explanation.

When the sack of San Pedro moved into the next operation, looting, it became plain that Tulio had an extraordinary co-commander: a dark, slim girl of about 20. The bandits called her Doña Edelmira; she wore men's clothing, carried two revolvers and a knife, seemed to be Tulio's girl. Edelmira directed the pillage. The bandits stacked the loot in the plaza, loaded it on stolen mules. Bandolera Edelmira enforced a stern rule upon the men; she permitted no raping or kidnapping of the village women.

The bandits found a single Liberal in the local jail, held on suspicion of aiding the bandits. Freed, this man showed Tulio's boys where there were two drums of oil fuel for the local power plant. "If only they hadn't found that fuel," mourned a San Pedro survivor later. Tulio ordered the homes of the town burned, to flush out any possible police ambush, but forbade his men to fire the church or the school.

With smoke still pluming into a clear sky, bandits not busy looting or loading lined up in the plaza to drink aguardiente from the local cantina. They hauled the little harmonium out of the church, tried to play it and failed, and smashed it with rifle butts. Then they found a phonograph. It provided wild music for a dance in the plaza's basketball court. Edelmira did not dance, and under her eye the bandits dared not seek the village women for partners. So the men danced together, one cavorting wildly in the cassock he found in the priest's house.

By mid afternoon, the bandits were ready to leave. At the cemetery they buried their single casualty with military honors. Then they marched away in good order, leaving smoldering ruins and 24 bodies. The surviving people of San Pedro stayed long enough to bury their own dead, to disinter the bandit's body and throw it to the buzzards. Then, the civil war's newest refugees, they struggled westward to seek shelter in the nearest towns.[9]

It was the hour of vengeance: an eye for an eye, a tooth for a tooth. The fearful power of the government not only held the Liberal majority in check, but reduced it to a cowering minority. Many Liberals fled the country, the leaders slipped away to foreign safety. A few Liberals, calling themselves Popular Liberals, criticized their fellows for not cooperating with the government, which, they believed, played into Gómez' hands. But the Liberal day had passed, lost to party anarchy and divisionism.

And so, terror stalked through Colombia. Forty thousand men had formed into one partisan army alone. Every Department was up in arms, and men thought only to sell their lives dearly.[10] Men lay down to sleep not knowing if they would ever again see the light of day. The destruction of herds and crops was so great that food became scarce in the cities. To meet the crisis, Gómez further restricted civil liberties, gave greater power to the Church, and began systematically to hunt down Liberal leaders.[11] The jails swelled with those unable to escape.

A traveler returning to the United States from Bogotá in 1953 told reporters, "Death has become commonplace in Colombia. The words 'assassination' and 'murder' are bandied about with no more emotion than we talk of beans, butter and bread."[12]

And *El Colombiano* editorialized wearily, "There will be enough hatred in Colombia for the next 150 years."[13]

DICTATORSHIP IS GOOD FOR BUSINESS

As the price of human life went down, commodity prices rose, bank balances grew, and the export market boomed.

Freed of wartime controls, coffee strengthened and brought dollar prosperity to the upper classes of Colombian society. And along with prosperity by inflation and plenty of money for the top echelons,

[9] Philip Payne, Courtesy *Time*; copyright *Time*, Inc., August 6, 1951, pp. 30–31.
[10] García, *Gaitán* . . . , p. 322.
[11] MacDonald, *op. cit.*, p. 406.
[12] Courtesy *Time*; copyright *Time*, Inc., August 18, 1953, p. 30.
[13] *El Colombiano* (Medellín), September 10, 1952, p. 8.

rigid wage levels and fixed incomes tended to impoverish the poor classes even more harshly. Between the years 1946 and 1950, media of payments in Colombia increased from 651 million pesos to 1,009 million—and the new name for inflation was coined in the documents of the Conservative regime: "the economy of prosperity."

Thus, while a civil war raged, the Gómez regime encouraged a speculative and expansionist economy. The peso fell steadily in value, eventually to lose a third of its value; and already there were too many pesos lying idle and available. The social effect was to create dizzy price levels, and to stimulate a national fever for quick profits which, in turn, led to frequent bad investments and the demoralization of the labor force.[14]

Ironically, in this period of social failure, 1949 to 1953, the value of exports almost doubled, making it the highest earning period in the history of the economy. Between 1948 and 1952, the percentage of capital formation jumped from 14.2 to 28.2 per cent. The trend was accompanied by great increases in bank deposits and money in circulation, while bank loans for expansion, commercial movement, and agrarian development rose to a new high. Corporate liquid assets increased from 170 millions to 249 millions, and the Ministry of Finance let it be known (1951) that less than one tenth of 1 per cent of those filing income tax returns based on corporate earnings had received 44 per cent of all such dividends.[15] The oligarchy was reaping the financial reward for supporting Gómez.

While Ospina Pérez was yet in office, the Currie Mission had arrived in Colombia to make a study for the International Bank, to be used as the basis for a developmental plan for Colombia. Under Gómez, many of the Mission's suggestions were put into practice. In the main, they benefited only the upper classes in the line of providing investment for idle capital. The new steel mill at Paz de Río in Boyacá was begun, intended as an organic basis for a new national economy; but the organic principle was abandoned when foreign participation was sought, and when forced contributions in the form of government bonds as required purchases by commerce and industry were resorted to.

But it was a prosperity for the upper classes coupled with a time of harsh lessons for the masses. Not only the brutal lesson of repression,

---

[14] *El Comercio Colombiano y la Economía Nacional* (Bogotá: Editorial Antares, 1951), p. 210.

[15] García, *Gaitán* . . . , pp. 327–31.

but the dreary knowledge that not even upper-level prosperity would, under the existing system, materially change the economic condition of the poor.

As Gómez adopted policies favoring the oligarchy, he also turned to methods designed to fragment labor, to strangle the independent unions, and to rob the labor movement of any organic tendency which might still make it a cohesive force. Laws passed under the López regime, particularly that prohibiting parallel unions in plants or industries, were anulled by Gómez. Consequently, with the corporations enjoying maximum liberty, agents of the state invaded the labor unions. The employers, free now to create their own unions, called upon the police to break up meetings of true unions; owners and managers prepared and exchanged blacklists of troublemakers and agitators among their workers; labor leaders were treated as conspirators against the public order; and representatives of the *Procesal del Trabajo* appeared in plants to tell labor leaders what was permissible and what was not. Of this period in labor development, Professor Adán Arriaga Andrade says, "With the prohibition against parallel unions anulled, the workers were guaranteed the right to destroy themselves, and rival organizations were encouraged ... in the budgets of the companies a systematic reserve was set aside to dissolve the unions or throw out the combative leaders; and the state set the example, eliminating from its own organs the labor union leaders, without permission of the courts...."[16]

The reign of corporate capitalism under Gómez became, therefore, the death agony of a free, independent union movement. In place of free unions, the bosses, the government and the Church sponsored the "confessional union." This brain child of Hispanism, modeled after Franco's captive labor movement, holds that "morality" is anti-communism, and "sin" is agressive unionism, or, by definition, communism. The view of the Colombian employers was generally that "syndical unity was a tremendous arm in the hands of Communists,"[17] and to be combated. Confessional unions, by this muddy line of reasoning, could not possibly be communistic. Strange as this may seem to North Americans, the reasoning is sound to many Colombians:

The Colombian people, the Colombian workers, are traditionally, spiritually and conscientiously Catholic. Which means that, if the practice and defense of

[16] Adán Arriaga Andrade, quoted in *Semana* (Bogotá), January 31, 1955, p. 15.
[17] Niño H., *op. cit.*, p. 37.

democratic and republican ideas do not prejudice the workers, nor divide nor weaken them, much less can they be divided and anarchized by professing and defending religious principles, because it is certain that these principles are the ... heart and hovering spirit of our nationality.[18]

From this premise, it was but an easy step for the government-industry-Church oligarchy to define the strike, the picket line, and collective bargaining as un-Colombian "sin," i.e., Communist-inspired. There seems little doubt that conservatism was out to break the labor movement, as it had broken the Liberal party:

> What Arriaga says about syndical parallelism describes a situation which had become rather notorious during the last years of the regime that was deposed June 13, 1953. The country had the feeling, about the time of the last Liberal regimes and the beginning of Ospina Pérez', that the working masses, agrarian and urban, inclined more toward the Liberal side, and some even affirmed that the masses, especially the workers, directed by their unions, constituted the "shock forces" of the Liberal Party. For obvious political reasons, Conservatism became preoccupied, once in power, with neutralizing these adverse forces. There was then initiated what the Liberals called the "counterreform," whose most visible political effects were the general weakening of the Leftists in the unions, accomplished by means of syndical parallelism.[19]

Out of industry-controlled unionism came a group of movements rivaling the CTC. Chief of these was the *Unión de Trabajadores Colombianos* (Union of Colombian Workers), a confessional, passive, and submissive union "which had the Sympathy of Ospina, Gómez, and Urdaneta, and which, because of Gómez' approval, has been called *'Laureanista.'*"

Weakened from within, assailed from without, fragmented and disoriented, labor had become under Gómez and Ospina a vassal of the oligarchy. Naturally, the oligarchy treated it without mercy. In 1951, hundreds of workers were fired from the brewing industry, and police prevented them from even exercising their rights to a final medical check-up. Men with fifteen and twenty years service were turned into the streets without bonuses or severance pay because they had "agitated," an "act of violence" under the Gómez laws. Between 1951 and 1952, 4,772 workers were discharged from the National Railways only because they belonged to the Liberal party.[20]

[18] *Ibid.*, p. 39.
[19] "Productores de Riqueza," *Semana* (Bogotá), January 31, 1955, p. 14.
[20] García, *Gaitán* ..., p. 332.

On the plus side, social security was advanced a bit, but agrarian workers were not included; the minimum wage of two pesos a day became operative (a shrinking peso), and workers were given the right to participate in the stock of the companies which employed them. But the two-peso minimum was unreal and far below daily needs; not one cent was distributed to the workers as dividends; and "in the same period . . . the workers were obliged to renounce gains already made; the brewery workers, by means of a collective agreement, gave up their premiums to compensate for the rising cost of living, and the petroleum workers abandoned the right to purchase consumers' goods at 'frozen prices.' "[21]

Moreover, while the upper levels rode the wave of prosperity, buoyed up by a regime that broke the power of labor; while Liberal employees were discharged only for being Liberals, the workers cost of living index in Bogotá rose from 368.5 in 1950 to 401.6 in 1951. Business was indeed good under the dictatorship, but it meant misery and economic attrition for the masses of people.

For the *campesino* and the worker, the counterrevolution had brought the loss of a class voice, persecution as organic forces in the nation's economic life, and, if either were of the Liberal party, possibly also the loss of employment.

Labor and the Liberal party were routed, defeated, and, finally, demoralized.

THE WAVE OF NATIONAL REVULSION AND GROWTH
OF OPPOSITION TO GÓMEZ

Although politically bankrupt, the Liberal party at first refused to admit defeat, and it organized its Directorate under Carlos Lleras Restrepo in the early days of Gómez' dictatorship. With Lleras Restrepo were Alfonso López and Eduardo Santos. These three men tried without success to heal the basic party split, and in 1951, during the heat of the repression, they sought personal safety abroad. With their departure, the state was firmly in Gómez' hands.

Late in the year of 1951, a heart attack forced Gómez to take a rest and leave active public life. This did not mean that his control was to wane. By-passing the party convention, Gómez hand-picked a committee to choose congressional candidates who, he knew, would ap-

[21] *Ibid.*, p. 326.

prove his choice for Acting President. This Blue Ribbon Congress, which "came to office in keeping with the strictest Nazi technique,"[22] did Gómez' bidding and named as Acting President Urdaneta Arbeláez, Gómez' Minister of War, who had masterminded the violent scourging of the "bandits."

But at about this time, too, the Conservative party began to demonstrate the fatal flaw of most Colombian parties: divisionism and personal ambitions began to weaken its solid hold on power. A challenge to Gómez rose in the person of Gilberto Alzate Avendaño, political *caudillo* of Caldas, who opposed Gómez' cooperation with the United States and the sending of Colombian troops to Korea. The Gómez wing in Congress was represented by the dictator's son, Álvaro Gómez Hurtado, and this group fell increasingly under the attack of Alzate's group and that of another alignment of Conservatives who "believed that their best choice in the next election would be Ospina Pérez, the man who had presided over the dissolution of the nation's democratic institutions."[23]

The situation created by the rise of Alzate and the re-emergence of Ospina Pérez is analyzed by a Colombian Conservative politician in these terms:

> The Conservatives, meanwhile, when they found themselves alone in the political field, began to dissent and divide. Alzate Avendaño organized a dissident faction which temporarily obtained a majority in both houses of Congress. Laureano [Gómez] who had previously retired on account of ill health, had to intervene personally, after it seemed that Alzate was defeating the pro-government forces in the Conservative National Convention, and he, Gómez, boycotted the election of a National Directorate of the party with a dissident majority, by putting up a list of names of his own, which were more or less widely accepted by the Party.[24]

And so the dreary, chaotic state of persecution of Liberals, of violence and terror, drew on. In September, the government announced that it had discovered the decapitated bodies of five policemen. After funeral services in Bogotá, a mob attacked and fired Liberal headquarters, and put the torch to the homes of Liberal Directors Alfonso López and Carlos Lleras Restrepo. Then, still not content, they

[22] Arciniegas, *op. cit.*, p. 185.
[23] MacDonald, *op. cit.*, p. 405.
[24] Private correspondence with the writer, cited above p. 119.

wrecked and set fire to two Liberal newspapers, *El Tiempo* and *El Liberal.*

Gómez' newspaper alleged that the violence was set off by shots fired into the crowd of mourners. The Liberals alleged that the mourners were actually Conservative government employees, acting under instructions to create an incident.

A roar of protests went up from newspapers throughout the hemisphere. For some days the government remained silent. Then Urdaneta took to the radio with a reply that gave cold comfort. He harangued the bandits and their atrocities, said nothing about punishing the mob leaders, and issued tighter censorship regulations which provided for "prior approval by the government of all material dealing with matters of public and political order, military and police questions, criminal and administrative investigations, economic affairs and international issues involving Colombia."[25]

In this crisis, many Conservatives joined with the Liberals in protest. On September 15, *El Diario Colombiano*, with fine irony, devoted three entire columns of its editorial page to the tourist attractions of St. Augustine, Florida! It explained, "For obvious reasons, we welcome to these pages an article on the tourist attractions of a distant city. Tourist travel today has a vital interest. It not only stimulates the economy, but broadens the view. We invite our readers to go in search of new horizons."[26]

However, the widening schism in the Conservative ranks was not due solely to personal ambitions of other leaders than Gómez. Many serious-minded Conservatives were concerned about their own liberties. Gómez had come up with a final scheme to alarm even the people in his own party: a culminating blow to fasten the Hispanic counterreform upon the nation, and thus to stamp out the last vestiges of dissent. To this end he planned a thoroughgoing Constitutional Reform. Around this plan gathered the opposition, gathering impetus as a "stop-Gómez" movement of some importance. That many of his partisans had become disillusioned with Gómez after two years of hard-handed rule, is attested by the words of a one-time supporter of the dictator:

At the same time the idea of a Constitutional Reform (I think this is a wider

[25] *Newsweek*, September 29, 1953, p. 53.
[26] *El Diario Colombiano* (Cali), September 15, 1952, p. 8.

term than your "Amendment") began to be accepted in government circles, who believed that modification of some clauses introduced in the 1936 Reform [under Liberal President López] was essential in attaining pacification of the country. This circumstance has been utilized by some Conservatives to advance peculiar ideas of their own which would radically alter the Democratic features possessed by Colombia. Laureano [Gómez] himself has come out with proposals that would establish a Corporative Senate ... while this has been taking place, the division within the Conservative ranks has widened enormously, by the appearance of a candidate for the next presidential period (1954–58). This is former President Ospina Pérez. His name attracted followers from both the dissident sector and from the government. However, it seems that Laureano and his *camarilla* had different plans for those years, and hoped to name a successor to Urdaneta of their own choosing.[27]

And so Ospina, who had presided as midwife at the birth of the dictatorship, now arose to disavow his handiwork. Naturally, he was distasteful to Gómez, first as a friend of coalition, and now, because he challenged Gómez' tenure. Ospina headed the fight against Gómez' proposed constitutional reform; the Gómez-Urdaneta group was determined to create a totalitarian state which would insure Conservative dictatorship for years to come. On these clashing propositions the battle was joined, Conservative against Conservative.

The comments of Antonio García upon the Gómez plan may serve as an interpretative prelude to a look at them:

> The last act was the Constitutional Reform, inspired by the absolutist philosophy of the Spanish counterreform: oligarchic deformation of the representative system; Caesarist centralization of power; creation of a corporative, dynastic chamber under the mantle of the Chamber of Labor; conversion of the Church into a political organ of the State as in the long-ago and archaic era of the Patronate; exhumation of the colonial ideals of confessional and monastic culture, uprooting the rationalizations of Caballero and Góngora. This was the last part of the program of the counterrevolution: the greatest power with the least liberty, the least responsibility of the State with the greatest force.[28]

Gómez' hand-picked Commission in Constitutional Studies began work on the new document late in 1952. In preparing its agenda, it was guided by instructions outlined in Gómez' message to Congress of January, 1953. The changes which Gómez desired comprised the following points:[29]

[27] Private correspondence cited above, p. 119.

[28] García, *Gaitán* ... , p. 336.

[29] This résumé is drawn from reports of Gómez' speech in *Semana* (Bogotá), January 10, 1953, pp. 5–6.

The House would be the center of political activity, and would be elected on the basis of universal male suffrage. The Senate, elected at another period, would be known as the Corporative Chamber of Labor, and would include representatives of professional groups, labor, the universities, trades, etc. It would not have concurrent power with the House over legislation, but would merely serve to debate, to air issues. It was to have neither vote nor veto. Congress as a body would have no initiative in fiscal matters, nor in making the budget.

Presidential power would be greatly increased under the reform. Although he would be elected by popular vote, the Chief Executive would have no responsibility to Congress, and the power to impeach him would be abolished. With his control over the budget and the national purse strings, with the Senate unable to oppose him, and the House elected by suppliant Conservative electors, the President would be a *de facto* dictator. This was hinted at by Gómez himself: "The Reform of 1953 would separate the parliamentary body from all judicial interference. The present Constitution establishes . . . almost certainly a conflict between the Legislature and the Executive." The simple solution: weaken the legislature, strengthen the executive.

The departmental assemblies would be converted into "administrative boards," or branches of the central executive. Membership was to be sharply reduced. This change was very dear to Gómez' heart, for he believed that the "small parliaments" as he termed the departmental assemblies, were "garrulous, dilapidated and scandalous." Under the new plan, they would consist of from seven to nine members, with the governor—a presidential appointee—presiding. The governor would have both voice and vote in all deliberations. The members of the assemblies would be elected by the town and city governments (firmly controlled by the oligarchy), rather than by popular vote.

Municipal government would be scaled according to size: in small cities, municipal councils would consist of four members; in those of medium size, of six; and in the larger, of eight. In all cases, the councils were to be elected by "fathers and mothers of families," thus disfranchising bachelors at the municipal level. The mayor (alcalde) would have a voice in deliberations, and a tie-breaking vote.

The judiciary—bête noire of the dictator and target of many of his repressive acts—was to be reformed to the end of "precluding political influence." Naturally, this meant "influence of the opposition party," for magistrates and judges were to be elected by a gathering of legal lights (who feed only off the government in power), thus insuring the self-perpetuation of a party-dependent legal oligarchy. All court administration, the general legal work, would be supervised by the Procurer General; and circuit judges would be elected from among the meritorious municipal judges, by the legal fraternity's majority vote. Justices of the Court of Justice (Supreme Court) would be similarly chosen.

As for the political parties, all parties would be "allowed as long as they conformed to the purposes of such a state, and operated for the general or public interest of the state."[30] One can readily imagine who would interpret the "general interest" in deciding which parties might freely operate.

Under Gómez' plan, the press would be considered to have a "public service or function," and as such it would be "subject to governmental control."[31] That is to say, it would be a controlled press, existing by the suffrance of a permanent censor.

True to his Hispanic dream of dual authority, Gómez proposed to re-establish the Church and the Catholic religion to its place of power. The nation would be considered a "Christian Democracy, and Protestant sects might worship," but they would be banned from making public demonstrations of their faith, and from proselytizing.

This series of proposed reforms stirred up strong opposition to Gómez. Republicans of all parties banded together to discredit the program. A first cautioning voice was raised by Forero Benavides, a Liberal director: "Liberals are more interested in the spirit than in the letter of reform . . . in knowing whether there will be a section on individual guarantees. The Constitution may be dictated by a single party, but respect for the institutions it creates must be unanimous."[32]

In addition to the Liberals, the Conservative wing which followed Ospina marshalled its forces to oppose. Ospina had been steadily drawing support away from Gómez. Those who had once supported the dictator had grown increasingly alarmed by the state of the nation. Early in January, 1953, Jorge Uribe, a spokesman for the *Ospinistas*, wrote, "The First Magistrate is disenchanted with universal suffrage,

[30] Private correspondence with Colombian politician cited above, p. 119, dated June 2, 1953.
[31] *Ibid.*
[32] Forero Benavides, quoted in *Semana* (Bogotá), January 17, 1953, p. 6.

[yet] he recommends it for the supreme government. It is inadmissible to blame all Colombia's woes upon the system. . . . President Gómez makes most of his changes in the representative bodies, yet proposes no new formula for elections in the House!" And, with tongue in cheek, he lampoons Gómez' plan to elect municipal governments by "heads of families":

Bachelorhood is no index for mental blindness, nor matrimony proof of brilliance. Marriage is not always an indication of intelligence, or even of good judgment. The election of municipal councillors by heads of families is not an infallible thesis. Nor is the designation of Deputies by "Roman magistrates" and as far as choosing the Senate by "guilds" goes, we would see them again using that execrable practice of one-half plus one, since they could not use the one-half minus one without defeating their own predominant will.[33]

By January 10, Ospina was ready to speak out openly in opposition. During a mass meeting in Cali in his honor, he called for Conservative solidarity "not in the name of the government, but in the name of the nation"—an obvious appeal for unity of all sectors against Gómez' personalistic government. Stirring hope in the hearts of all those who were sickened by blood and violence, he demanded military and spiritual "pacification" of the nation, the return of the political refugees "to their homes and fields," the restoration of "national spirit."[34]

As might have been expected, Ospina's temerity brought denunciation from the government and from the Alzate wing of the Conservative Congress. But the public was by now definitely critical of the "hybrid Senate" and other proposed reforms. Toward the end of January, *Semana*, the widely-circulated news weekly, ran an "Inquiring Reporter" feature on the question, "How would you change the Constitution, if you could?" A taxi driver summed up the sentiments of most people: "This country's constitutions came from constitutions. Lots of people are out of work. Most Colombians pay no attention to those fellows on the Constitutional Commission, because they have made us lose faith in written things. We want deeds, not words."[35]

In fact, a ground swell of unrest, together with Ospina's tactics of letting his followers do most of the talking, deprived the government

[33] Jorge Uribe, in *El Diario de Colombia* (Cali), January 11, 1953, p. 9.
[34] *Semana* (Bogotá), January 17, 1953, p. 6.
[35] *Ibid.*, January 31, 1953, p. 10.

of valid grounds for quashing the Ospina candidacy. Dr. J. A. Restrepo sums it up:

> The official opposition to Ospina's candidacy was reduced to gossiping and remained underground until the latter made a speech early in April, 1953, accepting the candidacy and accusing the government of having lured him back from abroad as a leader of the Conservative Party and its natural leader for the forthcoming term. Actually, this was true, as the government called him back when he was living in New York, in an effort to unite the party when Alzate's first attempts to divide it were being made. Later, when Alzate was crushed, [Gómez] felt that he had no need for Ospina, and began to think of someone else.[36]

And so it was that from April onward, the opposition, the events leading to the end of the regime, began to gather force and momentum. Most important, somewhere behind the scenes, the Army had begun to plot with the Ospina forces.

In mid-February, the Constitutional Commission handed Gómez a draft of the unpopular reforms. Bitter public discussion at once broke out. Then, in early April, Ospina announced his candidacy—an open challenge to Gómez and Urdaneta. The government fought back, first with alarms regarding the "pacification of the country," and with boastful bulletins claiming the restoration of order: "The centers of banditry in the Department of Tolima have been completely wiped out."[37] The motive, of course, was to create the impression that only the Gómez government could control the situation. But linked to this "panic" strategy were more direct moves to scotch the Ospina threat. On April 14, 1953, *El Siglo* carried an announcement by the Conservative Party Directorate to the effect that the Ospina candidacy was "deferred," as divisive of Conservative interests. Ospina was attacked for "conciliation toward the Liberals," and coalition government in general was blasted as disasterous. Nothing, said the leader of the Directorate, could cope with the internal situation save the "strong hand."[38] That hand, it was implied, was Gómez'.

Five days later, Gómez hauled himself out of retirement to personally handle Ospina. In a radio broadcast to the nation, he denounced Ospina and invoked an old law (put into effect by Ospina

[36] Dr. J. A. Restrepo, in private correspondence with the writer.
[37] *La Prensa* (New York), April 2, 1953, p. 5.
[38] *El Diario* (Bogotá), April 14, 1953, p. 1.

himself to muzzle the Liberals) which forbade political junketing and campaigning during a time of national crisis.

By now, Ospina had rallied a strong force of opposition. The strategy of Gómez and Urdaneta was to shift public attention to the internal situation. It was an open admission of weakness, for the very situation which they pointed to was that which gave Ospina his strength: the internal violence and civil war. The people of Colombia wanted less, not more, of blood and terror.

Perhaps old Laureano had read the thin tracing of handwriting upon the wall. At any rate, he followed his broadcast with censorship, stricter and harsher than before. Any mention in print or on the radio of anything relating to the political situation would bring the censor's hand smashing down.

With the media of information closed to him, with the public forum closed against him, Ospina said, "They should let me speak if they do not fear the truth."[39] Defying the government, he planned his campaign. Gómez was being steadily isolated. Only some final blow was needed to topple him.

THE ECHAVARRÍA PLOT: THE ARMY MOVES IN

Three days after Gómez made his appeal to the nation and mingled with it a denunciation of Ospina Pérez, General Rojas Pinilla, chief of staff, issued an Order of the Day which reminded the military of the "imperious necessity of not losing serenity in the difficult moments through which the country is passing."[40]

Colombian ears pricked up. When high-ranking Latin-American Army officers remind others not to *perder la serenidad* (literally: not to lose one's serenity), it may merely be another way of saying, "Hold everything, lads. The Revolution is not yet."

It is now known that the Order of the Day came after Gómez had ordered the General to go to Germany for the inauguration of a civil air line between Hamburg and Bogotá. Aware that the Army was plotting with the Ospina group, Gómez had decided to get Rojas out of the country, and then replace him the moment he departed.

In any case, the government's case of nerves was now visible. Public and party support had long since drained away from it, and the Army

[39] *La Prensa* (New York), April 19, 1953, p. 1.
[40] *Ibid.*, April 17, 1953, p. 2.

was slowly grinding into action: the most competent political force for arbitrating differences when other forces have failed to do so. Yet Gómez followed his blind course to the end. On April 19, *Diario de Colombia* was confiscated by the censor for publishing material banned by Gómez: pro-Ospina articles. At the same time, *El Especta-dor* and *El Tiempo* were warned by the censor not to mention Ospina's candidacy.[41] And the very next day found the Colombian Minister in Havana answering growing foreign criticism of the Gómez regime, branding such criticism as "Communist-inspired propaganda." And the Minister added, "We believe in the Communist danger because we have already suffered its effects."[42]

Meanwhile, the Ospina bandwagon gained momentum. To counter the swing to Ospina, Acting President Urdaneta appealed over the radio on April 22 for "serenity and reflection by all Colombians." Again, the promise of rapid pacification of the country was heard, and Urdaneta warned that the Constituent Assembly, soon to meet to approve Gómez' reforms, would require an atmosphere of calm. The question of candidates, said he, would have its day. The implication: this was not the day, nor Ospina the candidate.[43]

As the political pot came to full boil, the meeting of the Constituent Assembly was twice deferred. This in itself was disturbing. And then, on April 26, 1953, the Procurer General of the nation, Dr. Alvaro Copete, resigned the position which he had held since July, 1951. In resigning, Copete expressed "fundamental disagreement with the policy of the present government," and gave as his immediate reason the radio attack by Gómez on Ospina Pérez as a "menace to Colombian liberty."[44]

Copete was the highest judicial figure in the land. His resignation focused attention on the Gómez injustices, on the need for a change. It had a profound effect in both Liberal and Conservative circles. Rumors flew that the cabinet as a whole would resign. Soon, coupled with the talk of a cabinet crisis came a whispering campaign from "official sources" to the effect that that dearest of Gómez dreams, the Constituent Assembly, had been postponed indefinitely. Originally

[41] *Ibid.*, April 20, 1953, p. 4.
[42] *Ibid.*, April 21, 1953, p. 7.
[43] The Associated Press, Bogotá, April 22, 1953, in *La Prensa.*
[44] *La Prensa* (New York), April 26, 1953, p. 7.

scheduled for April 20, it was set back to May 11. But on May 4, the Associated Press reported from Bogotá that "an atmosphere of tense poiltical expectancy prevailed," amid indications that the Assembly would again be postponed. The observer noted that a cabinet crisis had "appeared imminent for weeks," and predicted the resignation of the ministers which would "take place simultaneously with the meeting of the Assembly," by way of protest.[45] This would, of course, give constitutional reform the kiss of death.

As the atmosphere of crisis deepened, the government sought to shore up its position with more of the same: it redoubled its efforts to "wipe out the rebels"; it confiscated the May 3 edition of *El Colombiano* for backing Ospina Pérez.[46] Nonetheless, it was now clear that if Gómez persisted in constitutional reform, the cabinet would abandon him. Now, too, the Liberals came awake to their opportunities, and from the background they showered praise on Ospina Pérez. Off in the shadows, the Army was moving quietly and efficiently.

The final *coup* which brought Gómez down was occasioned by the dictator's conviction that Rojas Pinilla was plotting against him. His consequent determination to get rid of the General touched off the final action.[47] In the best tradition of Latin-American conspiratorial technique, the Army developed a counter-counter plot to Gómez' gambit, and old Laureano lost. Here is how it happened:

Late in May or in early June, 1953, a young Army officer came to his superiors with a story to the effect that one Felipe Echavarría, a wealthy Conservative industrialist and businessman of Medellín, had approached him to suggest a plot to assassinate General Rojas Pinilla and nine other persons. The officer feigned interest and led Echavarría on. The latter gave the officer money and arms to carry out the deed. With Echavarría deeply implicated, the officer informed Rojas Pinilla, who ordered Echavarría's arrest.

It would seem that the plotter was "sweated" a bit to get a confession. For, when Gómez' son, Álvaro Gómez Hurtado, heard of the arrest, he and his brother interceded with the Army and tried to block the investigation, suggesting that Army officials have Echavarría declared insane and sent to an asylum. The official account suggests that

[45] *Ibid.*, May 4, 1953, p. 1.
[46] United Press, Bogotá, May 3, 1953.
[47] *La Prensa* (New York), June 15, 1953, p. 2.

they wished to halt disclosures which would implicate Laureano Gómez. But the confession of Echavarría, it was said, was freely made, before Rojas Pinilla and several cabinet members.

One thing is certain: the affair spurred Gómez to action, driving him headlong into the wall of opposition that had grown up about his regime.

When the Army refused to free Echavarría, Gómez took decisive steps. Rushing to the presidential palace, he summoned his ministers and closeted himself with Urdaneta Arbeláez. Some time later, he faced the ministers and announced that he had assumed the powers of President, pushing Urdaneta aside. Thereupon, the ministers resigned in a body, first refusing to accede to Gómez' request that they order Rojas Pinilla's arrest.[48]

Furious, old Laureano then personally ordered the General's detention. At that moment, Rojas Pinilla was waiting at the airport to board a plane that was to carry him to the United States on a military mission. Gómez decided to let him go, then replace him after he had taken off. But loyal Army officers sped to the airport and tipped off Rojas to Gómez' plans. Quietly, the General canceled his flight and returned to his suburban home.

That night, Army tanks, under orders from Rojas Pinilla, rumbled through Bogotá's quiet, dark street, out into the suburbs, where they trained their guns on Gómez' residence. The dictator was sealed off with a ring of steel. The next morning, Rojas assumed power, in the name of the people, as Provisional President.

Gómez' dictatorship had been abated by the only competent force left in the nation. The Liberals had destroyed themselves over reform questions. The victorious Conservatives had bickered and snarled over the spoils of victory. In a morass created by the failure of the traditional parties to lead and point the way, the nation wallowed in its own blood, and there was no public force capable of rescuing it, save the military.

All forces of resistance to the dictatorship had disappeared, save one. The same one in which the country had hopes in 1944 . . . one force: the Army. The *coup d'état* of June 13, 1953 was a blow against the victorious counter-revolution. The

[48] *El Espectador* (Bogotá), June 15, 1953, p. 5. This source gives the best account of events surrounding the ministerial crisis. The Echavarría story comes in fragments, the most authoritative found in *La Prensa's* United Press dispatches from Bogotá, between September and November, 1953.

Republic could not defend itself in 1953, save in the same way that it was created in 1810.[49]

"THE TERRIBLE NIGHT HAS ENDED": ROJAS BEGINS MILITARY RULE

Wild public jubilation greeted the downfall of Gómez. Liberals and Conservatives alike pledged support to the new government, in a great sigh of national relief. After five years of bloody strife, the peaceful transformation was all the more welcome, all the more dramatic.

When the news came to the nation, people gathered in public, in homes and clubs, to celebrate Gómez' overthrow. They toasted one another with a phrase from the national anthem: "The terrible night has ended." One Conservative daily used the line as its banner heading.[50]

Within a matter of hours, the Liberal party announced its returns to the political arena, and the government gave full guarantees to Liberal chiefs who had sought safety in exile.[51] Everywhere, people quoted the words of General Rojas Pinilla as he assumed power: "Let there be no more blood, no more depredations, no more fighting between the sons of Colombia."[52] And the people spoke it hopefully, prayerfully.

One of Rojas' first official acts was to lift the censorship on foreign news dispatches. At the same time, he promised a general amnesty to all *guerrilleros* who laid down their arms and surrendered, and freedom for all political prisoners jailed by the deposed regime.

And meanwhile, as the people rejoiced, the old dictator and his family took the familiar route to political exile, this time to the United States, and later, to Spain. *El Siglo* suspended publication indefinitely.

Three days after the bloodless *coup*, *El Colombiano* in an editorial spoke for the Conservative view:

Colombians rightly mistrusted the Constituent Assembly, as a result of the prejudicial campaigns used by the *camarilla* to satisfy political aspirations. We have been partisans of constitutional reform, provided that it be based upon the republican traditions of Colombia. The deceptive legality of the *coup* of June 13

[49] García, *Gaitán . . .*, p. 337.
[50] *La Prensa* (New York), July 15, 1953, p. 3.
[51] *El Espectador* (Bogotá), June 15, 1953, p. 1.
[52] *La Prensa* (New York), June 16, 1953, p. 3.

has been succeeded by the legality of a government which has the support of all good men, of the Armed Forces, of the Conservatives and the Liberals and their chiefs, of the Supreme Constituent Assembly.[53]

And the powerful mouthpiece of the Liberal party, *El Tiempo,* summed up the reaction on the other side:

> Individually, we as Liberals have received the political transformation, accomplished yesterday, with a satisfaction that we do not attempt to hide. It was apparent to all that the situation created by the partisans of totalitarian government could not continue. There was no other road ... and the Army, which has always been Colombia's maximum expression of democracy, Saturday fulfilled an essentially democratic function, in suppressing an adventure designed to eliminate the last vestige of representative government.[54]

Of course, there were the immediate, scattered fears that Rojas might turn his government into the traditional *Junta Militar.* But they were dissipated when, out of thirteen cabinet posts, only three went to military men.

Shortly after the new government began to function, Ospina Pérez, Urdaneta Arbeláez, and others revamped the Conservative Directorate, with Ospina as its head. Gómez men were ousted and replaced by *Ospinistas.* On the heels of this move, Liberal leaders called on Rojas and pledged their support in working for the restoration of peace and order.

True to his word, Rojas Pinilla very soon issued a general amnesty to the beleaguered "bandits," many of whom had been in the hills for five years. They came in by squads, companies, bands, individually, though those in the *llanos,* suspicious and unconquered, were to wait until the President personally came down to the plains country to tender the palm leaf.[55] Political prisoners were turned out of the jails, and a freer, cleaner atmosphere prevailed generally, though Rojas maintained censorship on material which might reopen the old wounds which he was determined to heal, in a gentleman's agreement with the press.[56]

And what of Gómez? As soon as he had made himself comfortable in New York, the old war horse began to issue grumbling blasts against the Rojas government. Furious, he pestered Rojas to decide

[53] *El Colombiano* (Medellín), June 16, 1953, p. 5.
[54] *El Tiempo* (Bogotá), June 14, 1953, p. 7.
[55] *El Diario* (Bogotá), July 29, 1953, p. 5.
[56] *Ibid.,* July 29, 1953, p. 5.

The northern part of the *llanos,* a great region of 270,500 square miles, is Colombia's Wild West. Proud, hard-riding *llaneros* follow herds of cattle over the open range along the Casanare and Arauca rivers. The big event of the year for these people is the annual roundup and cattle fair, when men, women, and children ride into Villavicencio.

whether as a "voluntary exile," he might return to the country. In August, 1953, he issued a manifesto giving his version of the events leading up to the *coup* of June 13. Reopening the Echavarría case, he viciously attacked Rojas Pinilla. Rojas permitted the New York version to appear in the Bogotá press, where the Associated Press summarized it:

> Gómez gives as the original cause for his overthrow the arrest by military authorities of one Felipe Echavarría, a wealthy Conservative businessman who had no particular political ties, on grounds of participation in a plot to kill an Army officer [not identified in Gómez' version] and other persons.
> Gómez affirms thatt Echavarría was "barbarously tortured and beaten," a fact which was brought to the attention of the Minister of War, Lucio Pabón Nuñez, who refused to entertain the charges, which caused the President [Gómez] to resume power as Titular President in order to punish the military authorities who were responsible; his fall resulting.[57]

Naturally, Rojas' version differed somewhat, a version given in a public address after he had authorized the publication of Gómez' charges. "Echavarría was detained by reason of accusations made against him by a junior officer of the Army, to whom he gave arms and money to assassinate ten persons including [Rojas Pinilla] the Commanding General of the Armed Forces."[58] (In other respects, the Rojas version bears out the résumé given above, on page 137.) And the General left it to "public opinion to decide if the Armed Forces should be loyal to individuals or to the nation's institutions."[59]

The controversy over Gómez' status ended by the government denying him the right to return to Colombia because his attitude was "openly subversive," and because his return might be "prejudicial to the national welfare and dangerous for his personal safety."[60] Gómez took the hint and headed for Spain.

Thus, for the time, the Gómez threat was ended. But his disappearance from the Colombian political scene did not mean, as Colombians generally had hoped, a full return of their freedoms. Gómez in exile was to exert a powerful influence upon his one-time followers, was to fire them again with the zeal of opposition. For, after the full, first flush of relief, Colombians were to look more closely at the Rojas

---

[57] *La Prensa* (New York), August 18, 1953, p. 3.
[58] *Ibid.*, August 19, 1953, p. 3.
[59] *El Diario* (Bogotá), July 28, 1953, p. 5.
[60] *La Prensa* (New York), September 12, 1953, p. 1.

regime. The political parties were to clamor once more for the center of the stage, were to agitate the old hates and strictures.

And out of the atmosphere of growing political impatience were to stalk the specters of the terror of 1949–53. The problems which had brought on the trial by fire had not been solved. With all their knotty paradoxes and contradictions, they were dumped into the lap of Rojas Pinilla. From acceptance there was slowly to emerge dissatisfaction; and from this, opposition to the soldier's government. But behind this opposition loomed a new political factor: the dormant threat of a people who had awakened and who were only waiting to see whether, this time, they would have their social revolution. If they did not—Galbraith states the potentialities of another popular disappointment very succinctly:

> The vast majority of the voters are either illiterate or totally uneducated, and the social system itself is unstable; the masses are subjected to emotional, impractical and self-interested propaganda, and now that they have learned their strength and tasted blood, it is going to be a hard task for any government to correct and control the political errors and exaggerations of the last thirty years.[61]

In terms of social struggle, the masses of Colombia have now been blooded in the field, against the might of those whom they consider their oppressors. Between them and the oligarchy which refuses to reform, reconsider, or revise its programs, stands Rojas Pinilla and the Army.

It would require only a slight scratch to strip the surface from the "150 years of hate" of which *El Colombiano* spoke.

[61] Galbraith, *op. cit.*, p. 135.

IX.   Some Tentative Conclusions Regarding the Rise of Rojas Pinilla

Even if Rojas Pinilla were to abandon power tomorrow, still he would have to be regarded as the culmination of the processes which have been at work in the Colombian society between 1920 and the present. He stands as a turning point in the nation's history which was created by the dramatic explosion of 1948 and subsequent events. Changing times, the changing popular temper, seem to require that he lead the country toward goals that were unattainable in the changing era that raised him to power.

What occurred in Colombia between April 9, 1948 and June 13, 1953, was not "just another Latin-American revolution." Donald Marquand Dozer writes, "No event since World War II has so violently revealed the revolutinary potential that exists among our neighbors to the south as the abortive revolution in Colombia on April 9 last. Analysis of this incident will bring to focus generalizations, for like a microcosm, it disclosed all the elements of a Latin American revolution."[1]

The statement does not go far enough. The troubles in Colombia were not the elements of the typical Latin-American revolution. It was, rather, a true social revolution whose bursting clamor and violent shock were felt where one had been accustomed to seeing only the usual *revolts* which constitute mere skirmishes for control of the reins of government.

Nor is Rojas Pinilla the typical military Caesar who creates a revolution in order to satisfy his own aspirations for power. The man, the circumstances, the social imperatives of the times, all serve to distinguish the case of Colombia. A summing up of certain factors may place Rojas and his regime in this clearer perspective.

THE ILLUSION OF FORTY YEARS OF DEMOCRATIC PROGRESS

The social, economic, and political facts of life in Colombia's last four decades rise silently to slay the genial fiction that, until

[1] Dozer, *op. cit.*, p. 284.

the troubles of 1948 erupted, the nation had enjoyed forty years of democratic progress.

It is understandable enough how this fiction originated and was perpetuated. The vocal and competent members of the society said it was democracy; the foreigners who observed, wished it so. And thus there was a harmless, well-meaning conspiracy set afoot to elect Colombia the Miss Democracy of the Good Neighborhood, largely because there had been no major public violence during that period.

But in the end, reality defrauded both Colombians and those who wished her well. The events of 1948–53 tore away the papier-mâché front of Colombian democracy and unmasked the inequalities, the weaknesses, the oppressive character of many Colombian institutions. Upon critical appraisal it became clear that the society was neither democratic nor even likely to become so for the majority of the people for a long time to come. What the closer view disclosed was a society in which a kind of latter-day Athenian democracy existed; but it was a democracy in which the vast masses of the people lacked almost entirely the bases upon which popular democracy might have even a slight chance to develop and survive.

Those who knew Colombia were long aware of this. Kathleen Romoli, whose excellent book won her the Colombian government's *Cruz de Boyacá* (its highest decoration, an indication of the critical tone of the work), wrote with complete candor in 1940, "Government by the people in Colombia has always meant 'by the people of the upper classes.' There is nothing approaching a common level of economic or cultural well-being."[2] This is a fair statement of the facts. "Democracy" in Colombia has always been that of the Athenian city-state—democracy for a small, privileged, educated, and wealthy oligarchy existing because of and far above a rigid class-caste system comprising various grades of poor mixed bloods. The stability which came at the turn of the century was due in large part to internal and external economic expansion, and it followed a long period of anarchistic violence. "From 1910 to 1936," writes Professor Eugenio J. Gómez, "the nation lived through the only era of true peace and of effective advance in intellectual and material prosperity. . . ."[3] But this does not mean that democracy developed. Peace, or non-violence, was equated with democracy when, in fact, only the cor-

---

[2] Romoli, *op. cit.*, p. 32.
[3] Eugenio J. Gómez, *op. cit.*, p. 13.

rosive effects of proletarian awakening, of realization by the masses of their true state when compared with that of others in other countries, was needed to throw the lower classes into conflict with the directors of the society. The shiftless misery of social and economic submergence did not honestly imply that the people were satisfied with the existing order.

During that forty years of the country's greatest progress, the rungs of the social and economic ladder were barred to the lower classes, as they always had been. They watched the game of progress from the sidelines. But then, as Dozer says, there were only two rungs to begin with: the highest, and the lowest.[4] High illiteracy, the high-level concentration of wealth, the apathy and ignorance, the endemic and epidemic (as well as the psychological) illnesses of the masses, all were factors making possible the perpetuation of the "genial fiction" of Colombia's democracy.

The record itself speaks eloquently of what the period of progress did for the people. With the influx of foreign capital, large fortunes were created and many of the oligarchy grew wealthy. But in this time, the Army slew peasants who had revolted against native and foreign landowners, and the police were used to break and suppress any budding union movements. As the rich profited, inflation and sagging wages pinched the poor. Even the López regime was terminated by the division, the bickering, and dissension of the parties over necessary reforms. Out of it, in the end, came the formation of a solid oligarchic front, formed of both Liberals and Conservatives, dedicated to opposing the march of the social revolution.

Consequently, it is difficult to view the period 1948–53 as a departure from a democratic norm. On the contrary, it was a return to a century-old norm, as the class-party truce of forty years was suspended, and the country reverted to political violence.

It is easy for a prosperous, contented oligarchy to assume the existence of democracy, so long as it averts its gaze from the condition of others. Such groups develop an easy, unconscious social arrogance that, in the final analysis, causes them to assume that *they* are the people. What is good for them, is good for the country. This is what happened in Colombia. Few students bothered to dig below the rich, flavorsome upper crust of the social pie. Had they done so, they would have found all the ingredients of a social revolution

[4] Dozer, *op. cit.*, p. 274.

simmering beneath the surface. And perhaps the Colombian oligarchs cannot be blamed for praising as "democracy" what they created of, by, and for themselves, even though the masses were not permitted to participate in it.

One may logically justify the organization, direction, and control of a society having a low cultural level by the competent classes. But this justification may become very tenuous when the directing class fails to take into account the basic human needs of the low culture groups. In Colombia, this disregard has long been so characteristic that it amounts to a major assumption by the oligarchy that the other 90 per cent simply do not exist—one does not plan economically for something which is not, or which exists primarily for the convenience of the oligarchy.

Colombia is predominantly agricultural; the whole society is still permeated with feudalistic thinking, with reverence for the Great Families, with the validity of the peasant-*patron* relationship. Half the national income is in the form of some type of dividend earnings from investment,[5] which means a few relatively idle rich existing on the labor of the masses. Three per cent of the people control 90 per cent of the wealth,[6] and the remainder is scattered through a 97 per cent composed of mestizos, mixed bloods, and Indians, whose lot is poor housing, no education, illness, and poverty, with the hope of living under such conditions to an average 39–40 years. This is the people of Colombia before, during, and after the "forty years of democratic progress."

People do not reject democracy when it works well for them. The masses of Colombia did not revolt against democracy, but rather, in the hope of *attaining* at least the substance of economic democracy. Their forty years had been four decades of want, of stealthy hunger, and never-enough-of-anything but poverty.

A study of the times leading up to 1948–53 shows, then, that the bases for popular democracy have never been laid down in Colombia. An orderly republicanism was present for a while, but it was a monopoly of the upper classes. When it failed, under the pressure of social demands, to serve the whole people, it collapsed. In the final analysis, it was top-heavy with privilege and monopoly; it was an edifice without a social base laid among the people themselves.

[5] *Elementos de Ingreso Nacional* ..., p. 15.
[6] Dozer, *op. cit.*, p. 274.

In summary, it may be said that during the "forty years of demo-cratic progress" popular democracy did not exist. It was a period of considerable material progress for the upper classes, but when the epoch ended explosively, it did so because the state of the masses of people had so grievously worsened. Hence, the "democracy" of Colombia was illusory, confined to an oligarchy of wealth, family, privilege, position, and political and economic control.

Nothing could be truer of the period than the saying that the Bogotanos have for their city: "It is the *Athens* of South America."

1948–53 : SOCIAL REVOLUTION OR INSURRECTION?

Men who are born in chains do not feel the hard cut of the shackles until they learn from free men how it feels to move unfettered.

In Colombia, the ages-old caste system had institutionalized social and economic differences between the two great classes into some-thing very closely approaching a normal state ordained by God. The humble were born to serve; the wealthy, to give orders and rule. But Colombian history has shown that mass misery alone is not good and sufficient reason to bring about a social revolution. If it were, half the world would be growling at the throats of the other half, and we should destroy ourselves forthwith. But in Colombia, as elsewhere, a characteristic of the humble people has traditionally been that they have "taken great contrasts of wealth and poverty for granted."[7] For many decades, they were unaware that any other kind of life existed.

This was changed by the outside forces already mentioned. They acted as catalysts upon the inert elements of social revolution, and the violence was generated to an explosive point. What happened was different from most of the revolutions for which the Latin-American area has become notorious.

The classical type of Good Neighborhood revolution is not a revolution at all. It is a revolt, a skirmish at the top between forces who wish to control the government, the budget, the administration, the making of policy. Save for the continuing Mexican Revolution, certain aspects of the Peronist Revolution, that of Pérez Jiménez in Venezuela, and the outbreak in Colombia, the whole dreary suc-cession of revolutions in Latin America have been palace revolts,

[7] H. B. Mayo, *Democracy and Marxism* (New York: Oxford University Press, 1955), p. 92.

however broad the fields in which they were fought, however great the numbers of men who have died for "Liberty and the Liberal Party."

In most of them, the institutions have remained the same; the winning side takes over the treasury, the customs, the palace; it gives its supporters jobs; the dust settles, the *vivas* die away in the distance, the smell of smoke clears away, the *aguardiente* bottles are picked up, and the dead "martyrs of freedom" are buried with full military honors. Only the leader and his coterie are different. Business begins as usual. The people sigh, shrug, and wait, hoping that the next time, *se acaba la cosa* (figuratively: the usual run of things will end).

Plus que ça change, plus que c'est la même chose, is the correct heraldic motto for the banner of ninety-nine out of a hundred Latin-American revolutions.

But the case of Colombia was different. New ideas, new norms, new demands had been created and agitated by industrialization, the inflow of capital, better communications, the spread of proletarian ideas, the growth of a laboring class of industrial workers. And along with these, "the western world also [sent] its disrupting ideas of efficiency and change, its principles of rational calculation, its technology, and the very possibility of an end to poverty."[8] Inequalities of wealth and status were put to the question, new frames of mass reference were created. The humble people began to realize that their status was possibly not necessary.

The elements of revolution existed, and the leaders came: Gaitán, López, the young intellectuals who stirred the fermenting brew of social discontent. López opened the way for the peaceful escape of the "pressure from below," only thus to force the alignment of the groups who opposed, who clung to the old ways, who wanted to push the masses back to their lowly estate. And with López' second term this counterrevolutionary movement gained momentum, to reach a climax under Ospina and Gómez. The people fought back— tentatively at first, then with a full-throated roar after Gaitán's death, that frightened the leaders of the society by its elemental savagery.

A character in one of Balzac's stories of the Napoleonic invasion of Russia says, "There is nothing more terrible than the rebellion of a sheep." The people of Colombia proved that, as they furiously

[8] *Ibid.*

reversed the tradition of political uprisings where, as Rafael Nuñez once said, "[Among us] revolutions come from the top down, and not from the bottom up, as ordinarily happens in other countries."[9] This time, the direction was reversed: no camarilla, no party, no *caudillo* began it. It was the people, demanding not a change of government, but a change in their way of life. The mobs which ran wild in the capital and in other cities, the partisans selling their lives dearly in the hills, were driven there by long social defeat and hardship. They had finally made their choice: no more of it.

In a sense, it was an imported revolution, which may account for its upward direction. For it was part and parcel of the world awakening of peoples, of the new demands and the new expectations of submerged peoples who have been told by their betters that a fuller life is on the way. It is the movement of which Toynbee says:

> In our day, we are seeing the old barriers fall. The entire...surface of the planet is going to be now a single home for the whole of mankind if it is not going to be a single *abbatoir* for all of us ... we are seeing all races, peoples, classes, and individuals demanding a share in the power and wealth that, till now, have been a monopoly of the few ... and perhaps the first thing we have to learn is that the missles raining down now upon our ... heads from Russia and Asia and from parts of Latin America are boomerangs that were once hurled into the blue by our own ... fathers and grandfathers.[10]

Perhaps this demanding, this clamoring, which accompanies what Ortega y Gasset called the Revolution of the Masses is the single greatest social phenomenon of our time. For the masses are there, awakened finally, and very vocal. The spear-carriers have moved downstage and, having pushed the divas and tenors into the wings, are staring down over the lights and yelling for the orchestra to play *their* tune, to *segue* into the chorus music, and hang the arias!

And the chorus sings in Spanish, as well as in Chinese, Arabic, Bantu, or Russian. Lleras Camargo, now head of the Colombian Liberal party, recently wrote:

> The most urgent necessity of Colombia is that of preparing a numerous group of people with the capacity to manage and resolve the elemental problems of a collective type of life which is extending over the planet with tremendous rapid-

[9] Rafael Nuñez, *Los Mejores Artículos Políticos* (Bogotá: Editorial Minerva, n.d.), p. 108.

[10] Arnold J. Toynbee, "The Revolution We Are Living Through," *New York Times Magazine*, July 25, 1954, p. 7.

ity. This type of life is the consequence of the great industrial revolution which enlarged and made more dangerous *the distance between the rich and the poor people, by virtue of which the latter, in addition to being poor, fell into another category, that of "backwardness", which makes them feel more keenly their inferior destiny* ... the new problems are, in the first place, more general, because *they concern impatient human beings, masses, with a very definite consciousness of their rights and ambitions....*[11]

Lleras, a Colombian, could be (and probably is) speaking of the state of the Colombian mass mind. We have seen proof of the danger in the vast gaps between rich and poor—the mobs made it explicit in blood. We have also seen the determination of the oligarchy to maintain the "inferior destiny" of these impatient people. These factors, more than the classical ones, brought Rojas Pinilla forward to establish order out of chaos; but the demands they place upon him are almost superhuman.

Out of social revolution, Rojas Pinilla and military government! It has a paradoxical ring, and also its social logic. In 1949, Germán Arciniegas wrote what could be both an explanation and a guiding principle for Rojas as he sets and follows his course: "[Our] revolution must transform our social customs to achieve the democratic ideal ... it is very possible that our revolution is not over, that it still has a long road to travel."[12]

What occurred in Colombia between April 9, 1948, and Rojas' rise was due to no accident; it resulted from the meshing of the forces behind an authentic social revolution. It was the one which came, at last, from the very bottom up; it belonged to the people, and was their handiwork. Inevitably, it was crude, brutal, bloody. And essentially, Rojas Pinilla was raised to power because of the anger, the frustrations, and the demands of the masses of Colombia, who deprived of any other medium for gaining their ends, struck out at the system which had failed them.

"THERE ARE TWO CONSERVATIVE PARTIES": OLIGARCHY *versus* THE PEOPLE

In looking backward over the events which wrote finis to republicanism and led to military government in Colombia, one is re-

[11] Alberto Lleras Camargo, "Preparándonos," *Semana* (Bogotá), February 28, 1955, p. 11.
[12] German Arciniegas, "What's Behind our Revolution?" *Americas*, March, 1949, p. 42.

minded of something that Ortega y Gasset says in his essay, "On Fascism":

> On being asked what fascism was, the first answer that all of us gave took the form of another question—"What are the liberals and democrats doing?" As if a certain intellectual instinct made us suspect that the key to the question, the essence of the phenomenon, lay not in the action of fascism, but in the inaction of liberalism. Our attention moved instinctively away from the political movement itself, to the atmosphere about it.[18]

So it is in the case of Colombia. Our attention is riveted not upon the positive program of the dictator—for we feel instinctively that this species is at best transitory—but upon the divisions, the quarrels, the weaknesses, and the lack of integration of the Liberals and the true democrats who succumbed by their own weakness rather than by the strength of their enemies.

It is interesting to recapitulate briefly the instances in which this fatal tendency was made explicit. In 1920–30 the Liberals grew strong enough to unseat the Conservatives; yet they surrendered their position as true Liberals and accepted an Olaya whose backing was a Liberal-Conservative coalition of oligarchs. Thus, Liberal "victory" was a Trojan horse operation by the Conservatives.

As Olaya's term ended, the Liberals made their strongest bid as popular leaders by electing López on an openly reformist platform. But the struggle to nominate López split the party, and from that moment on, many nominal Liberals became sentimental Conservatives because they feared their own party's program. This opposition, headed by Santos, came to be called the Moderate Liberal wing. It provided a common meeting-ground for many Liberals and Conservatives, and it triumphed in 1938 with Santos' election.

If Santos did not precisely turn the clock back, at least he stopped it. And the reformist Liberals, angered, became effective allies with the Conservatives in opposing the government. By the time the new election came around, the central issue was reformism, the Conservatives had sworn battle to the death, and the Moderate or Santos Liberals had become alarmed with the rabid demands of the López faction. Then it was that the Liberals first ran their two candidates: López and Arango Vélez. The latter, a fact which demonstrated

[18] Jose Ortega y Gasset, *Invertebrate Spain* (New York: W. W. Norton & Company, Inc., 1937), p. 192.

the affinity of the Moderates and the Conservatives, was supported by the Conservatives.

During the second López term, the community of interest of the oligarchs, whether Conservative or Liberal, became quite plain. The emergence of the vicious Gómez opposition as the chief weapon of the counterreform, was accompanied by López' naming many oligarchs to his government, by a watering down of the old López reformism to an innocuous political pap that satisfied no one.

The same combination of Liberal and Conservative oligarchs stood behind Lleras' transition government of National Union. And when the next election came along, it found the Liberal party hopelessly split, irrevocably divided, in effect, over the question of whether they were true Liberals, or, as Moderate-Santos-Liberals, spiritually and economically members of the Conservative collectivity. As a consequence, the battle between the Turbay and the Gaitán factions brought the Conservatives to power over the mutilated body of liberalism, and Ospina, nominally a coalitionist, took over. The revolution had been frustrated by the Liberals themselves.

Secure in the knowledge that the important forces in the society and the economy stood behind him, Ospina was able to pave the way for Gómez through his series of decrees that emasculated republican government. He was able to do this because in this crisis, as in all major ones where the interests of the upper classes were threatened, the Conservatives were able to count upon the support of their Liberal opposite numbers of the oligarchy. As a result, the masses, abandoned by their own party, were treated to the sight of Liberals expressing satisfaction with the election of Laureano Gómez!

The historic irony of this situation lies, of course, in the fact that the Liberals dug their own grave. In the time of decision, they abandoned the people and went over to the enemy. Because reform was disturbing to business and industry, they approved a swing over to repression. Even as did the Conservatives, they desired a government which could, and would, keep the masses of people firmly on their leash.

This, then, is what the Liberals and the democratists were doing: squabbling, arguing, dividing, judging basic issues in terms of dollars and cents in their own pocketbooks or bank accounts, subverting the true mission of the party to personal and class considerations. They lost their sense of historic perspective; those who realized and spoke up for their mission were drummed out of the "club"; and when the test came, Conservatives and Moderate Liberals stood shoulder to shoulder against the rising masses and their reformist leaders.

Yet they had *created* the masses, in the political sense. They had given them leaders, a voice, a program, hopes. And when the issues were joined they ran off into the Right, frightened by the thing which they had done. The people were abandoned. And thus, indirectly, the Liberals served to make possible both Gómez and Rojas Pinilla, for their abdication and rejection of leadership of the vast social movement gave Gómez the opportunity, and the ensuing chaos cried aloud for a Rojas Pinilla. By their actions they proved that, when the oligarchy is threatened by reform and mass demands, "there are, in effect, two Conservative parties."[14]

But the Liberal failure did not end with mere abdication. After April 9, 1948, neither Liberals nor Conservatives were willing to admit that anything had happened; neither would shoulder an iota of the blame; neither party saw its guilt or any serious omissions or shortcomings which could honestly be attributed to it. Looking around for a culprit, they chided the masses—with the proper degree of *noblesse oblige,* of course—for so far having forgotten their manners as to revolt!

The striking political fact of this period is simply that, under the test of modern demands, the traditional Colombian party system broke down. They were capable only of the old game of oligarchic politics: Liberal oligarchs testing the strength of Conservative oligarchs; and then, when the masses posed a real threat, joining forces of both sides on the basis of the true issues, the economic-social class issues.

As the revolutionary tide swelled stronger about them, the Colombian parties learned nothing, found nothing new. They took the old way: repression, violence, counterreform, a sterile procedure five centuries ago, but disastrous in the modern era. There was no force left to lead, to direct, to call a halt, to rationalize a ruined society. The parties had devoured one another with their ancient casuistry and their outworn dialectic. Some other force had to stop the bloodshed, fill the complete vacuum of power left by a bankrupt liberalism and a Conservative dictatorship whose only remain-

[14] "El Tercer Intento," *Semana* (Bogotá), May 9, 1955, p. 11.

ing recourses at the end were more police, more Army, to hunt down hungry, miserable little *campesinos* armed with shotguns and machetes.

Rojas Pinilla was not elevated to power because he sought it. This time, power sought him out.

At the outset of his administration, Rojas himself said, "When the parties throw themselves into desperate and violent battles, they are not fulfilling their duties to the country, and, on the contrary, are the instruments of ruin and desolation."[15] Someone had to teach the parties that *they* were not the nation. Yet they were fastened upon the nation in a parasitic strangle hold: "Administration was carried out with partisan criteria; public works were begun on a partisan basis; public aid was based on a party criterion; technical ability was judged on a party criterion, to such a point that in filling certain posts, the real credentials were ... whether a man was a good party man."[16]

Something of this is present in every party system, anywhere in the world. But possibly nowhere as in Colombia has the party battle been so openly of, by, and for, the oligarchs. Colombians delude themselves with political philosophical casuistry, but, "in the end, the problem is none other than the struggle for power, of the two great parties, who, in every official word, and in every public act, look only to their advantage or disadvantage in the war without quarter which has been declared."[17] Contrary to the general belief, the Colombian parties are not two different groups of philosophers who differ only in Olympian terms from one another. Economics, rather than great abstractions, are the motive force behind party activity, and this force had made of the nation " a country whose drama is simply the balanced influence of the two voracious and intransigent parties, which periodically destroy the nation in their struggle for power."[18]

Nor have the masses of people either directed or found answers to their own destinies through these parties. The peasants have

[15] Gonzalo Canal Ramírez, *El Estado Cristiano y Bolivariano del 13 de Junio* (Bogotá: Editorial Antares, 1955), p. 177.

[16] *Ibid.*, p. 178.

[17] "Ametralladoras y Paraguas," *Semana* (Bogotá), January 31, 1955, p. 7.

[18] Jorge Padilla, "Cabellos Cortos y Ideas Largos," *Semana* (Bogotá), May 9, 1955, p. 12.

voted, but they have never *participated* in the public life. "The cedula of citizenship has served only to permit the *caciques*, the slave-traders of our day, to line them up like beasts of burden to vote for lists whose contents they know nothing of."[19] In Colombia, the tail has always wagged the political dog.

The heroic butchery, the Homeric onslaughts of party against party, have been, until 1948, the joustings of oligarchs against oligarchs, followed by those who answered the *grito* of revolution in the name of some lofty abstraction. But that of 1948–53 was in the name of shoes, bread, a roof, a job. It started where the trouble lay, and the oligarchy, unaccustomed to such social dynamics, could neither control, understand, nor end it. Anarchy was the consequence; Rojas Pinilla, the complex result of that anarchy.

And thus, the paradox of Colombia in her time of trial: out of hyperpartisanship, no parties; the obliteration of the traditional system; the wreckage of conservatism, the bankruptcy of liberalism. Democracy did not fail. It never existed, for the party system tended to kill it a-borning.

And Rojas was "legitimized by the *coup d'opinion* of the people who saw in [him] the only possible solution."[20]

THE TRUE ROLE OF ROJAS

It is tempting to take the easy way out and place Rojas in the long tradition of Latin-American military men who have risen to power because they carry swords and issue commands. But this is the trap to lure both the disillusioned democratist and the habitual classifier.

The new pattern of military government which has emerged in Latin America has certain characteristics of the old. Yet, there are important differences. The new Caesars are prone to short cut procedural democracy by suspending parties, constitutions, and many civil rights. This is no innovation. But the purpose itself has changed. Rather than arbitrary rule for the benefit of a privileged oligarchy, the new military rulers frequently employ their power against the old-time oligarchs, in order to secure greater economic democracy for the masses of the people.

The programs of the soldier Caesars indicate at least the *intent*

[19] *Ibid.*
[20] Canal Ramírez, *op. cit.*, p. 177.

to change the emphasis in governing. And certainly, if they do govern in such a fashion as to spread the benefits of the society to larger numbers of the people, they merit serious consideration. After all, the arbitrarily-labeled "democratic" governments of the past—chosen sometimes in truly free elections—have been distinguished chiefly by a fine disregard for any but the privileged upper classes. Consequently, the fixing of Rojas' true role is rendered difficult by conflicting definitions.

Some help may be found in Ortega's test for fascism: the nature of the atmosphere in which the government comes to power. In the case of Rojas, it was one of bloody anarchy, of repression of revolutionary masses, of the failure of the society's institutions, and a breaking of party lines only to find them reforming in a solid oligarchic front to oppose needed reforms.

Good, bad, or indifferent, Rojas can justify his tenure of power only on the basis of the state of things when he came to the presidency. A time of great crisis called him up to restore order, but his task does not end there. For, more than a policeman, he was the product of forces pushing toward a change in the society's institutions, which had been thwarted. Therefore, he must also be the instrument for the orderly accomplishment of these things, or he will be merely one with the dreary parade of resplendent strong men who have had their day, strutted a little while, and then passed on, leaving nothing behind but some repetitious phrases of history.

So long as Rojas stands, he is at the apex of an evolutionary cycle in Colombian society. From that point he can push upward, or, disregarding the forces which raised him up, plunge the nation back into some ultimate chaos in which, in time, the basic conflicts must again be put to trial by fire. In short, he has the choice of directing the social revolution along orderly, progressive ways, or of holding it in check with the nation's maximum force. He cannot long stay on dead center, for politics, even as nature, abhors a vacuum.

There are two awkward facts about Rojas' government which one encounters in trying to appraise him. He has abated political party action and he is shored up by the Army, both of which are repugnant to true democratists. The absence of party activity seems to create a wasteland to those accustomed to popular democracy under a two-party system. However, this must be regarded as a relative matter. One must keep in mind that the Colombian parties were unable to govern or to meet the challenge. One must remember the horrible carnage which they sowed. Something of this is reflected in the words of Jorge Padilla, discussing the Rojas government: "The present government is bolstered up by the dialectic of the tanks, but from its very beginning it has found clamorous support from the people. No one honestly believes that in the present emergency there is any viable regime other than that of the Armed Forces."[21]

Rojas, then, insures viability: he enforces an armed truce between the parties and the classes which, three years ago, were tearing at each others' throats. If he has abated certain civil rights, one may fairly ask what these amounted to under Ospina and Gómez. If the parties are muzzled and straight-jacketed, what competence did they demonstrate when they were active and free? Rojas saved them from a mad drive toward national suicide. Who, then, should mourn their present suspension, at least until they have reformed, reorganized, or adopted programs in line with the real class and economic issues of the society? "The profound disturbances of April 9, 1948," says Jorge Padilla,

gave us a momentary glimpse of the bottom of the abyss. The thirteenth of June [Rojas' *coup*] arrested the national dissolution. The crisis had been produced within the framework of our institutions. There was no one, among the directing classes, free of responsibility for it. Only the people, the eternal victims, were innocent. They had wagered, without hope of indemnification, their faith, their dignity, their burned-out homes, their dead. The military coup had to take place, not only against the discredited government, but *against the political parties*. The Political Nation is the truly responsible agent for this historic crisis. The Conservative regime and the Liberal opposition are merely the superstructures of two collectivities. It was necessary to impose, with the sword, the recess which no one wanted voluntarily to adopt after April 9. All the difficulties which General Rojas' government has encountered have come, precisely, from the work of *caudillos,* the special groups, and the parties, in their drive for public power. And from the equivocal situation created by the fact that one party, as a *bloc,* has access to administration, and the other, as a *bloc,* is excluded from it.[22]

But the maintenance of a mere state of partisan truce is not sufficient justification for military rule under Rojas. One must begin with beginnings. And there, we find the absolute need to develop in Colombia, if necessary by enforced conciliation or compromise, some understanding of what Lleras Camargo called the "collective type of living" so essential in meeting modern social demands. The party

---

[21] Jorge Padilla, "La Dialéctica de los Tanques," *Semana* (Bogotá), February 7, 1955, p. 8.

[22] Jorge Padilla, "La Historia no es un Carrousel," *Semana* (Bogotá), April 4, 1955, p. 14.

system only heightened the vast, divisive gaps, social, economic, and political. Some force must close them and soften their fricative action on their opposites.

Some conclusions can, therefore, be drawn regarding Rojas:

He did not destroy popular democracy in Colombia, for it never existed.

Political necessity raised him to power, in order to halt bloody, anarchistic class and party warfare.

But a truce alone will not solve the problems; Rojas may be unable to do much about them, in fact, before the parties, impatient with silence and inactivity, begin some adventure designed to give them back their former positions.

On balance, it seems fair to say that Rojas' historical role is that of head of a transitional government; of a government which directs the society along the lines demanded by the times which created him; which imposes upon the parties the social responsibility of representing the general welfare rather than that of the upper classes predominantly; which, having done these things, having protected the nation during a period of enforced social progress and political tutelage, then restores the constitution and turns back power to the parties of the people's choice.

There are staggering obstacles in Rojas' way. Nonetheless, his main task is that of creating a true synthesis on national will, in which all classes share a broader social myth than the nation has ever known. In Colombia, there has never been a synthesis of such general will regarding national directions. Economic, social, and political integration is only just beginning. The "collective living" which Lleras recognizes as essential is inhibited by the divisive influences of race, the muddled ideological tradition of the Independence, the caste system, the narrow concentration of great wealth, the unreality of the constitution, the general conflict of social aims among the classes. All these things tend to divide rather than to integrate. Therefore, they must be examined in some detail, for they will, in the long run, be the deciding factors in Rojas' success or failure. Rojas must play out his role of chief of a transition government, leaving the old society behind and reaching out for the new, with a supporting cast most of whom speak unrelated lines, many of whom seek to take the leading part, and of whom very few, indeed, agree regarding the *idée maîtresse* of the drama in which they are all involved.

X. Basic Problems Facing Rojas: Incentives to Violent Solutions

HISPANIC ANARCHISM AND THE URGE TOWARD DEMOCRACY

The Anarchistic Legend, and the
"Pessimistic View" of Latin Society

The last thirty years of Colombian history is rife with evidence of the need for people who can, as Lleras Camargo says, "manage and resolve the elemental problems of a collective type of life."[1] In the sense intended by Lleras, "collective" means a life in which there is a reasonable consensus of national will, and some fair level of agreement among classes and groups regarding desirable ends for the society. Bolívar was speaking of the essence of the matter when he said, "To form a stable government, one must have as a national base a general spirit whose object is to incline everyone uniformly toward two points: moderation of the general will, and limitation of public authority."[2]

In Colombia there has not yet developed a major existing faith or social belief in some common terrestrial destiny for most of the people. Socially, economically, and, perforce therefore, politically, integration has not proceeded to the point where class compromises and fusion of interests in the general welfare can replace conflict of classes and groups. Hence, there is a basic, major division within the nation.

Not yet has the great common social myth taken shape or form or substance in Colombia. Consequently, there exists not even that ultimate, grudging, but rational agreement of all classes on final directions, which is so necessary to a democratic environment. And this unfortunately, is a *sine qua non* for the return of popular government to the nation. Some common group of ideals, certain aims for future achievement, and common memories of past striving shared by a majority of the people must be created before Colombia

---

[1] See p. 149.

[2] Cited in Francisco García Calderón, *Les Démocraties Latines de L'Amérique* (Paris: Bibliothèque de Philosophie Scientifique, 1920), p. 60.

has a reasonable chance of finding her lost directions. That social myth which makes for community of will in an orderly society is one that "contains an explanation of the existing social order, justifies its component relations in terms of accepted values, and depicts the social ideal, the future, toward which the society is moving."[3]

In Colombia, the upper classes have their own social myth; the masses have another, and who knows when or how, or under what circumstances, the twain shall meet?

The history, the traditional form of the institutions, all have created cleavages, rather than synthesis. At the root of the problem lies the human element: a seeming predisposition toward anarchism, the long tradition of personalism in government, the rigidity of group particularism. In public affairs, the Colombian experience has been part of the general Latin-American experience: something in the national *génie* tends to regard the *status quo* as a challenge, sets individual off from individual, region from region, class from class, and creates a latent antipathy toward joint effort or mutual striving.

A Colombian writer says, "A very marked characteristic of the Hispanic character is what Ortega y Gasset calls 'particularism.' This characteristic consists of assimilating experience through a private peep-hole, of using a very small screen to see the problems of life, in place of a large, ample one of Cineramascope size."[4] For the Colombian, this is a trait honestly come by. It arrived with the conquistadors, and neither time nor distance has quite obliterated it. The very anarchism of the past decade in Colombia requires that this characteristic be examined, for it is part of the "sociology of pessimism" which has oriented much of the thinking and writing on Latin America. It is the basis for the justification for the *caudillos*, the "Democratic Caesars," the "necessary gendarmes" as García Calderón called them. The Hispanic peoples, runs the reasoning, are anarchistic by nature. In times of stress, this tendency breaks out into public disorder, and creates semipermanent instability. Hence, the Strong Men, the dictators, are necessary to impose a stability because the masses are unruly and volatile by nature.

If this be wholly true, one may write off as an impossibility any future democracy for Latin America. One may also easily explain

[3] Nicholas John Spykman, *America's Strategy in World Politics* (New York: Harcourt, Brace & Co., 1942), p. 205.
[4] "Simplex," *Semana* (Bogotá), January 10, 1955, p. 38.

away what happened in Colombia in recent years: it was simply the anarchistic urge of the people at long last manifesting itself. Clearly, this is at best an unsatisfactory conclusion. However, since the dictator-anarchy relationship seems to be the only resort left when "democracy" breaks down in Colombia, or elsewhere in Latin America, the importance of the characteristic cannot merely be waved aside. The problem is to weigh its nature and assess its importance.

Hispanic Anarchism as an Ethnological Trait

Many writers believe that a basic factor in the Hispanic racial *génie* is a boundless individualism, often anarchistic and always anti-social in character. Analyzing this trait in the Latin-American people, García Calderón says:

> Individualism is the fundamental note of the Spanish psychology. An Iberian trait, it has the force of an imperious atavism. It exalts all forms of action, of affirmation of the self; it inspires a limitless confidence in force *per se:* it tends to develop human energy, to defend the national independence against all pressures from without, against the rigors of the law, against the moral imperative, the inflexible duty; it creates in excitable spirits an ardent will to dominate . . . wilful, mystical, the Spanish temperament is active, it affirms itself outwardly in conflicts; antagonisms, dissociations, thesis and antithesis abound in Iberian history.[5]

In accordance with this belief, there is, somewhere in the Hispanic spiritual labyrinth, an easily roused urge to criticize, to oppose, to impose one's personality upon other persons and other things. It is what Madariaga defines as "[a] tendency to widen gaps instead of bridging them over, and to turn a split into a ditch, a ditch into a gulf, [and it] is primal and permanent in Spanish psychology."[6]

Obviously such a tendency, if permanent, would stand in the way of the Latin-American, and specifically the Colombian, need for integration and the development of common social objectives. It is not the stuff of which modern democracy, with its requirements for compromise and individual subordination to the general will, is easily made. "If we look at ourselves in the mirror," says Alberdi, the Argentine philosopher, "we must confess the anarchy in our minds . . . the dividing lines that prevent unity."[7] Thus is this basic characteristic

---

[5] García Calderón, *op. cit.*, p. 16.

[6] Salvador de Madariaga, *The Fall of the Spanish American Empire* (New York: The Macmillan Co., 1948), p. 29.

[7] Juan Bautista Alberdi, *Fragmento Preliminar al Estudio del Derecho* (Buenos Aires, 1886), I, 119–23.

one which leads not to unity, but rather which makes of unity the occasion for antithesis, for a challenge to conspire; which regards majority rule as an imperative to form camarillas and cliques, and finds in stability sufficient reason to issue a *pronunciamiento*.

If one attaches true importance to the racial elements behind Hispanic peoples, there are, indeed, but few which seem to favor popular democracy. African Berber, Phoenician and Carthagenian, Jew, Greek, Celt, Roman, German, and Arab all fused their blood strains to make the Spaniard and his Latin-American cousin. More than any other European people, they are Oriental and African.[8] It was this same mélange of blood and temperament which caused Bolívar's "deep pessimism" regarding the political potentialities of Hispano-America.[9] Addressing the Congress of Angostura, the Liberator said by way of warning, "Let us keep in mind that our people is not that of Europe nor of North America; it is a compound of Africa and America rather than of Europe, since Spain itself ceases to be European by reason of its African [Berber-Moorish] blood, its institutions and its character."[10]

But there are other racial characteristics than anarchism which some scholars see as barriers to orderly democratic living in Latin America. Northrup enumerates them as stoicism, a laziness marked by enough energy to undertake great things, but inability to handle the detailed labor necessary to carry them through; and an individualism that makes excellent guerrilla fighters, but poor soldiers: a warlike people, but not a military one. It is this same individualism which makes it impossible for them to unite for the collective effort, either in war or politics: "One of the worst features of Spanish politics is the inability of the nation or even of a single party to unite in a common cause." And yet, paradox of paradoxes, this Hispanic individualism acts as the wellspring of the Latin's deep *personal* sense of democracy. However, one must admit that as of the present, such democracy is the democracy of egoism, well represented by the oath of allegiance which the four estates of Aragón forced upon their king: "We, who

[8] George Tyler Northrup, *An Introduction to Spanish Literature* (Chicago: The University of Chicago Press, 1925), p. 16.

[9] Rufino Blanco-Fombona, *El Pensamiento Vivo de Bolívar* (Buenos Aires: Editorial Losada, 1944), p. 22.

[10] Simón Bolívar, *Discurso Pronunciado ante el Congreso de Angostura*, ed. J. A. Cova (Buenos Aires: Librería El Ateneo, 1952), p. 70.

are as good as you, swear to you who are no better than we, to accept you as our king and sovereign lord, provided you observe all our liberties and laws; but if not, not." Dignity, too, says Northrup, a dignity which approximates a high sense of personal worth and honor, in the beggar as well as in the *fijo de algo*; readiness to take offense, a susceptibility to becoming rather pompously ridiculous—but behind it all a preoccupation with the self, the *ego*, the virtual deification of the individual.[11]

This complex of traits, many believe, easily leads Hispanic peoples to interpret democracy as some maximum freedom of the individual. Hence, in practicing what they think is democracy, they often create its antithesis. But the paradox of personal anarchism coupled with the democratic urge, is merely part and parcel of the total paradox of all Hispanism, a paradox that cannot be resolved, and which frustrates the student who searches for something tangible upon which to hang a study of Hispanic political and social institutions. For the country itself is a "vast paradox, compounded by little paradoxes, each region, and each class a world unto itself, with an outlook that is contradictory to that of other parts."[12]

Such an odd mixture of individuality and of democratic urges has, many believe, made the Hispanic peoples partisans of a kind of "Democratic Caesarism." The personalist *caudillo* thus easily rises over anarchistic, squabbling parties and regions rent by divisionism. But the basic popular reverence for authority sooner or later disintegrates under the impact of restless, leveling individualism. The language of Hispanic peoples is replete with *dichos* that tend to reduce everyone to some common denominator: "We are knights as the king is, only with less money," is a fair example.[13] It follows that this conflict of purposes is deadly to the collective action. It results in a fateful lack of social instinct, a lack which is underscored most dramatically in the era of modern living. Gregariousness the Hispanic peoples have in abundance. "But the moment the warm spontaneous glow of sociability passes into the cold, rigid limitations imposed by union in common enterprise, Spanish individualism

[11] Northrup, *op. cit.*, pp. 16–23.

[12] Danielle Hunebelle, "A Frenchwoman Sizes up Franco," *Réalité* (New York), January, 1954, No. 38, p. 42.

[13] John A. Mackay, *The Other Spanish Christ* (New York: The Macmillan Co., 1933), p. 3.

makes its presence felt immediately. The innate dislike to be bound together by obligation or mutual consent underlies the problem of Spanish regionalism, and has militated against the success of corporate enterprises carried on by Spaniards."[14]

The writings of Latin and North American scholars who support this pessimistic theme of anarchism and *caudillismo* seem rather to assume that political instability and its time-honored remedy, dictatorship, are racial characteristics transmitted with the genes. As a cure, Alberdi and Sarmiento recommended heavy infusions of European immigration. García Calderón concurred. Lucas Ayarragaray was of the same thought, because "ideas, like the blood to ennoble them, must filter down through the generations." *Caudillismo,* as a result of instability, was in his view a product of ethnic determinism. "Its arbitrariness was consecrated in tradition and in the [peoples'] predominating customs. Latin America's political incapacity is due to the crossing of the conquistadors and the Indian races."[15] And writing as late as 1955, Laureano Vallenilla Lanz says, "The American states have need of paternal care to cure the sores and wounds of despotism and war."[16]

This is all very well for Hispanic traits which may incline the people toward violent solutions, and which stand in the way of social integration. But granting, for the moment, their validity, can they be applied to the specific Colombian situation?

The Spanish Heritage in Colombian Society

The Hispanic past has left its mark on the people and the society of Colombia.

Diego Rafaél Guzmán, of the Colombian Academy, says, "There is nothing more based upon reason than that Latin-American society and peoples of Spanish origin should be, not a degeneration ... of their forebears, but ... a blending of it, more temperate and wholesome."[17] And Jose María Samper, a great Colombian scholar and a profound student of his own society, concludes that:

[14] *Ibid.*

[15] Lucas Ayarragaray, *La Anarquía Argentina y el Caudillismo*, cited by Jose M. Machin, "Caudillismo y Democracia en America Latina," *Panorama* (Washington: Pan American Union), 1955, IV, No. 13, 30.

[16] *Ibid.*, p. 31.

[17] Diego Rafaél Guzmán, *Importancia del Espíritu Español en las Letras Colombianas* (Bogotá: Editorial Minerva, 1935), p. 121.

Spanish society inoculated into the blood of Colombia all the sources of life and of decomposition that it contained; but with this difference: the second worked with all their unfortunate energy, while the first found themselves oppressed by the egoism of the colonial regime. A quick comparison of the Spanish race and the Colombian peoples would bring to the fore clearly the solidarity established by the heritage which blood and education have transmitted to us.[18]

Nor did the mere transformation of the Colony into the Republic change anything fundamentally, save add to a maladjusted society the impossibility of squaring feudalistic institutional structures with the lofty human ideals incorporated in constitutions that were inspired by the French and American revolutions. "Under the guise of republicanism," says García Calderón, "Spanish heredity, profound and century-spanning, has been maintained. The forms vary, but the *soul* of the race remains identical . . . the democracies of [Latin] America are therefore Spanish, although the elite has always been inspired by French ideas."[19]

Individualism verging into anarchism, deep respect for authoritarianism in politics and religion (Crown and Church), the dogmatic cruelty of the Inquisition, these and many other factors left their imprint upon Colombia as part of the Spanish heritage. Traditional authoritarianism evolved into *caciquismo* and *caudillismo;*[20] and "the natural arrogance of egocentricity showed itself in an inordinate desire to have power over others . . . Spanish arrogance became Creole arrogance."[21] In this atmosphere of personalism, of individualism enshrined, the common effort was foredoomed to failure.

And yet, the *environment* did change, modify, attenuate, and accentuate variously, certain of these characteristics. Dr. Eugenio J. Gómez of the National University of Colombia considers many of the basic Hispanic traits in a state of transition, in that time and environment may greatly alter them; but they will still "constitute facets which, transmitted . . . to the American colonists, [determine] in the new race *permanent* characteristics held in common with the

---

[18] Jose María Samper, *Las Revoluciones Políticas y la Condición Social de las Repúblicas Colombianas* (Bogotá: Biblioteca de Cultura Popular, n.d.), p. 251.

[19] García Calderón, *op. cit.,* pp. 81–82.

[20] The cacique is the local "big shot," country squire, lord of the manor, head of a numerous family, a region, etc.; the *caudillo* is the political boss, the arbiter of larger affairs, the man whom the caciques follow.

[21] Mackay, *op. cit.,* p. 14.

Spanish."[22] Colombians, says Gómez, let emotions predominate over sober reflection; they are impulsive and impatient with thinking matters through; in the realm of ideas, logical absolutism rules; in that of action, an absolute morality. Hence, extremes have dominated the nation's political life, leading to passionate and violent reactions. Lack of foresight, of planning, cause the nation to live by the moment: "Neither the government nor the people take from the past the lessons by which to direct the present and plan for the future." The result is a national life in which "miracles are always hoped for." But above all, says Gómez, the general conduct of the people is moved by a basic personalist envy. "Our race cannot stand, either in the individual or the collectivity, the success of our neighbor." And as an example, he cites the story of the peasant who, when the priest visited him to bless his lands, said, "Father, don't bless my fields, curse those of my neighbor."[23]

Such envy is, of course, the sublimation of the ego; it is runaway individualism, a need to be better than the next one, and it is deadly to social collaboration. Says Professor Gómez: "The Anglo-Saxon races show a spirit of cooperation, of collective enterprises . . . the Latins in general, and the Spanish in particular, recoil from their fellows." And finally, favoritism and nepotism in government, which make of the parties contending armies which must win the political wars for simple economic reasons of survival: privilege and gain.

> It is the favored [person] . . . who carries out the critical functions of the society. Thus, one sees doctors who have failed in practice acting as Ministers of the Interior; lawyers directing public works; fanatical and intransigent politicians directing the Department of Education; schoolteachers acting as Chiefs of Hygiene and Public Assistance; individuals who hardly recognize cooked vegetables direct agricultural societies . . . this favoritism, based upon what the public calls "pull" [rosca] demoralizes the masses and prostitutes civic criteria, even as it disorganizes administration.[24]

Clearly, this Hispanic anarchism-personalism-particularism was one of the factors at work during the times detailed in this study. It lay behind the drive of the parties to destroy one another; in the divisionism of the victorious Conservatives after they had, in effect,

[22] Eugenio J. Gómez, *Problemas Colombianos: La Unidad Política* (Bogotá: Gráficas Mundo al Dia, 1941), p. 72.

[23] *Ibid.*, p. 74.

[24] *Ibid.*, p. 76.

destroyed the Liberals; in all the "playing politics" when statesman-
ship was demanded; in the bloody civil war when the one thought
was, *destroy*. The net result of it was, of course, to create for Rojas
Pinilla such a deep divisionism of interest between parties, classes,
castes, that only a miracle will permit him to forge some broader
national interest so necessary to the collective life toward which
events are placably driving Colombia. "From the various elements of
[national] disorder," says Canal Ramírez,

> there has resulted popular disagreement, in place of the national spirit which
> Bolívar required. When the citizen does not fulfill his duties, nor feel sure of the
> satisfaction of his rights, he ceases to be a unit of some contribution to the common
> welfare, and becomes a unit of resistance, if not of contradiction to, the general
> welfare. Public opinion, an indispensable element of good government, then dis-
> appears. Criticism arises, negative and destructive, as does systematic opposition
> and the irrevocable division of the people into unconditional friends or uncon-
> ditional enemies of the government; and from their inevitable collision violence
> arises.[25]

Out of division, anarchy. The theme runs like a red skein through
the history of Colombia. The individual, the historical past, the
lay of the land, the political parties, the economic structure, all
these make their contribution to it, all are of the essence. No Colombian political collectivity has ever been able to comprise answers
to these dilemmas in its program. The claim that in Colombia "men
fight for ideas" is belied by the nation's history; rather, they have
explained or rationalized in terms of lofty principles, conflicts rising
out of other purposes. And in moments of crisis, the leaders and
the parties have shown themselves, far too often, to be only
Madariaga's "Spaniard in search of power."

It would be wonderful if this were not so. Yet most Colombians
know it for a fact, even though Colombian intellectuals and foreign
observers are unwilling to accept it. On this score, Jorge Padilla has
something interesting and pertinent to say:

> Our aptitude for anarchism is incredible. We are churlishly individualistic. No
> great movement has ever taken place here because there are as many opinions as
> people. In 1946, when Liberalism split over Turbay and Gaitán, the Turbay Di-
> rectorate sent a telegraphic circular around with the rules for the campaign. One
> day it received from a hamlet lost in the depths of the provinces a message, in
> reply, which said:

[25] Canal Ramírez, *op. cit.*, p. 195.

Liberal Directorate, Bogotá
Have received circular. Respectfully advise am only Liberal in this town. And *I* am divided. Regards.

Pedro Pirateque

We are an archipelago of opinions, of theses, of contrary interests. The greatest difficulty for a governor is, therefore, that of knowing exactly where our un-coercible, our unstable, our paradoxical public opinion flows. Every Colombian is a political party. If, in moments of foolishness, there should be established here, let us say, a parliamentary government like in France or England, our governments would have the ephemeral duration of the roses in the poem by Calderón de la Barca.[26]

The task of creating the common social myth in Colombia is great, but it hardly will require the remaking of Hispanic nature. One must agree with Professor Eugenio Gómez that certain apparently basic divisive characteristics need not be permanent. Time, environment, and other factors will operate to change much of what has been superficially designated as the "Latin-American nature." Yet something particularly and essentially Hispanic will remain. The question is: will it stand in the way of the development of stability and popular democracy?

The Requirements of Popular Democracy
versus Colombian Particularism

Basically, the question is not *whether* Colombian politics have been marked by anarchism and instability, but *why*. The fact itself is there, unshakable and stubborn. But behind it stand certain common fallacies. First, the assumption by Latin-American intellectuals that deep attachment to the principles of democracy can create democracy itself; and, second, the assumption by North Americans of the "optimistic" school, that assurances from Latin intellectuals that democracy exists is sufficient to make it so. Finally, coupled with this optimistic view is the counter assumption by the extreme pessimists that democracy can never develop in Latin America, because the Latins are basically anarchistic and not amenable to popular government.

This confusion of interpretations requires, for the specific case of Colombia, some explanation of what makes for political democracy, and what factors inhibit its growth.

From many reliable points of view, democracy is a public frame

[26] Jorge Padilla, "El Archipiélago," *Semana* (Bogotá), July 4, 1955, p. 10.

of mind expressed through institutions. This means "that any democratic organization, is prepared by a series of inclinations, feelings, convictions, and habits of thinking in the minds of the people, *long before* its historical realization."[27] At certain stages of a society's development these attitudes, frames of mind, and ways of thinking merge into a pattern of social behavior that is expressed in the society's institutions as a democratic way of life. "When this frame of mind is lacking, democratic institutions cannot grow: if they are introduced from outside, they are likely to be mutilated or to disappear altogether after a short time.... Democracy grows out of its own soil. This means that it requires specific experiences and specific mental changes in a community before appearing as historical reality."[28]

These public mental changes, these experiences, have not yet taken place in Colombia. Class is separated from class by vast gaps; social ends of major groups are not only different, but antagonistic; great contradictions in wealth exist. In this atmosphere, there not only can be no democracy, but even the beginnings of compromise are difficult to achieve. The Hispanic norm is individualism, the Latin-American ideal of democracy is unlimited personal freedom: "The truly essential quality of the Latin-American peoples is their affection for democratic ideals," says a Latin writer. "Their authentic expression is found in these ideals. Of course, they have not achieved them integrally in accordance with their aspirations... [but] the American ideal has been ... and is ... a tenacious effort to achieve what the people intimately feel: democracy."[29] One does not "feel" democracy; rather, it grows from the anguish of necessary conciliation.

But there is no reason to doubt the sincerity of these words. In all Latin America, and particularly in Colombia, there is much talk of democracy. But notably, it is mostly the talk of the intellectuals. Moreover, it is usually printed talk, and therefore, it is not for the people, for the vast majority of the people cannot read and write. Yet this overabundance of democratic verbalism is accompanied in Colombia by a disheartening lack of discussion of

[27] Zevedi Barbu, *Democracy and Dictatorship* (New York: Grove Press, 1956), p. 34.
[28] *Ibid.*
[29] Machin, *op. cit.*, pp. 33–34.

even the primary elements of which true popular democracy is made. There is much ado about ideals; almost nothing is said about *practical social cooperation*. And until Colombians learn the necessity of sociopolitical compromise, Colombian democracy will remain in the realm of semantics. Unfortunately for real democracy, the Colombian upper classes do not cooperate with the lower; often enough, not even among themselves. "Compromise, of course, is at the heart of the democratic process," says Charles Frankel.

Modern Parliamentary democracy has grown out of a series of bitter contests between different social groups . . . Protestants and Catholics, the landed gentry and the middle classes, capital and labor, and, in the United States, the North and the South. These contests have frequently been settled violently. But whenever they have been settled, and democracy has survived, *two principles* have presided over the solution. The first has been that each of the contending parties must have some accepted place, some access to power, in the social order. The second has been that neither of the contending parties could be given its maximum demands. In this sense, it is precisely the business of the democratic politician to make deals, to conciliate conflicting groups, to give as many people as possible something of what they want, and to give no one everything he wants. For a democratic social order exists under a constant pressure to create a balance of power and interests from which no significant section of the community is cut off.[30]

This analysis of the nature of popular democracy states almost the direct antithesis of the public situation in Colombia. Uncompromising struggle has always marked the Colombian party battle. The losers are liquidated and forced from office; they are made the "enemies" of the true believers. Access to government, to privilege, even to the benefits of the economy, is denied them. Parties and groups seek the maximum fulfillment of their own demands and objectives, to the exclusion of all others. Monopoly drives rule their strategy. Rather than seeking to conciliate conflicting interests, the parties and their leaders try to destroy the opposition. Instead of giving all the people a little of what each group wants, the winning group aims to get everything that it, exclusively, wants. Rather than seeking to create a balance of power and interests in the society, Colombian political leaders strive almost without exception to capture all power for themselves. As a consequence, significant areas of the social order are left outside the political and economic pale, dis-

[30] Charles A. Frankel, "A Plea for Moderation in Moderation," *New York Times Magazine*, May 6, 1956, pp. 56–58.

gruntled, antagonistic, and determined to treat the opposition in the same manner when fortune again smiles its winning smile.

This dynamic of social cooperation has a number of important corollaries. It implies that people in the society have a sense of social change, and a realization that they can have a hand in shaping and directing such change. Relatively few of the people of Colombia have been made aware of that. It means, also, the delegation of authority, rather than its transfer to a party, an individual, or a group; yet the majority of Colombians have for over a century placed their fate unquestioningly in the hands of the party, or the *Jefe Supremo,* and have found their interests ignored. It requires cooperation and compromise, but the Colombian political system is premised upon bitter-end antagonism and constant group strife. It assumes that every man will make his part of the society by his own efforts in cooperation with other men, yet the social and economic systems divide human beings into men, and those who are not quite regarded as men.

Consequently, despite the consistent preoccupation of Colombian intellectuals with democracy, one must conclude that they have been enamored of ideals, rather than faced with, or facing, realities. National living together is not "the passive and inert co-existence of a pile of stones by the side of the road, but an active and dynamic reality. Nations are built around important and stimulating enterprises which demand a maximum of sacrifice, discipline and mutual consideration from everyone."[31] The dynamic reality, to become Colombian democracy, must first give consideration to poor, ignorant Colombians, and abolish the passive role to which the upper classes have relegated them. Pile of stones by the side of the road, or human ciphers, they must be brought actively into the national life before democracy becomes a reality.

Actually, the fabled, inherent "Hispanic anarchism" is much less a deterrent to Colombian democracy than is the feeling of group *particularism* which pervades the society. Exclusiveness, a feeling of group apartness, stand firmly in the way of democratic compromise, supported by tradition, by custom, and by the class and economic prejudices of the society.

In Colombia, the social groups, the classes, and the parties, tend to

[31] Ortega y Gasset, *op. cit.,* p. 43.

think of themselves, alone, as the *nation*. All others exist by chance: they need not be taken into account. Each one, closed off behind the confines of its particular interest, busily grinds its own axes. If there are limitations, they belong to the other fellow, the other party, the other class. Few, indeed, have developed a sense of living in a society which is "a common home, lighted by a common inspiration and dedicated to a common destiny." Of just such a situation Ortega y Gasset wrote, in his classical condemnation of particularism:

> Since the current of sympathy is cut, the woes that afflict a neighbor have no effect on the other groups, and he is left abandoned to weakness and misfortune. On the other hand, hypersensitiveness to one's ailments is a characteristic of this social state. Disagreements or difficulties which are easily borne during periods of cohesion come to be intolerable when the spirit of a national life in common has disintegrated.[32]

For myriad reasons growing from the historic past, and from the social and economic systems of both Spain and the Colony-Republic, Colombians have come into the modern era as a collectivity of fragmented groups. Never have they really *lived together* in the sense of cooperating socially. On the contrary, they have known intimately the process of competing, of struggling and battling with one another inside the same national boundaries, for economic, class, racial, regional and, ultimately, political reasons. Only just recently have they awakened to the full realization that each group may have just complaints and aspirations. This is a beginning, of course, and may mark the start of a real transition from a feudalistic public frame of mind to a democratic one, in which social cooperation will replace rigidity, antagonism, and monopoly.

But essentially, Colombian social cooperation does not have to wait for some genetic mutation of Colombian character to render the Colombian people sweetly cooperative. Anarchistic traits or vestiges of them are, after all, found in every settled society at certain historical moments. "Hispanic anarchism" has very little, if anything, to do with the genes or ethnic influences, but considerable to do with socially conditioned reflexes. Particularly is this true of group particularism.

In plain terms, Colombia is going through the pangs of an industrial revolution which is creating new social norms. This is something that even Spain herself has so far largely escaped.[33] Hence the analysts

[32] *Ibid.*, p. 36.
[33] The Spanish Republic and the Civil War represented the ideological phase

of the Hispanic character are still on safe ground when they tag Hispanic peoples as anarchistic. They have not yet been faced with the ultimate necessity for compromise. But the growth of cities; the increase in money and production and consumption; the new vocality and influence of laboring classes and of borning middle classes; the inevitably greater interdependence of all groups, classes, castes, will break down the old Colombian standards, will erase many of the old prejudices and create new values and norms. Thus it was in the Anglo-Saxon nations. Why should it not be so in the Hispanic-American ones when the necessary socially formative factors operate? Democracy and social cooperation are not test tube factors, but socially-determined patterns of activity which represent conciliation forged in the heat of struggle and basic group interdependence.

In Colombia, wealth and good living are rapidly ceasing to be "subjects of contemplation" for the mass of people.[34] The masses are demanding change, and a government has now based its legitimacy largely upon its ability and desire to govern for the benefit of the humble as well as the great. If it be true that democracy cannot grow until the gaps between the very rich and the very poor have been shortened by creation of a standard of living that gives everyone a stake in the society; until education has made the majority conscious of their dignity as men; until the whole society has a sense of participation in the national life, then the obvious conclusion is that procedural democracy cannot come to Colombia until some government or another has done something about creating social or economic democracy.

When this has been done, social cooperation will be not only possible but logical, and perhaps inevitable. But the greatest influence in breaking down group particularism and apartness may very well come from the development of internal markets for business and industry. As Colombian workers become consumers as well as producers, they will establish community of interest with the upper classes, simply by becoming customers. In the meantime, the government of Rojas Pinilla enforces from the top down one of the important lessons of democracy. It is one which was learned in the Anglo-Saxon ex-

---

of revolution, but not the determining factors created by basic changes in modes of production and class realignment.

[34] Carlos Dávila, *We of the Americas* (Chicago: Ziff-Davis Company, 1948), p. 204.

perience by the struggles that began with the commercial revolution:
the classes must cooperate before democracy can hope to thrive. It
need not be willing cooperation. It may be, and often is, grudging
and bitter, but it does mean that each group eventually has to take
the other into account in forging national ends and objectives. Each
surrenders a part of its objectives and admits the legitimacy of the
other. Cooperation thus becomes normal.

For a limited time, Rojas and his government can enforce this
situation. It is to be hoped that the society may adjust progressively
and prosperously to the new norms, and that out of it will come a
recognition of mutual group benefit so great that voluntary cooperation will be the rule in the future. Almost certainly any attempt to
go back to the old particularism will mean violence and further instability. If Rojas succeeds, Colombians may one day have truly
popular democracy, the legend of "Hispanic anarchism" to the contrary notwithstanding.

Meanwhile, Rojas has tailored a government with certain enforced
attributes of unity. But he faces extremely difficult tasks. They grow
out of basic class, caste, and economic conflicts; out of the maldis-
tribution of the society's wealth, the use and ownership of land, the
divergent interests of regional groupings; out of the very nature of
the party struggle itself as legalized partisan warfare to the death.

Rojas' position is not enviable, for he must initiate important
changes in a national way of life. And in the meantime, he must
always remember that, lacking the experience of socially-conditioned
cooperation by groups and individuals, many Colombians still interpret *E Pluribus Unum* to mean, "Out of One, Many."

THE RACE-CLASS CLEAVAGE: DARK SKIN, DARK DESTINY

During the bloody civil war of 1948–53, a group of bandits burned
the home of a wealthy Conservative landowner, killed his foreman
and two sons, ravished his daughter, and left the owner wandering
dazedly before his flaming hacienda. In shocked horror, the man
mumbled over and over, *"Por qué?*–but why, *why?"*

And the scornful answer was: *"Porque usted es rico y blanco."* (Because you are rich and white.)

In this cruel, terse phrase is summed up the basic, unchanging eco-
nomic-racial cleavage between the classes in Colombia. Rich-white-
ness is identified with education, political control, and other

Most of Colombia's employment in industry now centers around textiles and food processing. Celanese Colombiana (affiliate of Celanese Corporation of America) furnishes acetate yarns and staple fiber to Colombia's textile industry, polyester resins to building industry, and polyvinyl emulsions to paint and chemical industry. Here, yarn is given final inspection before shipment.

attributes of the oligarchy; it is opposed to and by a poor-red-black-pastel mélange of humanity which, having awakened to a new conception of their place in life, are exerting a constant, dangerous pressure upon the established institutions of the society. In Colombia, the conflicts between men are equated by clashing colors of skin and economic status.

Although Colombians claim that there is no racial discrimination in the country, the truth is that discrimination has become so institutionalized that it is considered a social norm, and therefore not discrimination, which is, basically, a departure from a norm, or the application of a particular, restrictive one. No one is conscious of discrimination in Colombia, provided he is white. What the Colombian really means is that there is no Jim Crowism or segregation. The real segregation is by availability of opportunity. "In Latin America," said Humboldt at the beginning of the nineteenth century,[35] "the skin, more or less white, decides the place that a man will occupy in society." The rule is unchanged today.

The Spaniards who first came to Colombia were soldiers without women. They took the Indian women for concubines, and later, when slavery was introduced, the black woman and the white master cohabited and to the Indian-white cross was added the African bloodline. But the Spaniard's easy indifference to the color of a woman's skin did not, as had been generally held, imply a lack of racial prejudice. The need for a mate was something quite apart from a social judgment. If anything is needed to kill the fiction of "lack of racial prejudice," it is the premium which Colombians, along with most Latin Americans, place upon *pureza de sangre*.[36] The concupiscent conquistadors and their descendants took the native and slave women to their beds, but scarcely ever to their bosoms; they used them, but did not marry them. Rather, they made of "whiteness" a yardstick by which all social, economic, and political preference was measured. Children of cross-matings had better social chances than did the aborigine; and further "whitening" might bring them even closer to the select circle. Still, from the beginning down to the present in Colombia, the circle has been select.

The people who conquered and settled Colombia were not all

[35] Cited by García Calderón, *op. cit.*, p. 34.

[36] Purity of blood. See C. A. Hauberg, "Spain in Latin America," *Current History*, March, 1955, p. 130.

Spaniards as we loosely use the term. Strongly-developed local characteristics which tended to set them apart were, paradoxically, their common characteristic. All were daring, most were cruel, but it is difficult to distinguish among them any common social ideal.[37] They were hardhanded adventurers, fortune hunters. When fortune's smile was wide, they went back to Spain as quickly as possible; and those who remained did so because they could live well in a caste-ridden society, despite ill fortune, simply because they were white, and therefore lords and hidalgos.[38] From such men one might expect daring and high adventure, but not tolerance—especially not racial tolerance.

After the men, the institutions formed in their likeness. The encomienda and the *mito* (whereby the Indian passed as a chattel with the land to the *hacendado*, and others were levied as free labor in the mines) were anything but social levelers. On the contrary, they created the master servant, human chattel psychology long before slavery itself set economics and skin color at odds on the social scene. The white Spaniard found, or eternally sought, a life of ease and luxury, while those of darker color created the wealth and supplied the labor to maintain his illusions. "*Peninsulares* and Creoles," says Vila, "spent most of their year seeking leisure and recreation [*en la holganza*], on the pretext offered by the celebration of civil and religious fiestas."[39]

At the other extreme, the Indians' pattern of life fell into a caste-mold that has scarcely been cracked to this day. They labored for the white man, or they fled to the wilderness. Those who remained eventually became mestizised, and suffered the psychological shock of suspension between two cultures. And with the opening up of the slave trade to the Colony, a third factor was added to the tri-ethnic elements, again putting into operation the search for "whiteness" as an Open Sesame to acceptance. For, as with the Indian, so each Negro cross with a white meant a slight rise in the social scale, some small gain or hope of gain in economic status.

In the colonial period, there was one common factor between Negro slavery and Indian forced labor; each was part of a rigid social and economic structure, and each system deprived the bulk of the popula-

[37] Eugenio J. Gómez, *Problemas Colombianos: La Unidad Política*, p. 70.
[38] Vila, *op. cit.*, p. 126.
[39] *Ibid.*, p. 127.

tion of many human and personal rights.[40] Basically, the class structure was of only two main groups, the white conquerors and their
descendants at the top, and a vast, ethnically-mixed, servile, and sub-
servient class of Indians, Negroes, mestizos, zambos, and mulattos at
the bottom.

Writing in the last half of the past century, Jose María Samper saw
in this situation of mixed races a factor producing democracy, because it tended to "admit the equal competition of the castes, open
common ways for them, annul all social antagonisms, under the
threat, if to the contrary, of creating civil war. . . . "[41] Unfortunately,
there has never been "equal competition of castes" in Colombia. Perhaps it should have created democracy, and might have done so, had
not political parties become the property, respectively, of rich-white
Liberal oligarchs and Conservative oligarchs. The two groups used
and manipulated the lower classes for their own class interests, and
the political struggles were high-level affairs, untouched by lines of
influence from below.

Consequently, the castes did not compete until the coming of the
twentieth century. By that time, the antithesis of democracy had become established: a stratified caste system, and the institutionalization
of race-class division. In the rare instances where men of mixed blood
rose to positions of wealth and influence, they "whitened" themselves
by purchasing certificates of blood purification. From the start, the
class cleavage was based on economic differences and these were
closely equated with the color of the skin.[42]

It was a feudalistic society. The lower classes owed service to the
upper; and when, at length, the *repartimiento* was abolished, peonage
sprang up to entrap the Indian and the mestizo in a web of debt that
held him as effectively to the upper class as had the old system. Sup-
plementing these bonds of economic thralldom was a general lack of
education, and the momentum gained by a history of servitude. Nor
did the coming of Independence make essential changes in the class
relationship.[43] The freed slaves remained black and poor; the mestizo

[40] Sanford Mosk, "An Economist's Point of View," *The American Political Science
Review*, March, 1950, p. 130.
[41] Jose María Samper, *op. cit.*, p. 78.
[42] Mosk, *op. cit.*, p. 130.
[43] *Ibid.*

was still a mixed blood; and the Indian, through chicanery and fraud, lost to white speculators the lands which had been marked for division among the Indians. "The Liberal, individualistic criterion of the Independence created an atmosphere contrary to the survival of the Indian communities. What had survived up to the decline of the Colony, succumbed to the individualistic scope of the Republic."[44]

In much the same manner, too, the industrialization and allied advances of the nineteenth century sharpened, rather than softened, the race-class frictions. Industrialization widened the gap between the rich and the poor. It drew the humble to the cities to work for low wages, and as the agrarian population dwindled, new lands were needed for cultivation, for Colombian coffee was becoming a commodity of world demand. But the many small farmers were not independent yeomen; they were sharecroppers and peasants working for starvation wages; they were tillers of marginal and submarginal tracts so small that they provided at best only a precarious subsistence.

The combining of these factors brought on in Colombia what García Calderón calls the "war of the races." It was not always violent; sometimes it was latent and unseen. But it was always implicit: a basic struggle between the classes of skin colors. "The political conflict might know a change of names, but this antagonism was universal. In the diversity of these quarrels, we see one essential principle: two classes were in conflict ... the proprietors of the *latifundio* and the poverty-stricken people, the Spaniards and the half-breeds, or the oligarchs and the generals of a barbarous society."[45]

No truly revolutionary movement until that of 1948–53 has ever seriously challenged in Colombia this stratification based upon white-wealth and color-poverty factors. "I was born in a middle-class family in Bogotá," writes Germán Arciniegas, "a city where there were no Negro slaves because the climate was too cold for them ... and I remember that there were never fewer than four servants in my house, as well as many peons who cared for the animals and did the chores in the fields. The peons called my father 'my master' and they greeted me as 'my little master.' The women called my mother, and still do, 'Your Grace.' My home was typical."[46]

[44] Guillermo Hernández Rodríguez, *De los Chibchas a la Colonia y a La República* (Bogotá: Universidad Nacional de Colombia, 1949), p. 285.

[45] García Calderón, *op. cit.*, p. 214.

[46] Arciniegas, "What's Behind our Revolution?" *Americas*, p. 42.

It is still typical, though that is changing a little. Colombia's pre-taste of the true social revolution had housewives clucking their tongues over the difficulties they were experiencing with *el servicio*. But the old caste barriers scarcely bent, for the upper classes still cling tenaciously to the old *hidalguismo*, even though their world is vanishing before their eyes. Today, even, the low-caste who becomes rich invests his money in real estate: a country *finca* where he can have a *mayordomo* to boss a corps of peons; land, the mark of the *Gran Señor*, is still a yardstick of prestige.[47]

No matter how hard one tries to avoid it, sooner or later as one studies the Colombian race problem, one must recognize its economic implications. Merely putting on white man's clothing does not make for whiteness. Reichel says, "One must take into account the fact that the term 'Indian' designates a social status, and not an ethnically identifiable biology. An individual with predominantly Caucasian physical characteristics [still] is designated as an 'Indian' if he lives on an aboriginal cultural level, or if he *occupies a low rung on the social scale*."[48]

The mixing of the races in Colombia was not often accompanied by a change in the system of values. Thus, while the trappings of whiteness might be adopted, the mental and social outlook frequently remained Indian. Such contradictions are, of course, a dead weight upon the neck of social integration. But although the "inferior classes" have been a road block in the way of progress, the oligarchies have been too prone to take the easy way out: ignore the masses, or resettle them, or breed them up by mass immigration. Generally, the view is that they are a rather hopeless problem. And so, rather than elevate them—a staggering task, and worse, one that would require a redistribution of the society's wealth—the oligarchies have ordinarily ignored them. By ignoring them, the white elite thus find support for their basic prejudice: the belief that they and they alone are the proper custodians of the political power of the nation.[49]

The critic of this class system must admit that the exploitation of

[47] Olive Holmes, *Latin America, Land of a Golden Legend* (New York: Foreign Policy Association, 1948), p. 20.

[48] Gerardo Reichel Dolmatoff, "El Marco Cultural en el Estudio de la Vivienda," *Economia Colombiana* (Bogotá), June, 1954, p. 311.

[49] Arthur Whitaker, "A Historian's Point of View," *The American Political Science Review*, March, 1950, p. 106.

the mixed blood potential is a difficult task for a not-rich nation. "Whatever attempt to better the Indian sector of the society one makes," says Dr. Juan Comas, "it presupposes measures of great social amplitude, with the consequent political and economic repercussions for the nation. From this comes the difficulty that the solution of the problem faces."[50]

Difficult it may be, but there can be no true national integration until these masses have been given a stake in the society, and this will be extremely difficult to achieve short of forcibly breaking down the resistance of the influential sectors of the society. Legislation which makes deep social reforms costs money, and the upper classes will not voluntarily give up their wealth short of some threat of complete disaster. And the basic fact is that these very classes control politics so completely that they can oppose reform (when left free to act) with all the organized resources of public order. "Many times," says Comas, "these private interests weigh more heavily in politics than do the just demands of the aboriginal sector and its friends and allies; in consequence, the necessary legal steps are not taken, or, if they are, once having been legislated, they are not enforced."[51]

And yet, the race-class-economic gap may very well be the single most important obstacle to national integration in Colombia. It lay at the heart of the violence of recent years, and is the chief dynamic of the social revolution. In a recent book, Alfonso López Michelsen finds that one of the three main factors causing the present disturbed state of the nation is "the conflict between a minority class, economically powerful, which in its refinement *disdains national values and tries to ignore them*, and a people rooted to the land, primitive and violent, which is *searching for a government* which may be its genuine mode of expression."[52]

Rojas Pinilla has the opportunity, has been called on to give, that government. If he does not, nothing is more certain than that the very depth of the urges behind the people's searching will sometime force a solution satisfactory to them.

[50] Juan Comas, "Panorama Continental del Indigenismo," *Panorama* (Washington: Pan American Union) 1954, II, 47.

[51] *Ibid.*, p. 47–55.

[52] Alfonso López Michelsen, *Cuestiones Colombianas*, cited in *Semana* (Bogotá), July 11, 1955, p. 32.

Rojas is aware of this sharp class cleavage, and appears to be thinking of it. After a year in power he said, "The struggle of the classes has been the product of the greed of the very powerful, and of the immoderate ambition of the very weak. The class struggle which makes no sense in a democracy must be opposed by the concurrence of the professional people and the trade unions, within the framework of a Christian application of social justice."[53]

If social justice is Rojas' objective, this may mean something. The problem, however, goes deeper than passing laws or issuing decrees. Class particularism in the upper levels of the society simply assumes that no other class of true humans exists. "The essence of particularism," says Ortega y Gasset, "is that each group ceases to feel itself a part of the whole, and therefore ceases to share the feelings of the rest. The hopes and needs of the others mean nothing to it, and it does nothing to help them win their heart's desire."[54] Ortega could have been writing about the Colombian situation.

There has hardly ever been a practical political admission that both of the two main Colombian classes are members of the same society. Colombians have never coexisted in the sense that they stimulated each other to a conscious recognition of mutual rights and ends. Both political parties have subscribed to the Rights of Man, and then, in the pinch, have treated the vast majority as non-men. This was possible so long as the non-men failed to question the assumption that only the upper classes were men. Now, there is no other way but that, somehow, they forge a common destiny or dig a common grave. "The essential thing is that each should know, and to a certain extent incorporate in his own life, the ideas and desires of the other."[55]

Rojas must manipulate the divisive forces of Hispanic anarchism, forge from Colombian particularism a common social ideal through cooperation, and heal the wounds that have been cut into class-caste sensibilities for over a century. He must effect some redistribution of the society's wealth to bring about the viability which Lleras defines as the "collective way of life." The races, the factions, the classes, the fundamental Hispanic separatism of the people, all work against him.

[53] Rojas Pinilla, quoted in *Economía Colombiana* (Bogotá), June, 1954, p. 258.
[54] Ortega y Gasset, *op. cit.*, p. 36.
[55] *Ibid.*, p. 44.

Recent events demonstrate that the country has not attained the necessary degree of common viability to lift the state of siege. Unfortunately, the efforts of the government have succeeded in imposing public peace, but have not obtained between Colombians a sincere and real viability whose origin is not something other than authentic and autonomous will to concord. The parties, the groups, the factions, continue in the shadows to keep vigil with the arms of hate, which appear to be the only ones which they propose to use in the violent battle for power.[56]

Holding these forces in suspension are Rojas and the Government of the Armed Forces. And the logical and pivotal question arises from this state of suspended animation: "What would happen tomorrow if, as the impatient political leaders of the country desire it, they called us to an election in which there was to be decided, not the people's sympathy regarding power, but the fate of power itself?"[57]

Three per cent of the Colombian people control 97 per cent of the wealth; approximately 25 per cent are white and fairly well off, and the rest are colored and poor in varying degrees.

Very possibly the answer to the question lies in those cold, bare figures.

[56] *Semana* (Bogotá), February 14, 1955, p. 8.
[57] *Ibid.*

XI. The Conflict of Economic Aims: Class Division Rather than Community of Will

THE UPPER CLASSES, WHITE, PRIVILEGED, COMPETENT

The gaps between the classes in Colombia are so great and so rigid that in a time of social ferment violence is always potentially present. Even when social and economic resentments merely simmer below the surface, the stream of national life may give a deceptive appearance of placidity that belies the facts and misleads the observer.

To a very great extent, this is due to the frames of reference created by the upper classes themselves. Colombian upper-class people take their place in society by right of birth. The Great Families are still names to conjure with, and connections with them by marriage, bloodlines, or financial and social ties are both desirable and a kind of *Paz y Salvo* (safe-conduct card) to most areas of preference and privilege.

Due to the centuries-old tradition of caste, those born into the upper classes inherit the unshakable assumption that the lower classes are by nature inferior—they are those who cook, serve, clean, run errands, bow and scrape, and perform the hard and the menial tasks of the society. Moral judgments aside, this is literally true, and therefore, the assumption may be pardoned to a degree, provided that it is not subjected to examination and no one questions why this is so.

There is, actually, nothing necessarily unkind or uncharitable in such an upper-class assumption. It simply has about it the dreadful arbitrariness of a social categorical imperative, whose effects are hardly ever questioned because it is a dogma of group living. Colombian oligarchs are not unkind to the lowly, often are quite the contrary. But they resent the implication that the lowly should enjoy another state than that in which nature has placed them.

Objectively regarded, this attitude is at best socially dangerous in our day; yet there is some logic behind it.

Those who are to the manor born have long held a monopoly on education, wealth, political power, and private and public prestige.

The tradition runs back to the Colony and beyond. Their history, their public philosophy, their prejudices, their experience generally, have affirmed their superiority and their right to direct the society and to manage the destinies of the great mass of poor-colored along with their own. The Colombian Mass Man is not, in fact, as yet a good bet for democracy or a stable factor in the society. Russell Fitzgibbon pinpoints the reality, when he says:

> The Indian's contacts with the white man's government are usually with the police official, the recruiting officer, or the tax collector. None of these persons is the best possible salesman of democracy. It is no coincidence that the Latin American states which we usually assume to be most democratic are those with the largest percentages of European population: Uruguay, Costa Rica, Chile, Argentina.[1]

There is, then, considerable justification for the maintenance of control monopoly by the upper crust of Colombia's social layer cake. But that is not to justify, nor to indicate that the monopoly should be continued indefinitely. The real question, however, arises from the long tradition of the monopoly: how to break it without doing harm to the whole society; how to admit the masses to fuller participation as they impatiently demand a voice in directions.

This dilemma must be resolved in terms of the willingness of the upper class to share power, a willingness so far not demonstrated. Status in society in Colombia has always been determined by birth and by ownership of land. All other norms are unreal and untrustworthy to most Colombians. When the system of encomienda passed, most of the white landowners were able to establish title to land. Usually the lower castes remained with them, as peons, bound by debt or custom or inertia. Some few low-castes became owners of submarginal tracts near the great haciendas, but even in these cases the feudal relationship to the local cacique survived. *has always been*

Thus, from the start, the Colombian upper class was separated from the people: "a small, highly intelligent, white, aristocratic *élite* for whom nothing in the world was too good, and a great mass of humble, poverty-stricken, disease-ridden, uneducated, colored or mixed-blood *campesinos* at the bottom of the scale. As cities have grown, the fact that hundreds of thousands of the most demoralized segments of the

[1] Russell H. Fitzgibbon, "A Political Scientist's Point of View," *The American Political Science Review*, March, 1950, XLIV, No. 1, 124.

lower classes have flocked into them *has not changed the class system.*
It has merely transformed a part of them into an urban proletariat
at the very base of the social scale."[2]

But to say that the upper classes of Colombia are an elite percentage of the population is not to say enough. Basically, the white
Colombian is a Spaniard, with a complex racial heritage, and he is
therefore, a complex personality. Charming and witty, he is skeptical
often to the point of cynicism, capable of extreme violence and frequent cruelty. When he gives friendship, he does so warmly, *con todo
corazón*, and when he is crossed and forms a dislike, he can be a
formidable enemy.

Most of the Colombian upper class are devoted to politics as a way
of life. It is the great *raison d'être*, the *idée maîtresse* of the Colombian's Olympian existence. He has found that in politics there are
answers for his personalist urges, for his innate need for conflict and
opposition, for battle to the death; he has made it the source of his
great victories, and it is the cause of his most depressing spiritual defeats. He is adept, even gifted, at polemics and the high-sounding but
empty phrase. The poetry of his romantic soul finds expression not
only in neat tomes of verse published now and then, but in his tirades
in the public forum (a major speech on foreign policy by Luis López
de Mesa, Colombian foreign minister, in 1941, held the Congress
spellbound by his eulogies of Colombian orchids and the savage
grandeur of the Amazonian jungles, and other travelogue features).
Theories and disputations over abstractions charm him unutterably.
But he is also extremely clear-headed and practical in everyday affairs. This upper-class Colombian has made his mistakes, but he has
also done a first-class job of building the national economy and the
national culture into a respectable edifice worthy of admiration. In
brief, he is quite a fellow. His one blind spot is that he has always
felt that the economy was for *him*; that culture (not necessarily
esthetics) was for his sole consumption.

In questions dealing with social problems, the upper-class Colombian frequently (nay, usually) speaks in terms of polite hyperbole.
Always, he does so in the drawing room, when meeting you on the
street, when writing letters, and in the thousand and one small for-
malities of social intercourse. This charming exaggeration does no

[2] T. Lynn Smith, *Materiales Para el Estudio de la Clase Media en la América
Latina* (Washington: Pan American Union, 1951), p. 4.

harm except that it will cause foreigners to think that the Colombian is insincere. This is a mistake, for he will not hesitate to show his feelings if they turn to dislike.

Generally, he is quick to suspect and to resent comparisons—his pride and egoism again—and any criticism from foreigners, North Americans in particular, will instantly touch a raw, exposed nerve. Chances are that he is more aware of his shortcomings and those of his country than is the foreigner or the critical friend. But he prefers to live with them, or to reflect upon them, or to handle them in his own way. On the other hand, he is quick to criticize others. Generally on the personal level he will use good taste in this, but when it becomes a political matter, he pulls out full stops and uses very available lexicon of disparagement and vilification.

As a young man, this upper-class Colombian was probably educated in a Colombian prep school or university, and later went to the United States or Europe for further study. Very likely he plays polo, or did before easy living made the game too strenuous for both him and the horse. Still, he keeps up an interest in sports, gambles with moderation, holds large quantities of whiskey (Scotch preferred) well, and loves a good story, either from himself or others.

Quite often he is highly literate, having gone through a youthful period of writing doggerel, although now he prefers the stock reports to Valencia or Mistral. Rather earlier than North Americans, he learned about women, and he will maintain an active, practicing interest in them long after he has married the daughter of his father's best friend who, like himself, is of the elite. His interest in politics may take him to Congress or to a cabinet post, or to service on the directorate of his party, even while he heads his own company or runs his coffee business or hovers over his investments. Books and ideas will be a part of his life, running always a little ahead of practical matters, for even in the industrial age, he remains spiritually the child of a race which believes that "*la felicidad se encuentra sobre el lomo de un caballo, entre las páginas de un libro, y en los brazos de una mujer.*" (Happiness is found on the withers of a horse, between the pages of a book, and in the arms of a woman.)

All summaries are oversimplification, and this one does not tell all of the upper classes in Colombia. Perhaps it rather understates the case for the oligarchy: the culture, the industry, the tenaciousness, the vision in certain regards, the true gentility, the many-sided comprehension which marks these upper-class people. But it can never, on the other hand, overstate the case of the mental rigidity of the upper-class social outlook, a rigidity which prevents the development of a truly national outlook for all Colombians.

For, this same high-caste Colombian has tended, and still tends, to worship at the shrine of social immobility through the vertical stratum; to perpetuate a set of values which excludes the great mass of people from participation in the national life; and in this regard, he is both arbitrary and short-sighted.

This class is Rojas Pinilla's most formidable opponent in working for national integration. They have never lost a battle yet; they do not intend to begin losing now.

Russell H. Fitzgibbon says in a few words all that needs to be said regarding the impossibility of democratic cooperation between the classes as they are presently constructed:

It is inevitable that in a land thus divided in so many directions and on so many planes, democracy would find flimsy foundations. Democracy presupposes a tough-minded and tenacious acceptance of the nation as deserving a continuing loyalty which transcends loyalty to class. Democracy assumes that the proper adjustments and accommodations among classes, probably accompanied by vigorous debate and pulling and hauling, will be made peacefully within the framework provided. If loyalty to a class, whether a proletariat in the professional sense or an elite group, supersedes common loyalty ... democracy suffers correspondingly.[3]

The oligarchic political leaders who are presently barred from government in Colombia could do worse than ponder such principles as they skirmish for a return to power.

THE MIDDLE CLASS IS NOT IN THE MIDDLE

The most difficult task in studying the Colombian middle class is to find it.

History, political evolution, and the economic institutions of the nation followed a rhythm far different in Colombia from that in other countries. As a result, the composition, function, and vertical location of the Colombian middle class is entirely different from these indicators in other nations.[4]

Broadly speaking, there is no Colombian middle class such as we know in the United States. When Germán Arciniegas says that he was

[3] Fitzgibbon, *op. cit.*, p. 122.
[4] Smith, *op. cit.*, p. ix.

born in a "middle-class family in Bogotá," and then tells of the number of servants in the household as "typical," he may be believed. But he is not describing an equivalent of the middle class in the United States; rather, something which we would call the upper class.

There are two Departments in Colombia where genuine middle-class elements have developed: Antioquia and Caldas. Both of these regions were settled by the same industrious, business-minded, industrially-gifted "race" of Spaniards. Moreover, they killed off the aborigines, leaving their areas white from the bottom up, and as a result, only whites were available to perform the tasks which ordinarily fall into middle-class activity.[5] The fact that the *Antioquenos* and *Caldenses* went in more heavily for trade, commerce, and manufacturing than for lordly management of great haciendas also tended to bring up something of a middle class: small farm properties, small businesses, small manufacturing enterprises, placed white men between the top and the bottom social-economic rungs of the ladder.

This was the exception. "Elsewhere in Colombia, there continued to be well-defined and widely-separated classes of the elite and the lower orders, with hardly anything deserving of the designation 'middle class' present to help fill the great void between the two."[6]

It is true that the industrializing cities have their share of white-collar workers, public officials, and bureaucrats, and professional men of second category downwards. They are neither upper crust nor proletariat. Even in the large industries there are sons and relatives of the Great Families who are far below the rank of capitalist or enterpreneur. And the legal profession, the teachers, the doctors, the dentists, the accountants, the notaries, the minor government functionaries, would all seem, in strictest theory, to be middle-class people.

Therein lies the trap, the distinguishing characteristics of Colombian society. For a very high percentage of these people are the sons, the grandsons, and the great-grandsons of the people who once perched atop the apex of the social pyramid. Thus, most of the middle class are members of proud old families. They retain the prejudices, the basic beliefs, and the frames of reference of the class from which they are sprung. They try to emulate the mode of living of that class, and set their standards by those of the very top.

It is the rare child of the masses who, with the limited educational

[5] *Ibid.*, p. 9.
[6] *Ibid.*

facilities open to him, can rise above the "ignorant, illiterate, disease-ridden, malnourished, ill-clothed, poorly-housed, poverty-stricken, landless, dissolute mass which constitutes the bulk of the Colombian population."[7] The urge, if there, is killed somewhere along the line by sheer weight of tangible and intangible barriers erected in its way.

✓ This peculiar character of the Colombian middle class arises from the dynamics of social mobility and the birth rate. In the United States, the capitalist-managerial class does not reproduce itself: that is, births are highest on the lowest economic levels. Hence, it becomes necessary to "elevate" from the lower classes enough capable ones to fill the deficit left by the small birth rate among the managing classes.

In Colombia, the process runs contrariwise. Upper-class families have as many children as do the lower, and the survival rate of the well-born is much higher. Thus, there is a gain of whites of the upper classes over the lower ranks, in a percentage sense. The upper class gains on the lower. Moreover, the upper-class Colombian generally leaves a numerous posterity, all to the manor born, all suckled and nurtured on its concepts, standards, and prejudices. Most of them will marry early, and generally they will reproduce by the time they are twenty-five. Frequently, one sire may live to see one hundred of his descendants. The writer has been present at *reuniones de familia* where the numerous *parientes* ran well over two hundred, not counting *primos segundos*.

It is clear, of course, that not all these aristocrats and near-aristocrats can maintain even a precarious footing on the topmost rung of the economic ladder. Fortunes in lands, stocks, and chattels can be divided and subdivided only a limited number of times; *fincas*, so cut up, cease to be productive, and stocks to be worth much. Hence, second, third, and fourth sons, grandsons and great-grandsons, are pushed down the *economic* ladder by the inexorable pressure of mathematics. But as they go, they take with them the rights, perquisites, and prejudices of the top *social* rung, often coupled with a resentment against fate and a longing for their lost birthright.

Such people never can identify themselves with the proletariat, or even with the genuine "bootstrap" middle-class person. On the whole, they are people who feel that they were meant for better things, and they are against any scheme or system or ideology which preaches egalitarianism or leveling, for this denies that they will ever again

[7] *Ibid.*

achieve their lost world. Therefore, they turn to teaching, to the law, to medicine or dentistry, or any other activity which requires wit and intelligence, and in which their "connections" can profit them.

Never, short of complete degeneration, do they turn to the trades or skilled labor. Such work has always been for the peon, the Indian. As Smith points out, this view that work is either dishonorable or ignoble "is the thing which makes it most difficult for them to become full-fledged members of the middle class."[8]

Whatever class consciousness exists among these people is the tendency to identify themselves with the upper classes. They cannot become members of the middle class, because that would require remaking their whole past. As a result, they frequently spend their long, unhappy lives looking for "something good to turn up"—social Micawbers, minus Micawber's basic optimism and social resilience. Their social, economic, and political yearnings, consequently, are those of the elite, and are generally contrary to the objectives of the hungry mixed bloods. "As yet," says Smith,

a genuine middle class is largely lacking in Colombia. The bulk of those who appear at first glance to be middle class people, of those who actually live at a modest, middle class level, are merely the impoverished hangers-on of the old elite. They have not brought themselves to accept middle-class status, nor developed a solidarity of consciousness of kind, with those in a similar position, nor resigned themselves with a good grace to performing the indispensable labor function.[9]

This strange position of the middle class has important political implications. The well-founded assumption that an alert middle class is necessary for the development of democracy is harshly undercut by the true political orientation of the Colombian middle class. It is this class, in fact, which best proves Arthur Whitaker's contention that "it would be a mistake to assume that the Latin American middle classes can be counted upon as champions of democracy under all circumstances."[10] On the contrary, the Colombian middle class has traditionally supported the more Conservative elements who oppose mass demands. It was one of the strongest bulwarks of the Conservative regime of Laureano Gómez.

It is doubtful that the Colombian middle class as a whole, other

[8] *Ibid.*, p. 13.
[9] *Ibid.*, p. 14.
[10] Whitaker, *op. cit.*, p. 115.

than those who rise from the proletariat, will ever be a force to actively support necessary social reforms in the society's institutions. Certainly they will not function to moderate the class-economic conflict of the extremes, which is the central problem. Many of them are in a vise, squeezed between rising living costs for themselves and the costly proletarian demands. And it must be remembered that they have less money to pay for those demands than do the upper classes, to whom they sentimentally and spiritually adhere.

But it may reasonably be expected that if Rojas attempts state redistribution of the wealth by levying most heavily against the rich, the middle class will support him. This would be the preferable alternative to some more violent distribution effected from below. In the case of Colombia the middle class will be found on the side of entrenched wealth and privilege, because the real threat to them lies with the masses.

In short, the Colombian middle class acts neither as a liberalizing nor a stabilizing element in the nation's social struggle. It has gained no political competence of its own, for it has traditionally equated its interests with those of the oligarchy. In a general way, its function has been to sharpen the conflict, by tending to increase the numerical strength of the "enemies" of the masses.

However, in any choice that might be necessary between a popularly elected reformist government, and that of Rojas Pinilla (or, for that matter, if Rojas takes from the rich and passes over the middle class to distribute to the poor), the Colombian middle class, such as it is, would likely support Rojas.

There is nothing more conservative than a poor conservative with hopes of becoming a rich one.

THE URBAN PROLETARIAT

On the anniversary of his rise to power, Rojas Pinilla was hailed by most of the Colombian press. Among them, the official organ of the Comptroller General, *Economia Colombiana*, spoke wise words of advice to the President:

> The political chaos and all its consequences in which Colombia was [before Rojas] struggling was the exclusive result of its economic, social and political system, anachronistic for the period in which we are living ... for whoever wants to see Colombia freed, torn away from the interests who have enslaved the majority of Colombians in the name of political ideals, the masses of our good people

redeemed rather than kept in ignorance and poverty by their leaders, the thirteenth of June must be something more than a simple exchange of power. *It must be a social, political and economic revolution, which re-educates the country in the exercise of politics, implants a social system based on Christian justice, eliminating the class struggle, and establishing economic opportunity for whoever works, thus avoiding the unhuman and unchristian exploitation of the less favored of the society.*[11]

Even if this were no more than mere words, it states the general situation of the masses of Colombian workers and peasants as of the time Rojas took over. His success will be judged by the degree to which he changes this state, or fails to change it, by the time he relinquishes power or is forced to give it up. In the long run, his supreme tribunal will be the "less favored of the society."

The so-called "average man" loses dimension, character, being, when impaled upon the sharp point of statistics and scrutinized as some laboratory specimen. But some additional data about the masses may throw light on the powder keg of social discontent in the nation.

The masses of Colombia have been growing and moving. In sixteen years (1937–53) the population increased by almost 50 per cent, or 2.03 per thousand annually.[12] Average family size was about six persons.[13] In the same period, too, a demographic revolution was taking place, as industrialization drew to the cities a massive migration of depressed agrarians. In 1938, 74 per cent of the population was engaged in agriculture, but by 1949, this percentage had fallen to 60,[14] the remaining 14 per cent having gone to swell the population of the cities. In 1950, the British Board of Trade estimated that the urban growth had far outstripped the rural increase, "three towns in Colombia [having] an annual increase of over 40 per thousand, and seven over 30 per thousand."[15] Bogotá alone almost doubled in size between 1940 and 1954.

/ This demographic transformation was not due alone to the lure of jobs in industry. The civil war which raged in the provinces, the fear of violence, sent hundreds of thousands of refugees fleeing to

[11] "Notas Editoriales," *Economia Colombiana* (Bogotá), June, 1954, p. 245.

[12] *Demographic Yearbook, 1953.*

[13] *Problems of Housing of Local Interest* (Washington: Pan American Union, 1953), p. 24.

[14] *Elementos de Ingreso Nacional . . .*, p. 15.

[15] Scopes, *op. cit.*, p. 37.

the cities for safety. Some observers place the number of such refugees as high as 300,000.[16] Nearly all of these unfortunates remained, swelling the ranks of the urban proletariat, despite government efforts to relocate them in agriculture.

Again, in looking at the actual economic state of the worker, figures blur, distort, hide him. Usually, he appears in official statistics as a percentage-wise participant in the total national income: in 1950, the national income was almost three billion U.S. dollars. This came out to $252.16 per head, or $1,437.31 per family.[17] However, this flawless mathematical exercise fails to show that while the money supply had increased by almost 700 per cent since 1937, the traditional inequality of income and the distribution of wealth remained virtually unchanged. Stated more simply, the average individual and family income was much lower than the per capita distribution figures indicate. In fact, even certain real wage increases failed to change the great gap in wealth distribution.[18] In 1949, the second year of the civil war, the British Embassy in Bogotá reported that "one of the most pressing social questions is that of the increase of the cost of living. On official figures, which certainly do not overestimate the rise which has taken place, the price of 15 selected articles of diet had, by July, 1949, risen 272 per cent since 1935 . . . [and] the general level of wages has not risen proportionately, and the inefficiency of attempted measures of direct control of prices might easily lead to a serious degree of public discontent."[19]

The lot of the Colombian worker has always been one of struggle to make ends meet. In times of inflation, he has often failed to do so. Between 1937 and 1950, there was an over-all rise of 398 in the general cost of living curve, while wages lagged far behind.[20] How did this struggling creature spend his money? Two-thirds for food, one-sixth for shelter, the rest for light and heat, skimpy clothing, and tobacco and drinks. On a statistical basis, the national average (1948–49) gave the individual Colombian 2,280 calories per day, of

[16] Arciniegas, *The State of Latin America*, p. 155.

[17] *Problems of Housing of Local Interest*, p. 53.

[18] Simon G. Hanson, "Latin America and the Point Four Program," *Annals of the American Academy of Social and Political Science*, March, 1950, p. 66.

[19] Scopes, *op. cit.*, p. 35.

[20] *Secretariat Report on Economic Conditions in Latin America* (Washington: Pan American Union, 1950), p. 33.

which 19 per cent was of animal origin. This compares with 3,150 calories and 40 per cent in the United States,[21] and should be qualified by the known fact that the highest contribution to the percentage factor came from the well-fed few, while millions of Colombians consumed far below the national average.

A better index to worker prosperity is the amount of labor expended to earn certain commodities. In late 1946, the Colombian worker labored one and one-half days to buy a shirt, three days to buy a pair of shoes, and one month for a suit of clothes; and at that time, his United States opposite number had the shirt within his grasp in two hours, the shoes in five, and the suit in thirty-seven and one-half hours.[22] Moreover, since two-thirds of his labor was devoted to filling his belly, and this time increased as living costs overtook him, the Colombian worker was destined to give up one or the other: food or clothing. Even if he chose food, as he most certainly did, he was again defeated, for he could purchase only food items too high in carbohydrates (80 per cent)[23] and horribly deficient in proteins. Consequently, his hard labor was to the end of maintaining himself and his family in permanent sub-nutrition,[24] which led to goiter, anemia, scurvy, pellagra, and other ills of malnutrition. In many parts of the country, he was also the victim of rampant venereal disease, tuberculosis, and mosquito-borne fevers. In 1946, 10,000 new cases of tuberculosis were reported by Colombian health officials, and 104,000 old cases were treated; 24,000 cases of syphilis were diagnosed, and 28,000 of other types of venereal disease.[25] How many hundreds of thousands of such cases went unreported is anyone's guess.

What if he were sick and required treatment? In 1952 there were 4,212 physicians and 2,400 dentists in the nation, all priced out of the field for the Mass Man. If his wife had a child, she was attended by a midwife, of which 510 are registered in the country.[26] And,

---

[21] *Statistical Yearbook, 1953.*

[22] Serafino Romualdi, "Labor and Democracy in Latin America," *Foreign Affairs*, April, 1947, p. 478.

[23] Galbraith, *op. cit.*, p. 30.

[24] Moises Poblete Troncoso, *El Stándard de Vida de los Poblaciones de América* (Santiago: Universidad de Chile, 1942), p. 102.

[25] Scopes, *op. cit.*, p. 36.

[26] *Statistical Yearbook, 1953.*

rather than go to a hospital, the average worker had to care for himself as long as he could, and then let nature run its full course. *"No hay mal que dure mil años, ni cuerpo que lo resista"*[27] say the people resignedly, but still hopefully. The proletarian is a Stoic both by nature and force of necessity.

✓The growth of the cities has created critical housing problems. Slums have mushroomed over large areas around most of them. The government has tackled the problem, but bad planning and mismanagement are common. The cities are required to spend a percentage of their income on housing projects, but most Colombian building is of the façade type: public buildings, business houses, parks, country clubs, football stadiums, bull rings, parks, and the luxurious homes of the rich. Nearly every Colombian city appears at first sight bright and shining and modern, with *rascacielos* (skyscrapers) pointing skyward. But on the outskirts are the hovels where the future of Colombia may be decided, "dwellings which lack every amenity and are deplorably unhygienic."[28]

A study of worker community life in the *barrios obreros* of Medellín, made in 1953, discloses the stuff of the social revolution. An excerpt from the study follows:

Barrio Castilla: Situated northeast of Medellín, on sloping ground, where, when it rains, water runs through the streets, making [them] impassable ... somewhat isolated from the city, [its location] has encouraged the neglect which the city *generally shows* for these workers sections ... it is chiefly inhabited by people of scarce economic means, who for the most part are political exiles [of the civil war in the provinces].

Public hygiene, of the streets as well as the houses is deplorable. The only sewers are the very same gutters which are used for washing clothes. Installations of electric current and services are found in some houses; water service in a very few. For transportation, certain buses come to the main street. Service is very slow, due to the bad condition of the road.

Although it [has] very few community resources, one discerns among the people common unrest, and now leaders interested in the general welfare are beginning to stand out.

The outstanding problems include: from the political standpoint, frequent rivalry between the two opposing parties; in municipal administration, the barrio lacks official sanction, and as a consequence has incomplete installation of water, electric power and sewage system. From the medical-hygiene point of view, the

[27] "There is no evil which lasts a thousand years, nor the body which can endure it."

[28] Galbraith, *op. cit.*, p. 32.

outstanding fact is the use of midwives without previous training in maternity cases.[29]

Two other barrios studied were on about the same level. Las Estancias has 6,000 inhabitants, is built on a hillside, without central plaza, on land that "formerly belonged to three wealthy families from the city, who sold it to a gentleman who, in turn, sold unimproved lots to the present proprietors; for this reason it, too, is without official approval."[30]

In existence for thirteen years, its recent growth is due to the migration from the provinces. The people are *personas poco instruidas* (poorly educated people), bitter and resentful. "Among the inhabitants a common vice is to criticize destructively . . . possibly this is due to envy . . . in general, they hope that they will 'be taken care of' without any personal effort, in the way which some of our people have been helped . . . [but] they are of good moral character, and are searching for a healthy organization of the family and the society in which they live."[31]

Barrio Santa Cruz was also typical: 6,500 people living in 650 houses; deficiencies in water and electricity; the people, workers, "very poor"; little effort made to get to know one another, scarcely ever offered to help one another; a barrio of abandoned wives and illigitimate children, which felt no ties to the city as a whole, a feeling of isolation; two primary schools, one kindergarten, and a hygiene center "nearby."[32]

As an average of three barrios studied, the wages of those who worked were three pesos (peso: .40 U.S.), and daily income per family was $3.95 or .65 per capita. Of 118 houses surveyed, 88 were without either light or water, Eighteen had both light and heat, and 12 had water and light. Children formed the bulk of the population, most of whom were under ten years of age.[33] One wonders what these slum-raised children will mean for Colombia's political future.

/ Recent estimates place the number of urban and rural workers in Colombia at six million, which "would indicate that half of the

[29] Caroline F. Ware, *Organización de la Comunidad para el Bienestar Social* (Washington: Pan American Union, 1954), pp. 227–28.

[30] *Ibid.*, p. 228.

[31] *Ibid.*, pp. 228–29.

[32] *Ibid.*, p. 229.

[33] *Ibid.*, p. 228.

population of the country daily creates wealth with its hands, and the other half lives at its expense."[34] This is, of course, an over-simplification, for the "other half" includes private and public employees in service capacities, vagrants, children, unemployables, and those who live solely from income on investments.

Although the worker and peasant are the backbone of the nation's developmental potential, the place of the worker in society has fluctuated widely on his low level.

Throughout the nation's history, the workers and peasants have been not only the theme of speeches and articles, and the object of electoral campaigns and sporadic social reforms, but the target of political violence. On the other hand, not infrequently they have been sought out to fill the ranks of "new" parties, new campaigns, new "movements." When a worker claims his severance pay or goes to the Social Security; when a farm laborer asks the patron to recognize the "improvements" due him, he is unaware of the details of the parliamentary debates and the legal texts which serve as a written base for them. Few people know them.[35]

The Magna Charta of Colombian labor was the Constitutional Reform of 1936 under López, which gave labor the "special protection of the State."[36] It served as the basis for the organization of the CTC, mentioned above, and under the last Liberal regimes, labor flourished to a degree, until the Conservative counterreform began to cut away its position. The onslaughts of organized business and industry made it necessary for President Santos, who certainly was no wild-eyed reformer, to announce in 1940 that social and labor legislation had been placed on the statutes "to stay" and that his administration would enforce labor's rights.[37]

But the Conservative counterreform forced through laws which required an extraordinary number of signatures for labor union petitions to organize. Defeated by the Liberals again in 1938, the provision was voided, and by 1939 there were 82,893 members in 520 unions, of which 425 were of the "craft" type.[38]

Following this beginning, legislation under López in 1940 set up

[34] "Productores de Riqueza," *Semana*, p. 13.
[35] *Ibid.*
[36] Poblete Troncoso, *op. cit.*, p. 17.
[37] Ernesto Galarza, *Labor Trends and Social Welfare in Latin America* (Washington: Pan American Union, 1941), p. 29.
[38] *Ibid.*

special labor courts and established permanent machinery for collective bargaining. In the same years, petitions from the convention of the CTC were indicative of workers' needs: requests for aid in forming producers' cooperatives; educational facilities for the Indians; better enforcement of the right to organize; protection from dismissal for union activities; free medical service; food and rent price control; the six-day week; scholarship opportunities for workers; the eight-hour day in agriculture; the forty-four hour week for women and children.

Most of these gains were later made, only to be invalidated or to remain unenforced under the Conservative regimes that followed Lleras Camargo. Professor Adán Arriaga Andrade, who took part in the period of "flowering" of the labor reform under López, finds that the new era for labor—that of a recapture of the movement by the government—was marked by "codes" which squeezed the organic life from the labor movement.[39] Under the Procedural Code (as we have shown) the Conservative governments approved parallelism, permitting the owners to set up "confessional" and competing unions bound to the bosses, and so to undercut the true labor movement. Furthermore, provision was made for fines and penal punishment for anyone serving as a union director or policy-maker, or as an interpreter of union laws, other than as authorized under the Conservative reforms, a harsh blow at radicals and "red labor agitators." It was frank, open, government-sponsored union-busting: "In the budgets of business concerns a mathematical reserve is set aside for breaking unions or getting rid of leaders who are too combative."[40]

At present, the status of labor has again shifted, with certain unions still trying to organize organically, others staying with the companies, and still others groping for some sort of a labor front to support Rojas. In general, the Colombian labor movement is disorganized and demoralized, not yet having recovered from the shock of the Conservative attack, and still basically uncertain of what form it should take vis-à-vis the Government of the Armed Forces.

There is a social security system for workers, but only recently has the government considered extending it to agrarian laborers. The law provides for disability, old age, and death benefits, with annual contributions of salary totaling 8 per cent. Of this, the worker

---

[39] Arriaga Andrade, cited in *Semana*, p. 14.
[40] *Ibid.*

and the state each contribute 2 per cent, and the employer, 4 per cent.[41] It is a beginning, but is obviously without much meaning until the notoriously low wages are raised to a decent level. The basic law for social security (passed by Ospina as a crisis move just before the violence erupted), says one writer, "is full of faults because basically it establishes a typical system of industrial security." Hence, it is limited to industry and urban populations, and the quality and costs of the service, as well as the means of financing it, are beyond the reach of the great mass of casual workers, peasants, and the very needy, low-class common laborer of the nation.[42]

In general, the condition of the urban proletariat is one of explosive potentials. Attempts to better it have been sporadic, half-hearted, and marked by reluctance to face the issue of making the worker also a consumer. Present wage levels leave workers not much better than half-starved, underpaid producers of wealth for a small percentage of the population. As of 1947, "the *lowest* income group, which comprised seven-eighths of those with some income, obtained less than 60 per cent of the total income, while at the other extreme, less than 1/40 of those with income accounted for almost 30 per cent of the total. In other words, about 90 per cent with income received less than an average of 1,073 [pesos], while 2.5 per cent had incomes on an average ten times greater than the general average."[43]

The weaknesses of such a system are obvious. The roots of most of Colombia's troubles are economic, but the effects are primarily psychological and political as regards the mass of the people. For, it is from this unfortunate complex of economic inequalities that there arises the organic structure of the worker's family, the level of popular morality, the use of alcohol as a palliative, and the generally degenerative psychology of the working classes. A Colombian sociologist, writing shortly after the outbreak in April, 1948, pointed out that the rise in crimes against persons and property, the increase in prostitution, alcoholism, and gambling immediately before the revolution, had their roots in hunger, want, and defeat. "The principal cause of delinquency in Colombia," declared Dr. Humberto

[41] *Problems of Housing of Social Interest,* pp. 66–67.

[42] Aurelio Caycedo Ayerbe, "El Problema de la Seguridad Social," *Economía Colombiana* (Bogotá), November, 1954, p. 12.

[43] "Las Escuelas Industriales y Artesanales Como Factor del Desarollo Económico del País," *Economía Colombiana* (Bogotá), September, 1954, p. 255.

Carrasquilla, "is an economic cause; that is to say, a tremendous social inequality which causes citizens to lose moral perspective and ethical frames of reference."[44] The remedy: attack the high cost of living, unemployment, and depression, and so raise the general cultural level.

Rojas Pinilla's problems in the field of labor are great and many. The masses of workers must somehow be incorporated into the national life more fully, made part of the national drives, given a share in the social myth of the present and the future. But this means, essentially, that they, too, must be turned into *consumers,* productive citizens with a stake in society. In the meantime, they must have a backstop: a social structure in which permanent social values are being created on the basis of minimum standards of nourishment, better social security for all, regular employment, and better wages and living quarters.[45]

Rojas Pinilla will be opposed every step of the way along this route, even if he does not become discouraged and abandon it. The sheer bulk of accumulated opposition forms a tradition that must be reversed: "Power has always been in the hands of a Conservative class which has taken the names of 'Conservatism' and 'Liberalism' to identify themselves in some fashion in the struggle for the budgetary loot. In the beginning, the method of rotation was by civil wars. Later, this costly process was replaced by the voting booth."[46]

Antonio García's summation of the general tradition squares with most of the facts. But the masses are expecting, and will sooner or later demand, a better deal. There is a power in them that comes from knowing the smell, the feel, the taste, of poverty. They will give Rojas his chance, but if he fails them—

The upper classes say: "the workers and peasants." The official bulletins speak of the "working people." The politicians cry heart-rendingly, "the masses!" And the worker and the farm hand smile thinly. They smile with something of what a leader would call "native cunning" [*malicia indigena*]. For they have been learning as they go along, through successive disappointments, that only very rarely can *words* be seen and touched.[47]

[44] Humberto Carrasquilla, "Causa Especial del Delito es la Desigualdad Social del Pueblo," *Heraldo de Antioquia,* (Medellín), June 19, 1948, p. 1.

[45] *Habitaciones Obreras y Cooperativas de Vivenda* (Washington: Pan American Union, 1952), p. 4.

[46] García, *Gaitán* . . . , p. 35.

[47] "Productores de Riqueza," *Semana,* p. 13.

Until the status of the Colombian worker is basically changed, any appearance of national unity, peace, cohesion, or stability will be merely a façade thrown up to cover some oligarchy's weaknesses. The fundamental view of the upper classes must undergo appreciable change, for they "have not held, through their history, any marked affection for the working classes; they are scarcely remembered at election time, when their vote is necessary to support the existing order. That has been the tragedy of the Colombian proletariat. It is true that social laws protecting them have existed since 1915, but they have always been no more than simple palliatives."[48]

And so, despite laws and regulations, the state of the Colombian masses remains a deplorable one. Nor is it because of simple uncaring neglect. There is a positive principle of submergence at work: "The Colombian people is demoralized by those above them on all levels and in all hierarchies . . . the proofs are clear: there is the ninth of April, 1948."[49] And yet, the people of Colombia, fragmented organically, economically exploited, and socially outcast, are not beaten: "Everything in Colombia indicates that the working people are ravenously hungry for the social and economic betterment which has been awakened in them by the constant impact of new social doctrines . . . in this state of indigence of the workers, when they are gorged with ideas of progress . . . the situation is critical and indicates that a fundamental change in social policy must take place."[50]

The parties refused to make that change at the time when it was most urgently needed. Largely for that reason, Rojas Pinilla came to power.

If he cannot make it, there will be no justification for his regime, and his contribution will be only another failure of a Colombian government to answer modern demands.

But the need for the change will go on, and until it is answered, by some government, the social revolution will hang like a sword of Damocles over the orderly existence of the nation.

[48] Londoño, *op. cit.*, p. 115.
[49] *Ibid.*, p. 117.
[50] *Ibid.*, p. 119.

XII. The Land Problem: The Too Small Farmer

It has long been generally believed that the numerous small proprietors of land are a force working toward democracy in Colombia; that, contrary to most Latin-American nations, the curse of the *latifundio* does not plague Colombian society.

"Contrary to general opinion," says Romoli, "Colombia is not parceled out in vast estates that cover all arable land and exclude the possibility of small holdings."[1] And Duggan has the comforting reassurance, "In Colombia [these] small farmers are in the majority. Elsewhere, the great bulk are landless peons or rural workers."[2]

The inference to be drawn from these genial misconceptions is that the state of the Colombian peon and *campesino* is just the contrary of those where the *latifundio* prevails.

Small proprietors do indeed own much of the Colombian land. Although many properties are great *fincas* and ranches, the typical farm unit is between four and five acres.[3] Coffee-growing itself is mostly in the hands of small farmers, 87 per cent of the *cafetales* having less than 5,000 trees, and the average running about 3,000. Thus, for what comfort it will give, Colombia *is* a land of small farmers. The total number of proprietors possibly goes as high as 700,000.

But mere parceling of land overlooks location, size, and fertility, as well as general productive capacity relative to farming methods. On this basis, Colombia's land tenure system has created as many evils as any in Latin America. It has been, and still is, a main source of social and political discontent. From it stem the evil of the *minifundio,* or too small tract, a grinding system of peonage, and a basic inequity in property that periodically brings the discontented *campesino* up in arms against the public authority.

Over the years, the farm laborer and, to a lesser extent, the small

---

[1] Romoli, *op. cit.*, p. 33.
[2] Laurence Duggan, *The Americas* (New York: Henry Holt & Co., Inc., 1949), p. 24.
[3] Galbraith, *op. cit.*, p. 87.

farmer, has become increasingly disenchanted with his lot. Although not bound to the land, except by debt where peonage is rife, the peasant looks more and more to the city for a betterment of his economic status. In his study of the *minifundio*, Luis Duque Gómez says "the best fitted [peasants] almost always abandon farm life to go on to the urban centers in search of greater prospects and an easier life."[4]

Nor is it strange that he should do so. "The farm laborer, who devotes one day a week to his own plot, one (Sunday) to a trip to the nearest market, and one to recuperation from the exhausting joys of the Sabbath, makes little enough in cash. His chief purchases are meat, panela, and *miel* (molasses). The last two serve principally for making chicha and *aguardiente*, the crude liquors with which he and his defeats fatigue, illness and the infinite weariness of a life without horizons. Most of his provender comes from the garden.... His house, such as it is, cost him nothing; and he has no expenses for light, gas, heat and water, because for him these services are nonexistent."[5]

Hardly ever does the peasant get his hands on hard money in any reasonably useful amount. Between 1936 and 1940, farm labor earned on an average forty centavos to one peso per day (the peso: .57 U.S.). In some cases the rate was higher, provided the worker furnished his own meals.[6] At this same time, the government made feeble efforts to improve peasant housing, but the root of the matter—wages—was left untouched. Small loans were made available for lower class agrarians in 1939, but the Territorial Credit Institute usually saw to it that loans were granted to those who already had some property and collateral. Consequently, the major problem went untouched, except for the government's efforts to "induce" employers on the great estates to "require" better housing for their employees.[7] Under such circumstances, the lure of the city for the peasant and farm laborer is understandable.

But not even the lives of the small farmers of Colombia are enviable by the most minimal standards. A good picture of typical con-

[4] Luis Duque Gómez, "Los Problemas del Minifundio en Colombia," *Economía Colombiana* (Bogotá), January, 1955, p. 577.

[5] Romoli, *op. cit.*, p. 33.

[6] Poblete Troncoso, *op. cit.*, p. 30.

[7] Galarza, *op. cit.*, p. 30.

ditions is drawn in the study of Tabio, made by the Department of Agriculture, Washington, in 1945.

In Tabio, an area of about twenty-nine square miles, the land was mostly level, only about one-fourth being located on the mountain slopes—an exception to the average small farming community. About half of the population was farm laborers, there were a few large landowners, and the rest were small proprietors. *Half of the land was controlled by 3 per cent of the population.* Labor was predominantly carried on by hand, the standard of living was very low, and most of the produce was consumed locally.

"The typical house in Tabio," says the report, "is a two or three room affair of wattle and daub, covered with thatch. Its floor is of bare earth, and there were either no windows or merely openings with shutters, and the house is without ceiling. The average home's furnishings and conveniences do not include electricity, running water or any sanitary equipment."[8]

In such places, the stove was ordinarily three stones on the floor, or a pipeless brick stove covered with galvanized tin. Four, five, even six people live in each room, and sanitary conditions are as bad as might be expected. Socially, the family life is no unifying factor. Three-fourths of the families were without a man at their head, many were under some abandoned married woman, one-sixth were broken by the death of a parent, and one-fifth were informal arrangements headed by a married man or woman.[9]

There were rudimentary schools in the area, but no agricultural instruction for the youths. Many of the girls of all families left as soon as they could, to seek domestic service in Bogotá. Neither the land, nor the family, nor the conditions of life was a source of satisfaction for the needs of most people in this typical community.

Conditions somewhat better were found in a study of agricultural communities in the Magdalena River Valley, made by the Currie Mission for the International Bank.[10] In this area, annual income for a family of six averaged about 1,200 pesos (peso: .48 U.S.), but almost all of it was used in purchasing food, beverages, and liquor. Housing was of bamboo and mud, with thatched palm leaf roof.

[8] T. Lynn Smith, *Tabio, a Study of Rural Organization* (Washington: U.S. Department of Agriculture, 1945), p. 31.

[9] *Ibid.*, p. 33.

[10] *Basis of a Development Program for Colombia,* pp. 8 ff.

Colombia's land problem centers around the *minifundio*, or too small farm. However, there are some large farms, particularly those which produce sugar cane and rice (pictured here), where farming methods are efficient and high labor productivity has been gained through use of mechanized equipment.

Houses contained no chairs, and beds were a rarity, most people sleeping on mats or blankets on the floor. When water was needed, it was carried from the river. For toilet installations, there was usually a wash basin. Privies were inadequate, but the fields wide. This study found a diet somewhat better than that of the peasant in other parts of Colombia since meat was available at low price; still it was considered inadequate. In general, existence was a precarious matter. Most workers lived so close to the margin of subsistence that illness, accident, deaths in the family, or unemployment were disastrous events, which would plunge the family into debt from which they hardly ever recovered. Only the unusually gifted individual, the person with foresight and determination, could hope to rise above such conditions, the Mission concluded.

"At this level," says the report, "the rungs of the economic ladder are widely spaced and difficult to scale. From our observation, the conditions of the small freeholders and tenants in this area do not differ significantly from those of the worker."

The tragedy of this, for the nation, lies in the fact that the peasant is still the base of the economy, and the disregard which has been accorded him and his problems is the real cause for much of Colombia's turbulent history. Arturo Botero Arias, writing in *El Colombiano* of Medellín, hits at the heart of this paradox:

> The existence of the Colombian peasant is a drama which causes one to flinch at its prospect. Illness, the anarchy of the tropics, usury, impassable roads, buyers' monopolies, the worst of the bandits who rob and burn and kill, artificial urbanism . . . costly and devouring . . . the quarter-share which the hoe and harrow yield him . . . all these daily assail the peasant, impoverish, weaken and defeat him. Nonetheless, his labors have paid for the importation of a material culture which is very superior to the requirements of our environment, our history and economy. The Columbian peasant does not go to movies, doesn't walk on asphalt streets, wears no Manchester cloth, but he pays for the excesses and mistakes of a minority which has forgotten the austerity of life and its sense of proportion.[11]

The Colombian peasant, for all these reasons, remains back in the dark shadows of the national life. The directors of the society want him there; but they frequently forget that he is all the more susceptible to any light that may come his way. For when it does light up his drab existence, it comes not as a beacon, but as a bursting conflagration. Therefore, he is dangerous.

[11] Arturo Botero Árias, cited by Londoño, *op. cit.*, pp. 108-9.

There are, of course, special aspects of the land problem which set the small landholder and the tenant apart from the laborer, even though their basic social and political problems are similar. For, if the farm laborer flirts with starvation as a paid hand, the small freeholder well knows that same grim lady, even though his want be dignified by a title to a plot of earth.

The present land tenure system in Colombia is a direct heritage of Spanish colonial land policy. From the latter stems not only the problem of the too small farmer, but also the thoughtless treatment of the native population, the extensive system of tenancy and share-cropping, and even the reluctance of the Republic to change fundamentally the system which provided, and still provides, a cheap supply of low-class agrarian laborers.

The effect of the encomienda system was to transfer the Indians to the Spanish overlords along with the land, much in the nature of other permanent fixtures. Thus, they became chattels, serfs, workers owing the *patron* their toil and sweat. Worsening the system, there was the practice of giving "free hands" to the labor of Church lands, which eventually grew into a permanent system of labor tribute due the Church. Another onerous burden was added to the crushing load borne by the indigenous labor forces when the *mito* was resorted to in order to recruit slaves, servants, and workers for the mines. At the top of the system, of course, sat the Spanish or Creole overlord, supported by the labor of men half-free.

Contrary to popular belief, the system was not radically changed by the Independence. The Republic replaced the Colony, and that was about the extent of it. As Luis Emiro Valencia says, "economically, there was a change of masters, but not of system," so far as the masses of people were concerned.[12] Under the colonial regime Creole groups and classes had developed along lines that made a relatively few families and oligarchies all-powerful when the Colony came to an end. But the indigenous casts had not supported the revolution of the upper-class Creoles against the Crown, which had occasionally intervened in their behalf with the rulers of the Colony.[13] Consequently, Bolívar's act of turning back to the Indians their "reserves" following Independence stood as a challenge to the land-hungry,

[12] Valencia, *op. cit.*, p. 295.
[13] Hernández Rodríguez, *op. cit.*, p. 284.

the avaricious, the patriot who felt that the Indian deserved little or nothing from the revolution.

The decree which gave lands back to the Indians provided that the land should be parceled according to the size of each family.[14] It was intended to make it easy for the Indian to become a republican proprietor. But the politicians had other ideas. Soon it became necessary to pass laws to require the Indian to hold on to his lands, to not sell to the white man for a figurative bottle of rum. Hundreds, thousands, knowing nothing of the law and little of economics, sold their properties for next to nothing. Then, landless and rootless, they manned, and their lands were integrated into, the great *latifundios* of the white men. "[Those who lost them] in the economic struggle [were] dispossessed of the land which was the cement of their ephemeral liberty, and they chose the way of the paid laborer, while others returned to the land as sharecroppers."[15] So was the colonial system perpetuated under the Republic: the oligarchy got the land, the Indian and mestizo became laboring peons or tenants, and nothing had changed but a flimsy legal status. "The Republic did not fundamentally change agrarian policy."[16]

There were still other devices employed by the upper class to get their hands on the land and turn it into haciendas and *latifundios*. Indian lands were parceled in the form of many small tracts, so that there would be an active market for competing buyers. Maps in existence today of Indian lands which were parceled in the Department of Cundinamarca indicate that many of the old Indian reserves are now covered by "great *latifundios* and haciendas of considerable importance."[17]

One of the most common practices of defrauding the peasant was that of buying title to the lands of the reserves before they were parceled out. This practice became very common after 1850. Ignorant peasants, bewildered by the legal red tape and the conflicts of title under the Civil Code, often sold their tracts for a "few centavos." Since the laws on title to real estate were purposely made "very

[14] *Ibid.*, p. 286.
[15] *Ibid.*, p. 292.
[16] *Ibid.*, p. 293.
[17] Diego Mendoza Pérez, *Ensayo Sobre la Evolución de la Propiedad Privada en Colombia* (Bogotá, 1897), p. 93.

complicated," the peasant, when he saw his title challenged by one who claimed anterior rights, simply gave up, for he had neither the money nor the intelligence to effectively support his claim. Hence, "it happens that with only a few pesos, one may acquire great holdings of land."[18]

The Church, too, had gotten title to extensive lands under the Colony. In theory, this was changed with Independence, but in fact the matter was scarcely touched until the Mosquera administration of 1861. Mosquera's reform of the *Manos muertas* expropriated lands held by civil and ecclesiastical bodies which were "out of the commercial current and held by entities of perpetual existence."[19] The intent was to parcel out lands of the Church and the absentee corporate owners in order to bring unproductive land into some social use. But here again, the oligarchy defeated the social ends. "The radical businessmen bought up the Church haciendas with depreciated public bonds. Neither the peons, nor the renters, nor the poor peasants participated in this quartering of the lands of the Church, because the haciendas were sold in blocks, and on cash-on-the-barrel-head terms."[20] The net effect of Mosquera's "liberal" reform, then, was to create a new landed aristocracy of radical businessmen who had pledged allegiance to the ideas of the French Revolution of 1848.

Contributing to this lodgment of land in already rich hands, the practice of granting large estates to the *beneméritos* (well-deserving) who had served the Republic in the civil wars created many large landholders. Much public land was also alienated to pay foreign debts. Another thriving practice was to include in the patrimony of deceased citizens of towns or villages title to public lands or commons of the municipality. This type of official connivance, the difficulty of disproving title once granted, outright fraud, and legislative spoilation of Indian properties, all tended to build up substantial estates at the expense of the public and the lower classes. (It was by no means accidental that the many Indian "reserves" were expressly located adjacent to the great haciendas of important men.)

There has, of course, been a substantial countercurrent to this trend running through Colombia's history. Peasant agitation, the

---

[18] *Ibid.*
[19] Hernández Rodríguez, *op. cit.*, p. 294.
[20] García, *Gaitán . . .*, p. 63.

urging of liberals, and the prodding of intellectuals have given rise
to a series of steps in the direction of agrarian reform. Unfortunately,
most of them have been no more effective than the reform of the
Manos muertas of 1861.

In 1874 a law was passed which provided for squatters rights to
any cultivated land, together with thirty hectares adjacent, after
five years of uninterrupted tenancy. It was out of this law that there
arose the pleasing fiction that Colombia was a nation of small farmers.
However, the fact is that the successful claims staked under it were
largely on "expendable" land: areas on the mountain slopes, on the
rough, rocky, hard-scrabble fringes of the great haciendas, and on
the marginal and submarginal lands near the towns and cities or
at the very edge of the forests. This is, unfortunately, the essence of
the tenancy of the Colombian yeomanry.

By López' Law 200 of 1936, squatting was permitted on the great
estates themselves. However, it was made subject to a difficult procedure of eviction which backfired in favor of the landowners.
Minimal improvements were supposed to vest title in the squatter,
but this hazy title ran into conflict with the Civil Code which vests
title in the person having written and notarized deeds to the land.
Courts tended to respect the longstanding Civil Code, and since the
legal conflict was not clarified by the law, its effect in the long run
was to "foment a flood of lawsuits and controversies which did the
farmers no good whatever, and by reason of which the nation has
[but] few more proprietors."[21]

The "reform" of 1944, known as Law 100, had counter-productive
effects regarding land distribution. Some observers, in fact, believe
that it was only intended to increase agricultural production, and
not to create more proprietors. As interpreted by the courts, conflicts between sharecropper, parcel cultivator, and proprietor or
owner were always to be decided in favor of the landed party.[22]
The strong presumption of right on the owner's side, as Valencia says,
"permitted abusive use of the land by the large landholder."[23]

After the violence of 1948 broke out, President Ospina Pérez
adopted a land parceling policy through the Department of Parceling and Colonization. The purpose was to extend credit to farm

[21] Londoño, *op. cit.*, pp. 158–59.
[22] Valencia, *op. cit.*, p. 298.
[23] *Ibid.*

families without land, or with too little.[24] The government engaged to buy certain large farms for distribution to the peasants, or to facilitate their settlement on public lands. But no provision was made for the already penniless *campesino* who could provide no collateral whatever. Therefore, the law was only a palliative, operating essentially for the benefit of those who already had something in the way of tools, goods, money, and minimal collateral. It left "the *campesino* like an island within a capitalist market."[25]

An important study of the Colombian land problem by Eduardo Jiménez Neira finds that a major evil of the system is a national underproduction which makes necessary the importation of food. Civil war uprooted the peasant and drove him to the cities in a mass emigration sparked by fear and panic. Consequently, any reforms in the so-called "land revolution" are at best a paper revolution, for production ends were defeated. The decrees and laws, begun by López and continued by Ospina after panic struck the government, have operated to favor the *latifundio,* and leave vast areas untouched. They give the *parcelero* (parcel owner) no real protection, and have done practically nothing for the peon and the simple farm laborer. "In fact," says Jiménez,

the "Land Law" only served to consolidate the position of the landholders, to provide them with legal instruments against settlers and cultivators without title. The only provision of real interest, to bring about the transformation of a feudal economy to a social one, was suspended. Article 6 of the law, which established "the extinction of the right of dominium or property over rural lands on which possession might cease to be exercised for ten consecutive years" was suspended. The conservative mentality of the Great Fortunes which direct the country could not permit this constitutional provision to take a course contrary to their personal interests. With things thus, *the uncultivated large holding continues to be a reality, while the nation needs more production, and while there exists an absurd number of peasants without land.*[26]

In all probability the law, if enforced honestly for the purpose for which it was originally intended, would solve many phases of the problem. There are certainly a number of landowners who would sell land to the government near the cities, where cultivation would be most beneficial. But demagoguery, traditional thinking,

[24] *Basis of a Development Program for Colombia,* p. 64.

[25] Duque Gómez, *op. cit.,* p. 298.

[26] Eduardo Jiménez Neira, "Bases Para una Tecnificación de la Agricultura," *Economía Colombiana* (Bogotá), September, 1954, p. 290.

class-slanted judicial decisions, and a certain degree of land speculation in hope of future sales to the government have all militated against its effective enforcement.[27] "Our contracts of parceling," says Samuel Hoyos Arango,

totally disappeared. There ensued a battle to the death between the hacienda owner and the agrarian worker; the houses of foremen and of peasant families were destroyed by the owners for fear of permanent occupation by "squatters"; the worker who considered himself an owner by right of improvements made, expelled from the land the rightful owner and proprietor, or the latter expelled the former for fear of permanent occupation. Rather than being collaborators toward a common end, rather than complementary forces, they became antagonistic forces. The nomadic worker replaced the permanent worker, and temporary encampments took the place of farm family abodes.[28]

There is ample evidence, therefore, that the mere existence of many small farms is no guarantee either of social justice or high agricultural production. On the contrary, the chief characteristic of the Colombian system is the fact that these small, unproductive farms are a deterrent to a decent national productive level, and that they exist side by side with the great *latifundio* and the important *fincas*, which still dominate the agricultural picture. The best land is held by the biggest owners; and most of the settlement of agrarians and colonizers has taken place in remote areas, far from markets, or on unproductive lands.

Essentially, the mere number of small holdings is, therefore, a false criterion. There is considerable reason to believe that the large number of small tracts in Colombia produces merely a multiplication of misery, inefficiency, and unproductiveness. For there, as in "many Latin American countries, *minifundios* [small holdings] abound, agricultural developments of reduced size, while simultaneously there are properties which include great areas [*latifundios*]. Properties of medium size are few as to be not important. In these countries, the ... great number of small holdings is not due to the scarcity of land ... the problem is due in part to the unequal distribution of the land, and in part to lack of colonization programs."[29]

The best historical study of the development of the Colombian

[27] Samuel Hoyos Arango, "Parcelación y Crédito Agrícola," *Economía Colombiana* (Bogotá), November, 1954, p. 105.

[28] *Ibid.*

[29] *Progresos en Materia de Reforma Agraria* (New York: United Nations, 1954), pp. 221–22.

land tenure system has been made by Professor Guillermo Hernández Rodríguez, of the National University of Colombia. On this matter of the small parcel as a predominating type, he says, "One must distinguish between the numerical majority of units and the general economic importance."[30] In a detailed study of 12,693 properties in ten municipalities (roughly, counties) of the Andean section of Colombia, Hernández found that 4,038 were valued at only between 100 and 300 pesos. On the other hand, 3,732 of the total were worth between 300 and 1,000 pesos, and 1,582 ranged from 1,000 to 5,000 pesos in value. Counting 2,406 tracts which ranged from no value up to 100 pesos, this added up to more than 11,000 of the 12,693 small farms ranging downward in value from 5,000 pesos to nothing.

But, and this is the significant fact, 105 tracts were valued between 25,000 and 50,000 pesos; 47 up to 100,000; 30 between 100,000 and 250,000 pesos; and 7 were worth more than a quarter of a million pesos.[31]

Stated otherwise: 96 per cent of the 12,693 properties were small and worth less than 5,000 pesos; the 96 per cent of the *units* accounted for only 27 per cent of the *total value*; and 1½ per cent of the *units* represented 52 per cent of the value of them all.

Professor Hernández reaches a conclusion that slays definitively the comforting fiction that Colombia's small farms are a factor producing stability, democracy, and contentment: the holdings between 25,000 and 250,000 pesos in value *"constitute the predominant type in Colombian agriculture, because they represent more than half the value of rural property, and value logically expresses location, extent and size, and the quality of the land."*[32]

The hard fact, the core of the trouble, is that Colombia is a land of too small farmers: too small for their own, the nation's, or the social, good.

The problem of the *minifundio* lies at the heart of much social discontent in Colombia, and production-wise is the major cause for high costs of living. The land is simply not producing enough for the people, and it is failing because the small tract is not capable of giving back more than a mere subsistence to those who till it.

[30] Hernández Rodríguez, *op. cit.*, p. 296.
[31] *Ibid.*, p. 297.
[32] *Ibid.*

This conclusion is borne out by a study recently undertaken by the Colombian Ministry of Labor. Headed by Dr. Luis Duque Gómez, the problem of the *minifundio* was studied exhaustively, using the *Municipio de Manta,* in the Department of Cundinamarca, as a typical case.

In Manta, land had been subdivided into so many parcels that its utilization was uneconomical. Properties of more than two hectares (2.47 acres per hectare) comprised only *17 per cent* of the land. A shocking 71.6 of the parcels contained *under* two hectares. Such tracts, even when intensively cultivated, could produce little more than meager subsistence for the tenants or owners. But the story gets worse: of those of less than two hectares, *43 per cent were of less than one hectare, 30 per cent were less than one-half hectare, and a miserable 6.12 per cent were less than one-eighth of a hectare in size—scarcely more than overgrown garden plots.*[33]

Dr. Duque Gómez has an interesting comment upon these diminutive parcels of land:

> It was not at all rare to find parcels whose area varied between one-eighth and one-twentieth of a hectare, on which, as on the others, there gravitates the principal economic base of a *peasant family which has an average of seven members,* whose subsistence is derived in great part from agricultural activity, in a primitive system of exploitation of the earth, sustained by the hand sower and the wooden plow.[34]

As one would expect, the health of the people of Manta was found to be very poor, and the diet extremely deficient. For the most part, they lived off the land, but what could not be raised had to be bought. A survey of fifty families showed that rarely did the head of a family spend more than fifty pesos a week for a family of seven, and the average was twenty-four pesos (peso: currently .26 U.S.). Usually, all members of the family worked as farm laborers when the large haciendas needed hands.

The result of short crops and scarce cash created what Dr. Duque calls the Fair of Hunger, whereby an unreal surplus of goods appears at the local markets for sale, despite the hunger of the seller:

> Many of the heads of working families barter with eggs, milk, meat, rice, wheat, fowl, etc., for clothing, for the services of a dentist, for the prescription of a

[33] Duque Gómez, *op. cit.,* pp. 577 ff.
[34] *Ibid.,* p. 580.

quack, for the drug which alleviates pain, when he does not turn to the liquor for which he pays the State, and which gives him a moment of forgetfulness in this painful and sterile battle for existence.[35]

This "small farmer," then, lives a life of robbing Peter to pay Paul. And when he awakens and tries to increase production, turning to the official credit sources, he again faces frustration. Applications are surrounded with red tape, long in processing, and they require lengthy inventories and the assignment of farm animals to the state as collateral. And so, in desperation, the *campesino* turns to the private loan sharks, who charge usurious rates up to 24 per cent per annum for twelve months. Nor have the higher wages in the cities helped the peasant. "The rural worker is the last to derive some benefit from higher day wages, the payment of some improvement, or even a better market for his so-called 'surplus' products . . . rural wealth has been exploited directly by agents from the city, doing nothing for local welfare, and taking a final flight towards the centers of capital and derived profits."[36]

Although one might expect a somewhat better situation among the small coffee planters, the backbone of Colombia's coffee industry, a study recently made by Dr. Ernesto Guhl proves otherwise. Between 1932 and 1940, the number of small coffee holdings in the Department of Cundinamarca increased from 13,812 to 30,270. This was as the result of a few additional lands put under cultivation, but basically it represented an aggregate halving of the tracts themselves. Yet, despite the increased number of properties, total coffee production increased but slightly, and that was probably due to strong world coffee prices.[37] Among the coffee growers, health, social security, housing, and diet conditions were found to be deplorable. Guhl concludes that any program of agrarian reform must include health and education measures, to interest the peasant and the small freeholder in his role. "With workers lacking a healthy and progressive set of aspirations, and having a world of dire necessities and a very low standard of living, no region, wherever it may be, could be converted into an

---

[35] *Ibid.*, p. 591.

[36] *Ibid.*, p. 582.

[37] Ernesto Guhl, "Seguridad Social Campesina," *Economía Colombiana* (Bogotá), November, 1954, p. 21.

economically prosperous area. The worker should produce, but he should also consume."[38]

Most of these data have referred to the small freeholder, the favored class of the humble agriculturalists of Colombia. Impossible as it may seem, the situation of the peon and the sharecropper is even worse. These less favored groups spend their lives locked in mortal combat with poverty, and in the end are defeated and die without realizing their humble dream of someday owning a piece of sterile earth of their own, in order to continue cultivating crops—and poverty—as *terratenientes* (landowners).[39]

Sharecropping and tenancy are found at their worst in the great tobacco-growing areas of Colombia. By far and away the vast majority of growers in the northern regions of the Departments of the Santanders are families who have no land of their own. When they have cash, they rent a small parcel, or take it on shares, under a system which, says *Semana*, "is a colonial system of exploitation of the land, nourished by the necessity of landless people for work and land, of people born and raised in the country."[40]

As the system presently operates, the landowner turns over to the family or a group of families very limited tracts for them to work, the product to be shared by the owner and the tenant. By means of a verbal contract, and depending upon the amount of cash which the proprietor wants to invest, the tenant returns a half, a third, a fourth, or a fifth of the harvest. In any case the owner receives an excellent profit without worry or care or management duties. His labor force is always there, caring for the crop. It is an investor's dream: maximum return, with minimum work and investment.

The sharecropper and his family, on the other hand, work from sunrise to sunset on a crop that requires constant care. More often than not, his share will not get him out of debt. Thus, he is held to the land and to the proprietor for making another crop, his only hope, the illusion that the next season's bounty will set him free.[41]

Generation after generation of Colombian free men have lived like this, under a kind of legal feudalism that narrows all alternatives.

[38] *Ibid.*, p. 22.
[39] "Los Esclavos del Humo," *Semana* (Bogotá), February 14, 1955, p. 12.
[40] *Ibid.*
[41] *Ibid.*

No schools, no money; worst, no hope, for economically, socially, and culturally, they are serfs. Turning over the leaves that help to build the great fortunes of the nation, the peasant thinks his long, long thoughts. He has heard of different things now, and has begun to examine his prison. It is "a ring of steel and tobacco [which] brings no return to those who cultivate it." And the peasant is becoming impatient. He and his fellows now know that "they pay excessively for the usufruct of the earth, and receive low prices in the market which is virtually dominated by a few buyers, who purchase and use it in the industrial production of cigars and cigarettes."[42]

Perhaps the knottiest problem that Rojas Pinilla has to face is that of elevating and integrating the peasant and the small freeholder into the national life. Peasants are again up in arms in many places in Colombia. And in this, they are following a tradition of sullen non-acceptance of their status which began with the revolt of the *Comuneros* in that same tobacco country in 1781. They revolted in the banana zone in 1928; they swung their machetes in Tolima and Valle del Cauca and Cundinamarca and Boyacá many times between 1930 and 1948. Hundreds, thousands, of them were still harrassing the Armed Forces in Tolima as late as July, 1956. They have not finally accepted their fate.

As in the case of the great gap between the upper classes and the urban proletariat, Rojas Pinilla must face in the area of agriculture, the necessity of a revolution in landholding and production. If he fails to do so, the most important segment of the population will not become identified with the core of the national life. The complex sequel of evils that deprive too many men of land and keep others in *de facto* serfdom must be broken up to achieve this. The entrenched oligarchy of landholders will oppose this with every device which they have developed in their long period of privileged ascendancy.

Against Rojas' need to integrate the peasants stand the combined wealth, influence, and prestige of the Great Families. Yet it is a task which he can shirk only at the risk of some later, necessary, and perhaps violent attempt to solve it.

> The immense majority of the Colombian population lives and works in the country under a system of surviving enslavements from the colonial era. The backward methods of exploitation of the *latifundio*, the precarious position of renters and land laborers subject to a system of corvees, the small property

[42] *Ibid.*, p. 13.

strangled by the scarcity of easy and low-rate credit, and the absence of state interventionism in the economic field to plan and direct animal husbandry, make this problem the most difficult and important one in a nation which still has to import agricultural products that could easily be produced on its own soil.[48]

The "small farmers" of Colombia will continue to be a factor of divisionism in the national life until many, many more of them can pick up a handful of Colombian soil, crumble it through their fingers, and say, *"Esta es mi tierra, mi propia tierra!"*[44]

[48] Hernández Rodríguez, *op. cit.*, p. 298.
[44] "This is *my* land, my very own!"

XIII.   The Party Struggle: A Search for Directions

An article in *Semana,* the thoughtful news weekly of Colombia, in reflecting upon the nation's political dilemma as of mid-1955, had this to say:

> With the same passionate attitude with which they defended their sovereign autonomy and their nationalism a century ago, Colombians lately have been discussing which of the two parties failed, which of the two carries the responsibility for the ills which grieve the people. The evil which besets them is, evidently, the gravest of any that they have suffered: the collapse of their institutions, of the institutions which constitute, over the course of the people's history, a bond of unity almost unique, a point of reference to understand the existence of the country called Colombia. Its present moment, together with the favorable signs, poses a question: Will it be able to find the lost road? Colombia today is a country with an emergency government, a country under a state of siege, whose inhabitants have confidence in the skill of a chief of the Parade Ground. But now some have pointed out that everything should not be left to the responsibility of a single man. The siege is not being maintained by those from without, but by the hate of the besieged themselves.[1]

In this searching statement of the Colombian political problem, there are two assumptions which stand on shaky ground when held against the recent history of the nation: the institutions which failed may fairly be said to have done so because they had not created unity of will or served all the people; and, therefore, there was no "unique bond" of unity among all the people. And, again, one may seriously question whether Colombia as a nation had *ever* found the right road. The crux of the problem, in fact, seems to be that those who have faith in the "chief of the Parade Ground" want almost anything but a return to the road the nation was following when Rojas took over.

The present searching, the examining, the condemnation, and the blaming; the very inability to attach responsibility to either party beyond hope of contradiction; the admission of lost ways, indirection, and indecision; the satisfaction of so many with a military government; the implied admission that the party-created institutions

[1] "Eterno Retorno," *Semana,* p. 18.

served the nation badly—all these factors emphasize the failure of the political parties to direct the society along lines acceptable to a majority of the citizens.

For the truth seems to be that *both* parties failed; that under them, comprising the "traditional order," Colombia consistently failed to find the right road.

It is easy to forget, under the reassuring myth of Colombian "democratic stability," that the nation's history has been one of political anarchy. Jorge Holguín, writing in 1908, counted twenty-seven civil wars in Colombia up to his time, which had cost the nation thirty-seven million gold pesos, and hundreds of thousands of lives.[2] Estimates place the dead in the War of a Thousand Days (1899–1903) at 100,000; the losses other than in human lives, "were incalculable."[3] And, of course, this heroic butchery was far outstripped by the civil war of 1948–53.

The issues over which Colombians have performed their Homeric devastation for more than a century have been beclouded by rather superficial explanations, many of which were perpetuated by Colombian partisan politicians. Federalism *versus* centralism; Church against state; abstraction running counter to philosophical credo— somehow, the tradition has accumulated that Colombians have always grabbed up their muskets for the defense of Olympian principles, for the purest of philosophical and intellectual motives, for the protection of great truths against barbarian hordes. "In Colombia," says García Calderón, "men abandon fortune and family, as in the great religious epochs, to fly to the defense of a principle."[4] And Mary W. Williams finds the Church at the core of the trouble: "The Church question [was] one of the chief reasons for factional strife for the next hundred years."[5] Austin F. MacDonald couples federalism *versus* centralism with the Church "problem": "The Conservatives believed in a strong central government and the maintenance of intimate relations with the Roman Catholic Church. The Liberals, on the other hand, favored local autonomy and secularization."[6] And later he, too, adds, "The nation has a long history of civil war. Per-

---

[2] Jorge Holguín, *Desde Cerca* (Paris, 1908), cited by García Calderón, *op cit.*, p. 180.

[3] Arrubla and Henao, *op. cit.*, p. 519.

[4] García Calderón, *op. cit.*, p. 180.

[5] Williams, *op. cit.*, p. 532.

[6] MacDonald, *op. cit.*, pp. 388–90.

haps, however, there has been less fighting for the personal glory of ambitious dictators than in most of the other countries of Latin America. Colombians have shed their blood instead for vital principles." There is substantial fact in all these assertions.

But the plain, unvarnished truth is that Colombia had her anarchy for much the same reason that caused it in other Latin-American countries: the party struggle, however masked by a patina of idealism, has been toward the end of capturing, controlling, and using the public budget, the customs receipts, and the administration through which funds and favors were disbursed. This is neither better nor worse than in most countries everywhere. But it is neither a vital principle nor a great abstraction. It is simply bread-and-butter politics. If it can be explained in terms of some major philosophy, that is philosophy's gain. But it does not explain the nature of the party struggle, nor why the problem now perplexes most Colombians as they peer warily into their troubled future.

Between 1811 and 1886 the country had ten constitutions, six of them embodying the principle of strong central government, while four established governments which gave the provinces or states fairly wide to almost absolute autonomy. These documents, as Gibson says, "furnish the evidence of the difficulties which the Colombian people have surmounted in their search for a government both beneficial and practical for their society."[7] Since these words were written in 1948, Gibson may be pardoned the assumption, popular enough for all that, that Colombia had solved her problems, rather than only having approached the point where the whole system would crumble. For, shortly after he penned these words, the constitution was suspended, and remains suspended to the present, with no certainty that it will be permitted to operate in the near future.

The fact that Colombians have perpetually vacillated between strong central government and local autonomy would seem to place the abstract principle of location of power at the heart of the problem. But a far more pertinent question would seem to be: who wanted power locally, and *why*; and who wanted it in the national government, and *why*?

As a point of departure, one may say that the constitutions of Colombia were not patterned for the realities of the society they were to serve. They were a cloak for a Spanish hidalgo, cut on a Manchester

---

[7] Gibson, *op. cit.*, p. vii.

pattern, by a French *philosophe* acting as tailor, whose sewing was done by Thomas Jefferson. Consequently, the main struggle in Colombia has been to fit political theory to social practice. In general, therefore, the constitutions have remained ideals for future achievement,[8] and always, those who subscribed to them in theory eventually are forced to choose between the uncomfortable application of principles which upset their way of life, or the suspension of the letter of the constitution in practice. "Our constitutions, whether centralist or federalist," says Jose María Samper,

have fallen into the grave error of substantially imitating, as regards the executive power, the traditional forms of monarchy and unipersonal rule. In this, two things are revealed: an erroneous conception of the essential character of a democratic republic, and complete forgetfulness of the physical and ethnological conditions of Hispano-Colombia.[9]

In Colombia, the institutions did not emerge from the nation, but rather, they have come down as intellectual *concepts* from the early days of the revolutionary movement. Nariño and his clandestine translations of the Rights of Man left a far greater impression upon the upper classes than did the revolt of the *Comuneros* for social justice and acceptance by the elite as *men* in their own right. As Jorge Padilla points out, the Colombian systems "have been architectured on paper without sociological foundation." And he explains by leaving a portentous question hanging in the air: "Are the inhabitants of the byways any freer because they exercise, on that fateful Sunday election morning, the same rights that the Manchester workers, or the Lords of the City enjoy? Or perhaps because of that tiny piece of cardboard they possess, for which they suffer exile, persecution, and death? Up to the present, in this barbaric Republic, run by Anglo-Saxon institutions, each election day leaves some number of orphans, children without a father."[10]

The Creole intellectuals who fostered and pushed through the revolution to a satisfactory climax for themselves were true men of the Age of Enlightenment. Mistrustful of runaway democracy, still,

[8] See Russell H. Fitzgibbon's excellent discussion, "Constitutional Development in Latin America: A Synthesis," *The American Political Science Review*, June, 1945, pp. 511–22.

[9] Jose María Samper, *Ensayos* (Bogotá: Biblioteca de Cultura Colombiana, n.d.), p. 225.

[10] Padilla, "Cabellos Cortos e Ideas Largas," *Semana*, p. 12.

the intellectual ferment of the times and the lofty human doctrines which fed it, tantalized and captivated them. Says Professor Eugenio J. Gómez, "The French Revolution fascinated the Latin-American spirit . . . . The Rights of Man came to our land like the Decalogue of Moses to the Israelites. The example of the Jacobins and the Montagnards seduced our emancipators more than did the example of the Christian martyrs in Nero's arenas. These doctrines . . . continued as the guide for democratic conceptualism in the Republic."[11]

Perhaps this was the first great mistake of the Colombian Founding Fathers. For the true Hispanic constitution is not to be found in the *idearium* of Franks or Saxons, but in the racial and social complexes of Goths and Visigoths. Liberty did not come to Latin America from France or North America. It came from the *cabildos* or the *municipios*, and from the pulpit. It was both liberty and dogma—a substantial, satisfying mélange to the Spanish soul. The natural organ of expression for the Spanish colonies was the local *cabildo*. Behind it stood the sanction of a vote by the people, and it provided them with political liberty, the necessary unity, administrative decentralization, collective economic interventionism, resistance to excessive authority and authoritarianism, and defense and independence of the natural region.[12]

For the reality is that the true constitution of Hispano-America is *conciliar*, both in theory and in practice. It is the people electing tribal elders, the antithesis of the popular shout of "yea" and "nay," for it is a strange blend of popular participation and the elevation of dogma and authority above the popular will. In Colombia, the nation has vacillated, under the spell of democratic republicanism, between extremes of excessive liberty and of dogmatic authoritarianism. "For this reason we have had so many 'constitutions' which can be reduced to two: centralist and federalist. The first desired that the alcalde direct the *cabildo*; the latter that there be no alcalde at all."[13]

This indecision between the demands of a general, central government and the deep passion for local autonomy, tended over the years to create a political schizophrenia from which Colombia has never recovered. Always, the frame of reference was the locality, the prov-

---

[11] Eugenio J. Gómez, *Problemas Colombianos: La Unidad Política*, pp. 88–89.
[12] Fernando Guillén Martínez, "Retratos Provisionales," *Semana* (Bogotá), February 28, 1953, p. 38.
[13] *Ibid.*

ince, the municipality, before the nation; for there, and not in the nation, were rooted the political, economic, and social frames of reference. "The Wars of Liberation of Latin America began, and to a high degree ended, as municipal affairs."[14] It was Bogotá and Cartagena, but not the *nation*, against the Crown. Naturally, strong municipalities and provinces implied lack of unity, and the leaders of Independence quite rightly saw anarchy in this. Local *versus* national views; the cities and the localities against the central government. "It was natural that the two extreme theses should be presented, in a society which was struggling with the paradox of an experience completely authoritarian on one hand, and the ideological influences of the humanists recently come from France and the French Revolution on the other."[15]

Neither was to win. Federalism, autonomy, and the *"cabildo* instinct" wrote the constitutions. But when the national government began to operate, it soon came under the sway of the Strong Men who centralized power and ignored the federalist deviation.

The constitutional pattern, then, has been one of basic documents conceived on the high level of the Rights of Man, but articulated more often than not through authoritarianism and the suspension of all rights; of conflict between central authority and local autonomy; of a searching and groping for the spiritual Hispanic constitution among a hodgepodge of foreign and illsuited concepts derived from French and Anglo-Saxon political theory. Small wonder that Jose María Samper says, "Above all, the Hispano-Colombian republic must . . . bring ethnological Colombia and the political constitution into harmony."[16]

In practice, the many Colombian constitutions based upon agreement regarding the Rights of Man have been employed by both parties—as though only the upper classes were actually *men*. Quite frequently, when others insisted upon thus identifying themselves, the constitutions have, perforce, been suspended. Some of the blame for this can be laid to the fatal attraction which most Colombians feel toward abstractions. The nation revels in theory, and rejects often enough the practice of that which theory finds good. "Doctrinal cri-

[14] "Deterioro del Municipio Latinamericano," *Economía Colombiana* (Bogotá), January, 1955, pp. 545–46.
[15] *Ibid.*
[16] Jose M. Samper, *Ensayos*, p. 220.

teria, which, applied to social sciences, often are deficient, have prevailed in our country over experimental criteria, the only kind which can solve the problems of governing. From this comes the costly, interminable series of constitutional experiments, which have given Colombia not one day of prosperity or an hour of repose."[17]

There has been an equal abundance of experimentation with laws. "If paper were asphalt," says one writer, "with the paper of our constitutions and laws, we could pave all our roads and maybe even enough would be left over to pave certain city plazas."[18] This may be literally true, but laws and constitutions which fail to mirror the needs of the society as a whole are better unwritten. There has never yet been a faithful transcription into either laws or constitutions of the whole Colombian nation and its spirit. Very possibly the spirit of the nation is not popular-democratic in the Anglo-American sense; and the laws have failed deplorably to express the will and needs of most of the people. Of necessity, therefore, these constitutions of Colombia are fragile things: they are artificial in basic conception, and out of tune with the structure of the society. "Our innumerable constitutions, regarded as portraits of the society, since 1810," says Fernando Guillén Martínez,

have a close symbolic resemblance to the gift which one of our presidents received, bearing the following legend:

> "Portrait of the Honorable President of the Republic, by John Doe, painted without his having studied art, or having seen a photograph of, or having had the pleasure of meeting, His Excellency."

With such a system, it is clear that all "portraits" must be different, and all have to be provisional.[19]

THE ECONOMIC AND POWER BASES OF FEDERALISM: LOCAL OLIGARCHIES

Behind the local resistance to central authority in Colombia there has always lain a firm economic base, comprising locally entrenched interests, the jealous authority of small privileged groups, the position of caciques or local big shots, and a basic provinciality induced by physical barriers and lack of transportation and communication.

[17] Jose de la Vega, *La Federación en Colombia* (Bogotá: Biblioteca de Autores Colombianos, 1952), p. 172.
[18] Canal Ramírez, *op. cit.*, p. 167.
[19] Guillén Martínez, *op. cit.*, p. 38.

The immense distances and the difficult terrain that once isolated Colombians from one another "continue to isolate country regions and some cities."[20] Many of the civil wars of Colombia's history, although taking the administrative pretext, had geography at the heart of the difficulty, and economics and local areas of control provided their *raison d'être*.

Colombians have always been highly regionalist, stay-at-home, and provincial. Although nurtured on the Rights of Man, much of their basic democratism derives from their dislike of being governed by some distant, central power. There are nine hundred municipalities in the nation, of which fifty have most of the characteristics of cities.[21] And most of them have grown from and have perpetuated, strong local characteristics which hardly ever bow before national ones. "Generally the man in the street, or on the road, considers the Governor of the Department more important than the President of the Republic, and the Mayor is more essential than the Governor. The Colombian does not like to have his rulers at arm's length ... he likes to touch them and live with them, and an excess of power in a single hand irritates him, although very few could sustain these sentiments with philosophical and political theses."[22]

Localism, then, a sealing-off of the locality from the nation, was a main force in developing the peculiar characteristics of Colombian politics. From the Colony to the Republic, nothing much changed in the environment, and even less in the basic character and thinking of the people. Essentially, independence meant only that new interests were elevated to control, but they were interests which, as Creole interests, had already spread their network of influence and prestige and competence throughout their physical region. And along with their new and more important control of the society, there came to them greater opportunities for profit in commerce, industry, lands, and the general exploitation of government and governing.

In these basic facts is found much of the explanation for the struggle between federalism and centralism. Belaunde says the

... decisive factor lies in the very nature of the revolution and the *interests which created it*. When the central authorities had been swept aside and the authority of the mother country no longer recognized, *the government fell necessarily into*

[20] "Eterno Retorno," *Semana*, p. 15.
[21] *Ibid.*
[22] *Ibid.*

the hands of local oligarchies or of the caudillos who took the lead in the popular insurrection. So much for the fact. As for the doctrine [of liberal democracy] what we have is the logical result of the application of the principle of communal sovereignty when the Peninsular authorities disappeared. This doctrine was exaggerated by Jacobin and Federalist agitation. This is the true origin of American federalism. In a general way, it was not badly applied ideology which created the movement or tendency [of federalism], but *the tendency supported by determined interests which encountered its ideology.* Naturally, the effects react on the cause. That explains what we may term the double political base ... psychological and economic ... of federalism in [Latin] America.[23]

The initial impetus, then, was the determined interest of locally entrenched and powerful leadership groups. And when the oligarchies, the caciques and the *caudillos* learned to mask their interests behind Jacobin liberal ideology, the tradition of the conflict over "vital principles" was born. Into the hands of these powerful local oligarchies fell the plums from the toppled tree of colonial life. Supreme, happy, prosperous, and powerful in their small areas, they naturally opposed any central control which might shift or attenuate the lines of power. Nor is this type of social control which they represented without considerable logic. Professor Eugenio Gómez, while admitting the absorbent and aristocratic nature of caciquism, even its corruptive influence, holds that it "exercises a certain influence for direction in incipient societies which perforce carry within themselves the noxious ferment of anarchy." And he adds:

> The people who, by reason of learning, intelligence, wealth and contacts, acquire a certain ascendancy in a region, if they use it only for their own benefit, or for that of their friends and cliques, they descend and degenerate into caciques. ... Among us Colombians, caciquism is customary; it has consummated many outrages, but it has also restrained many foolish pretensions; and it will exist until the people are educated and raised to a higher level of culture, and the social ties are strengthened.[24]

The strong federalist tendency, then, grew from the drive of local, privileged groups to maintain monopoly and continue privilege as their right. Such groups fastened themselves upon the ignorant, retarded people, and became institutionalized as a device and even a philosophy of government. Hence, they combated, often to the death, any attempt of the central government to invade their baronies. This,

[23] Victor Andres Belaunde, *Bolivar and the Political Thought of the Spanish American Revolution* (Baltimore: Johns Hopkins Press, 1938), p. 132.

[24] Eugenio J. Gómez, *Problemas Colombianos: La Unidad Política*, p. 82.

in essence, is the root of Colombian federalism. And that is as high as one can place it on the slopes of Olympus, despite the cloud of rationalized Jacobinism which was used to justify and veil it as a doctrine. At best, the doctrine made the reality palatable for the uncritical, but it changed nothing of the motives.

But particularly in the past two decades of the modern era, the former isolation of the regions has tended to disappear, little by little. And as a result, the power of local caciques and oligarchic minorities is being seriously challenged by the need for central administration.[25] Moreover, the main support for such control—mass ignorance and incompetence—is slowly but surely being undercut. This trend results in certain important consequences in the legal-administrative order:

> Science and technology have moved into the remote regions, and the growing interrelationship of these regions with others in the general socio-economic development has moved the center of gravity from the former "politicos" toward other orbits which take direct control over them. There is being produced, no doubt of it, a shift of control over the social and economic patrimony to other hands. But it is still impossible to say precisely toward *whose* hands.[26]

And yet, with the shift of the center of gravity, there has been no substantial gain for the "great abstractions" over which Colombians have long been said to butcher one another and create their poetic havoc. With the change of control direction, there has come merely a change in the secondary objectives of the oligarchies and the *caudillos*. Since the state has moved toward interventionism, the oligarchies now move to control the bureaucracy, to capture more firmly the legislative committee, the *chef de bureau*. From the old days when control of power meant free use of the budget, the modern emphasis has shifted to control of those elements of government which can create the atmosphere favorable to doing business. "The struggle for power, which was, until 1930, for control of the public budget, *in a country without any business larger than the budget*, changed, in 1950, into a battle for the most elemental goods [import licenses, exchange permits, etc.] between the two implacable factions."[27]

One is forced to the conclusion that the reputedly high-level in-

[25] Jaime Quijano Caballero, "Teoría de la Función Económico-Social del Poder Público," *Economía Colombiana* (Bogotá), August, 1954, p. 57.
[26] *Ibid.*
[27] Guillén Martínez, *op. cit.*, p. 306.

spiration of Colombia's anarchical political past rests upon more mundane motivations. The stuff of Colombian politics has changed little from the day of which Miguel Samper said, "Anarchy has not quite dissolved us, because we still have the strong binding tie of hate which the parties profess for one another, and the mutual tie of the budget of income and expenses."[28] Samper, once himself a candidate for President, had a clear view of the "principles" behind the centralist-federalist struggle. He called it "this tremendous and tenacious struggle of interests and parties which, in politics, has led us from centralism to federalism, and, in economics, from monopoly and isolation to free trade with the civilized world."[29] Perhaps these are vital principles, but there are others more deeply rooted in the souls, rather than the purses, of men.

As with the "great abstraction" theory, so with the use of the "Church Question" as an explanation of Colombian political dynamics. Colombians simply have not ever divided into two parties because of differing views of the place of the Church in their society. They have, on occasion, disagreed over Church control of education. They have grown angry and bitter over an archbishop meddling in the choice of a presidential candidate; but basically, the Conservatives "pray in public," and the Liberals "pray in private," which is another way of saying that they both pray and both parties are firmly Catholic because that is their tradition. There is no French anticlericalism in Colombia, though some may, on occasion, claim to see it. "There are twelve million Colombians," says *Semana* in a thoughtful analysis of the nation's political thinking,

and the twelve million, minus 3 per cent, belong to the Catholic, Apostolic and Roman Catholic religion, have been born and have multiplied under the same moral norms of the Church, or have violated its precepts with the same indiscriminate decision, and have repented and ordered masses and built temples with identical fervor, with equal assurance of reaching Heaven ... there is not, then, fundamental difference. But sometimes the men of liberal ideas have called "Goths" those with conservative ideas, and the latter have replied by calling the former "reds," and on this point the people have become bitter: small causes have led to great consequences.[30]

The Colombian political parties have, in fact, been moved by a

[28] Miguel Samper, "La Protección," from *Escritos*, p. 179.
[29] *Ibid.*, p. 220.
[30] "Eterno Retorno," *Semana*, p. 17.

desire to divide the public loot, as has been the ancient urge of political parties in nearly all times and climes. Originally battles between oligarchies in the capital and other oligarchies in the provinces or regions, the character of the struggles has changed in recent years chiefly in that the provincial oligarchies, displaced by government interventionism, have moved their command posts to the capital where they can exert pressure directly upon the administration. It was precisely this evil against which López railed in his bitter moment of resignation. "Our parties," says Jorge Padilla, "are monstrously personalist. Here, ideas have less value than men. And behind every political situation is a vast network of created interests."[31]

And, despite the new emphasis upon infiltrating and pressuring the modern control agencies (which often necessitates the improvisation of doctrines to fit the old centralist-federalist "philosophies"), the motivation of the parties is the same: a desire to capture and exercise power for gain. "When the conquest of the presidency can, and does, signify the exclusion of the losing party *from all material good*, the result can only be what we have suffered," writes Fernando Guillén Martínez, "disguised as it may be in the name of diffuse principles and myopic and superficial doctrines."[32]

Behind the façade of "ideals," of "vital principles" and "great ideas," the Colombian parties move to defeat state control for the general welfare; to retain oligarchic control, now under the banner of centralism, again, under the name of liberalism or federalism.

The result is that economic policy expresses not the joint will of the nation's diverse classes, but the will and interest of the strongest class, which has the capacity to be *coactive in the two political parties of the state.* The history of the customs duties, of control of foreign exchange, of price control, is animated by no other philosophy, nor can it give any other lesson. Thus, *the political struggle has taken a new turn:* it is not only a matter of capturing the State to remake the nation in our image and likeness; it is a matter of taking it over *as an inexhaustible source of enrichment, as a source of nourishment for our own electoral clientele, as booty, and, finally, as an industry.*[33]

All things considered, it is impossible to discount the central place of the economic motive for the party struggle in Colombia. One must

[31] Jorge Padilla, "Por Una Sonrisa del Presidente," *Semana* (Bogotá), February 14, 1955, p. 8.
[32] Guillén Martínez, *op. cit.*, p. 306.
[33] García, *Problemas de la Nación Colombiana*, p. 151.

admit the sheer lure of politics as a source of personal and class prosperity. Behind the thin veil of verbal idealism there operates, and has operated, the compulsion to control the budget and the bureaucracy; to maintain local privilege, profit, and ascendancy against central control; to equate liberty and freedom with a minimum of control by government over one's own position of control of many of the humble; to regard government as a safeguard of privilege, rather than a force restraining it in the general welfare.

It is this solid fact which indicates that the Colombian parties have not lost their way, as *Semana* suggests; rather, they are trying to return to the old way in times which demand a bold striking out in new directions. The "crisis in the traditional order" is merely the culmination of a crumbling process in the institutions and in the public morality which began long ago. The real crisis is the failure of the parties to understand that the old order was a type of Creole feudalism inherited from the Colony, and that it cannot endure under the social questioning which marks the twentieth century.

THE CONQUEST OF POWER: NATURE OF THE PARTY STRUGGLE

We must repeat it to the point of weariness: the primordial cause of the backward condition of our nation ... *is the nature of the political battle between the parties.* Among us, the practice of politics *is not a struggle for the domination of ideas,* carried on by sermons intended to make new converts. Here, one is born with the Mark of Cain on his forehead, with a political denomination which he inherits, with a foreordained baptism, but without, as in the Catholic religion, a sacrament of Confirmation upon attaining the use of reason. And those who have the misfortune to bear the wrong mark are heretics whom it is not worth while to convert, but rather, who must be exterminated by assassination, fire, and the confiscation of their goods.[34]

Colombians have been divided by much more than the lack of roads. In the past, and still to an important degree today, "more than other notorious factors such as economic equality, what divides Colombians is a slightly abstract concept, a vague intuition, which they have agreed together to denominate 'politics.' " *La Politica* is at once the common denominator and the explosively divisive agent in the society. To some people, it has been the mystic source of some hope of a future good; and for the upper classes it has been at once the leading

[34] "Los Beneficios de la Paz," *Economía Colombiana* (Bogotá), August, 1954, p. 5.

avocation and the instrument whereby they maintained their power and found and husbanded their wealth.

Not only has the party battle been singularly unmarked by the supposedly high-level ideology which many have ascribed to it, but it has, in fact, been characterized frequently by the ferocity of rival bands of brigands fighting over literal loot. Arrubla and Henao say of elections in Colombia:

Most have been accompanied by fraud and violence, the incumbent chief executives often attempting to dictate their successors. Between 1864 and 1884, the Conservatives frequently found all attempts to participate in national elections futile. They were proscribed or defrauded while the Liberals often had personal combats over rival candidates within their party. Then, between 1886 and 1904 the Liberals usually suffered the fate which they had previously inflicted upon their opponents. The Liberals were so disgusted with the treatment they received in 1918 and 1922 that they refused to participate in the elections of the year of 1926, and were preparing to abstain in 1930, until a split in the Conservative Party offered them their first opportunity to return to power in forty-four years. *Perhaps there have been six or seven reasonably fair national elections in Colombia during the century of its national life. Proscription, violence and fraud have characterized almost all the rest.*[35]

In the political writings of Carlos Martínez Silva there is an excellent description of how the Congress of 1880 raided the Treasury: pensions to anyone who asked for them, gifts to Liberal heros, to relations of those heros, the pardoning of debts, back salaries with interest, a flood of public works construction, portraits of heros authorized, others commissioned of presidents and martyrs, appropriations for ironclad boats, arsenals, and nautical schools to raise Colombia to the first rank as a sea power, salary increases for all government employees, the naming of a host of consuls and ministers.[36] But Martínez adds:

We must in all conscience declare that the corruption which we censure is not an innovation of the independent party. Before it, the radical party had struck out along the same dangerous road. And if the abuse of power today seems unduly alarming, it is because in everything, and most of all in the evils, there is a logical development. The seed that the radicals sowed has borne fruit which, through unforeseen circumstances, is being gathered by other hands.[37]

[35] Arrubla and Henao, *op. cit.*, pp. 540–41.
[36] Carlos Martínez Silva, *Prosas Políticas: Sobre el Congreso de 1880* (Bogotá: Editorial Minerva, n.d.), pp. 41–42.
[37] *Ibid.*, p. 43.

The history of the parties and the writings of the political essayists teem with references to the ferocity of the party battle in Colombia. Mere accumulation of evidence adds nothing to the fact. Politics in Colombia has long been both a way of life and an integral part of the economy for the winning party. The winner has controlled the budget, handed out jobs, and acted as the source of all economic good for the faithful partisans and the members of the ruling camarilla. The losing party has been denied access to the fount of plenty, and in many cases losing an election has resulted in outright economic hardship for whole families whose income had been based upon service with and in the government. Consequently, from the top echelons down, the ferocity of the struggle. For the masses, winning an election offered some chimerical hope that their miserable state might somehow be bettered. For the upper classes and their relatives and hangers-on, the struggle had nothing to do with the masses: it was a question of retaining power to maintain personal prosperity, or of losing it and facing economic depression.

In general, such are the "vital principles" which have moved the political contests in Colombia. From the very beginning of the nation, party aims have been to invade, conquer, and exploit government for party welfare, excluding *all* other party members if possible, until the cycle might swing around and displace the conquerors. Frequently this led to hasty and open pillage, for anyone who failed to make hay while the sun shone was either a poor farmer or a hopeless idealist. It led, too, to the fraud and violence of elections, for any measures were legitimate in the struggle for economic survival which, in essence, party politics became under such a system. As for the poorer classes, they "function as blind instruments of the power of ambitious intriguers, while the upper classes ... see only in [the suffrage] a means of exploitation, of corruption and of surreptitious violence."[38]

Writing in 1954, Fernando Guillén Martínez says:

The problem continues, simple and terrible, without solution: why do Colombian parties always initiate a fratricidal battle, a battle to the death, for control of the political government? Why has it been necessary that a force apart from this struggle assume political control in order to save the essential part of the society? There is only one answer: because in Colombia, access to the presidency signifies,

[38] Jose M. Samper, *Ensayos*, pp. 227–28.

for either of the bands in the fight, absolute control of the economic life of the country, and exclusion for those who do not share political authority.[30]

The change which took place about the thirties, when the worth of the economy passed the total value of the national budget, has brought only a difference in emphasis for the directing political classes, but a far deeper one for the masses. The oligarchies still exert themselves to capture and invade government, but now it is for the end of controlling not so much the budget as the actions of the state which bear upon a growing, expanding economy. But the masses, far more than the dictators, have still retained their simple, naive belief in the principle for which, they have always been told, the parties stood. They cannot forget that each party has offered lip service to the Rights of Man, and they are becoming increasingly hungry for fulfillment of those rights.

Hence, the conflicts of direction, the dilemma forced upon the directors of both parties. The conflict between material aims and ideals, between directors and masses, has split the two parties along lines which bare the true cleavage within each: the wide differences in class and economic status and social aims.

It is this peculiar dynamic which brings the Liberal-Conservative oligarchy to close ranks and oppose the masses—whether Liberal or Conservative—when reform threatens. It is the reason for Antonio García's contention that "there are two Conservative parties." It is beyond doubt the reason for Rojas Pinilla, because the social tensions are dividing and shattering the old party alignments. In the process, the masses of both parties are being thrown behind the *person* of the *group* which will try to answer their needs, as opposed to the directing groups (again, Liberal and Conservative) which oppose such an answer.

Here again, we are faced with a contradiction. So deep is the Liberal-Conservative division, so important the "Mark of Cain" tradition of party affiliation, that only recently have the masses learned what the oligarchy knew from the start: that these party denominations are not *basic*; that the party labels have masked similar social and economic objectives for the upper classes, leaving only small areas of fundamental disagreement. And now, at length, the masses of people have learned a part of that lesson, and they are tending to express

[30] Guillén Martínez, *op. cit.*, p. 306.

political preference by deeds and their own class aims. The times when a Conservative proletarian would reject common action with a Liberal proletarian is passing. The sense of a common destiny is breaking down the old party distinctions, and forcing a *de facto* party alignment.

For the fact is, there is precious little basic difference between the upper-class Liberal and his Conservative counterpart. Says *Semana:*

> The spectacle of the political battles in Colombia, the arduous and stubborn will that the political parties inject into their contests, the collective tragedies that one and the other have provoked (the most recent leaves a balance of 300,000 dead according to general estimates)[40] would seem to indicate the existence of two absolutely opposed concepts with relation to the government and the society. But still this is not so. A Liberal differs no more from a Conservative with regard to the value and ends of government than does a Carib from a Chibcha. One of the most perspicacious presidents of Colombia, Alfonso López, once said that between the parties of the country "there existed no ideological frontiers." And this is true. They do not exist, and they did not exist, even in the first years when, in the flush of independence, there aligned opposite the Creoles or Republicans a few timid royalists or "faithful ones." The most outstanding figures within the parties, at least until the end of the nineteenth century, were alternately Federalists and Centralists. On the other hand, and despite the fact that the Conservatives supported systems of strong government, Liberals and Conservatives alike were always enemies of militarism, and the military were always friends of Civilism.[41]

The firm bond, the basic cement holding upper-class Liberals and Conservatives together in likeness has always been the identity of social and economic position and aims, when these were challenged from below. Hence, López stated a mere truth in denying the existence of ideological frontier between the parties.

The fact is, that the true party differences are to be located vertically, rather than horizontally. They exist between the upper and lower *strata of both parties.* When the winds of revolution blow hard, these strata are laid bare. The differences, class-wise, stand out in bold relief, and the horizontal differences disappear. From this true cleavage came the failure of the traditional party mechanisms—neither based upon, nor recognizing, the essentially social alignment of the nation—to meet the challenge in a time of crisis. From it springs the need for new party organizations in Colombia which recognize its importance and devise programs accordingly.

[40] These latest figures from the weekly *Semana* are the highest estimates yet of the carnage brought by the civil war of 1948–53.

[41] *Semana* (Bogotá), August 8, 1955, p. 17.

Should Rojas return power to the parties, or should they seize it back from him, in the near future, they would unquestionably put the old political treadmill into operation. One would win after bitter battle, one would lose, and no matter what the central government labeled itself, the hidden government would be that of the possessors, and the losers would be the dispossessed. Governors and directors would govern, and those of the other party would be governed. Under present conditions, no other system or solution seems possible, for Colombia is politically "a country where all the economic activities have come to depend directly and increasingly on the action of the absolutist [interventionist] state."[42] Control of the administration means prosperity and progress for the controllers; failure to control may mean economic disaster.

The traditional parties of Colombia failed because they used government as an instrument for perpetuating class privilege and economic ascendancy, in almost total disregard of the needs of the people. Consequently, when the crisis came, the people had no where to go in the political sense, no political collectivity through which they could channel their drives and resentments. Partisanship in all phases of life, the superficial expression of the economic motives of the party oligarchies, ramified through everything in the private and public order. And while the oligarchs of both parties devised new stratagems to fit the modified objectives of governing (the control of economic interventionism, or evasion of it), the ideas, the aims, the desires of the masses remained the same. Still, they expected the state to be used to fulfill the century-old promises.

The parties slowly lost the truths of their doctrine and their myths, until, finally, there was left to them only the state, not as an organic expression of the society (which they were supposed to direct with the orientation of their doctrine and the fervor behind their myths), but as a bureaucratic booty to enjoy when they had come into it, or to reconquer when they had been driven from it.[43]

These were the motives developed over the years by the directors of the society and the parties. As for the masses of both parties, they "remained true, loyal to their old ideals, but slowly, painfully, they became convinced of how their leaders were fighting for other and different things; slowly, too, they lost their faith, until the most intelligent part of the masses had fallen into sheer weariness and

[42] Guillén Martínez, *op. cit.*, p. 307.
[43] Canal Ramírez, *op. cit.*, p. 178.

indifference for their party. The political crisis provoked crisis in other institutions . . . which had been so contaminated politically, and were destroyed by the political criterion. And while the parties created crisis in these institutions, they left unresolved the basic problems of social justice and education. From the union of these latter two, the final crisis was precipitated."[44]

The vital principles behind Colombian politics have always been based upon the fundamental divisions of the society: local, class, caste, economic, and racial preferences, which the oligarchs and directors of the society strove to maintain. Stripped of all lofty verbalism, this is the "road" which the parties followed, and which led, in the end, to the destruction of false institutions which served only a small minority of the population. "Traditional order" or "lost direction"; "national crisis," or "national pause," something had to change the orientation of the nation, to call a halt and enforce a moment of reflection.

The tragedy of Colombian politics is that the parties were unable to do this. But surely the tragedy would be greater if, under present circumstances, these same parties "found the lost direction," and that direction were to be the one which they followed for more than a century—down to the very brink of national disaster.

Reorientation of Colombian society must be stated first through a reorientation of party objectives. It must include a new view of party functions and responsibilities. The new collective demands will not permit the old, narrow way again. The unpleasant truth seems to be that Colombia was never, for long, on the way which meant the achievement of some common social goal and good for the majority of her people.

[44] *Ibid.*

XIV. Rojas and the Challenge of the Economic Class Cleavage (1953–1956)

HEAVIER TAXES ON THE OLIGARCHY

As Rojas went into his third year of governing Colombia, there was considerable anguished talk, in Colombia and abroad, of his having put an end to the nation's "democracy." Much of this was traceable to the bitterness of the upper classes over new taxes. These taxes produced funds which, providing services and benefits for the lower classes, were plainly a forced redistribution of the wealth which heretofore had concentrated at the top of the economic structure in a few hands. In Colombia this kind of thing is as unpopular as it has been in other countries when first initiated.

From the moment that Rojas assumed power, tax revision was high on the agenda. Shortly after taking office, he established a minimum one-peso tax on all incomes above 1,000 pesos and on all patrimonies over 5,000. This hit the habitual low declarant, and the lower salaried and propertied classes who had before been exempt. Also, the personal income tax was revised to ease the burden on the lowest-level earners, while rates went up on all incomes over 12,000 pesos. Again, the bite was sharper on the preferred groups of the economy. It was not, however, oppression of business, for, even though exemptions were grouped, they were doubled in many cases, and corporations were given larger deductions for the payment of salaries to high officials.[1]

Probably the most controversial provision was that which included as taxable income the dividends from stocks and bonds of corporations. Until that time, personal incomes from investments in industrial corporations and certain financial stock companies were tax-free. Since all the wealthy people invested heavily in these fields, fortunes from stock dividends piled up at a phenomenal rate, innocent of any levy by the government. Such earnings were taxed only

[1] "El Gobierno de Colombia Aprobó Reforma Tributaria," *La Prensa* (New York), September 22, 1953, p. 3.

at the corporate level, and thus thousands of wealthy Colombians enjoyed huge incomes from stocks which frequently paid as high as 15–25 per cent annually, and the government took nothing from them. Not even López' tax reforms had levied upon personal earnings from shares and industrials.

This blow at the oligarchy was not well received. Strong opposition was soon organized by the *Asociación Nacional de Industriales*, the Colombian equivalent of the U.S. National Association of Manufacturers. A move to effect tax relief for the corporations gathered the financial, industrial, and commercial elements together to work for reform. There was considerable evidence that ANDI had a case. Between 1953 and 1954, the capital of corporations was reduced by about half,[2] and businessmen and manufacturers charged that this shrinkage was attributable to the withdrawal of the funds of small investors, discouraged by the new tax on dividends. Hence, this "double taxation" became one of the gravest differences between Rojas Pinilla and the moneyed oligarchs.

In January, 1955, another government decree struck at the great concentrations of wealth. Decree 058 suspended previous laws which had made banks and insurance companies subject only to income and direct national taxes, levied by the national government, and it authorized local governments to tax the branches of banks and insurance companies. Thus, they were in the same category as industrial capital associations.[3] Opposition came quickly from ANDI and the Bankers Association, and they were promptly joined by the Colombian Association of Insurance Companies.[4] The oligarchy was solidly against Rojas' fiscal and financial policies. The Rojas attempt to get the upper classes to pay a heavier share of the society's costs was aimed at the very heart of the oligarchy: banking, insurance companies, and industry, all of which had enjoyed privileged treatment and the purest of laissez faire environments under both civil parties. And, as *Semana* pointed out, "there is no reason why the most modest storekeeper should be taxed locally, when the rich and powerful financial entities were exempt from such taxation."[5]

Nonetheless, Rojas fell under sharp criticism in "economic com-

[2] "Arcas Cerradas," *Semana* (Bogotá), January 24, 1955, p. 26.
[3] "Cargas Nuevas," *Semana* (Bogotá), January 31, 1955, p. 28.
[4] *Ibid.*
[5] *Ibid.*, p. 29.

mentary" programs on the radio, and in the party press, not only for these tax reforms, but also for the size of his budgets and the nature of the expenditures. The 1955 budget was set at 1,268,446,546.26 pesos, a sizeable sum by any standards. The major portions of it were itemized as follows: public works (directly productive of wages), 283 million; public health, 41 million; agriculture, 18 million; education, 65.5 million; and the Armed Forces, 252 million.[6]

The business, banking, and financial communities, pinched by the new taxes, were in no mood to finance such budgets. In February, the National Federation of Businessmen joined the other opposition groups to lobby for tax reform which would "allay the uncertainty of businessmen." At the end of that month, ANDI announced a program designed to stimulate private investment, to seek "stability" in economic and tax policy, to encourage private initiative, and to loosen facilities for credit and technical assistance.

But much of this agitation was pure "crying wolf." Mainly, it served to divert attention from the substance of Rojas' broader economic aims. The February, 1955, report of the Bank of the Republic showed that 1954 had been "generally satisfactory for the development of the various sectors of the Colombian economy."[7] Agricultural production had risen sufficiently to permit a rise in internal consumption, which was reflected by a slight drop in the workers' cost of living index (a decrease of 6 per cent as compared with a rise of 17 per cent the previous year). The same trend was notable in the middle class cost of living curve. *Semana* interpreted the Bank's report as follows:

> The campaign which the government has for some time been carrying on to increase agricultural production has now begun to bear specific fruit. During the year, the *Caja Agraria* increased loans by 98 million pesos over the previous years, most of it for the purchase of machinery, seed, fertilizer and the fostering of new techniques."[8]

Credit was also given to the government in the report for "vast accomplishments" which took place during the year: many new industries were established and others undertaken. "To these," said *Semana*, "may be added the steel mill at Paz de Río, the oil refinery

[6] "La Plata Que Nos Rodea," *Semana* (Bogotá), March 21, 1955, p. 7.
[7] "Índices Favorables," *Semana* (Bogotá), February 7, 1955, p. 29.
[8] *Ibid.*

at Barrancabermeja, and several hydroelectrical centers, all of which received their impulse from vigorous official action."[9]

There were other optimistic and favorable reports. According to a study of the three previous years of Colombian economic activity, made by the Popular Custodian Corporation of New York, the money supply had risen from 1,309 million pesos to 1,847 million between 1952 and 1954. The production of most basic items was up to a new high, and collections of letters of credit had almost doubled between January, 1954, and the same month in 1955.[10] This analysis concluded: "Finally, it may be said that the present situation will benefit the development of industrial establishments, and this period of adjustment makes it ideal for those in developed areas of the world to enhance their investment relations and dealings with Colombia."[11]

In addition to loosening the budgetary purse strings to plow back Colombian funds into the nation, Rojas Pinilla actively sought foreign capital investment for developmental purposes. An ardent supporter of Colombia in this regard is the South American Gold and Platinum Company, which has invested several million dollars in the country. In January, 1955, Lewis B. Herder, president of the company, said of the Colombian situation:

> Colombia is a dynamic economy which is just beginning to boom...productivity of labor is rising, and industrialization is increasing rapidly. Consumer purchasing power is also rising rapidly as a result of industrialization, and this will make further industrialization possible...one [of our] guiding principles was to *invest in new industries where labor costs were not the determining factor, since...wages are certain to rise in Colombia.*[12]

Rojas' policy of fostering internal development despite violent partisan sniping is well exemplified by the Cauca Valley "TVA" project. In mid-January, 1956, a study mission for the International Bank for Reconstruction and Development, which had been considering a regional development plan in the Cauca Valley of Colombia, rendered a favorable report. The plan includes works for the generation of electric current, its transmission to industries and homes in

[9] *Ibid.*
[10] *Colombian Newsletter* (Bogotá), April 18, 1955, p. 2.
[11] *Ibid.*
[12] "U.S. Capital Lured to South America," *New York Times*, January 5, 1955, p. 34.

the area, flood protection of valuable agricultural areas, and a vast irrigation network.[13]

The Cauca Valley is one of the most important sectors of the nation's economy. Cali, with a population of 500,000 is an important manufacturing center, and the region itself contains about one-fourth of Colombia's population. Says *Time* of the project of the Cauca Valley Corporation: "The objective, as finally visualized, became nothing less than a quick and dramatic boost in the standard of living of the Valley's 3,000,000 people, to be achieved mainly by power production and control over crop-destroying floods, but also by related programs of education, road-building and better farming."[14]

In January, 1956, the CVC asked President Rojas Pinilla for the large sums of money needed to get going. Rojas unhesitatingly committed the government to spend 64 million dollars. The plan will cost about 187 million dollars over all. In addition to Rojas' commitment, the World Bank report indicates its willingness to lend between 20 and 27 million dollars.[15] The government will make up the difference between the amount now pledged and the total cost. According to Rojas' Minister of Finance, Carlos Villaveces, "the government will see this through, come what may."[16] Already Rojas has doubled land taxes in the Cauca Valley by way of underwriting his determination to carry the project to successful completion.

Rojas Pinilla has also acted with considerable sagacity in the matter of petroleum resources. Certain lands optioned by American companies were returned to government control when found not profitable to operate or exploit. One such tract was El Carare, which no other foreign company wanted to take over. After title had been cleared in favor of the government, the government formed its own corporation known as *Empresa Colombiana de Petroleos* (Ecopetrol). In December, 1955, Rojas' government entered into a contract with Cities Service Company of the United States to jointly develop the El Carare concession. The area has always looked like a winner, lying close to heavy producing areas. Thus, this 2.2 million-acre tract

[13] Informe Económico Sobre Colombia," *La Prensa* (New York), January 17, 1956, p. 3.

[14] "Go Ahead for CVC," Courtesy *Time*; copyright *Time*, Inc., February 17, 1956, pp. 38–39.

[15] *Ibid.*

[16] *Ibid.*

should provide good income for both the government and the U.S. company. Cities Service is in the deal for a 75 per cent cut of both costs and profits.[17]

In a further attempt to nationalize industry, the Colombian government in February, 1956, bought out the *Aerovias Nacionales de Colombia* (AVIANCA), the country's largest air line, at a price of twenty-two million pesos.[18] Forty airstrips and installations were included in the deal. The system is now operated by a government corporation.

Despite the wounded cries of industrialists and businessmen, the business level of the country was better "in 1955 than in 1954, which was also a good year."[19] The *New York Times* called this a "tribute to the strength of Colombia's economic position, and her even vaster potential." At the end of December, 1955, *Time* reported: "Colombia's economic health is good; the cost of living has remained stable for a year, and the country's major crop, coffee, selling at a satisfactory 62 cents a pound, should bring in a fat 500 million this year. [President] Rojas' public works, depicted in pictures, maps, and models at the exhibit he opened last week, are impressive: pipelines, airports, irrigation projects, and badly needed roads."[20]

Rojas' public works program was paralleled by financial encouragement to the growth of Colombian construction companies which would be employed by the government on a continuing basis. All elements of the press and the economy approved this.[21] But his revaluation of lands lying along highways for the purpose of raising more taxes for development from the rich drew the unanimous fire of the wealthy landowners.

Housing for the workers and small salaried groups was included in Rojas' program. In April, 1955, he announced an agreement with the Lewis Construction Company of New York for the building of 10,000 low-rent homes in Bogotá, at a cost of fifty million dollars—a

[17] "Good Partners," *Time*, January 2, 1956, p. 25.

[18] "Colombia se Hace Cargo de Aeródromos de Avianca," *La Prensa* (New York), February 15, 1956, p. 3.

[19] Henry Joy, "Instability Blurs View in Colombia," *New York Times*, January 5, 1956, p. 49.

[20] "Going Strong," Courtesy *Time*; copyright *Time*, Inc., December 26, 1955, p. 39.

[21] "Plan Vial en Grande," *Semana* (Bogotá), January 10, 1955, p. 10.

long step toward meeting the housing problem of the lower classes, and a source of employment for many humble workers.[22]

Rojas, in short, has actively sought the development of all sectors of the economy on a broad front. Industry has boomed, and profits have been high, though not as high as before Rojas' taxes on industry, business, and finance. On the whole, the loud complaints must be weighed against the long-range effects of taxing the great concentrations of wealth for the purpose of spreading more prosperity farther through the economy. In general, these taxes are paying for self-liquidating projects of general utility.

To a reporter of *Visión*, Rojas recently stated that there is "no area of public works in which the government is not carrying out an important program." As evidence, he cited the Atlantic Railway, which will link the Pacific and Atlantic coasts, passing through Bogotá; the Paz de Río steel mill in Boyacá; several international airports, particularly those at Bogotá and Leticia, and many smaller ones which supplement the national air network; the construction of trunk highways and the improvement of secondary roads; port renovation; construction of hospitals, rural and urban housing, irrigation, and hydroelectric projects, schools, etc.[23]

In August, 1955, another *Visión* reporter wrote of one of Rojas' improvement projects:

In San Andres there used to be neither communications services, hotels, factories nor banks. In November, 1953, President Rojas Pinilla visited the islands of San Andres and Providencias and declared San Andres a free port, and converted Providencias, which was formerly a dependent of San Andres, into a municipality. He appropriated considerable money and created facilities for tourism. This correspondent, who was in the islands in 1953, and has just returned for a second visit, found these islands ... completely integrated into the territory of Colombia and on the way to prosperity. They have an airport under construction, a fine hotel for tourists, a factory for the manufacture of fats, and a branch of the *Banco Popular*.[24]

Inevitably, this use of the taxing power and of the budget to make economic advances all along the long, diverse national line of classes and interests, aroused the opposition of those who were accustomed to

[22] *La Prensa* (New York), April 28, 1955, p. 3.
[23] *Visión* (Santiago), October 14, 1955, p. 17.
[24] *Ibid.*, August 5, 1955, p. 8.

making the only advances. Moreover, certain economists believed that
the expansion should be curbed, and the money diverted into more
specific programs for small industry, rather than spent in public
works. Others wished a general boost in production as a counter to
high consumers' prices, and many viewed the expenditure of pesos on
nonproducing projects as an undesirable stimulus to high prices. The
manufacturers, the businessmen, the banks, and insurance companies
finally presented a specific bill of complaints to the Minister of Finance in May, 1955. The main points of their criticism were, that
tax reform was necessary to loosen credit and insure development;
that the budget included "sumptuous and unnecessary expense
items"; that imports must be reduced; that industry was being "punished" by the tariff policy; and, again, that tax relief for industry was
an absolute necessity.

The Minister replied orally to the president of ANDI and the
gathered industrialists and financiers. The government, said he,
would continue its policy of advances on a broad front. That program
was backed by these six main objectives: (1) maintenance of the internal price of coffee (the price paid to the small producer) even when
it was not exported, by "compensatory" budget appropriations (basically, this is a price support plan for the help of small growers who
are always at the mercy of coffee brokers); (2) utilization of the budget
to maintain general wage and consumer levels when falling coffee
prices cause a reduction in economic activity through loss of foreign
exchange; (3) control of inflation and deflation by manipulation of
credit and reserves; (4) import preferences for those raw materials
which maintain a high level of employment in industry; (5) restriction
of nonessential imports when necessary; and (6) in case of necessity,
sharp restrictions upon the importation of capital goods, i.e., machinery and allied lines.[25]

The oligarchs of industry, finance, and commerce had great difficulty in adjusting to a government program which recognized the
worth and importance of the lesser sectors of the society. They were
reluctant to accept the small farmer, the peasant, and the worker as
co-equals with the giants of the economy, and possibly would not do
so until they realized that the best guarantee of national prosperity
is a producing class which also has high consuming potentials.

To those who have long been accustomed to such mild measures of

[25] "La Procesión Va Por Dentro," *Semana* (Bogotá), May 30, 1955, p. 30.

state control in the general welfare, Rojas' schemes seem tame enough. They must be judged in the light of the privileged position which the upper classes have enjoyed for so long, and also by the new norms whose fulfillment is being demanded by a majority of the Colombian people.

The true nature of the conflict in which Rojas finds himself involved in working out a redistribution of the society's wealth was stated not long ago in an article by the president of the National Committee of Employees:

> The middle, working and peasant classes, that is to say, 95 per cent of the population of the country, are inclined to support the government in the task of national renovation and salvation.
>
> The working and middle classes cannot accept as indexes of social progress the fact that four or five industrial enterprises and as many banking federations have profited by several millions of pesos in the course of the last ten years, under the protection of the tariff policy, while hunger, misery, sickness and ignorance camp on the doorsteps of the workers.
>
> The government has understood that its duty is ... [to change this] and in this sense all the people go along with it ... in leading the country toward a better life whose boundaries of free thought and opinion are reinforced by economic security. Thus, and thus only, can the Colombian people claim that they fully enjoy the total realization of the noble ideals of our liberators.[26]

THE "OTHER 95 PER CENT": MAIN SOURCE OF ROJAS' STRENGTH

Labor Under Rojas

Since 1953, when Rojas moved into the presidency, there has been little gain for Colombian labor as an organic force in the national life, even though the government has, in general, favored the social aims of labor.

Under the Conservative counterreform of Gómez, who fostered "parallelism" and the "confessional union," labor has become fragmented and has lost its sense of unity. As a result, there were three groups which mainly served as nuclei for many scattered locals. The *Confederación de Trabajadores de Colombia* (CTC), was composed of the old die-hard, true *laboristas*. The *Unión de Trabajadores Colombianos* (UTC), Catholic, confessional, had been favored and actually established by Gómez, Ospina, and the Conservatives, and it

---

[26] Rafaél Vieira Moreno, "El Papel del Gobierno en la Economía," *Economía Colombiana*, December, 1954, p. 311.

showed depressing tendencies toward collaboration with the bosses and compliance with the Conservative tenets of the Church's "syndicalism." Finally, there was the *Confederación Nacional de Trabajadores* (CNT), which was affiliated with the Peronist labor movement that gathered strength in many countries under the name of the *Asociación de Trabajadores de la America Latina* (ATLAS).

In general, the UTC may be considered a "Catholic unionism" group; the CNT as "justicialism in Colombia," after the fashion of Peron's movement; and the CTC as true labor unionism, searching for organic autonomy. This divisionism, of course, rendered the Colombia labor movement vulnerable to any strategy designed to weaken its total influence on the economy.

There is little doubt that the battle within labor itself was made more bitter by Rojas' obvious favoritism toward the CNT. In 1954, the government accorded this group juridic status by rather arbitrary methods, the Minister of Labor even writing the doctrinal aims and objectives of the group, an act which drew the fire of the CTC and the UTC.[27]

It was not surprising, therefore, that the Church hierarchy of the Department of Antioquia, the seat of the CNT's greatest strength, condemned the union through a pastoral letter in January, 1955, as being "Peronist and anti-Catholic." The main objection seemed to be that the CNT was opposed to "social teachings of the Church on questions of unionism." This could factually be interpreted as meaning that the CNT refused to become a "confessional" union and submit to Church-oligarchy domination. Of course, the charges were denied by the CNT, which stood on its main points of opposition to confessional unionism, and the rejection of the Church's right to intervene in social affairs; refusal to make any agreement with the Church; willingness to admit to membership any local of the CTC; and, finally, the right to have Communists in the upper levels of its leadership.

The CNT had been active from the start in trying to form some type of third party, and was militant in the *Movimiento de Acción Nacional* (MAN), which for a time seemed to be going in the direction of Peronist "justicialism." It was extremely vociferous in support of Rojas Pinilla, a fact which, together with its third party tendencies, alarmed both the Church and the traditional two parties.

[27] *Semana* (Bogotá), January 31, 1955, p. 15.

This force, which proved a menace to the Church, to the political parties, and to industry itself, drew sufficient disapproval from influential sectors that, following the end of the Peron regime in Argentina, it was liquidated by its own directors. At that time, however, it was announced that the leaders of the CNT would "work for the creation of a new organism which would be a sort of Great Workers Center to include all workers (laborers and salaried employees) of the State."[28] Many former officials of the CTC joined in this endeavor, and shortly the move drew fire from the "confessional" UTC, whose spokesmen "rejected any kind of state syndicalism."

By the middle of November, 1955, the political parties had become alarmed, and the party press was hoisting danger signals against the *Gran Central Obrera*, a master government-sponsored labor organization which had been put under the charge of the Central Committee of Syndical Unity for the purpose of controlling labor activity.[29] It was feared that this was a government move, or at least one inspired by the Minister of Government, Lucio Pabón Nuñez, to align behind Rojas Pinilla a "political force of its own," to compete with the two traditional parties. The UTC, of course, bitterly inveighed against the movement, as a means of "converting the workers into a new unit of the official machinery." The Church-dominated UTC drew attention to the fact that many of the leaders of the new movement were those same persons who had agitated for the MAN as a third and only party for the nation.[30]

As for the government, Rojas defined his own position as the agitation went on, stating that the "government has no interest in fostering state syndicalism, but that he would favorably regard syndical organization in accordance with conditions which would permit labor to achieve a program of Peace, Justice and Liberty."[31]

By the end of November, the press had launched an all-out attack on the new labor group, and the Church had joined in the fray to condemn it categorically. But the Minister of Labor, Castor Jaramillo Arrubla, at a meeting of the Workers Union of Cundinamarca, explicitly answered the critics, by admitting the social role of the Church, while adding, "but it is necessary to have unity of labor

[28] "La Otra Unión," *Semana* (Bogotá), October 24, 1955, p. 17.
[29] "Nuevas Siglas," *Semana* (Bogotá), November 14, 1955, p. 11.
[30] *Ibid.*
[31] *Ibid.*

around the ideas which the Church supports." There was still doubt as to the extent of official sanction and action behind the new labor movement, although certain opposition newspapers charged that the funds for its labors came from the government.[32] There was no doubt at all that the Church regarded it as a challenge, that the parties feared its power to become a medium of support for the government, and hence a deterrent to their drive to regain power; nor was there any doubt that the masses of Colombia seemed to be groping for some vehicle through which they could express in organized fashion their support for Rojas and his program.

But essentially, the groping and searching of labor was utilized by the main forces of the society as a weapon in their long struggle for power: behind the UTC stood industry, the oligarchy, and the Church, backed by the press which has always voiced their interests; behind the Great Workers Center stood the government and the masses of people who had come to realize that their interests were more likely to be served by the Government of the Armed Forces than by the old social-economic-political alignments.

Rojas has made every reasonable effort to keep employment at a high level, and to combat the cost of living for the workers. By the use of the budget he has given them not only employment, but a considerable hedge against the lows in the economic cycle—as much as is possible in a nondiversified economy.

For 1955, fifteen million dollars were earmarked for the Ministry of Labor. This was to finance a varied program of worker betterment. Some of the projects were: the Institute of Worker Training, which gives night classes in elementary, technical, and union education; the National Syndical Council, where representatives of all unions may meet to discuss common problems; the establishing of a family wage, or a supplementary compensation for workers based on the size of the family; the compilation of an Agrarian Statute, or Labor Code for Agricultural Workers; the rationalization of the minimum wage by regional and occupational differences; the fostering, by government financing, of workers cooperatives through their unions; and the revision of the Public Workers Code, a long-deferred objective of the white-collar middle-class employees which is now about to be realized.

Most of these ends were well on the way toward realization by late

[32] "Paternalismos," *Semana* (Bogotá), November 21, 1955, p. 15.

A view of a part of the Barrios Quiroga, a $10,000,000 housing project for workmen and their families, which is nearing completion in Bogotá. Playgrounds, schools, churches, medical and shopping centers are included in the development which eventually will provide homes for a total of 55,000 persons. The project is being financed by the Colombian government through its National Public Service Corporation.

1955. In themselves, they were not revolutionary, but they indicated a new proccupation of government with the place and status of labor and the employee classes in the society. They were eloquent justification for the popular support behind Rojas and his government.

In January, 1955, *Semana* queried labor leaders regarding their views of the government's aims and achievements on behalf of the workers. The opinions of the CNT and UTC bosses were synthesized as follows:

> The good will of the present government for the working classes is simply undeniable. Among the most positive benefits...[are those] which refer to the reserve clauses [to maintain employment in hard times], the rights of the unions, and the duration of collective agreements for the workers...but those reforms upon going into force become largely inoperative, and the National Syndical Council is the first real step toward true unification.... In order to strengthen the labor movement, the leaders of the unions must be given true, organic, juridic status and exemptions.[33]

And the CTC said, "The Executive Committee believes that the President's program corresponds to the necessities and aspirations of the workers ... we have confidence in seeing it realized."[34]

Rojas' solicitude for labor has ramified to at least one important Colombian industry. In June, 1954, the textile industry, headed by Coltejer (the second largest mill in South America) announced the voluntary adoption of a family wage for laborers and mill workers, to go into effect in July of that year.[35] If Rojas has done no more than set a good example for manufacturers, he has served an important purpose.

The Peasant and the Small Farmer

From the very outset of his regime, Rojas Pinilla demonstrated grave concern for the uprooted, homeless, and penniless peasants who had flocked to the cities everywhere before the raging storm of violence in the provinces.

In September, 1954, he demonstrated that his concern was sincere, by establishing a National Secretariat of Social Assistance (SENDAS), with his daughter, Maria Eugenia Rojas de Moreno, as head of the organization. While the appointment of the young woman was sur-

[33] "Productores de Riqueza," *Semana*, p. 15.
[34] *Ibid.*
[35] *Visión* (Santiago), June 11, 1955, p. 32.

reptitiously derided by the politicos and used by many to draw a parallel between Rojas and Peron (Evita having performed something of the same function in Argentina as Señorita Rojas did in Colombia), the Secretariat quietly and unobtrusively went about restoring hope to thousands of miserable Colombians. This was not, as in the case of Evita Peron, a personal dispensing of largesse for political purposes, but rather, the gathering of all social assistance functions of the government into one office, where they were coordinated with public and private social beneficent activities.

In February, 1955, the Office of Rehabilitation and Help, a bureau of the Secretariat, made its first report. The report was eloquent both of the past devastation and the steps which had been taken to rebuild popular morale. Said *Semana:* "The figures permit the contention that only [our] extraordinary national vitality kept the country from complete ruin. These data show that the regions declared Zones of Violence in the civil war reached 332, or the equivalent of 39.9 per cent of the territory of the Republic. Also, they reveal that no less than 40 small towns and thirty thousand (30,000) peasant homes were wiped out."[36]

Acting through SENDAS, the Rojas government has done a great deal to rebuild peasant and farmer life. As of January, 1955, it had granted 9,000 loans to peasants and small farmers (totaling 7.4 million pesos) in the *llanos*, which was hardest hit by the violence. In other areas of the nation, it had lent to 11,700 persons similarly affected a total of 16.6 million pesos; 18,500 persons were given assistance to incorporate them into the life of Bogotá and other cities; 500 persons were repatriated and re-established after having fled to Panama, and 1,000 similarly assisted who had crossed into Venezuela and other countries to escape the terror. Subsidies of 173,000 pesos were given to children left orphans by the civil war; 26,000 petitions for restoration of property lost through sale or illegal occupation were acted upon; and work was begun on the model town of Yacopí (which had been razed to the ground during the civil war) to the end of accomodating 1,500 inhabitants.[37]

In her first public appearance as head of SENDAS, Señorita Rojas made an excellent impression on the newspaper women, one of whom

[36] "Lo Que el Odio Destruyó," *Semana* (Bogotá), February 21, 1955, p. 5.
[37] "Si Podemos," *Semana* (Bogotá), February 21, 1955, p. 8.

said with some admiration (and for the ears of her male colleagues), "And there are still those who think that women do not have the ability to carry out major national tasks!"[38] Moreover, Señorita Rojas defended her position with pride and firmness, telling the press:

> There are those who think that I should remain at home, a sort of recluse, dedicated to the role of the spoiled child who sees the days pass in a series of fiestas and diversions; who think that my taking part in public life can be prejudicial to the policy established and headed by my father in the name of the Armed Forces, but quite another thing is the need of the humble people, and even my own conscience.[39]

Certain interesting aims of SENDAS were made public at that time. Among them were a plan to establish nursing homes for infants, and kindergartens and social welfare centers in all the principal cities; obligatory social service for women between eighteen and forty, except in special cases; the creation of a special certificate of *Paz y Salvo con la Nación* (a certificate of merit for all authorities to recognize) for any woman who, during any year, taught the alphabet to an illiterate; and, finally, the establishing of a psychotechnical institute which would direct the orientation of Colombian children and the re-education of juvenile delinquents.

Under SENDAS, social security has for the first time been extended to peasants. In case of the death of a father, agrarian families were assured a minimum of 1,000 pesos. The organization also announced plans for a National Chattel Mortgage Bank, financed by SENDAS, and the *Banco Popular*, with very low rates of interest for the borrower, and provision that if the borrower could not pay within the term of the loan, the object used as collateral would be sold at public auction and the selling price, minus interest and principal due the bank, would be returned to the borrower.[40]

In September, 1955, after one year of service in the social field, SENDAS was recognized as having done an excellent job for the needy. Said *Semana:* "[It] has given evident public services, with the establishment of councils in 500 municipalities of the country, with direct aid to private beneficent organizations, with the establishment

[38] *Ibid.*
[39] *Ibid.*
[40] *Ibid.*

of child and infant centers, and in the reorganization of homes and the readaptation of thousands of peasant families."[41]

But Rojas has otherwise given evidence of his sincerity in behalf of peasant welfare. In December, 1954, the powerful *Compania Colombiana de Tabaco*, one of the largest industries in the nation, raised the price of cigarettes five centavos per pack. There had been no corresponding increase in the price paid the sharecropper and poor peasants who raise most of the tobacco for the company in Santander, under arrangements with wealthy absentee landlords. Nor had the company increased salaries for its workers.

In a public address at San Gil, Santander, where he had gone to inaugurate a new airport, Rojas expressed the government's concern with this failure, pointing out that the increase had gone "to support the powerful stockholders, who annually take out millions in dividends."[42] Therefore, he added, the government was forced to "think in terms of the company's nationalization, and the Government of the Armed Forces would not hesitate to nationalize it if the company did not rectify its attitude."[43]

Within the same week, Rojas was able to announce that the company had doubled "participation of the peasants and workers in the recent price increase in cigarettes."[44]

One of the most vicious phases of the civil war was that which took places in the *llanos*. The plainsmen were the first to fight, they fought the hardest, and they resisted longest, laying down their arms only after Rojas Pinilla himself had gone to the *llanos* to confer with the partisan chiefs and to assure them that they would be treated justly and given every opportunity to resume their normal way of life.

Only two months after he became President, Rojas founded the town of San Luis de Palenque, along the shores of the Rio Pauto, in the very center of the *llanos* of Casanare. Various government agencies were coordinated to bring about the rehabilitation of the *llanos*: the Office of Rehabilitation and Help of SENDAS, the Agrarian Bank, and the Army. Loans were provided for individuals and families, health and technical facilities were put to work, provisions were brought in, and construction begun. A "traveling office" of the

[41] *Ibid.*
[42] *La Prensa* (New York), December 15, 1954, p. 1.
[43] *Ibid.*
[44] "Política Económica," *La Prensa* (New York), December 20, 1954, p. 3.

Agrarian Bank went through the region on wheels, and in the first two months lent nearly half a million pesos to those who had been uprooted and despoiled by the war.[45] At first, loans were for rehabilitation only, but later were put on a continuing basis for the purpose of development, and a permanent branch of the Bank was established in the *llanos* to serve the people who had always been forgotten, save in time of war.

By May, 1954, the government had made 8,936 loans for a total of 10,548,882 pesos to help the plains people get back on their feet. Roads and towns were under construction, agricultural experts were working in the region, side by side with the peasants, and hope of a better future had come to the *llanos* at last.

In January, 1955, Rojas Pinilla visited the *llanos* to check on the progress that had been made. His progress through the region turned into a triumphal procession. At Yopal, he was met by a thousand mounted plainsmen. Someone told him, "Most of them traveled two and three days to get to the village. These men are tireless on horseback. And for a friend [referring to the Chief of State] we're capable of riding a long, long road."[46]

At the distant pueblo of Tamé, Rojas was met by the toughest chief of ex-guerrillas and a band of his former riders: Guadalupe Salcedo shook the President's hand and chatted with him, and then insisted that he and his men accompany Rojas everywhere he went as a Guard of Honor. Finally, they left him at the airfield where Rojas' plane had put down. An old peasant, who had fought for three years in the civil war, told one of the newsmen at the airport: "*Bueno*. We're not losing on this deal. Now not only we, but our land, is being reclaimed. Maybe it was first necessary that they send us powder and ball [the Army] before they realized that we needed seeds and plows."[47] And another mused wonderingly, "I was working my lands over there beside the Cravo Sur. When the fighting started, I lit out for the hills. I don't know how many months it was that I never tasted salt. And now, they have me here, again, but this time to do whatever they ask me."

A reporter for *Semana* summed up the reaction of the *llaneros* to

[45] "La Caja Agraria y la Rehabilitación Llanera," *Economía Colombiana* (Bogotá), August, 1954, p. 20.

[46] "Puertas Abiertas," *Semana* (Bogotá), February 7, 1955, p. 11.

[47] "Arados y Semillas," *Semana* (Bogotá), January 31, 1955, p. 5.

Rojas' accomplishments and his visit to the plains: "And it is certain that they traveled the long roads gladly, not to ask for anything, nor to claim favors, nor even out of curiosity to know a president, but simply 'to say hello to a friend, to show him that we're grateful.' "[48]

The *llanos* remain under Army control, but chiefly as an administrative and developmental agency, headed by Colonel Luis Carlos Turriago. In May, 1956, Colombian and foreign newsmen were permitted to visit the *llanos*. The report of the *New York Times* correspondent indicates the progress, though grudging due to natural difficulties, that continues under Rojas:

> All in all, the "Wild East" appears to have been pacified, although there is still cattle rustling, wife-stealing, and an occasional vendetta murder. But prospecting for petroleum by foreign concerns is again in full swing. Migrants from western Colombia are receiving government assistance to modernize agriculture and cattle ranching. Several artifical insemination stations and experimental farms have been established. The new residents feel, too, that the region, if properly developed, can produce considerable quantities of rice, cocoa and timber ... blueprints have been drawn for a brick factory in Araúca ... slowly, wattle-walled, thatched-roof shacks are being replaced by modern, pre-fabricated houses ... [Colonel Turriago] and his deputies agreed that illiteracy and the difficulties of transportation were the chief hindrances to the region's development. ... To bring medical assistance into many remote *llanos* regions, teams of physicians and nurses, often accompanied by a priest, are being formed to make the rounds of outlying settlements and isolated homesteads. A number of modern, well-equipped hospitals have been set up at key points [and] intensive efforts are being made to furnish water and better housing and non-profit markets for essential staples to the residents, but the military leaders know their hopes for better living will be realized slowly.[49]

Slowly, perhaps. But for the first time in the life of the *llanos*, a government—of soldiers, rather than politicians—is *trying* to better the lives of people who have been utterly neglected by civil governments for over a century. Rojas is trying to make them a part of the national life, to integrate them into the whole society. That is more than the traditional parties, their preoccupations centered on the capital and the control of power, have ever done.

Since December, 1953, an Agrarian Planning Commission under the leadership of Dr. Ernesto Guhl, a German-trained geographer, has been carrying out for the government an extensive study of agrarian conditions in Colombia. Fifteen thousand rural families

[48] Puertas Abiertas," *Semana*, p. 11.
[49] "Colombia Pushes 'Wild East' Plan," *New York Times*, May 12, 1956, p. 8.

were being used as "subjects," and preliminary reports indicated that the *minifundio*, or too small holding, would be the villain named as chief cause of the nation's production difficulties, and, indirectly, the source of low consumption levels and high living costs.[50]

Rojas has not yet begun to break up the large estates to rectify the landholding inequities. His chief problem has been that of re-establishing the peasant on the land from which he fled in terror during the civil strife, of getting him to digging in the ground once more, of offering him a certain measure of security, the beginnings of an education, decent homes where possible, and the feeling that he, too, has a stake in the society. In this regard, Rojas Pinilla has made an important beginning. Better credit facilities, social security, rural health education, and housing have all received attention. However, there is much still to be done, and in many ways, Colombia's agricultural problem is its most important one.

On Rojas' invitation, a study commission of the World Bank spent most of 1955 in Colombia making a detailed analysis of the nation's agriculture. The group found that at present population growth rates, Colombia would have to increase its agricultural productivity 25 per cent in the next ten years merely to maintain present nutritional levels—which are low. In order to attain self-sufficiency, the next ten years must see steps taken to utilize lands now given over to pasture, for food production; landholding revision to equalize the size of properties; taxation based on the productivity of land rather than on the size of the tract (the present basis); education in agronomy for young men interested in an agricultural career, and technical training for farmers; governmental agencies for planning, land utilization, forestry, land engineering; broader use of machinery and fertilizers; and, finally, increased budgetary assistance to provide wider and easier credit for small producers.[51]

There is every indication that Rojas will adopt this Ten-Year Plan for Agriculture. But doing so will mean a slowdown in industrialization. The trade debt of the nation is now large, due to heavy foreign purchases for internal development, and the only way that farm machinery can be bought is to cut down on imports of consumers' goods and industrial equipment.[52] It is much less glamorous to buy tractors

[50] Caycedo Ayerbe, *op. cit.*, p. 15.

[51] "El Progreso Tiene Yugos," *Visión* (Santiago), May 11, 1956, pp. 34-37.

[52] "Needed: Farm Reform," *Time*, July 2, 1956, p. 28.

than steel mill equipment, but the fact is that the development of Colombia, like so many of the other Latin-American nations, is uneven, with agriculture lagging behind capital equipment investment, with a resultant steady rise in cost of living and inflation. However, since Rojas has enlisted the World Bank, the chances are good that financing the plan through that agency and through private institutions may not be too difficult. At least, he is thinking in terms of agriculture and farming as organically allied to the nation's prosperity. His years in office have indicated that he has a grasp of the problem, as well as an understanding of the need to raise the level of living and of productivity of the 60 per cent of Colombians who work on the land. Here again, he has gone farther than any administration which preceded him.

One need only point out, however, that should he follow the World Bank's suggestion that he tax heavily the lands of rich absentee landowners (who now graze potentially rich crop land, or simply hold on to it as an investment) in order to force their sale to farmers or to the government for distribution to peasants, there will be redoubled cries against his "tyrannic" dictatorship. Plans of land reform have always been successfully opposed by the oligarchy, who, in any case, feel very little pinch from high food costs, since much of their food is imported in any case.

But in a general sense, Rojas Pinilla's major contribution to the lot of the worker and peasant is a psychological one. He has treated them as men worthy of the government's consideration, where before they have been treated as human ciphers. By using the power of government to restore men and their families to homes and lands, he has given them a sense of human dignity that nothing can destroy, regardless of the fate of the Rojas regime. This contribution is one which every Colombian government in the future must take into account. After Rojas, there can be no return to the past of yesterday or the day before. The 95 per cent will not permit it.

Trouble Ahead: Rising Living Costs

Rojas' good intentions with regard to the welfare of the masses were increasingly threatened in 1955 by rising living costs which seemed to ignore all government attempts to halt them. At the end of April, *Semana* summed up the situation in these terms:

Flour, fats, potatoes, milk, eggs, rice, sugar, meat, bought as a group at the value of the peso in 1946, today would leave an empty space impossible to fill. With the same 100 cents, one could hardly get 4 of the 9 indispensable items or articles, that is, less than half. The Colombian reality simply is this: that John Smith, with a discolored, crumpled peso in his pocket, would have to admit to his wife that she was right when she told him that with his peso he could buy only four things: half a pound of rice, 25 centavos; a quarter of a pound of meat, 45 centavos; a pound of potatoes, 18 centavos; and a plantain, 12 centavos. The lunch which these would produce would be evidently modest, far from the dreams of the dieticians. In buying a bottle of milk, more than half of John Smith's peso would disappear.[53]

A break in coffee prices in February, 1955, lay at the heart of the matter, but the situation was not helped much by a government decree that restricted imports by categories of necessity, so as to favor foodstuffs and items of general use.[54] The influx of foreign capital, high living at the top levels, the increase of money in circulation, and the heavy purchase of luxury items have all been factors in jacking up the general price level. But the "economic disequilibrium was accentuated, for the rise of modest salaries did not compensate for the cost of living. Those with least resources were, as always, hardest hit. They had to 'pay for the broken plates.' "[55]

Rojas moved to alleviate the pinch on the needy when, May, 1955, he convened delegates from employers' groups, labor leaders, and government officials to fix a new minimum wage scale. Meanwhile, the government wrestled with the rise of living costs in other ways. The worker's cost of living index had risen to 442.5 as compared with 1937 as 100, and that of the middle class had gone up almost as sharply. *Semana* reported:

It is evident that workers in general have continued to face a growing deficit, and this deficit has been met by them with privation and hunger...it is no secret that a minimum wage of 4 pesos, if the generosity of the Commissioners extends that far, will still be far below the needs of the worker...no one tries to hide his worry about it, and *En Marcha*, an organ of Catholicism in Santander, states very exactly something that is on the conscience of all the people when it says, "Let's be frank. The peasant and working classes are dragging their way, literally, through a life of misery, hunger and privation."[56]

Many economists agreed that the only solution to the cost of living

[53] "El Peso Liviano," *Semana* (Bogotá), April 25, 1955, p. 29.

[54] "Clasifican Artículos de Importación," *La Prensa* (New York), February 24, 1955, p. 5.

[55] "El Peso Liviano," *Semana* p. 29.

[56] "Seamos Parcos," *Semana*, p. 8.

dilemma was a lessening in the stream of money flowing into Colombia, together with an increase in the production of foodstuffs and in the purchasing power of the masses, rather than a ballooning of upper-class purchasing power. But these were long-range solutions, and on their face unacceptable to the influential elements of the society who are determined to push "internal development."

Quite a few Colombians called the question of the control of the cost of living curve an "imponderable." They held that no government could solve it, but could only put the lid on at certain price levels to prevent, possibly, further rises.[57] But unquestionably, one of the chief causes was ready and plentiful money on the upper levels, while scarcity marked the lower levels of the society. A major contributing factor, too, was the tendency for population to increase geometrically, while food production increased slowly and in mathematical proportion, as did mass purchasing power.

Such a problem could not be solved overnight, but it was there for Rojas to solve. The plans, the studies, the long-range solicitude for the poor, would all inevitably be swept aside before the too hard economic pinch of hard times, should they become unbearably hard. That was the lesson, in part, of 1948.

But there was a difference under the Rojas regime, for the budget would be employed to cushion the masses somewhat, as they had never been cushioned before, from the hardest shocks of economic hardship. And the emphasis was generalized, rather than focused upon the welfare of the oligarchy.

Consequently, as 1955 ended and 1956 got underway, the masses of the Colombian people looked upon Rojas as the protector of their interests and their loyalty to his government and his program was diminished slightly, if at all, by the rise in living costs. They believed in him and were willing to give him his chance to work for long-range major solutions.

For, as between a government which emphasized mass needs and ends, and one which governed for the primary welfare of the oligarchies, there was no difficult choice for the people to make. They were used to hard times. The oligarchies had schooled them in that. And this Government of the Armed Forces was, they believed, working for a better life for the small people as well as for the great.

[57] *Ibid.*

XV. The Resurgence of Partisanship and Violence: The Honeymoon Ends (1953–1955)

THE UNREPENTANT PARTIES REACTIVATE

The world changes, societies and nations also change, and consequently, political parties, unless they want to perish, have to change, in order to adapt to the society in which they are active.[1]

These words, uttered by Darío Echandía, head of the Liberal party, soon after Rojas Pinilla took over, seemed to voice a prevailing sentiment in Colombian politics. For a time after the violence had ended, it was as though a sober mood of reflection, of private stock-taking, had come over the two great political collectivities. But events showed that this soul-searching was neither profound nor sincere. By February, 1954, Colombian politicians were using among themselves a phrase which was the gauge of their self-examination: "The honeymoon is over."

More significant still, political murder was on the rise once more by the end of 1953. Even though Rojas Pinilla announced the end of public violence, more than a hundred dead were attributed to factional strife by the end of the calendar year in which he came to office. Gómez Conservatives, still active in the provinces, hacked fourteen Liberal farmers to death in the Department of Huila in November. Caicedonia, only 125 miles from Bogotá, became a battlefield. Rojas sent troops, and replaced the police officials with men of his own choice. These measures proved only partially effective. In the year-end résumé of the internal situation, *Semana* reported:

At the year's end in two Departments there had taken place dangerous incidents which seriously preoccupied the government and the citizens. In Huila, thieves and assassins, styling themselves government agents, had appeared in groups to commit atrocities ... in El Valle ... continuous crimes had taken place.[2]

[1] *Semana* (Bogotá), August 29, 1955, p. 15.
[2] *Semana* (Bogotá), January 18, 1954, p. 5.

With the renewed outbreak of the violence which he was sworn to halt, Rojas Pinilla gave increasing indications that he was changing his mind about his possible length of tenure. But another factor had intervened to disturb the situation: Gómez partisans had begun to reopen the old, bitter party strictures. A group of young Gómez Conservatives from Barranquilla sent to Rojas an open letter in the form of a questionnaire, which embarrassed the government and angered the Liberals. Pointedly, it asked the Conservative Directorate to answer: whether the "banditry" was planned and directed by the Liberals; whether Rojas' government was responsible for public order, and if so, why it did not pacify the nation; whether the Conservative party should ask for a definition of its relationship to the Rojas government.

This type of polemics had just brought the nation recently to the brink of disaster. Hence, it was both ill-advised and badly timed. Still, from his exile in Spain, Laureano Gómez seized the opportunity to publish an answer to the queries from Barranquilla. The letter, widely circulated and commented upon by the entire national press, was summarized by *Semana:*

> The results of what is happening in Colombia will determine the extinction of the Conservative party, or its youthful ressurection if there are strong clean hands to hold high the banner of pure doctrine.
> But the Conservative party will not die. "That would be the same as believing that noble convictions, just sentiments and sincere acts would disappear from Colombia." The name of Conservative cannot be used as "the flag of piracy to cover cowardly acts which betray [Conservative] principles."[3]

This letter, coupled with an article by Belisario Betancourt which designated Gómez as the "incarnation" of political legitimacy and urged his followers to work for a return to the presidency,[4] roused the Liberals from their lethargy. The Liberal press fired back staggering broadsides. Tempers of Liberals and Conservatives grew edgy; and the atmosphere of incipient violence returned as both sides turned to public name-calling through the press. In effect, the newspapers, always primarily partisan organs, became the reincarnation of the contending armies which Rojas had disbanded.

The recent near-disaster had been forgotten in the safety and security of the peace which Rojas and the Army maintained. The parties, unrepentant and unchanged, were returning to the lists.

[3] *Ibid.*, p. 6.
[4] Belisario Betancourt, in *Semana* (Bogotá), January 11, 1954, p. 10.

In the restless wondering about how long his tenure of power would go on, Rojas was moved, in November, 1954, to state publicly, "God is witness that I will continue to head the public destiny only until the fratricidal hate has been crushed and we may again take up the path of peace and recover our prestige as a cultured, Christian nation."[5] This indefinite promise only served to make the parties more demanding, to whet their appetites for agitation.

Consequently, it was inevitable that Rojas, seeing violence and bitter partisanship again spring up, should think in terms of retaining power until the dangers of another outbreak had passed. In Santa Marta, on December 16, 1953, he issued a warning that the parties should have heeded:

The complete re-establishment of institutional normality cannot be achieved without first winning the battles which we are waging against partisanship ... there is great necessity for a sincere and cordial union, which should place the Fatherland *above the parties*, in order that the progress of the nation may proceed along the ways indicated to it by the unified and indiscriminate efforts of its sons. The "Conservative Republic" or "Liberal Republic" are national misnomers, and have caused fatal dissension and tragedies which have bitterly convulsed the nation.[6]

This talk of "rising above party" had an ominous ring to the politicians, to whom it sounded as sensible as asking a starving man to rise above food. But there was logic in Rojas' view, and it lay in the temper of the times. Given the intransigence of the parties, their return to power at that time would have been a serious threat to an already disturbed state of public order.

At the end of 1953, Rojas issued a document entitled "Six Months of Governing." This paper denounced the Gómez regime and the "clique which seized power and employed it as a monopoly." There was harsh criticism of the Left also, particularly for its "resistance to the state." And again Rojas spoke of the "absolute impossibility of the old traditional parties to meet the problems of the moment." His justification for continuing in power was couched in these terms: "Power never needs to be justified dialectically. The existential fact of being able to direct and conduct is superior to logic."[7]

After six months in the presidency, Rojas' popularity had diminished to a degree among the higher levels of the society. His program

[5] *La Prensa* (New York), November 13, 1953, p. 1.

[6] *La Prensa* (New York), December 15, 1953, p. 3.

[7] *Semana* commented: "This is an affirmation whose implications could be wholly unforeseen if it were adopted as a norm." See January 11, 1954, p. 6.

of taxing the rich, his apparent determination to hold the political parties in suspension until internal stability had been achieved, the spending program to alleviate the condition of the masses of people, had alienated from his regime all those upper-class representatives who had at first believed that he would govern conservatively for a time, then hand power over to the Conservative party.

It seems fairly clear that it was during this time, when the Liberals and the Conservatives were renewing their bickering and snarling; when the violence was once more growing in the provinces as a result of public political agitation of issues through the press, that Rojas made up his mind.

There is more than a hint in his utterances and in the official decrees of the time that he had swung around to the view that his period of power must be one of educating the parties in their true social role in the nation; that they should be made to see the imperious necessity of formulating and being responsible for comprehensive national policies before they could again assume leadership of the society.

These were dangerous assumptions, but completely in keeping with the history of party accomplishments in Colombia. The parties had come very close to assuming that *they* were the nation, that their responsibilities lay only to the party directorates, composed of the most powerful oligarchies.

And in any case the masses of the people were for the time content to let the soldier speak for them. They had grown unutterably weary with mere words. Now they demanded deeds.

Perhaps at this stage of development neither the people nor Rojas knew what a heady incentive to autocracy could be brewed from a combination of popular support and the need for a strong hand to direct at a moment of crisis.

ROJAS AND FREEDOM OF THE PRESS

The conflict between Rojas and the press was inextricably woven of three basic strands: the fundamental right of a free press in a free society; the continuance of public political violence, assassinations, and general disturbances; and, finally, the tendency of Colombian newspapers to exploit every instance of violence for partisan advantage. To understand both sides of the problem, one must be mindful of certain distinctions between the press in North America and in Colombia.

The running fight which has flared between Rojas and the newspapers has been commented upon in the United States in such a way as to indicate that Rojas not only is the worst, but the first and only, President of Colombia who employed press censorship. Actually, it has been used by many: Nuñez, López, Ospina Pérez, and Laureano Gómez, to name some of the more recent Chief Executives who used the press muzzle when they saw fit. This tendency is not only based upon hoary tradition, but arises from the peculiar view of the press in the Colombian constitution. Article 42, Title III says, "The press is free *in times of peace*; but *it is responsible*, in accordance with the laws, *when it attacks* the honor of persons, the social order, or *the public tranquillity*."[8]

In other words, when the press acts in such a manner as to disturb public order, or in times of "non-peace," the press can constitutionally be made responsible by law. There is abundant authority for the President to enforce this responsibility, under the constitution, by imposing conditions that amount to censorship. In doing so, he is not necessarily acting as an arbitrary killer of newspapers.

It scarcely need be pointed out that this is a fundamental difference from the place of the press in the United States, where anything goes, subject to laws of criminal libel or to security measures in wartime.

Rojas' trouble with the press must be judged, then, in the light of a power granted him by the constitution, and, further, in the light of the persistence of violence and political murder in the public order. That the Colombian press has contributed to the continuance of the disturbed state of affairs is beyond question when one follows the record.

Colombian newspapers and periodicals are primarily party organs. Only the rare one, such as *Semana*, a weekly, is neutral and reasonably objective. The great dailies and their satellites in the provinces are frankly, unabashedly, and characteristically spokesmen for the party line of their owners and the interests behind them. Just as *El Siglo* dominated the activity and expressed the doctrinal and strategic views of the Conservatives under Gómez, so have *El Espectador* and *El Tiempo* of Bogotá established Liberal doctrine, strategy, and tactics throughout the nation. It is by no means accidental or coincidental that owners and editors of the leading dailies have always been presidents of Colombia, candidates, or party chiefs. A similar situation

[8] Noguera Laborde, *op. cit.*, p. 209.

would prevail in the United States if Eisenhower owned the *New York Times*, William Knowland the *Washington Star*, Adlai Stevenson the *Chicago Tribune*, and Harry Truman the *St. Louis Post-Dispatch*. Party leadership and newspapers go hand-in-hand in Colombia (recall that López founded *El Liberal* to oppose President Santos, who owned *El Tiempo*, and both fought with Laureano Gómez who owned *El Siglo*).

Always, the capital newspapers have been looked upon as the official voices of party heads, even of factional chiefs. It is no exaggeration to say that the provincial adherents of the parties scan the great capital dailies chiefly to keep abreast of the party's grand strategy as it emanates from Bogotá. There is, thus, an organic character, a political unity on partisan lines, to the Colombian press that is inconceivable in the United States, where other things than political opinions are used to sell newspapers and build circulation.

This strong equation of the press with political leadership and control raises a considerable doubt as to whether it can rightfully claim immunity from control as a public forum. Neither of the parties has historically spoken for the whole nation, but for the interests of its controllers; hence, the organs through which they speak are particularist and extremely personalist. Partisan first, informative incidentally, the Colombian press has always enjoyed a maximum political freedom with a minimum of public responsibility. As a result, it often has, at times of extreme political agitation, tended toward inflammatory polemics, irresponsibility, and a seeming disregard of the public consequences of its fervent partisanship. In a society where politics always runs along the margin of violence, such a "free press" can easily incite public disorder, even though such is not its intention.

When Rojas Pinilla took office, he lifted the censorship which Gómez had imposed, and asked the press to voluntarily refrain from publishing material which would exacerbate the hateful partisan passion which had lain behind the violence of the civil war. The representatives of the Liberal and Conservative press reasonably agreed to this voluntary censorship. At that moment, the memory of terror was still fresh in their minds. They knew that the nation could find peace only in an atmosphere of partisan amity.

But as the incidents of political violence in the provinces multiplied, as the Gómez Conservatives began to hurl charges at the Liberals and to question the right of the government to continue in power, the gentleman's agreement between Rojas and the press broke down. Partisan politics was renewed, and the press became the medium for the mutual onslaught.

Rojas, disapproving the aspirations of the parties, told a gathering of engineers and architects in June, 1954:

It would be well for the future and effectiveness of the campaign for a viable national life if the traditional parties clearly defined their ideological programs, *so that the masses might know in their consciences what postulates they are to defend, and which separate them in the political field*; and because, when many of the prejudices of the past are forgotten, *they will find themselves equally identified with many things that benefit them equally*.[9]

But the parties defined no programs. They had none, in fact, but that of mounting a drive to regain power. Rojas created a merit system and opened careers for professional government services. The parties, accustomed to finding their most ardent supporters among the beneficiaries of the spoils system, saw this without joy. Said *Economia Colombiana*, "It is curious that the establishing of an administrative career service has not, up to the present, aroused much enthusiasm among public employees. It may be that they consider it too Utopian for our [Colombian] environment."[10]

In the initial stage of feeling his way among the shoals of party struggle, Rojas turned to a mélange of government interventionism, slightly tinged with *caudillismo*, and cemented by streamlinings and reforms applicable primarily to the Colombian situation. The specifics of this dose of governing were to be: "worker discipline" and the elimination of the struggle between the classes; practical schools for training workers as both artisans and citizens; social justice—"the ideal is not that there be fewer rich men, but rather, fewer poor people"; stimulation of property-holding in land, by parceling out land to those who needed it; nonpolitical labor unionism by unions whose main function would be protection of the workers' rights rather than support of any party; just taxation, so that social costs might be borne by those best able to afford them (this lack of vision of the more favored classes has probably been the major cause of the revolution); reinforcement of municipal life and the development of the backward areas; "redemption of the peasant" through rural education, modernization of farming methods, stimulation of land parcel-

[9] *Economia Colombiana* (Bogotá), June, 1954, p. 257.
[10] *Ibid.*, July, 1954, p. 471.

ing, and elimination of the *minifundio* (redeeming the peasant from a "simple number on the voting lists" exploited by political hacks, and converting him into a useful citizen, at least as worthy as the city dweller); protection of the family and of small business by giving them living space among the growing and absorbing monopolies.[11]

Most of these aims struck directly at weaknesses of the Colombian society. But they would be costly. They would break up oligarchic control, redistribute wealth, and create among the masses an independence and sense of their own destiny which would shatter all former lines of influence, privilege, and preference.

Consequently, the oligarchy, which at first had tended to regard Rojas as a "restorer" of the old way, came to realize that he had different ideas. He was actually on the side of the social revolution which they had opposed, bitterly and violently. Hence, as the memory of the past terror receded, the parties easily convinced themselves that *their* democracy was being extinguished; that *their* nation was falling under dictatorial control. In place of an integrated Republic, the dream of the "Liberal" or the "Conservative Republic" was reawakened.

And the parties adopted not even some reasonable equivalent of what Rojas was attempting to achieve. They talked in the old, stale terms of doctrine; they advanced no plans for the future but the recapture of power; they admitted neither responsibility to the nation nor the validity of some general advance on broad fronts.

But they could not take the field to oppose as political collectivities. Hence, they transferred the battle lines to the pages of the party press. And there, once more, the ancient cycle began to grind out its bitter, inflammatory pattern.

VIOLENCE, PRINTED AND PERSONAL

The essential evil of the reappearance of the party battle on the front pages lay in the fact that it reported violence in such a manner as to incite further violence.

Here was a condition which the government, in an effort to bring the nation back to peace and rational living, was trying to stamp out. To that end, Rojas had asked for the gentleman's agreement. But each new disturbance provided ammunition for the parties in their bitter struggle for position. Charges, countercharges, and irresponsi-

[11] This résumé of the main points of Rojas' program is taken from *Economía Colombiana* (Bogotá), June, 1954, pp. 245–47.

ble insinuations rushed into print. Personal violence bred printed violence, and this, in turn, incited unregenerated partisans to further outrages. And behind it all was the basic discontent of the traditional parties with the new directions chosen by Rojas, and this lent the motive power to the vicious circle.

The press of both parties seemed to have forgotten, in just this short time, the terrible price that the nation had paid for this kind of partisanship.

On November 7, 1954, *La República* reported the killing of eleven Conservatives, all farmers, "by certain bandits in Tolima bent upon maintaining an atmosphere of terror and uneasiness." Five columns of the front page were devoted to this story and its "political implications."[12] Four days later, *El Espectador* headlined a clash between the Army and irregulars in the municipality of Genova, Department of Caldas, in which there were "thirty dead and many wounded." This incident prompted the Liberal Party Directorate to protest to the government that "nineteen peasants" had been among those killed. "We are sure that we express the sentiments of all hierarchies of the Party," said the letter of complaint, "in condemning as contrary to the national interest, *and the interest of Liberalism,* all direct and indirect acts which disturb the fixed social order by the absurd sacrifice of promising Colombian lives."[13]

These new outbreaks and the Army failure to stop them, had fallen under bitter attack by Alberto Galindo, a former editor of *El Liberal,* in a radio program devoted to "economic commentaries." With this affair at Genova making news, Galindo turned upon the Army. He implied that it had been a methodical slaughter of Liberal peasants, merely a part of a general plan. Then, complaining that the recent import regulations hit hardest at the lower classes, he pointed out that "there existed commissaries or military cooperatives in which all kinds of goods were sold [to the Army] at far below cost." Special criticism was leveled at the practice of computing at double length all military service which took place under the "state of siege."[14]

The meeting of the National Press Conference in Cali in November

[12] *La República,* November 7, 1954, p. 1.

[13] "Protesta Liberal en Colombia por la Matanza," *La Prensa* (New York), November 19, 1954, p. 3.

[14] "Demandarán Militares a Diario 'El Tiempo,'" *La Prensa* (New York), December 18, 1954, p. 3.

further agitated matters. Some of the delegates left the session because of the presence of "elements foreign to journalism who were interested in promoting political movements."[15] This reference to the attendance of Army officers was not calculated to soothe ruffled feelings. Some of the delegates approved a message of greeting to Rojas, but in general, partisan divisionism marked the conference and harshened the political differences.

Relations between the Army and the press took a turn for the worse when the commanders of the Army, Police, Air Force, and Navy filed suit against Alberto Galindo and *El Tiempo* for slander and calumny. In a joint statement, the officials categorically condemned "the tendentious and subversive campaign against public order which certain written and spoken areas of the press have been carrying out against the Colombian people."[16] By the end of November, 1954, public feeling had grown heated, and the Army, feeling itself impeded in the task of restoring order, felt that it had just complaints against the partisan press. *Semana* describes the situation as follows:

> Last week many Colombians were right in thinking that the government should take steps to prevent the re-igniting ... due to political partisan heat ... of the blaze that swept the nation with fire for so long a time. Taking as a pretext the tragic acts of bandits in Genova, and some similar occurrences in Tolima, two or three Conservative dailies, especially *La República* of Bogotá, began *a vehement offensive against Liberalism* to the end of convincing their readers that Liberalism was undertaking a new subversive plan.
>
> The Liberals defended themselves with no less heat. They threw the hand grenade back, suggesting that *the events might have a Conservative origin*, since some sectors of Conservatism oppose the government of the Armed Forces, and it was the Conservative Party which was pushed from power by the government which came in on the thirteenth of June, 1953.... Things went from bad to worse. And then there was a moment when the Governor of Caldas, Colonel Gustavo Sierra Ochoa ... said, regarding the events in Genova, "They were part of a plan of vast proportions...." This declaration capped the enthusiasm of the Conservative newsmen, one of whom commented in his column in *El Día*, "After spending a year on their knees before the government, the directing clique of *El Tiempo* would naturally return to 'Faith and Dignity'.... From the day that Eduardo Santos announced his return to the country, we predicted dark days in wait for the nation."[17]

[15] "Congreso de Prensa en Colombia," *La Prensa* (New York), November 3, 1954, p. 3.

[16] "Demandarán Militares a Diario 'El Tiempo,'" *La Prensa*, p. 3.

[17] "El Gobierno: Granaderos," *Semana* (Bogotá), November 29, 1954, p. 10.

This flare-up of press polemics caused the government once more to invite the press to "abstain from commentaries and news regarding the public order in these particular days."[18] The Minister of Government explained the request: "[The newspapers] go to extremes and wage a feverish battle over the party affiliation and beliefs of the victims and the affected property, in such terms that . . . they provoke reprisals and dangerous feelings which affect the public welfare. It is the duty of the government to watch over . . . the general peace for all Colombians."[19]

As the year came to an end, with reports circulating that the government would establish an "official newspaper,[20] dedicated to the defense of the government," Diario de Colombia reported more bloody clashes between the Army and "outlaw" forces.[21] And again came the charges and countercharges. The government was slaughtering innocent Liberals; the "outlaws" were Liberals bent upon exterminating peaceful Conservatives.

But something else had been added to the opposition to Rojas: a campaign of rumors and slander which embraced the Army itself. It was somehow reminiscent of the filth campaign which Gómez had sponsored to bring López down. Rojas and his generals, the stories ran, were enriching themselves at public expense; the President's country home was an example of oriental luxury straight out of the Arabian Nights; the Armed Forces were systematically pillaging the nation.

The opposition seemed only to strengthen Rojas' determination to bring the country to its senses. Nonetheless, a new bitterness came into his public announcements. In an address in Pacho, early in March, the President reaffirmed his intention to hold the country to the course he had set, economically, politically, socially. "Public opinion is not that which is artificially created by certain journalists to defend personal economic and political interests," he said. "The public writers and newsmen represent the interests of the enterprises which pay their salaries, and the points of view they express are those of the publisher or stockholders."[22]

[18] Ibid.
[19] Ibid.
[20] "Periódico en Colombia," La Prensa (New York), December 12, 1954, p. 3.
[21] "Muertos en Colombia," La Prensa (New York), December 28, 1954, p. 1.
[22] "Rojas Pinilla Ratifica Orientación Política y Económica de su Gobierno," La Prensa (New York), March 5, 1955, p. 1.

The President had, in fact, begun to act on that assumption. About the first of March, an official program over the National Radio had begun to state the government's point of view: "Public opinion, the authentic national will, is not ... the opinion of the newspapers. Nor does the future of Colombia shape itself through the liverish reactions of the magnates of journalism ... the common man in Colombia is beginning to free himself, as he has in countries of more ambitious culture, from the dictatorship of the reporters ... the national reality is not the reality of the newspapers."[23]

The press turned on Rojas. *El Colombiano* pointed out, "the country has a high opinion of Rojas Pinilla's intelligence, his patriotism, his Catholicism, and his desire to come to the point ... [but] does not approve his economic policy ... the official radio-newspaper ... and other things."[24] And *Diario del Pacífico* and *El Día* reminded Rojas that the government is not public opinion either, unless such opinion goes along with the government.[25]

And to the government's insistence that the public approved the establishment of an official newspaper, *Semana* countered:

> All governments, we all know, are transitory; if they do not count upon the support of the citizens ... expressed through the press or through the representative bodies ... they inevitably fall. The only stable thing is this public opinion of the streets with which we, the hated reporters, come into daily contact.... If liberty of the press is suppressed or cut off, the government will have to struggle with the phantasm of the tendentious, uncontrolled, whimsical versions of public opinion, which is about the same as the infidelity of a woman: the last to find out is the husband.[26]

And so the verbal battle drew on: Rojas trying to control inflammatory writing as he fought both the "bandits" in the provinces and the two parties; the parties indiscriminately hurling verbal brickbats at the opposition and at Rojas, each of which stood in the way of a return to power. But there was considerable substance to Rojas' claim that restraint was necessary in the press if the government was to succeed in re-establishing public order. A résumé of the known events describes a chaotic situation.

On March 17, two bands of partisans, accompanied by Indians

[23] "Transmisión Oficial," *La Prensa* (New York), March 3, 1955, p. 3.
[24] *Ibid.*
[25] "Libertad de Información," *Semana* (Bogotá), March 7, 1955, p. 26.
[26] "La Dictadura de los Reporteros," *Semana* (Bogotá), March 14, 1955, p. 27.

from the Tierradentro region, raided two villages west of Belalcázar, killing a number of citizens, sacking the town, and hacking up the bodies of the police defenders.

The Army's Rook Battalion (named after General Rook of the famed British Legion during the Wars of Liberation), on March 18 encountered a strong force of irregulars, and in a running fight killed six and took a number of prisoners.

More than sixty armed men attacked a hacienda in Chili Rico on March 19, killed the manager and a young man, and fought with the police when they arrived. This encounter brought the total dead in the Department of Tolima to twenty-eight; known wounded, four.

On the same day, in the Department of Valle, a retired Army officer was ambushed and killed by "persons unknown." Twelve were arrested on suspicion.

Between March 19 and 22, in El Valle, two brothers were assassinated by pistol fire; a coffee-roaster was killed by stab wounds and his place of business sacked; a man was shot and killed by "long-range" fire; the body of another was found dead of bullet wounds on a lonely road; and a hacienda owner was killed by seven bullets fired at close range. Total in El Valle killed by persons unknown, seven.

In these same days, many people fled for safety from the district of Monteloro (El Valle); a Cali newspaperman was threatened with death because of stories he had written about the violence; panic spread through the area.

On March 19, in a "political discussion" in the Department of Boyacá, one was killed and three wounded, including the mayor of the town of Toca.

Semana (the source of this résumé) added dryly, "the civil and military authorities of Tolima, and the Departmental Governors of El Valle and Cauca, as well as the military authorities and the press of both parties, have said that it is mere banditry, without political origins."[27] But these incidents were only a prelude to more generalized violence.

In its March 23 edition, *El Tiempo* headlined an outbreak in Tolima in which twenty-eight persons were killed. The military commander of the region claimed that he had "irrefutable proof"

[27] "De Donde Vienen?" *Semana* (Bogotá), March 21, 1955, p. 9.

that Communists were responsible.[28] The violence grew quickly from this clash. On about March 27, a battle occurred between 100 soldiers and 500 partisans near Villarica, Tolima. Newsmen flew over the battlefield during the engagement, in chartered planes, and the fighting went on until darkness fell. After six hours of sharp fighting, it was a draw. Reporters stated that the "bandits" used long-range weapons and machine guns. Villarica is the heart of a rich coffee-producing section, and apparently the irregulars were bent upon seizing the harvest of 100,000 sacks of coffee which is seasonally produced there.[29]

Following the action at Villarica, Rojas declared the area a Zone of Military Operations, and began mounting a major offensive to root out the insurgent elements. By that time, most observers had become convinced that Communist agitators were behind the trouble, Army officials claiming to have proof that the movement was Communist-led. This brought a denial from Gilberto Vieira, the Communist leader, who stated, "The Colombian Communist Party has always denounced the interests linked to violence against the Colombian working masses . . . which is due in great part to influential interests."[30]

By the spring of 1955, the state of public order had become a matter of grave public concern. The nation was, in fact, suffering from a bad case of nerves induced by the memory of past horrors, by the constant atmosphere of crisis created by the political juggling, and by the fear that the armed clashes could be a prelude to a return to generalized civil war. It was not surprising, therefore, that the Colombian government contracted the services of medical specialists from the United States to "work to combat a war neurosis among thousands of Colombians." Their main task was to aid the Colombian Korean veterans, but the United Press, in reporting the matter added, "The war psychosis has grown and extended, due to the state of public order shown in recent years, and which has again broken out in isolated areas."[31]

The public uneasiness probably was not allayed by a government announcement on April 21, 1955, that between March 27 and April

[28] "Matan los Bandoleros a 28 Personas," *La Prensa* (New York), March 22, 1955, p. 3.

[29] "Batalla en Villarica," *La Prensa* (New York), April 8, 1955, p. 1.

[30] *La Prensa* (New York), April 12, 1955, p. 3.

[31] "Contrata Médicos de EE. UU. para Combatir la Neurosis de Guerra," *La Prensa* (New York), April 18, 1955, p. 1.

12 the Army had evacuated 2,314 persons from the "war" zone. The announcement affirmed that the partisans in Tolima were threatening the coffee crop, and that the Army would undertake further operations to protect it.[32] But the very next day "between 70 and 100 bandits" attacked the town of Sambaló, killed the tax collector and two members of the municipal council while the body was in session, quartered the corpses with machetes, and sacked the town. At the moment that this outrage was occurring, the Army was fighting another band in an engagement which took eight lives. Thereupon, the Army ordered the civilian evacuation of Villarica.[33]

By the end of April the situation had become so bad that the Army was using heavy and light bombing planes against the partisans. Refugees were streaming into Ibagué, the central metropolis of the area, where the Army cared for entire families at refugee stations. Nearer the "front," groups of peasants "who had taken part in the campaign and felt that they had been misled" were surrendering under the heavier military pressure, and turning their arms over to the Army.[34]

The official mention of insurgent peasants was the first public mention of a possible economic basis for the conflict. But such a conclusion seemed to find confirmation in a message of May 1 from the Liberal Party Directorate to Rojas Pinilla. The message "applauded some of the steps taken by the government to control the situation," and also contained a complete analysis "of the social and economic aspects of the situation." Too, the government's plans to stabilize the area came in for praise: "the construction of hospitals, of schools, the amplification of facilities for housing and the *revision of titles to land,* in order to take care of the claims to rights of numerous peasants."[35]

This final official admission of the real base of the disorders simply recognized what had long been generally known. Many of the "bandits" still were what they had been under Gómez' repression: miserable and dissatisfied peasants striking out at a system which robbed them of hope. Yet, there was clearly Communist organization and direction of the insurgents.

In its May 5, 1955 edition, *Colombian Newsletter* carried photo-

[32] "Gobierno Colombiano Informa Sobre Actividades Subversivas en Tolima," *La Prensa* (New York), April 21, 1955, p. 3.

[33] *La Prensa* (New York), April 24, 1955, p. 1.

[34] "Causas Económicas," *Semana* (Bogotá), April 25, 1955, p. 8.

[35] *La Prensa* (New York), May 2, 1955, p. 2.

static reproductions of "Lenin and Stalin contribution stamps" which the peasants of the area were forced to buy; photographs of bonds sold to aid the cause of the "Workers-Peasants Alliance," and other types of Communist propaganda which indicated that the peasants were being led by militant Communists who knew their business. (Among the leaders was one referred to as "Lister"; hardly the Lister of Spanish Civil War fame, however.)

The reporter for *Colombian Newsletter* visited refugee camps and interviewed peasants, officials, and prisoners. He reported that the Army was caring for 3,000 refugees, who were "being shipped to the town of Ambalema on the Tolima side of the Magdalena, and from there re-shipped to haciendas in the region, where they are employed by official and private farming enterprises."[36]

Some of the other interesting finds which pointed to Communist direction of the movement were printed instructions to guerrilla groups: "How to Form Guerrilla Units"; "How to Organize Civilian Spy Units"; "How to Make Bombs, Guns and Ammunition" (*Colombian Newsletter* used photographs of several homemade rifles taken from the prisoners, which appeared to be efficiently deadly). One booklet of instruction on guerrilla warfare which the Army confiscated stated in the preface "that it is a translation of a similar piece of literature, originally published in Chinese, by Mao Tse Tung, the present leader of China."[37]

A fragment of an interview between Henry Janschitz, the *Colombian Newsletter* reporter, and a captured "rebel" is enlightening:

Question: "Why are you in jail, what happened to you?"
Answer: "Well, really I don't know, everything is so much confused ... first, some weeks ago, we came to the village to pay our taxes to the government.... Later on, some of these other *señores* came along and told us that the government and the Army are just fooling us, that first they will take our harvests and homes and our money, and that finally they may even kill us.... These *señores* promised us protection from the soldiers, and asked us to pay fees, 'protective taxes', to them.... Some told them that they did not have any money, so they were forced to join the guerrilla units ... some refused to have anything to do with them ... these were assaulted at night, killed, and their homes burned.... I, for instance, paid my taxes, both to the government and to these *señores*, and look what happened to me.... I had to join the guerrillas anyway, and the Army has taken me

[36] *Colombian Newsletter* (Bogotá), May 5, 1955, p. 4.
[37] *Ibid.*, p. 5.

prisoner ... and now I can see that I was all wrong, but you see, everything is so confused."[38]

In commenting upon Janschitz' report, *Semana* added further data. Estimates of the best sources held that there were about 2,000 partisans up in arms in the Tolima region; monetary losses in property destruction approximated a third of a million dollars; Communists were heading the movement, and were effectively playing upon peasant discontent and drawing them into the partisan forces; and finally, Colonel Forero, commander of the Zone of Operations, was convinced that the causes of the trouble were political, social, and economic, with the economic factors weighing most heavily.[39]

By the end of April, the Army claimed to have "stabilized" the region, but between the middle of May and the third week of June, trouble once more broke out. The troubled state of public nerves was reflected in all political sectors. On May 22, eleven public figures, all former governors of El Valle, sent Rojas Pinilla a letter which suggested a National Peace Commission and denounced unabated disorder in the Department.[40] On the same day, a university students' strike culminated a long battle between Rojas and the universities, a quarrel which found Rojas deploring the political influence of the schools on the students.[41]

Tolima remained turbulent. In mid-May, twenty-seven were killed and four wounded in a "bandit attack"[42] and a week later military authorities announced that 104 peasant families had been seized by the insurgents, to be used as hostages. On June 10, university students demonstrated in commemoration of the twelve students killed by the Army on that date in 1954; police broke up the demonstration with swinging billies. Three days later, *Semana* spoke pessimistically:

Colombians who, thanks to the silence regarding the matter of public order, had begun to think that peace had been imposed at last in Tolima, last week had an unpleasant surprise when the government issued a communique which states that the Armed Forces are getting ready to carry out the third and final phase of their operations ... the first reflection which sticks in one's mind, in the face of

[38] *Ibid.*
[39] "Pruebas Evidentes," *Semana* (Bogotá), May 16, 1955, p. 8.
[40] *La Prensa* (New York), May 23, 1955, p. 3.
[41] *Ibid.*
[42] *La Prensa* (New York), June 3, 1955, p. 3.

the persistence of a state of things that everyone thought finished, is that something very deep, something whose true nature had escaped the understanding of the nation, must be behind this incredible and useless action of a group of Colombian people.[43]

Social revolutions are, in fact, incredible to those who are unused to the conditions which cause other men to turn to violence. Where there is no sharing of basic aspirations, there can be no mutual comprehension of purpose.

And so, the Army moved in its final phase of clean-up operations. In late June, it announced the extermination of the Tolima guerrilla bands.[44]

But in July, trouble flared in El Valle, and the newspapers which reported it felt the swift hand of censorship. Nonetheless, the United Press reported from Bogotá on July 20:

In the city of Tuluá ... several well-known citizens have been the victims of surprise attacks. In other places in the Department there have occurred similar attacks and killings. Among the victims are the newspaperman, Emilio Correa Uribe and his son, who was manager of *El Diario* of Pereira. The latest victim was the lawyer Arístides Arrieta, a notable personage of Tuluá. In Cartago and other places, attacks have occurred, with several victims. Some months before, a distinguished Liberal politician was killed. The Liberal newspapers have affirmed that the most noteworthy victims have fallen because of their party affiliations.[45]

With the partisan charges regarding "banditry" once more flying, the government issued still another decree intended to still the clamor. This decree was flaunted by *Diario de Colombia* on October 8 with a front-page account of the murder of eleven Conservatives, including the Conservative director of the Municipality of Gutiérrez.[46] On the following day, the secretary of the National Conservative Directorate blamed "political banditry by Liberals" for the murders in Gutiérrez.[47] The printed-personal cycle of violence seemed to have no end, one inciting the other, and the government damned for censoring the printed violence, while it was cursed for not being able to halt the physical violence which fed on the printed kind.

Rojas, in all justice, tried for a considerable time to handle the

[43] "Parte Conturbador," *Semana* (Bogotá), June 13, 1955, p. 7.

[44] *La Prensa* (New York), June 22, 1955, p. 1.

[45] "Mas Violencia en Colombia," *La Prensa* (New York), July 21, 1955, p. 3.

[46] *Diario de Colombia* (Bogotá), October 8, 1955, p. 1.

[47] "De la Violencia en Colombia," *La Prensa* (New York), October 12, 1955, p. 1.

problem of violent partisanship fairly. The gentleman's agreement was not official censorship, but a reasonable plea for self-restraint in a matter which could ramify (and gradually did) into explosive acts contrary to public order. The Army needed the tranquillity of opinion in order to reassure all factions, and to calm passions which had too long run out of control. The manner in which the highly partisan press agitated and exploited public disturbances for the sake of political advantage was entirely contrary to the best interests of the nation. In this alone there was justification for Rojas' use of censorship, once the press had demonstrated its partisan irresponsibility. Beyond that, the constitution imposed responsibility upon the press, in times of public disorder. In effect, Rojas was not acting against the interests of the press, but in the interest of the whole people, of the Colombian nation. Any objective analysis of the relationship between press polemics of a partisan nature and the actual physical violence would establish their cause-and-effect character.

The Colombian press is strongly equated with the factional party lines, with *caudillo* ownership and control, with the economic and political interests of special groups in each party. In times of national instability, such a press can become a weapon of incalculable effectiveness. It is very questionable whether it speaks for the nation as much as it does for a clique, a group, an interest, a high-level complex of interests within a party. As such, it has shown itself lacking in true public responsibility.

Rojas' handling of the press problem drew together the lines of resistance to his regime, but in view of his basic objectives, there was little else that he could do. Possibly his greatest mistake was at first assuming that the press was more patriotic than partisan, that the newspapers would put the interest of the nation ahead of their respective political interests. Justice is with Rojas when he says that the press broke the gentleman's agreement.

There has been much more criticism of the regime permitted under Rojas than one would suppose in a country which has been stigmatized by the United States press as laboring under censorship. From the beginning, the emphasis was not upon stilling opposition, so much as upon getting the government's point of view before the nation—an almost impossible feat when half the newspapers are dominated by Liberal politicians who oppose Rojas, and the other half by Conservative politicians who want him to surrender power to them.

In this battle between the government and the press-party tycoons, the masses of the people had little to say. They seemed to be content with social and economic gains and an emphasis in governing which recognized their importance, rather than exercised about the freedom of the press. To the oligarchy, this was proof that the masses do not understand democracy.

But the common people rallied in public demonstrations of their support of Rojas when he closed *El Tiempo*. If, in that act of the President, they had lost some of their democracy, they did not seem aware of it.

XVI. Political Tug-of-War: Rojas Pinilla *versus* the Liberals *versus* the Conservatives (1955–1956)

Until Rojas Pinilla, his patience exhausted with an intransigent press, closed the great daily, *El Tiempo*, the political parties were unable to find a rallying point for their attacks designed to recapture political power. But that questionable culmination of the question over whether the press should enjoy liberty or license seemed to establish definite trends where before there had been blind, indecisive groping.

Shortly before the outbreak of violence in November, 1954, Alfonso López suggested a bipartisan government, in which Liberals and Conservatives would share policy-making, power, and responsibility. López explained:

> Bureaucratic monopoly, organized and maintained as a system of government by a party invariably left unpleasant memories ... it is the principle of a process well enough known in the political annals of Latin America, which is begun by assuming that it is the legitimate right of the victor in the political battle to make of the public administration a sort of booty of war, and, beyond that, carrying the system to its extremes, to prevent the defeated party from recovering its position and influence in the popularly elected bodies by the same means in which it lost them. The paralysis of representative institutions thus determined, the process is usually completed by concentrating in the hands of the executive the faculties of governing and legislating by decree.[1]

But this was a questionable solution, regardless of the evils of the party battle to get their hands on the budget and the administration. For the dreary facts of Colombian history indicate the impossibility of bipartisan government. A certain limited collaboration has been worked out when mass agitation has threatened the upper classes of both parties. But always, when the pressure from below has eased, the collaborating parties have ended up in a slam-bang fight to the finish for the whole prize.

[1] "Liberales: Respuesta Tardía," *Semana* (Bogotá), November 29, 1954, p. 8.

279

Possibly for this reason, López' suggestion was not taken seriously. But other trends soon appeared. In early November, 1954, a vague kind of "Third Force" made its first showing, when a Conservative, Felix Arango Vallejo, suggested to the President a movement in support of the government comprising elements from both parties and supported strongly by the (Peronist) *Confederación Nacional de Trabajadores*, now defunct. This group would "fight against political sectarianism and the phenomenon of political violence," which had so long plagued the nation.[2] But Rojas at that time withheld his approval, and the movement died a-borning.

Nonetheless, pressure grew upon Rojas to end the "state of siege" and return political power to the parties. Throughout the entire year of 1954 the Liberals and Conservatives skirmished, jockeyed for position, and sought to draw from the President some definite word regarding when he would step down and declare elections.

Naturally, therefore, there were downcast countenances when, in his New Year's Message, 1955, Rojas declared that the state of siege would not be lifted "while I am in power."[3] His justification for this stand: "To throw the country back into electoral debates would be the equivalent of paving the way for the return of the horrible epochs which we cannot sufficiently condemn."[4] He was right. He spoke thus at the moment when violence was sweeping through Tolima and the parties were charging one another with masterminding the savagery.

And all the while, the hazy idea of some demonstration of mass support to counter the opposition to Rojas by the party oligarchs seemed to grow in the background. Liberals and Conservatives were worried, for they did not doubt the true sentiments of the masses of people. "What Liberals and Conservatives fear with equal apprehension is that President Rojas wants to pass into history for more than having pacified and governed the nation in its most critical period: that he wishes to add to his deserved laurels that of founder of a party which would not be precisely a third one, but the first of militarist character in Colombia," *Semana* reported.[5] And it pointed out that a careful reading of political editorials of the weeks leading up to the New Year's Message indicated that the professional poli-

---

[2] *La Prensa* (New York), December 9, 1954, p. 3.
[3] *Time*, January 3, 1955, p. 40.
[4] *La Prensa* (New York), January 3, 1955, p. 3.
[5] "Perspectiva," *Semana* (Bogotá), January 10, 1955, p. 7.

ticians were fearful that Rojas might exploit *"the momentary disillusionment or coldness of the masses of the two traditional parties to found a 'force' . . . which could use the platforms announced by the Office of Propaganda as a program."*[6]

But it was already late for the political oligarchs to start worrying about strayed sheep. The masses of the people notably did not oppose Rojas.

The upper classes did not accept with good grace Rojas' announcement that the state of siege would continue. "There are many voices raised in nonconformity, and many angry voices,"[7] said *Semana* with admirable self-restraint. And by way of protest, a magistrate of the Supreme Court, Eduardo Rodríguez Piñeres (who had been appointed by Rojas), resigned his post.[8] Rojas offered polite regrets, but accepted the resignation.

During January, the movement for a popular demonstration favoring Rojas gathered force. February 26 was agreed upon as the date. The "Third Force" now had a name: *Movimiento de Acción Nacional* (MAN). It was not, however, an organic, spontaneous movement of support. Rather, it was born of the desire of disaffected politicians from both parties to define *something*, at a time when all political trends were completely without definition.

The major support for MAN came from a group of insurgent Conservatives, a somewhat smaller number of Liberals, and the Socialists.[9] The Peronist labor union, the CNT, lent its support also, a fact which tended to discredit it in the eyes of many. Naturally, the party oligarchs were "very preoccupied" by the movement, as it posed a threat to them by offering a possible new medium for masses of the people to express their aspirations.

But very possibly the CNT was the major factor in MAN's failure. Long before the date of the proposed demonstration, the propaganda for the movement began to take on a dangerous and explosive classist coloration. "In Bogotá and other cities, placards appeared which demanded support of the government and battle with the oligarchies." In effect, this may have played into the hands of the traditional parties, for they were "not unaware that these [devices] acted as stealthy

---

[6] *Semana* (Bogotá), January 10, 1955, p. 7.
[7] "Política Colombiana," *La Prensa* (New York), January 6, 1955, p. 3.
[8] *Ibid.*
[9] "Tirando la Cobija," *Semana* (Bogotá), February 7, 1955, p. 5.

propaganda against the government, when the people go through the cities and towns proclaiming the necessity of supporting a government which wants nothing to do for and nothing to do with the traditional parties because it has no confidence in them."[10]

It now appears that MAN overstated the issues by its appeal to violence. Rojas had from the start been opposed to inflammatory action, and he was now averse to open calls for a class struggle.[11] Therefore, in early February he forbade the demonstration, and MAN was killed by the man whom it was intended to honor.

There were other factors, too, which made MAN undesirable. The Liberals and Conservatives backing it had adopted the outworn mechanics of "collaboration" between the parties, while the two great collectivities were reluctant to express through MAN their own opposition vis-à-vis the government. These factors, says *Semana*, "produced the fall of the political apparatus so precariously set up. The government realized the reality of these facts, and, moreover, that the thermometer to judge its influence and the state of public opinion was actually not in the hands of new leaders, drawn (as it had thought) from Liberalism, Conservatism and Socialism."[12] The CNT, taking the initiative, had driven away the "respectable" political elements.

And yet, this manifestation of dissatisfaction with the old parties was deep and strong in many sectors. Many signs pointed to mass support for the Rojas regime, to disillusionment with the political maneuvering of the party oligarchs. The people were aware that the parties offered nothing new. "One of the gravest symptoms of the national crisis," wrote a commentator,

is our incapacity to bear up to the past. Colombia, as Forero Benavides sagely observes, is the only country in the world where, after a catastrophe, there are neither those who repent, nor those who are guilty. Everybody is right. All raise high the flag in their hands. Everyone speaks for a principle. No one was wrong. No one cares to rectify mistakes. No one modifies his historic posture before the march of events. Everyone goes ahead, a step more, a step less, with exactly the same influence in the life of the nation.[13]

The events of 1948–53 had apparently left no major lesson with the two political parties. This in itself was sufficient justification for Rojas

[10] *Ibid.*
[11] *Ibid.*
[12] "No ... MAN," *Semana* (Bogotá), February 14, 1955, p. 5.
[13] Padilla, "La Historia no es un Carrousel," *Semana*, p. 26.

to continue in power. The leaders were the same: Laureano Gómez, Ospina Pérez, and Alzate Avendaño on the Conservative side of the aisle; Alfonso López, Eduardo Santos, Carlos Lleras Restrepo on the Liberal side. Moreover, "the parties had not changed their positions, had not made any recommendations for betterment, had not proposed to the nation any fundamental readjustment of customs or political systems. Both would like to return to a civil regime. But ... democratic reconstruction cannot consist merely in setting up again the scenery for the old farce, in order that, on the same stage, the same men, with the same system, lead the Republic again into the same errors."[14]

Politically, Colombia was dissatisfied and uncomfortable under military government, but the former ruling minority was unable to find any formula which met both their own aspirations and those of the masses of people who supported Rojas.

On April 10, a public act of homage took place in memory of the slain popular leader, Jorge Eliécer Gaitán. Organized by the Liberals with the permission of the government, the affair drew thousands to the *Parque Nacional*. Gaitán's voice was heard on recordings. One Conservative and two Liberal leaders spoke. Attempts made by the Conservative Directorate to sabotage the meeting had been unsuccessful. But the oligarchs had their revenge: this major demonstration of popular political feeling *was completely ignored by the major Liberal and Conservative newspapers*. Three small newspapers gave it coverage, while the great dailies of both parties joined in a "conspiracy of silence" to minimize this homage of the masses to a dead leader.[15]

But three weeks later, *La República*, raising the phantom of class struggle, identified this mass gathering with the defunct MAN: "Now, when we are newly menaced by the belligerent presence of a Third Party which, from all signs, *is nothing more than a revitalization of Gaitanist Liberalism*, it is necessary that we recall traditionalist principles."[16]

In this statement is to be found the essence of the blind weakness of the two traditional parties. Gaitán was important because he voiced the aspirations of a social revolution. MAN, essentially, tried

---

[14] *Ibid.*

[15] *Semana* (Bogotá), May 2, 1955, p. 12.

[16] *Ibid.*

to (fumblingly) do the same thing. The support of the popular masses behind Rojas was evidence of continued faith in the fulfillment of that revolution; and the honoring of the dead leader spoke of the same faith and hope. Fear of that faith kept the party press silent—the typical "ostrich-head-in-the-sand" psychology which marked their reaction to the whole violent course of the revolution—and when at last they spoke, it was to issue a call for the faithful to rally around the same doctrine that the people had rejected with five years of bloody struggle.

This fear came to the party oligarchs at a time when the violence was flaring in Tolima and El Valle; when rumors persisted that a third party and a government newspaper would soon be a reality. These rumors deepened that fear and excited many of the bitter press attacks of the time. On April 19, *El Tiempo* affirmed that a third party was a certainty, and that it would be organized along corporate lines, to the end of "swallowing up elements of the two traditional parties for the purpose of supporting the government."[17] A few days later the major capital newspapers quoted "sources worthy of credence" to the effect that an official newspaper, capitalized at eight million pesos, would soon be a reality.

During this period of oligarchic fear and uncertainty there became current, too, many ugly rumors concerning President Rojas' personal enrichment since taking over the reins of government. They reached as far as the Pan American Union in Washington where, according to one official, it was common talk that Rojas was going in for large-scale pillage. "Not that he is grafting outright. But in return for a favor, someone gives him a prime bull, let us say. Well, what good is a bull without a few cows? And then, one must have a *finca* to pasture the herd. *Entiende, Senor?*"[18] And at a meeting of the Socialist party in May, Antonio García was roundly applauded when he called upon "men of state to publicly declare their incomes."[19]

Rojas had become a prime target for the angry, the envious, the political oppositionist. Therefore, most of the rumors probably were not true. At any rate, in early May, when the Rojas-press-party struggle was coming to full heat, and violence was rising in Tolima and El

[17] "Rumórase Creación de Partido Colombiano," *La Prensa* (New York), April 20, 1955, p. 3.

[18] As told to the writer by an official of the Pan American Union.

[19] *Semana* (Bogotá), May 9, 1955, p. 7.

Valle, he invited a group of labor leaders, politicians, and newsmen to his country home, probably in an effort to counteract some of the slanderous gossip. *Semana* reported:

> The invitees came to one conclusion: the summer home of the President is a little more modest than one of those which serve the oligarchs of lesser capital to spend their holidays. The conclusion was important, because many of the visitors had heard of the fabulous richness of that house, which they supposed would be surrounded by guard walls and a moat. Another conclusion which others reached: President Rojas is no enigmatic Buddha surrounded and isolated by a vigilant and jealous community of monks. The President demonstrates that he is well informed of the facts, of what the politicians do and say, and even of the jokes, good and bad, that the gay gatherings at the clubs and cafes heap on the shoulders of the president himself and his ministers.[20]

That there was a stubborn sense of justice behind Rojas' handling of the press was demonstrated by his imposition of censorship on *Diario de Colombia* on May 17, 1955. The managing editor of this paper is Rojas' son-in-law, Samuel Moreno Díaz. The publication had printed an account of the killing of twenty-three "bandits" by the Army, at a time when the press had been warned to forego comments upon public violence in the general interest.[21] Consequently, although known as a partisan of Rojas' government, the paper was subjected to censorship.

In the welter of conflicting interest, with the parties skirmishing for position around the government, and the Army fighting insurrectionists in Tolima, *Semana* sounded a sober note of warning:

> The political problem will remain insoluble while we fail to recognize that something broke on June 13, 1955. It is neither possible nor desirable to return to the past. Neither to Conservative "normalcy" nor to "Liberal normalcy." When will we convince ourselves that the military regime is a bridge between the old order and the new, between the Republic in crisis, and the fatherland so desired by people without hate? ... And as the President says, peace is not a simple idea, nor a mere desirable condition, but an essential atmosphere for life and work in Colombia.[22]

But the peace was far away as, with the mounting violence in the provinces, physical violence was paralleled by printed partisan violence, forcing Rojas to require prior censorship of all material affect-

[20] "Hombre Tenaz," *Semana* (Bogotá), May 9, 1955, p. 7.
[21] "Sanción Gubernamental," *La Prensa* (New York), May 18, 1955, p. 3.
[22] Jorge Padilla, "El Gobiernómetro," *Semana* (Bogotá), May 30, 1955, p. 12.

ing the public order in nine more important newspapers between June and July, 1955.[23] And by that time, ill feelings and tension had grown to climactic proportions. The true climax came with Rojas' closing of *El Tiempo*; and this incident grew out of his visit to Ecuador, to repay a state visit from President Velasco Ibarra. The incidents leading up to the ban on the great daily are worth recounting, for they are part and parcel of the events already described. Moreover, in this affair, Rojas provided his opposition with the stimulus and the weapon to forge a united front against his regime.

Rojas, with a large retinue, arrived in Quito at the end of July. On August 1, he was interviewed by foreign newsmen regarding his recent imposition of censorship on *El Tiempo* and *El Espectador*. As a result of that interview, a Quito correspondent sent a story which said, in part, "[Rojas Pinilla] declared that *El Tiempo* and *El Espectador* exploited for political ends the recent deaths in a traffic accident of three persons."[24]

Upon reading that, Roberto García Peña, editor of *El Tiempo*, on the same day sent the following cable to Jorge Mantilla, managing editor of *El Comercio* of Quito:

> According to an Associated Press report, President Rojas declared that *El Tiempo* and *El Espectador* had, for political reasons and purposes, exploited the deaths in a traffic accident of three persons. Possibly the President was referring to the assassination of Emilio Correa Uribe, director of *El Diario* of Pereira, and of his son, the lawyer, Carlos Correa, by assassins who, in the *Valle del Cauca* are known by the name of "birds" [pajaros], criminals in the pay of political violence. The assassination was not a traffic accident, as they are trying to make it appear; it is being investigated, but the material authors of the crime, now well known to all, have not been arrested and the crime continues to go unpunished. I beg you to make this clarification over my signature, because it is not possible that truth be deformed with the aid of your generous Ecuadorian hospitality. Cordial greetings.
>
> Roberto García Peña

This message, which said, in effect, "The President of Colombia lied," was printed in Quito. Under the circumstances it was at least bad taste, and at worst, an unwarranted transferral of the partisan fight with Rojas to the territory of a friendly nation. In the Quito version, the phrase, "over my signature" was omitted, and the title "Managing Editor of *El Tiempo*" was placed beneath García Peña's signature.

[23] *La Prensa* (New York), July 29, 1955, p. 3.

[24] This résumé from *Semana* (Bogotá), August 15, 1955, pp. 9–11.

On August 3, García Peña was summoned to a conference with the Chief of Staff, General Rafaél Calderón Reyes. The General transmitted to him, verbally, orders from Rojas Pinilla: *El Tiempo* was to publish for thirty consecutive days on its front page, without additional comment, a retraction of the substance of García Peña's cable. The text of the retraction had been prepared, and the General handed it to García Peña for study. The alternative to accepting the conditions stated was simply that troops would prevent *El Tiempo* from publishing and circulating.

This was a serious matter. The editor asked for time to submit a counterproposal. Time was granted him. In a matter of a few hours *El Tiempo* submitted its counterproposal: it would publish the prepared text between quotation marks, together with an additional clarifying statement of acceptance of the government's explanation.

Two hours later, police occupied the offices and plant of *El Tiempo*.

The next day, another attempt to settle the matter was rejected by the government. In the evening, Lucio Pabón Nuñez, minister of government, went on the National Radio to advise the nation that the great daily had been closed. What he told the people threw a bad light on the intemperate text of the telegram to Quito by *El Tiempo's* editors.

It was untrue, the Minister pointed out, that the culprits had not been punished. The prosecutor in charge of the case was a member of the Liberal party (the party to which the victims belonged). The three occupants of the automobile which had hit that of the Correas had been quickly identified, and two had been immediately arrested and were being held. A search was on for the third, but he had not yet been apprehended. Moreover, it appeared from the investigation that the death of the Correas was not an act of political violence. Exploiting it as such was censurable, because it impeded justice and disturbed the public order. As for the cable to Quito, the bald implication was that the President was lying; and the false statements and implied charges it contained were punishable under the penal law. Particularly did it lack justification because it was an attempt to turn the matter into an international crisis, by making it appear that Rojas had abused the hospitality of a friendly nation.[25]

Nonetheless, the shocked reaction of the nation and of the inter-

[25] *Semana* (Bogotá), August 15, 1955, p. 10.

national press at the closing of *El Tiempo* was followed by a heavy barrage of criticism of Rojas' "dictatorial regime and tactics." But if there remained any doubt as to how the masses of the Colombian people felt about it, the popular demonstration in support of his action, which occurred on August 13, dispelled such doubt. "If the masses were not fickle and inconstant," mused *Semana* in reporting the interesting event,

it could be said that they issued, on Saturday, August 13, the death certificate of the two Colombian political parties, or at least their exclusion for an indefinite period from active life. In fact, the demonstration carried out by the public on this day, as evidence of support of the President of the Republic and the Government of the Armed Forces, brought together a vast multitude which not only howled its agreement with all that the government has done (particularly with regard to the closing of *El Tiempo*) but *also, through its thousands of mouths and those of seven orators, proclaimed the necessity of a new political foundation, despite the fact that innumerable demonstrators carried blue flags to indicate their adherence to Conservatism, and also despite the fact that some of the orators, among them Darío Samper, spoke in the name of Liberalism.* The common denominator of the speeches was none other than a reiterated desire for radical change, a vehement condemnation of all that our political bipartisanship is.

The demonstration of the thirteenth indicates that the government, through the force of adherence which its proposals awakens, *can mobilize masses of humanity such as formerly Liberalism and Conservatism did.* The road then is cleared, the way open ... for the appearance of a program which will be challenged neither from the Left nor the Right. The new policy, nonetheless, could be none of those announced by the orators ... but another very far different: that which President Rojas Pinilla had in mind and which he announced to the people on June 13, 1953 ... a policy "over and above the parties."[26]

There seems little doubt that Rojas has earned for himself over the months, two very important things: the enmity of the oligarchs, social, economic, and of the parties; and, more important, a strong mass support which constantly acts as a force driving him toward some *de facto* third party movement or coalition to give battle to the oligarchies. This popular support, so long as it is valid and continuing, carries grave responsibilities. "[It] places upon him an historic task such as only two of his predecessors in the presidency have faced in this half century: Enrique Olaya Herrera and Alfonso López."[27]

There is good reason to believe that he is aware of this, despite his ill-humor with the partisan press. In his address to the multitudes who

[26] "Punto de Partida," *Semana* (Bogotá), August 22, 1955, p. 7.
[27] *Ibid.*

demonstrated in his support, he said of the program which he has tried to carry out on behalf of the masses, "it constitutes for the government not an objective reached, but a point of departure." And again he reiterated his determination to make further agrarian reforms and to foster more workers' cooperatives in the future; gave unions the right to hold meetings after merely notifying the authorities (until then, they needed affirmative permission) of their intention; and again called upon all Colombians to abandon their blindly partisan pursuits for the search for a national welfare.

But not all Colombians were in accord with Rojas.

On August 10 a large crowd of women demonstrated in Bogotá against press censorship. They were dispersed by police, one report saying that they were scattered by the use of "water and tear gas."[28] (A distinguished figure of this "mob" was the wife of former President Mariano Ospina Pérez, who had used press censorship lavishly in his preparation for the Gómez regime.)

Naturally, too, intellectuals, party directors, and many public figures joined forces to deplore the closing of *El Tiempo*. Rojas answered with further censorship, and by barring *Time* and *Visión* from the country.[29]

But it would be a grave error to assume that Rojas had dried up news sources. Quite the contrary had occurred. If anything, he had unwittingly stimulated journalism more than anything else since the invention of the rotary press. The closing of *El Tiempo* alone "resulted in a notorious growth of circulation for the provincial dailies," according to *Semana*, and many former staffers of *El Tiempo* were soon hired by those expanding enterprises. *El Correo* of Medellín, for example, opened a Bogotá editorial office manned wholly by ex-*El Tiempo* writers! Moreover, there was feverish activity in the outlying regions "to create new dailies or reorganize the existing ones."[30]

As one would expect, the fall of Peron in Argentina caused the gentlemen of the Fourth Estate to dip their quills in not-too-mild acid. The press broke out in a rash of admonitory editorials. By insinuation, choice of heads and key words, the writers "tried to convey and present similarities with the Colombian situation. *La República* and

[28] *Visión* (Santiago), September 2, 1955, p. 13.

[29] "Nuevo Golpe Contra la Prensa," *La Prensa* (New York), September 2, 1955, p. 1.

[30] "Panorama," *Semana* (Bogotá), September 5, 1955, pp. 15–16.

Diario Gráfico stated more than once that the Argentine case held a 'lesson' which should not be inadvertently overlooked. Said *La República*: 'The dramatic fall of the Argentine dictator proves once more those old ideas, given new vigor by events, on which the author of *The Spirit of the Laws* based this thesis: in order that liberty and order be maintained, it is necessary that power check power ... this great juridic and traditional theory is the very equilibrium of social and political forces ... the fall of Peron carries profound lessons for the whole world. ...' "[31]

To this, *Semana* added its own commentary:

> The insistence upon the use of the word "lesson" was universally interpreted as an effort to establish parallels with the Colombian situation, despite the fact that parallels are impossible in as much as so many and such profound differences exist [between the two countries]. The careful reader of the commentaries could make a complete map of the position which each Colombian group occupies vis-à-vis the national government.[32]

Nor was Rojas unmoved by the "lesson" of Argentina. On September 23, the day after Peron's fall, he announced the end of press censorship—and promptly established new restrictions. Significantly, there was to take place that very night a banquet-rally of highly placed Liberals to honor Eduardo Santos, owner of *El Tiempo*. The new decree forbade "publication of any material directly or indirectly disrespectful of the President of the Republic, or the head of any friendly nation, or compromising Colombia's international position." (Press commentaries had been drawing attention to the recent *rapprochement* between Peru and Venezuela; Rojas' visit to Ecuador was regarded as a counter to this alignment of two powers not notably friendly to Colombia.)

All in all, these moves indicated Rojas' awareness of a gathering pressure from the interests most powerful in the nation's life. And the meeting of Liberals to honor Santos represented a coalescence of that pressure. Present at the Hotel Tequendama banquet were "representatives of the fifty families who once governed the nation, mingling in their hands economic and political control within a framework of liberalism." Notably present, too, were many powerful and influential Conservatives, dining side by side with their opposite numbers of the oligarchy.

[31] "Reflejos," *Semana* (Bogotá), September 26, 1955, p. 8.
[32] *Ibid.*

The principal address was that of Alberto Lleras Camargo, whose understandable theme was, "We, too, are Colombians, and we have a right to participate." His words stirred vast enthusiasm as he reviewed his listeners' hopes of regaining "what all those present had agreed upon calling, in continental parlance, 'democracy.' "[33]

But there was one thing lacking: although Lleras and Santos spoke in rousing terms of a "civil front" to oppose the military regime, they offered no program, no revision of the old concepts. Opposition was the keynote, not reformation or reconstruction.

Yet this meeting had deep significance. "The [two] parties have faced up to the Government of the Armed Forces, and seek its disappearance. And even though they are minority groups, because of the instruments which they have at hand in the physics of politics, they constitute a weight that cannot be underestimated."[34]

This Liberal rally acted as the stimulus which excited a Conservative political response as predictable as that of Pavlov's dogs. Awakening with a start, *Diario de Colombia* noted that "not only the government, but the Conservative Party and the whole country would be profoundly wrong in thinking that Liberalism had lost its force in the national life."[35] Still a danger, liberalism was to be regarded as sufficient reason for the disunited wings of the Conservative party to unite in support of the government.

But when the movement for unification came, it came as a pact between the Conservative factions of Antioquia binding them to common effort in opposition to the government, and using the closing of *El Tiempo* as their *modus vivendi* with one another and with the Liberals.[36] The union in Antioquia seemed to stir optimism in the National Directorate of the Conservative party, which called for a convention in December, the government permitting, which would "include persons from all the Conservative elements, [even] those who remained loyal to Laureano Gómez."[37]

While this party maneuvering was beginning, Rojas Pinilla told a reporter from *Visión*, "I am aware that the great contemporary problem of the press is that of moving between two extremes equally

[33] "El Retorno," *Semana* (Bogotá), October 3, 1955, p. 13.
[34] *Ibid.*
[35] "Balance," *Semana* (Bogotá), October 10, 1955, p. 16.
[36] "Convención Conservadora," *La Prensa* (New York), October 24, 1955, p. 3.
[37] *Ibid.*

dangerous: that of the abuse of authority by governments, and the abuse of liberty by the press. I began my governing by turning back full freedom of the press. Unfortunately, some newspapers brought up the dangers of the second extreme, that is, the abuse of the power of the press, which obliged my government to take steps which neither I nor any of my ministers desired to take."[38]

[38] *Visión* (Santiago), October 14, 1955, p. 15.

XVII.   The Battle Lines Are Drawn (1956–?)

As 1955 passed and the Rojas regime began its fourth calendar year in government, upper-class Colombians were unhappy and restless. The parties were drifting toward the old pattern of collaboration, this time, to try to unseat a military government which was avowedly trying to effect a social revolution just as in the past they had joined hands across party lines to keep down similar movements by civil reform groups. There was, in fact, little difference, since it was the oligarchs of both parties against a popular-based movement. But this time, they had on their side the justification of pleading for a return to civil government. Those who did not look behind the real lines of control of public power could accept without question the complaints of the civil parties that the military government was tyrannical and dictatorial. Nor would they be bothered by the knowledge that the civil governing parties had notoriously been so, too, for the opposition party.

But as the year ended, violence again struck in the western provinces. Shortly before Christmas, 1955, the bodies of eleven persons were found, dead of gunshot and machete wounds, near Armenia, killed, apparently, by one of the roving bands of desperadoes which still infest the area. *La República* of Armenia reported that "many peasant families were moving into the cities nearby to escape the attacks of the *bandoleros*."[1]

Again, three days after Rojas Pinilla delivered his 1956 New Year's Message to the nation, a party of six hundred irregulars attacked San Pedro, in the Department of Tolima, destroyed the town, stole cattle, and killed thirty-two peasants. Reporting the attack, *Diario de Colombia* added that on December 31, bandits had killed twenty-five in two other regions of the Department, bringing the total to fifty-seven in a matter of a week.[2]

But on the whole, the parties did not seem to weigh too heavily the alternative to a Rojas Pinilla: a possible return to public anarchy.

[1] "Forajidos en la Cordillera," *La Prensa* (New York), December 18, 1955, p. 3.
[2] *La Prensa* (New York), January 5, 1956, p. 1.

293

Yet, significantly, there was no concerted move to unseat the regime. Reasons for this were many, but essentially, thoughtful Colombians knew that without Rojas, the nation would again face the abyss. Said a *New York Times* dispatch from Bogotá:

> Opposition to the President and his "Government of the Armed Forces" is not taking a more open form because the dictatorial apparatus makes it impossible, and because many Colombians feel that General Rojas' rule is preferable to the horrors of civil warfare.... Even those who deplore General Rojas' methods point out that anything short of his drastic policies could have meant total disruption of the national life. They recall that the period between independence in 1819 and the turn of the century was characterized by almost continuous bloodshed and that violent solutions are part of the national psychology.[3]

But "in the same breath" that they made this admission, these same Colombians pointed out that Rojas stands in the way of a "restoration" of democracy, and that there should be no price on freedom. To this question, Rojas himself gave the answer in an address opening a great public works exposition in Bogotá: "I ask myself how the government can be losing prestige? Formerly, the Liberal governments persecuted Conservatives, and many Conservative authorities persecuted Liberals, while today every Colombian knows . . . morning, noon and night . . . that the Armed Forces vigilantly guard his life, his honor and his property."[4]

Nonetheless, upper-class Colombians, schooled in making their own public decisions, found this kind of paternalism extremely galling. They were faced with a difficult choice: anarchy, or order at the price of paternalism. Moreover, "the opposing politicos of both parties are, by long tradition, well-bred, cultured, often wealthy men, not prone to lead revolutionaries to the barricades. Admitted one: 'If you gave me 50,000 men, I still would not know how to capture the presidential palace.' "[5]

Contrary to general belief, Rojas did not destroy the traditional parties. He simply rendered them ineffective for the time being as makers of public decisions. They remained active, well-organized, and still vocal and active as an opposition to the government. He did not touch their organic character, but imposed a moratorium upon

[3] Tad Szluc, "Colombians Find Peace Costly," *New York Times,* January 23, 1956.
[4] "Going Strong," *Time,* p. 39.
[5] *Ibid.*

their use of the public polls, for reasons which are apparent in Colombia's recent history. At times, this seemed to bother his conscience, as in an address he made in December, 1955: "The former *guerrilleros*, who gave us military people such a fight, today are the most in favor of the government; and it is curious that the government has to be fighting against the intellectuals, against the best-educated people in the nation, because they want to become intellectual *guerrilleros*."[6]

In his New Year's Message of January 1, 1956, Rojas alluded to the still disturbed state of public order, affirmed his determination to permit no further transfer of the party battles to the pages of the press, and castigated the critics of such agencies as SENDAS and the *Caja Agraria* and *Banco Popular*, "whose object is to favor the working classes." Such criticism, he pointed out, only added a dangerous stimulus to the class struggle, and further disturbed the public state of mind.[7] For the Civil Front of opposition—the term adopted by united Liberals and Conservatives seeking to regain civil control of the government—he laid down this challenge:

> The gentlemen of the opposition, or of the so-called Civil Front, abusing the full liberty of the press which is at their service, may well criticize the acts of the government and deny the swift progress which the country is making, which is a matter of astonishment to nationals and foreigners in every region of the nation and in every phase of living; they may well say that Colombian engineers do not fulfill their duties, and that because of professional incompetence or administrative lack of integrity public monies are being misspent, even when before their eyes there is in progress a plan of public works which, in a few years, will make Colombia into a modern nation, thankful and proud of native engineering and engineers.[8]

But the gathering discontent with Rojas and his government was inevitably to show itself in some public fashion. The occasion came at the bullfights on Sunday, January 29, 1956.

With the arrival at the arena of Alberto Lleras Camargo, who has come to symbolize the civil opposition to the Government of the Armed Forces, the crowd cheered long and lustily. Some minutes later, after the excitement of Lleras' arrival had abated, there arrived in the presidential box Don Samuel Moreno Díaz, Rojas' son-in-law, and publisher of the progovernment *Diario Colombiano*. With Mo-

---

[6] *La Prensa* (New York), December 15, 1955, p. 1.
[7] "El Presidente," *Semana* (Bogotá), January 8, 1956, p. 9.
[8] *Ibid.*, p. 14.

reno were his wife, Maria Eugenia Rojas de Moreno Díaz, daughter of the President, and an aide, Colonel Rengifo, together with other officers.

While this party took their seats, the Colombian version of booing started. From all parts of the amphitheater whistling broke out and continued. There were no boos against the President's daughter, but the whistling continued for some minutes. Occasional fist-fighting took place. Soon the Moreno Díaz party rose and stalked from the stadium. The whistling subsided. Periodically during the afternoon, the crowd cheered Lleras, forcing him to rise and acknowledge the plaudits.[9]

Next day, the incident was reported by only one morning paper, *Información*. Without mentioning either the cheers or the whistles, it editorialized briefly on the "volubility of the spectators at the bullfights." That afternoon, it was told to submit all its material for previous censorship.

However angry this rude insult to his daughter may have made Rojas, it probably sobered him just as much. For it was concrete evidence of the widening gap between those who support his regime and those who clamor for a return to civil government.[10] This may have been the reason why he chose to go to Barranquilla that week, where he delivered two important addresses. In these, he outlined his social and economic programs, and defended both the acts and the ends of his government. Again he asked for the support of the masses, and denounced his enemies. Smarting possibly from the affront to his daughter, he told Colombians that the politicians should abandon their illusions about recovering their domination over the electoral masses, because the government will not call for elections during the next two years; he warned that his binominal government, Government of the People-Armed Forces, had not yet used all its "material power" against those who oppose the redemption of the lower classes; and he spoke of using force, if necessary, in securing "public tranquility and fraternal viability."[11]

But fraternal viability between his backers and the opponents of the government slipped farther away almost daily. In fact, the day

[9] "Lucha Sin Cuartel Contra Políticos Resentidos, Anuncia," *La Prensa* (New York), February 6, 1956, p. 1.

[10] "Sangre en Bogotá," *Visión* (Santiago), March 2, 1956, p. 15.

[11] "Lucha Sin Cuartel . . . ," *La Prensa*, p. 1.

after his talks at Barranquilla, it seemed to be on the point of total disappearance.

The afternoon of Sunday, February 5, saw political violence and death in the Bogotá bull ring. Even as Rojas spoke in Barranquilla, the government announced its intention to suppress political manifestations at the *corrida*. Says *Time:*

> The measures turned out to be novel as well at fitting: the regime bought $15,000 worth of tickets and distributed them to thousands of policemen, plainclothesmen, and government employees. On bullfight day the official ticket-holders were waved through the gates; other fans were carefully frisked for weapons. Inside, the government boys took up their positions and sent up lusty *vivas* for President Gustavo Rojas Pinilla. Soon anti-Rojas spectators began to give themselves away by their glowering silences or muttered retorts. When the oppositionists were fully identified, the bullyboys opened up. Whipping out blackjacks, knives and guns, they attacked in milling fury. Victims were tossed screaming over guard-rails high above exit passageways; hundreds of others were toppled into the arena. Pistols banged away. The toll: at least eight dead, fifty hurt ... the one Colombian paper that got the story into print, Medellín's responsible *El Colombiano*, was closed down by the device of moving the government's censorship office to an out-of-town military post, where editors were ordered to bring all copy.[12]

An eyewitness of the affair stated that the police at the entrance gates searched both men and women. Once inside, the spectators saw an extraordinarily large number of police officers, and groups of "forty, thirty, ten men, in civilian dress scattered about, waiting." The account continues:

> Suddenly, from a microphone, a strange thing in itself, a voice was heard which repeated, "one ... two ... three ... one ... two ... three." And to our surprise, groups of people shouted *vivas* for Rojas Pinilla, the Administration, the Minister of Government. Down with the Politicians, etc. We thought that the demonstration would be limited to this, and we kept on waiting for the beginning of the fights, in silence.
>
> In front of the section in which we were, we suddenly noticed the beginning of a quarrel. A moment later we saw another, then another and five more, ten more, twenty, a hundred, until it was impossible to count them. Searching for whatever pretext, for not having joined in the *vivas* for the government, or because someone did not speak, without respect for women, adolescents, or children, twenty or more ruffians would jump on one of the helpless victims.
>
> Among the sights that I remember is that of a man, who had fallen in a pool of

[12] "Bull-Ring Massacre," Courtesy *Time*; copyright *Time, Inc.*, February 20, 1956, p. 34.

blood and lay absolutely alone in between the cement steps, being dragged by the feet to the bottom, while his head banged from step to step.[13]

Visión gave the total for this tragic afternoon as 8 dead, 112 wounded. A United Press dispatch from Bogotá on February 8 said that at least 9 were killed. The total may never be known, officially or publicly, but whatever the number, it was too many.

By February 9 the government felt the need to comment, and did so in an official statement by the Chief of Intelligence, who blamed progovernment elements for attempting reprisals against the antigovernment "thugs" for the previous week's demonstration. The bull ring battles were roundly condemned by the Cardinal Archbishop of Colombia, both in pastoral letters and in the official organs of the Church. But no official statement with regard to the matter had been made by Rojas up to the end of May, although in late February, in an address at Vélez, he said, "in the future, necessary means to insure that similar happenings will not occur will be strictly enforced."[14]

Despite Rojas' avowed battle with the political oligarchs—one which he calls a "battle without quarter"—it is not likely that he knew of the planned demonstration or reprisal, or, if he did, that he would have condoned the things which occurred. His whole period of governing to date had been marked by a positive determination to prevent all such instances of public partisan violence. Naturally enough, his enemies charged him, personally, with the blame.

In 1956, Rojas' rear-guard action against the press continued unabated, with the fortunes of government and press, respectively, shifting but little. It should, however, once more be emphasized that there was a considerable amount of criticism of the government permitted; that political comment and press freedom *in all but certain lines* (violent partisan polemics, insults to the President and the Armed Forces) was much more prevalent than was generally believed in the United States. Rojas' "tyrannical dictatorship" was basically an effort to keep Colombians from again going over the brink; to prevent Colombian journalists from exacerbating public tensions that are already explosive (and have long been so) through unrestrained partisan polemics.

[13] *Visión* (Santiago), March 2, 1956, p. 16.
[14] "Rojas Pinilla Reprueba y Condena Sucesos," *La Prensa* (New York), February 20, 1956, p. 3.

Actually, the censorship *was* aimed at maintaining public peace, a precarious thing in that unhappy Republic (there is no doubt that it was also aimed at keeping the regime securely in the saddle). But there was little or no censorship of foreign news, and Associated Press, United Press, and other news services continued to send news of Colombia abroad. In Colombia in recent times, the raw edge of violence lay just below the surface of daily living. If a similar situation existed in the United States, those editors who deplore Colombian censorship would probably exercise their sense of public responsibility and temper political reporting with enough wisdom to hold a civil war in abeyance. In Colombia, where the newspapers are the very spearhead of the party attack, the advance guard of physical violence, this is impossible.

An interesting example of the correlation between public violence and the party press battle is found in the outbreak of organized insurrectionism in the Department of Magdalena, where the government is actively pushing the construction of the Atlantic Railway. In late June, one of the engineers in charge of this work was abducted, tortured, and murdered by guerrilla bands.

The June 20 edition of *Diario de Colombia* published a strong editorial with a partisan slant and charges against the Liberals as authors of the new outbreak. It did not, however, publish details, nor did other dailies, all of whom had been warned by the censor to refrain from reporting the matter. Said the United Press dispatch from Bogotá: "The Government issued a communique for the international press agencies and for foreign correspondents, but in it, it warned that the news cannot be published in Colombia 'for evident and logical reasons of public order.' "[15]

This was, obviously, censorship. But after the burial of the engineer, Santiago Berrio Gonzales, at which the Minister of Public Works spoke, the Liberal *El Intermedio* (formerly *El Tiempo*) said, "His [Berrio's] death admits no excuses. Bitter sequel of barbarity, there will be none who will not condemn it energetically, as we condemn it from the bottom of our hearts, shocked by the stupidity of this abominable crime."[16]

[15] "Alega que una 'Turba Liberal' Mató a Berrio" (United Press dispatch), *La Prensa* (New York), June 22, 1956, p. 1.
[16] *Ibid.*

And although the censorship was in effect on the case, *Diario de Colombia* editorialized:

> While the President of the Republic exhausts all means at his disposal to bring an end to destruction among Colombians, just a few kilometers from Puerto Berrio *there is assassinated by Liberal rabble* one of the most promising youths of the present generation ... these deadly acts should be publicly reproved *by the directors of the revolt*, by whose [approval] is fed in one way or another the fronts of subversion, and by whom correspondence with the bandits is maintained, who thus merit the public contempt.[17]

"The last phrase," added the United Press, "is a clear reference to the Liberal Directorate, recently accused of 'close ties with elements which have risen up in arms.' "[18]

Thus the censorship. Thus, too, the avid urge to turn every act of violence into partisan political profit, or discredit for the political "enemy." The cause-and-effect relationship could not be proved, but some credit for honesty must be given to Rojas, who has consistently affirmed that the physical political violence spreads in proportion to the amount of press agitation of political differences. However it may be, by July 6, the government was forced to announce the issuance of a Public Order Bond, whose purchase would be applied in part to income taxes for 1957 and 1958, and whose proceeds were to be used in "re-establishing order in certain regions of the nation, principally the Department of Tolima [the perennial region of conflict] and in the valley of the Magdalena River [to which the violence spread with the killing of Berrio]." According to the United Press, this means of raising money for pacification of the insurgent areas was taken as an alternative to "reduction of the public works program," the prime concern beyond that being an acceleration of the military's action against the *guerrilleros*.[19]

Two days after the announcement of the Public Order Bond, three more engineers, an American, a Hungarian, and a Colombian, were hacked to death by armed bands in the Magdalena region. The Army moved into the region and began the old, dreary game that it had played, and continues to play, in Tolima.

Many Colombians were justified in believing that Rojas alone

[17] *Ibid.*, p. 4.
[18] *Ibid.*
[19] "Medidas Económicas en Colombia," *La Prensa* (Bogotá), New York, July 7, 1955, p. 3.

held the nation back from the old chaos. Others just as strongly held that the chaos was the result of his failure to return power to the parties. On balance, historical logic seemed to lie with the former.

The newspaper-destroying propensities of Rojas were not, upon examination, as strong as his critics indicated. In the justified outcry against his closing of the great Liberal dailies, *El Tiempo* and *El Espectador*, it was almost overlooked that in February, 1956, Rojas gave both papers permission to again publish. *El Espectador* appeared under the name of *El Independiente*, using "the plant and personnel of *El Espectador*."[20] The editor was Alberto Lleras Camargo, sworn enemy of the Government of the Armed Forces, a national symbol of opposition to Rojas, and organizer and head of the Civil Front.

This amounted, in essence, to again opening the arena of opposition to Rojas' enemies. Yet, such was much the same story in the case of *El Tiempo*. At the time that *El Independiente* was warming up its presses at the plant of the "suppressed" *El Espectador*, Enrique Santos, leading columnist of *El Tiempo*, was readying the appearance of *El Intermedio* to replace *El Tiempo*. Commenting upon these facts, the United Press reported from Bogotá:

> In the two cases, the only visible change is in the name of the newspapers, and the name of the directors. . . . The publication of the two newspapers, particularly for the exactitude of typography and the similarity of orientation, has been considered *almost a reappearance* of the country's two most important newspapers which were suspended in the thick of the fight between the government of General Rojas Pinilla and the independent press of Colombia.[21]

Going still further, Rojas in May, 1956, gave Enrique Santos permission to publish *El Intermedio* "in the future with its true name of '*El Tiempo*.'" But although *El Intermedio* devoted five columns of its front page to the texts of the letters exchanged between Rojas and Santos, still some stubbornness remained on both sides with regard to attaching blame. As of July, the name "*El Tiempo*" had not been set at the masthead. Apparently Eduardo Santos, the owner and director, was determined to have a complete moral victory without shouldering any of the blame in the affair. From his retreat in Paris he announced that "the question cannot be reduced to whether the right of a paper to publish or be suspended

[20] "Rojas Pinilla Reprueba y Condena Sucesos," *La Prensa*, p. 3.
[21] United Press, Bogotá, in *La Prensa* (New York), February 22, 1956, p. 3.

be recognized or not recognized . . . in reality, what is at stake is freedom of expression, freedom of information." And, although he indicated that he will "study" the possibility of again using the name "*El Tiempo*," he added, "let things be as they ought to be, or not be at all."[22]

By mid-1956, the press situation had bettered somewhat, internal development was progressing at a rapid rate, but violence had again broken out in Tolima and in new sections of the country. The opposition within the upper echelons of the Conservative and Liberal parties seemed to be slowly coalescing in the formation of a strong Civil Front under Lleras Camargo, with its aim set at harrassing the government until it was either forced out or voluntarily gave up power.

Formidable obstacles stood in the way of that objective. Rojas had consistently voiced his intention of staying in power until Colombians learned to live together in some cooperative major way. He viewed, possibly rightly, the parties as persistent inciters to social conflict. "The 55-year old general feels that mutual hatred and agitation by these parties has been at the root of the civil strife and holds that resumption of free political activity would signal new outbreaks."[23] Moreover, he had the Army behind him, and claimed the support of 95 per cent of the masses of Colombians, whether rightly or wrongly. Many responsible Colombians of both parties also supported him. As for the Army, he had raised officers' salaries, made gifts of cars and TV sets where they would do the most good, built a munificent officers club, and established post exchange stores where the military can get anything, virtually, at wholesale prices.[24] Under Rojas, the Army has the important task of administering the nation, and with it, a sense of new importance. He had gained much support, too, from the manner in which he had pushed the nation's internal devolopment forward. On the whole, the masses of people were better off under Rojas than they had been before, at least with regard to economic democracy. Finally, he had the support of the Church, which was flattered and happy to take on the work of organizing the labor unions.[25]

[22] "Habla en París Eduardo Santos," *La Prensa* (New York), May 16, 1956, p. 3.
[23] Szluc, *op. cit.*
[24] "Going Strong," *Time*, p. 39.
[25] *Ibid.*

Consequently, the dramatic show of opposition to him, and his sometimes strident defense of his program could not be taken as proof that he was universally disliked. "Most foreign observers believe," said *Time* at the turn of the year, 1956, "that Rojas at present is not popular ... but not hated. Sime think that if he relaxed his harsher measures, notably the six-year-old state of siege under which he rules by decree, he could even win back the genuine popularity of his first hopeful months."[26] This was, of course, wishful thinking. Primarily, he could not do so because decree-laws passed under a state of siege may be voided when a representative regime comes into power. Most of Rojas' program, his administrative agencies, the more substantial provisions for mass betterment, would thus be vulnerable to the political oligarchs who would undoubtedly control Congress should elections be permitted. There seemed no way but the hard, arbitrary way for Rojas to bring the social revolution to Colombia, so long as the main classes and the parties remained in conflict; so long as they pursued antagonistic ends and had such disparate stakes in the economy.

Nonetheless, the Civil Front under Lleras Camargo pushed its fight against Rojas and the Government of the Armed Forces. In this battle, Rojas watched with care, but at first not with apparent alarm. Lleras Camargo had adopted the old device of seeking union of Conservative and Liberal leaders to form a front of opposition. Although bipartisan fronts in Colombia have traditionally been for the purpose of slowing down or holding back mass reformism, Lleras Camargo was apparently aware that this time the issues went deeper and the demands were stronger. He was quoted as saying:

> Colombians evidently cannot permit themselves the luxury, after such long years of institutional disorder, of re-establishing the political game as though nothing had happened. Politically, there is no other way out of the emergency regime or the martial state of siege, than *through an understanding of the two parties* which will group together the near-totality of the national body ... a government of the two parties, not for purpose of opening another campaign for both of them to seek total power, but to acquiesce in a national regime in which neither predominates.[27]

Lleras Camargo is unquestionably the outstanding Colombian, possibly the outstanding Latin-American, of his era. His views are

[26] *Ibid.*
[27] "Política Colombiana," *La Prensa*, p. 3.

outward, stemming from an intelligence which grasps most of the intricacies not only of his own nation, but of the troubled world as well. In many ways, he is, intellectually, a man of the universe, rather than a Colombian. If anyone were capable of welding the classes and the oligarchies into an intelligently-operating national political front, it would be Lleras. Possibly he was the only Colombian capable of giving the kind of civil government which the nation needs, at least under present circumstances.

But implicit in the public violence, in the harshly partisan press polemics, in the constant exchange of threats, charges, and recriminations, was the implied reality that Lleras was fighting a losing fight. Perhaps the party oligarchs would join hands again, to restore civil government. Yet they gave no evidence that they would abandon the struggle for monopolistic control of government for their individual selves, once the danger had passed. The record indicated that once a Rojas was replaced, at some time in the future group and party particularism would again bring on the old, bitter struggles with their violence and dissension. The "Mark of Cain" was indelibly stamped upon the Colombian political brow. The disastrous years of 1948–53 had taught the partisans no lessons, given them no sense of blame, no feeling of guilt. It could hardly be expected that they would join forces for any other purpose than opening the political arena to the free competition of the parties, with all that that implied of the old practices, once the Army had decamped.

Nor did the existence of the Civil Front necessarily imply that politicians and oligarchs alone would make the basic decisions in the future. There was more to it than the Army *versus* the civilian politicos. There were the people, masses of them, the people who had demonstrated to support Rojas' closing of *El Tiempo*. And there were the partisan guerrilla forces still on the rampage in the more remote Departments. Something of the public state of mind, as opposed to the upper-class state of mind, was shown on a trip which Lleras made to Cali, to speak in behalf of the Civil Front opposition. The United Press reported on this occasion:

> The Liberal chief came in the interest of his plan to contact the Liberal *masses*, and was received by a large group of people at the city airport. Simultaneously, another group began to shout cries of support and backing for the government, and "Down with Lleras." When someone loosed a "Viva" for Lleras Camargo,

from the other group came stones and rotten fruit. None hit the mark, and Lleras came out of the incident unscathed. Later, at various points in the city itself, there were groups which shouted "Vivas" for the Government and "Down With Lleras," but there were no other incidents.[28]

One wonders what would happen if, suddenly, Rojas should say to the parties: "Take it back. It's all yours."

As head of the Liberal party, Lleras continued his efforts to form a National Front or Civil Front to replace the Rojas regime. Indications were that he had gained the support of important sectors of Liberal and Conservative thought, and would not stand in the way of Liberal support for even a Conservative candidate for President to succeed Rojas.[29] In July, Lleras traveled to Spain, where he visited the ex-dictator, Laureano Gómez in exile, for the purpose of "agreeing on the bases of a general policy of opposition to the present government of General Gustavo Rojas Pinilla."[30] This was, indeed, evidence of the desperation of Colombian Liberals. It could not be overlooked that Gómez was the titular head of an important wing of the Conservative party. It could scarcely be forgotten that Gómez had turned on the blood bath which Rojas Pinilla had been called upon to bring to an end. Any union of Lleras Liberals and Gómez Conservatives could scarcely promise the "collective living" or the "viability" which Lleras recognizes as necessary for Colombia. Viability exists between the lion and the lamb usually only until the lion rouses himself and feels the pangs of hunger.

There was no doubt, on the other hand, that Rojas and his followers were taking the Civil Front of Lleras seriously as 1956 drew on. To them, it became apparent that the challenge could no longer be ignored. Therefore, as the third anniversary of Rojas' accession to power approached, they readied their counterstrategy.

On May 30, the weekly *Sábado*, published by a group of dissident Liberals who support Rojas, announced that on June 13, Rojas would publicly proclaim his support of the long-discussed, often-abortive Third Force. On that day, a great public demonstration was scheduled to take place commemorating Rojas' advent to the presidency. Huge posters were prepared depicting a crossed rifle and shovel, and bearing the slogan, "People-Army-Third

[28] Carlos Villar-Borda, "Lleras Camargo Dice que Seguirá sus Esfuerzos por Crear 'Frente Nacional,'" *La Prensa* (New York), May 29, 1956, p. 3.
[29] *Ibid.*

Force."[30] On July 10, the Administrative Council of the Department of Caldas proclaimed the candidacy of Rojas for the term to begin in 1958. The resolution denounced the "situation of anarchy" in the nation, which it laid to party agitation, and it attacked the "old directing classes."[31]

Two days before the celebration, Rojas conferred with an assembly of governors, military chiefs, and authorities of the Departments. On the agenda: the formation of the Third Force. The United Press reported, "The Third Force has risen under the auspices and with the support of the Government, which has announced that it will put the organization in the hands of the Minister of Government and of the Governors. According to other sources, the Council of Governors will also concern themselves with the question of public order, giving it priority, which still agitates some sections of the nation."[32]

Three years to the day after Rojas pushed hot-eyed old Laureano Gómez from power, he took the oath of allegiance from the officers of Army, Navy, and Air Force, and officially proclaimed the Third Force in Colombia. *Time* described the occasion as follows:

> To get the movement started, Rojas marshalled army, navy and air force men in Bogotá's broad Plaza Bolívar.... Ranged on a platform at the foot of a statue of Liberator Simon Bolívar were a tall crucifix and eight urns containing the ashes of Colombian soldiers who fought in the Korean war and in the country's own backlands guerrilla war. Rojas then read off a solemn oath, swearing the servicemen, in the name of Jesus Christ and in the memory of Simon Bolívar, to "fight for the domination of the Third Force until Colombians lay down their political hatreds before the national banner." They took the oath. Next afternoon, at Bogotá's Campin stadium, Rojas likewise swore in a throng of youth, labor, farm and women's groups.[33]

The United Press, reporting the affair, said: "The so-called Third Force, often announced and praised by the First Magistrate, has aroused fears among the leaders of the political parties, who are afraid that it is an attempt to face them with an officialist party.

---

[30] "Grupo Liberal Asegura que Rojas la Respalda," *La Prensa* (New York), May 31, 1956, p. 1.

[31] "Procláman Candidatura Presidencial del Gral. Rojas Pinilla para 1958," *La Prensa* (New York), July 11, 1956, p. 1.

[32] *La Prensa* (New York), June 12, 1956, p. 1.

[33] "Third Force," Courtesy *Time*; copyright *Time*, Inc., June 25, 1956, p. 33.

Ceremonies in Bogotá's historic Plaza Bolívar in June, 1956, drew thousands to mark the third anniversary of the accession of General Gustavo Rojas Pinilla as President, and to hear him proclaim his support for a Third Force. The General and his wife, Doña Carola Correa de Rojas Pinilla, kneel in prayer at the temporary altar set in the Plaza for the religious ceremonies attending the anniversary.

The President, nonetheless, has been emphatic in affirming that the Third Force is the union of the People with the Armed Forces, in the service of peace, justice and liberty.[34] It is notable that at the ceremony at the Campin Stadium, the "vast throngs" were composed of "women's groups, industrial workers, peasants, businessmen, athletes, railway workers, children and youth groups."[35] How much of this was regimentation, how much voluntary support, is problematical. The creation of the *Gran Central Obrera,* the public demonstration of support to Rojas in his troubles with *El Tiempo,* the continued groping toward some kind of organic support of the government demonstrated by the defunct MAN, all evidence some justification for Rojas' use of the term "People-Armed Forces" to describe the nature of his power base. That the same instinct of approval lay behind the mass demonstration at the Campin Stadium may be doubtful. There is an uncomfortable similarity between this scene and the well-remembered mass demonstrations in Peron's Argentina, even though circumstances in the two countries differed, and still differ, sharply. And, if 1,200 oligarchs turned out to honor Eduardo Santos at the banquet at the Hotel Tequendama, it is no less significant that in October, 1955, 60,000 people appeared voluntarily to cheer Rojas when he visited Armero (a Liberal stronghold) in the Department of Tolima, where much of the bloody violence had occurred.[36]

Three years of governing, then, have alienated from Rojas the support of nearly all the Liberal political leaders, and quite a few of those of the Conservative party. The press is not free. Violence continues to stalk the provinces. Apparently, the Army remains firmly behind their General. The country is developing at a rapid pace under Rojas' direction, and the masses of the people are for the first time coming in for some important official consideration. The matter of a "return" of democracy is largely a quibble, for political democracy was never generalized for all the people.

Rojas, in this situation, is faced with a knotty power dilemma. He must not entirely alienate the political elements which have traditionally enjoyed the wealth, power, prestige, and economic leverage in the society. If he appeases them too greatly, he will fail

[34] *La Prensa* (New York), June 14, 1956, p. 3.
[35] *Ibid.,* June 15, 1956, p. 3.
[36] *Semana* (Bogotá), October 31, 1955, p. 12.

in his mission of making broad-front advances. It is no longer possible to hold their tentative support, by letting them believe that on such and such a date candidate A or candidate B will be permitted to assume power in a civil regime. The die has now been cast. Short of a miracle, or revolution, Rojas will be the candidate of the Third Force for the presidency in 1958. Military candidates have a consistently good record of wins in Latin-American elections, particularly when they run to succeed themselves.

The tragedy of the Colombian case lies in the impossibility of the parties to take Rojas at his own terms, as he first laid them down. To them, partisan politics proved stronger than national viability and progress on a broad front. Unable to find common ground, Rojas and the parties were gradually pushed to extreme positions, until the parties adopted the Civil Front form of opposition, and Rojas at last created the Third Force, or People-Army alignment to constitute a base for his regime. Both of these forces are, to a degree, uncertain supports. Masses of people are fickle and difficult to manipulate. In Colombia, there is still a strong tradition among many of the humble of expressing their political desires through one of the two parties. Rojas must make good on the major phases of the revolution which they want, or they will seek it through the traditional collectivities.

The Army seems to be his surest bulwark. They have profited in benefits, importance, and vital tasks under his administration. But always, in Latin America, there is the question of which way the Army will go—all or part of it. In Colombia there is an old joke or saying which has an Army officer asking a retiring brother officer: "And what do you intend to do now, after you retire?" And the other cocks a surprised brow and replies, *"Pues claro, hombre, conspirar!"* ("Conspire, naturally!") Rojas must frequently muse upon the fact that *he* is in power by reason of conspiracy with the Ospina Conservatives.

There seemed, as 1956 drew toward a close, to be two imperatives facing Rojas: carry out his essential mission while keeping the Army loyal and unimpressed by the blandishments of the oligarchic opposition; and weld the masses who apparently support him into some manipulable organic structure which can be imposed as a power factor or articulated so that their potential acts as a deterrent to his enemies. Most important, from these two aims, he must forge a major result: that of truly making broad-front progress while he imposes upon the classes and the parties the necessity of cooperation rather than antagonism and struggle, of taking each other into social, economic, and political account, rather than following their old, traditional particularist drives.

Only time would tell whether Rojas had become so enamored of power that he would forget the forces and social imperatives that raised him to power. There was evidence that he would not, but his persisting references to abolishing partisan political hates, to the need for national class and party viability, had to be weighed against the plain fact that hates have increased, and that viability for the Army and the masses of people still is one thing, and quite another for the political leaders and the important interests which they represent. Nor was it arguable that Rojas had lost important areas of support, despite his claims that 90 per cent of the nation stood behind him.

Colombian social viability under Rojas had developed into the viability of an enforced, unpopular truce. True cooperation seemed as far away as ever. And yet, if Rojas fell, if the now angry and determined political parties returned to the civil arena, the results might be disastrous for the nation. Said *Semana*: "If tomorrow the uniforms disappeared from the command of the nation, before we have rectified our common errors, or if, in some suicidal undertaking, the unity of the military should be broken, we would find ourselves [again] submerged in civil war. The irresponsible and rapacious elements should not forget that."[37]

Past events supported this view: the horrible carnage which Rojas brought to an end; the irresponsible party revival of violence, potential and actual, almost before Rojas had found his way around the presidential palace; the outbreak of civil war and insurrectionism in the provinces; the unrepentant attitudes of the parties; their failure, save in the lone case of Lleras Camargo, to reorient themselves, to put forth programs which comprised the recognition of a social revolution, rather than a desire to return to "doctrinal orthodoxy."

The hard fact was that a Rojas seemed a necessity—an unpleasant one, an uncomfortable reminder that Colombians had not used their freedom wisely. No better alternative had been presented, for

[37] *Semana* (Bogotá), November 14, 1955, p. 17.

the sterile, archaic party dogmas, the social and economic credos which once pushed the nation to the brink of total disaster would not again be acceptable to most of the people.

Beneath the surface of the whole nation there was an uneasy, ominous stirring of the demands which the parties had failed to heed, and which under Rojas, they attacked and castigated. In a society caught up in the implacable march of change between an old order and a new, the imperatives of history brush aside all man-made obstacles. Only at their own peril could the Colombian parties again stand in the way of an organic, autonomous labor movement, or oppose the plea of the peasant for land and a decent life, or try to regain the monopolistic organization and control of the society which looked upon only the upper classes of the nation as men. There is very little evidence that the Colombian political parties were aware of that, or that any civil regime would be other than what Colombian civil regimes have always been: instruments for upper-class control, privilege, and class-partisan "democracy."

Therefore, it mattered little, essentially, whether Rojas left office in a day or a month, or died of old age in the President's chair. Already, despite his many shortcomings, he had served a major purpose of the times: he had made human ciphers conscious of their importance, their strength, their rights, as humans. For once, *a government had governed for them.* They would not forget that. And no Colombian government of the future would long be allowed to turn the clock back beyond that point.

That is the way of social revolutions and the people who make them.

XVIII. Summary and Conclusions

The study of recent developments in Colombia, together with an analysis of the trends which historically preceded and created them, leads to the following conclusions:

1. President Gustavo Rojas Pinilla came to power as a result of the inability of the traditional parties to cope with a long-smouldering social revolution. The roots of that revolution lay in the social, economic, and political institutions of the Colony, and they survived, largely unchanged, under the independent Creole Republic.

2. In essence, this revolution was the delayed revolution, the one that did not come with the Liberation, which was frustrated by vast social and economic inequalities between the directors of the society and the masses of the people for over a century. And to this overdue revolution was added another in the modern era, when better communications, the spread of proletarian ideas of reform, the influx of foreign capital, and incipient industrialization widened the gaps between the classes and gave the common people new norms and knowledge by which to judge their condition in comparison with that of other peoples of the world.

3. The awakening of the Colombian masses created strong pressure upon the social, economic, and political oligarchies. The two parties, the public expression of the system of oligarchic privilege, made only those concessions which were necessary to maintain "peace" and "stability." Although they equated this public non-violence with "democracy," they failed utterly to reform the basic institutions to conform to changing times, to modern demands. In order to effect this hold-the-line policy, the oligarchs of both parties joined forces, at times of greatest agitation, across party lines to form what they called "coalition" or "nonpartisan" or "National Union" governments under presidents who were acceptable to the oligarchs of both of the political collectivities. Nonetheless, a characteristic of such alliances was that when the pressure from below ceased or materially abated, the partisan differences again appeared in a battle to the death for monopolistic control of the budget and the administration.

4. The result of this system was to throw up road blocks of re-

pression in the face of mass enlightenment and a growing clamor for mass satisfaction of basic needs. Inevitably, as the gap widened between the classes, the two parties drew farther away from the social mission demanded of them. The times required them to move the whole society forward on a broad front, toward some common, mutually satisfactory destiny in a modern, integrated, awakened, 'and collective world. But they tended increasingly to think of *themselves* as the nation; *their* class as the people; *their* democracy as "Colombian democracy." Disintegration, rather than integration, was the result.

5. In the wake of World War II, inflationary prosperity came to the Colombian upper classes. For the masses of people, there was only greater awareness of inequities, without appreciable change in their social or economic status. Consequently, the dormant conflict became more active. Some basic reforms were made under Alfonso López; and then the counterreform began to turn the clock back, at the very time when the common appetite for betterment had been whetted. When the Liberal party itself split over the question of reform or conserving the old order, the Conservatives came back to power with Mariano Ospina Pérez, a minority president.

6. The failure of the Liberals to stand up to the crisis made it increasingly clear that the two-party system in Colombia was unable to speak for, or to direct, the whole nation. The steadily worsening condition of the masses pushed the people closer to violence, and their needs were answered by a strange mixture of "panic concessions" and repression by President Ospina. During this time, Jorge Eliécer Gaitán, the champion of the common people, gave them a strong sense of some common destiny. Thus, when, at a time of dire economic stress, Gaitán was assassinated, mass resentments and anger broke in a tidal wave of violence that threatened to sweep the country under.

7. Out of this momentary explosion rose the dictatorship of Laureano Gómez, whose way was paved by Ospina Pérez' closing of Congress and other decrees which banned the Liberal party from public life. But the people did not accept the counterrevolution which had been mounted by Ospina and given direction by Gómez. Violence spread to the provinces and soon became a civil war whose destruction of life, of property, or moral values, still has not been fully calculated. From this blood bath there emerged

two unshakable facts: (1) the masses would always henceforth be a major factor in the nation's political life, and (2) the traditional two parties had proved their incompetence to direct the nation until such time as they might reform their policies and adopt new objectives for the entire nation.

8. It was this failure of the organized political forces to halt the national suicide, and to articulate and direct the social revolution in orderly fasion, that brought Rojas Pinilla to power. His immediate role was that of restorer of the nation, of the healer of wounds. The times made strong demands on him, both immediate and long-range. They required that he first pacify the nation, and then bring the people, the classes, the divergent interests, together in a viable, intergrated national life which recognized the necessity of collective living. It was his task to forge a sense of unity and of common destiny to replace the old order which had created only divisionism, particularism, and a sense of apartness for most Colombians.

9. Many basic counterfactors stood in the way of Rojas' achieving his purpose. There was the nation's historical tradition, which enshrined caste-class and economic-class differences as good, and perhaps necessary; the basic Hispanic tendencies toward divisionism and violent solutions; the Latin-American urge toward anarchistic individualism and the personalist view of problems large and small; the general seeking after individual goals rather than the general welfare. And, finally, there was the bitterness of partisan politics in Colombia. All of these were inimical to the group sense of interdependence and cooperation which had to be created to permit national living together.

10. This character of the political parties, which made politics literally an economic way of life, was perhaps Rojas' major obstacle. It was a tradition in which both parties regarded government not as an instrument of the society, but as an economic end *per se*. The parties existed, acted and survived on the theory that government was an objective to be assaulted, captured, invaded, and exploited monopolistically by the winner, while the "enemy"—the losing party—was to be denied access to power, and to the benefits of the administration.

11. In adopting the familiar "state of siege" device to restore order, Rojas tried to soften the worst features of Gómez' regime. He asked the cooperation of both parties, worked out the gentle-

man's agreement with the highly partisan press, and sought the cooperation of all elements of the society in his work of reconstruction. Rehabilitation of the peasants was begun, industry and public works were fostered, and programs were undertaken to raise wages and better the condition of the working classes.

12. But tax reforms, hitting the great concentrations of wealth and finance, soon alienated the oligarchs from Rojas' regime. They took the fight to the press. Violence broke out in the provinces, and a running fight developed between Rojas and the party oligarchs who used the newspapers to combat both the government and each other in a skirmishing for position. Barred from the electoral arena, they transferred their bitter partisan activities to the headlines and the front pages. Charge and countercharge exacerbated the physical violence, and tore the nation apart emotionally at a time when Rojas demanded and needed national unity to get his job done.

13. Toward the first months of 1955, the press problem and the violence in the provinces became inextricably woven with the party opposition to Rojas. Along with the general line of opposition there were increasingly critical comments on his tax policy, his use of the budget to maintain lower-level prosperity, and what many called—probably without substantial basis—the pillaging of the government by the Armed Forces. This complex of factors, all fuel for the raging fire of press polemics, culminated finally in the closing of *El Espectador* and *El Tiempo,* two of Colombia's greatest dailies.

14. Although possibly not without justification, in view of the state of public order, Rojas' closing of these newspapers was a major political mistake. It roused the Liberal party to action, to a semblance of unified opposition. This act, in turn, caused the Conservatives to search for some formula upon which to settle their differences. The net result was a *cause célèbre* which served as a nucleus for the formation of a Civil Front or National Front of Liberals and Conservatives, basically oligarchs and near-oligarchs, which, under the leadership of Alberto Lleras Camargo, sought actively if gropingly the end of the Rojas regime.

15. On the other hand, labor, the peasants, the masses of the people, seemed to support Rojas, and demonstrated their support in a public demonstration to back up his closing of *El Tiempo.* The

alarmed politicians of both parties saw in this a threat to their control of the multitudes. And, in fact, the masses of Colombia seemed to be groping toward some type of Third Force which would fill the vacuum in popular articulation left by the assassination of Gaitán. They tried with MAN, and failed. They sought an organic role for labor and got the *Gran Central Obrera*. Under the flags of both liberalism and conservatism, they rallied to Rojas to approve his closing of *El Tiempo*. A force was present, but undirected, ineffectually organized, still largely mute, but dissatisfied with the old parties, the old system.

16. As the Civil Front became more active, differences between the government and the politicians widened and deepened. Rojas' permission for *El Espectador* and *El Tiempo* to again publish did nothing to reconcile differences. Conflict broke out between the backers and the opponents of the Government of the Armed Forces in the bull ring fights in January. Rojas reacted by telling the nation that he would not tolerate "intellectual *guerrilleros*," and by again calling upon the people to support him against the political oligarchs. Increasingly, he turned to the use of the term, "People-Armed Forces" in describing his regime, his program. The lines were clearly drawn. It was Rojas, the Army, and the masses against the formerly privileged and competent elements of the society.

17. On June 13, 1956, three years after taking office, Rojas Pinilla declared the Third Force as the official party. His supporters announced that he would be put forward for another term in the presidency in 1958. Chances were that unless death, revolution, or weariness dictated otherwise, he would be elected. Rojas had traveled a long road from the day that he assumed charge of the nation in an atmosphere of harmony and with the support of both parties.

18. Rojas' three years in office had tended to bring out more sharply than ever the hazy lines of social revolutionary conflict in Colombia. The elites had been given the choice of cooperation in the achievement of that revolution, or of opposition to it. They had chosen the latter. But this time, the struggle was of a different character. The government and the Army stood on the side of mass demands, not unfriendly to the champions of the old order, but determined that they would not govern for their sole welfare as they had so consistently done in the past.

19. Rojas' opponent is wily and powerful. The influential forces

of the society have the economic, social, and, to a degree still, the political leverage. In order to fight them off, he must retain the loyalty of the Army, which has been raised on a tradition of conspiracy, and he must weld the mass support into a power factor that can be used positively in his favor.

20. It would seem, therefore, that Rojas' only chance of fulfilling the complete role which the times demanded of him when he came to power lies in winning the battle against the oligarchy for control of the government. If he fails, the country will again have strife and bloodshed, unless the party which might unseat Rojas adopts as its own the major reforms which he has sponsored, and, perhaps more important, abandons the practice of proscribing the opposition party.

21. Rojas gave few indications that he considered himself a permanent fixture, or his government more than transitional, but unquestionably his estimate of the transitional period has lengthened substantially. He has given ample indications that he holds the purpose of his regime to carry the country through the progress from the old order of social inequities institutionally enshrined, to the new in which some common national myth may be developed, socially, economically, politically. But there is little doubt now that he will not surrender power voluntarily to the civil parties until he has both accomplished his economic aims and brought the whole nation to a realization that group cooperation and conciliation must replace conflict and divisionism.

22. But whether Rojas stays in office long enough to complete his task or relinquishes power in a matter of days, his essential historical role cannot be changed. He was raised to power by the demands of a major part of the society for the articulation of a frustrated revolution. The inscrutable force of events decided that. And after all the political soul-searching has ended, after he either fails or succeeds in his major designs, and regardless of how he leaves the office of President, Rojas will be found to have made two major contributions. First, he has given the masses new importance; and, second, he has made it impossible for the oligarchy ever again to ignore the needs and demands of the people for long.

Rojas has turned the clock forward on social achievement for the masses. He has given them status, and a sense of their importance, if only because his government has emphasized their welfare. That lesson they will never forget, and nothing less will be acceptable from other governments to come. No regime in Colombia's future will be able to ignore successfully the needs of the "95 per cent."

In this sense, paradoxically, the military dictator is making a substantial contribution toward democracy. Every social, educational, political, and economic gain in status is a step toward the creation of the substantive bases upon which true popular democracy may one day rise in Colombia. It is an irrevocable departure from the lopsided "Athenian democracy" which applied the Rights of Man to only a few in the nation. And without these fundamental bases, it is as useless to argue over the existence of democracy in Latin America as to speculate upon the number of angels that can dance on the point of a needle.

In fact, the ultimate accomplishment of the process may require many Rojas Pinillas, many times of troubles. But the military dictators make their necessary contribution, a lasting one, with their emphasis upon substantive democracy as an essential prerequisite for procedural democracy. Nothing will be quite the same after they have come, spoken to and for the masses, and gone their way. It does not even matter, in the long run, whether they were sincere in their solicitude for the people, or merely self-seeking. The important thing is that the masses will not forget. They will slowly grow into the new concept that they, too, are men, and they will demand more from the parties in the future than ever they dared demand before. Some time, sooner or later, those demands will be met. And when they are, the national sense of "living together," of each class taking the other into account, may be realized.

Even though it may appear negative and temporary, this contribution is a gain for the future of popular democracy in Latin America.

It is a step forward for all the people, one step more into the background for the supremacy of oligarchies. Out of it may someday come the type of collective thinking and living which will produce real democracy, rather than its pale, spurious reflection.

Bibliography

A. References Cited

Books

Alberdi, Juan Bautista. *Bases para La Organización Políca y Económica de la Confederación Argentina.* Vols. I, II. Buenos Aires: El Ateneo, 1913.

——. *Fragmento Preliminar al Estudio del Derecho.* Vol. I. Buenos Aires, 1886.

Arciniegas, Germán. *Caribbean: Sea of the World.* New York: Alfred A. Knopf, Inc., 1946.

——. *Los Comuneros.* Bogotá: Editorial ABC, 1938.

——. *The State of Latin America.* Translated by Harriet de Onis. New York: Alfred A. Knopf, Inc., 1952.

Arrubla and Henao. *History of Colombia.* Translated by J. Fred Rippy. Chapel Hill: The University of North Carolina Press, 1938.

Bailey, Thomas A. *A Diplomatic History of the American People.* New York: Appleton-Century-Crofts, Inc., 1950.

The Basis of a Development Program for Colombia. Baltimore: The Johns Hopkins Press, 1950.

Belaunde, Victor Andres. *Bolívar and the Political Thought of the Spanish American Revolution.* Baltimore: The Johns Hopkins Press, 1938.

Bernal Jiménez, Rafaél. *Hacia Una Democracia Orgánica.* Madrid: Afrodisio Agudo, 1951.

Blanco-Fombona, Rufino. *El Pensamiento Vivo de Bolívar.* Buenos Aires: Editorial Losada, 1944.

Bolívar, Simón. *Ideario Político,* ed. J. A. Cova. Buenos Aires: Librería El Ateneo, 1942.

Bolívar y su Época. Carácas: Conferencia Interamericana, 1953.

Camacho Carrizosa, Jose y Guillermo. *Artículos Varios.* Bogotá: Editorial Minerva, n.d.

Canal Ramírez, Gonzalo. *El Estado Cristiano y Bolivariano del 13 de Junio.* Bogotá: Editorial Antares, 1955.

Cano, Luis. *Periodismo.* Bogotá: Editorial Minerva, n.d.

Colombia: Trade Problems. Washington: U. S. Department of Commerce, 1943.

Colombia's Economy in 1944. Washington: International Reference Service, U. S. Department of Commerce, 1945.

El Comercio Colombiano y la Economía Nacional. Bogotá: Editorial Antares, 1951–52.

Davila, Carlos. *We of the Americas.* Chicago: Ziff-Davis Co., 1948.

Debate sobre la Situación Financiera y Económica del País. Bogotá: Cámara de Representantes, Imprenta Nacional, n.d.

De la Vega, Jose. *La Federación en Colombia.* Bogotá: Ministerio de Educacion Nacional, 1952.

Demographic Yearbook, 1953. New York: The United Nations, 1954.

Duggan, Laurence. *The Americas.* New York: Henry Holt & Co., Inc., 1949.

Ebon, Martin. *World Communism Today.* New York: McGraw-Hill Book Co., 1948.

Fernández de Soto, Mario. *Una Revolución en Colombia.* Madrid: Ediciones Cultura Hispánica, 1951.

Gaitán, Jorge Eliécer. *Las Ideas Socialistas en Colombia.* Bogotá, 1924.

Galarza, Ernesto. *Labor Trends and Social Welfare in Latin America.* Washington: Pan American Union, 1941.

Galbraith, William O. *Colombia.* London and New York: Royal Institute of International Affairs, 1953.

García, Antonio. *Gaitán y el Problema de la Revolución Colombiana.* Bogotá: Artes Gráficas, 1955.

———. *Problemas de la Nación Colombiana.* Bogotá: Editorial Nuevo Mundo, n.d., post 1951.

García Calderón, Francisco. *Les Démocraties Latines de l'Amérique.* Paris: Flammarion, 1920.

Gibson, William Marion. *The Constitutions of Colombia.* Durham: The Duke University Press, 1948.

Goez, Ramón Carlos. *Geografía de Colombia.* México, D.F.: Fondo de Cultura Económica, 1947.

Gómez, Eugenio J. *Problemas Colombianos de 1863 a 1945.* Bogotá: Editorial Antena, 1945.

———. *Problemas Colombianos: La Unidad Política.* Bogotá: Editorial Gráficas Mundo al Día, 1941.

Gómez, Laureano. *Interrogantes Sobre el Progreso en Colombia.* Bogotá, 1928.

Gunther, John. *Inside Latin America.* New York: Harper & Brothers, 1940–41.

Guzmán, Diego Rafaél de. *Importancia del Espíritu Español en las Letras Colombianas.* Bogotá: Editorial Minerva, n.d.

Habitaciones Obreras y Cooperativas de Vivienda. Washington: Pan American Union, 1952.

Hanson, Simon G. *Economic Development in Latin America.* Washington: Inter-American Affairs Press, 1951.

Investments in Colombia. Washington: U. S. Department of Commerce, 1955.

La Izquierda ante el Presente y el Porvenir de Colombia. Bogotá, 1944.

Jorrín, Miguel. *Governments of Latin America.* New York: D. Van Nostrand Co., Inc., 1953.

Lafond, Georges. *Géographie Économique de l'Amérique Latine.* Paris: Payot, 1947.

Larco Herrera, Rafaél. *Por la Ruta de la Confederación Americana.* Lima, 1948.

Londoño, Carlos Mario. *Economía Social Colombiana.* Bogotá: Imprenta Nacional, 1953.

López, Alejandro. *Problemas Colombianos.* Bogotá, n.d., post 1934.

MacDonald, Austin F. *Latin American Politics and Government.* New York: Thomas Y. Crowell Co., 1954.

Mackay, John A. *The Other Spanish Christ.* New York: The Macmillian Co., 1933.

Madariaga, Salvador de. *The Fall of the Spanish American Empire.* New York: The Macmillan Co., 1948.

——. *The Rise of the Spanish American Empire.* New York: The Macmillan Co., 1947.

Martínez Silva, Carlos. *Prosas Políticas: Sobre el Congreso de 1880.* Bogotá: Editorial Minerva, n.d.

Masur, Gerhard. *Simon Bolivar.* Albuquerque: University of New Mexico Press, 1948.

Mayo, H. B. *Democracy and Marxism.* New York: Oxford University Press, 1954.

Mejía Córdoba, Juvenal. *Geografía de Colombia.* Bogotá, 1945.

Mendoza Pérez, Diego. *Ensayo Sobre la Evolución de la Propiedad Privada en Colombia.* Bogotá, 1897.

Mensajes del Presidente López al Congreso Nacional. Bogotá: Imprenta Nacional, 1938.

Mensajes del Presidente López al Congreso Nacional. Bogotá: Imprenta Nacional, 1945.

Navarro y Lamarca, Carlos. *Compendio de Historia Hispanoamericana.* New York: Scott, Foresman & Company, 1925.

Niño H., Alberto. *Antecedentes y Secretos del 9 de Abril.* Bogotá: Editorial Pax, n.d.

Noguera Laborde, Rodrigo. *Constitución de la Republica de Colombia y sus Antecedentes Documentales Desde 1885.* Bogotá: Fondo Rotario, Pontificia Universidad Catolica Javeriana, 1950.

Northrup, George Tyler. *An Introduction to Spanish Literature.* Chicago: University of Chicago Press, 1925.

Nuñez, Rafael. *Los Mejores Artículos Políticos.* Bogotá: Editorial Minerva, n.d.

Ortega y Gasset, Jose. *Invertebrate Spain.* New York: W. W. Norton & Company, Inc., 1937.

Ospina Vásquez, Luis. *Industria y Protección en Colombia, 1810–1930.* Bogotá: Editorial Santafe, 1955.

Pereyra, Carlos. *Historia de América Española.* Vol. IV. Madrid: Editorial Saturnino Calleja, 1927.

Pérez, Francisco de Paula. *Política Social.* Bogotá: Editorial Lumen, 1939.

Poblete Troncoso, Moises. *El Standard de Vida de los Poblaciones de América.* Santiago: Universidad de Chile, 1942.

Pombo, Manuel Antonio, and Guerra, Jose Joaquín. *Constituciones de Colombia.* Vols. I–IV. Bogotá: Ministerio de Educación Nacional, 1951.

Problems of Housing of Social Interest. Washington: Pan American Union, 1953.

Progresos en Materia de Reforma Agraria. New York: United Nations, 1954.

Restrepo, Felix. *Colombia en la Encrucijada.* Bogotá, 1951.

Rippy, J. Fred. *The Capitalists and Colombia.* New York: The Vanguard Press, 1931.

——. *The Historical Evolution of Hispanic America.* New York: F. S. Crofts & Co., 1945.

Romoli, Kathleen. *Colombia: Gateway to South America.* New York: Doubleday & Company, Inc., 1941.

Samper, Jose María. *Ensayos.* Bogotá: Biblioteca de Cultura Colombiano, n.d.

———. *Las Revoluciones Políticas y la Condición Social de las Repúblicas Colombianas.* Bogotá: Biblioteca de Cultura Popular, n.d.

———. *Selección de Estudios.* Bogotá: Ministerio de Educacion Nacional, 1952.

Samper, Miguel. *Mejores Escritos.* Bogotá: Editorial Minerva, n.d.

Scopes, L. A. *Colombia, Economic and Commercial Conditions.* London: British Board of Trade, 1950.

Secretariat Report on Economic Conditions in Latin America. Washington: Pan American Union, 1950.

Secretariat Report on Economic Implications for Latin America of Defense Programs Abroad. Washington: Pan American Union, 1951.

Selected Economic Data on the Latin American Republics. Washington: Pan American Union, 1954.

Smith, T. Lynn. *Materiales Para el Estudio de la Clase Media en la América Latina.* Washington: Pan American Union, 1951.

———. *Tabio, A Study of Rural Organization.* Washington: U. S. Department of Agriculture, 1945.

Spykman, Nicholas John. *America's Strategy in World Politics.* New York: Harcourt, Brace & Co., 1942.

Statistical Yearbook, 1953. New York: The United Nations, 1954.

Vila, Pablo. *Nueva Geografía de Colombia.* Bogotá: Libreria Colombiana, 1945.

Villegas, Silvio. *No Hay Enemigos a la Derecha.* Manizales, 1937.

Ware, Caroline F. *Organización de la Comunidad para el Bienestar Social.* Washington: Pan American Union, 1954.

Williams, Mary W. *The People and Politics of Latin America.* New York: Henry Holt & Co., Inc., 1945.

Periodicals

American Political Science Review
Americas
Annals (Pan American Union)
Current History

Foreign Affairs
Foreign Commerce Weekly
Economía Colombiana
Inter-American Affairs
Newsweek
New York Times Magazine
Semana (Bogotá)
Time
Visión (Santiago)

Newspapers

El Colombiano (Medellín)
Colombian Newsletter (Bogotá)
La Defensa (Medellín)
El Diario (Medellín)
Diario de Colombia (Bogotá)
El Espectador (Bogotá)
El Liberal (Bogotá)
The New York Times
The Pittsburgh Press
La Prensa (New York)
El Relator (Cali)
El Tiempo (Bogotá)

B. RELATED REFERENCES NOT CITED

Books

Bemis, Samuel Flagg. *The Latin American Policy of the United States.* New York: Harcourt, Brace & Co., 1943.

Brunn, Geoffrey. *The World in the Twentieth Century.* Boston: D. C. Heath & Company, 1948.

Christiansen, Asher N. *The Evolution of Latin American Government.* New York: Henry Holt & Co., Inc., 1951.

Crawford, William Rex. *A Century of Latin American Thought.* Cambridge: Harvard University Press, 1945.

Daniels, Walter M. *Latin America and the Cold War.* New York: H. W. Wilson Co., 1952.

Davis, Harold E. *Latin American Leaders.* New York: H. W. Wilson Co., 1949.

Downes, J. E. and others. *Latin America and Hemisphere Solidarity*. Boston: D. C. Heath & Company, 1943.

Estudio Económico de América Latina, 1951–1952. Mexico, D.F.: The United Nations, 1954.

Major Problems of United States Foreign Policy, 1954. Washington: Brookings Institution, 1954.

Plenn, Abel. *The Southern Americas*. New York: The Creative Age Press, 1948.

Periodicals

Annals of the American Academy of Political and Social Sciences
Estadística
Panorama

Index